MW01252849

Tibetan Buddhism in Diaspora

The imperialist ambitions of China, which invaded Tibet in the late 1940s, have sparked the spectacular spread of Tibetan Buddhism worldwide, and especially in western countries. This work is a study on the malleability of a particular Buddhist tradition; on its adaptability in new contexts.

The book analyzes the nature of the Tibetan Buddhism in the diaspora. It examines how the re-signification of Tibetan Buddhist practices and organizational structures in the present refers back to the dismantlement of the Tibetan state headed by the Dalai Lama and the fragmentation of Tibetan Buddhist religious organizations in general. It includes extensive multi-sited fieldwork conducted in the United States, Brazil, Europe and Asia and a detailed analysis of contemporary documents relating to the global spread of Tibetan Buddhism. The author demonstrates that there is a "de-institutionalized" and "de-territorialized" project of political power and religious organization, which, among several other consequences, engenders the gradual "autonomization" of lamas and lineages within the religious field of Tibetan Buddhism. Thus, a spectre of these previous institutions continues to exist outside their original contexts, and they are continually activated in ever-new settings.

Using a combination of two different academic traditions – namely, the Brazilian anthropological tradition and the American Buddhist studies tradition – it investigates the "process of cultural re-signification" of Tibetan Buddhism in the context of its diaspora. Thus, it will be a valuable resource to students and scholars of Asian Religion, Asian Studies and Buddhism.

Ana Cristina O. Lopes is Research Associate in the Center for Anthropology, Performance and Drama (Napedra) at the University of São Paulo, Brazil.

Routledge critical studies in Buddhism

Edited by Stephen C. Berkwitz
Missouri State University, USA
Founding Editors: Charles S. Prebish
Utah State University, USA
and
Damien Keown
Goldsmith's College, London University, UK

Routledge Critical Studies in Buddhism is a comprehensive study of the Buddhist tradition. The series explores this complex and extensive tradition from a variety of perspectives, using a range of different methodologies.

The series is diverse in its focus, including historical, philological, cultural, and sociological investigations into the manifold features and expressions of Buddhism worldwide. It also presents works of constructive and reflective analysis, including the role of Buddhist thought and scholarship in a contemporary, critical context and in the light of current social issues. The series is expansive and imaginative in scope, spanning more than two and a half millennia of Buddhist history. It is receptive to all research works that are of significance and interest to the broader field of Buddhist Studies.

The Resonance of Emptiness
A Buddhist Inspiration for
contemporary psychotherapy
Gay Watson

American Buddhism
Methods and findings in recent
scholarship
*Edited by Duncan Ryuken Williams
and Christopher Queen*

Imaging Wisdom
Seeing and knowing in the art of
Indian Buddhism
Jacob N. Kinnard

Pain and its Ending
The Four Noble Truths in the
Theravada Buddhist Canon
Carol S. Anderson

Emptiness Appraised
A critical study of Nagarjuna's
philosophy
David F. Burton

The Sound of Liberating Truth
Buddhist–Christian dialogues in honor
of Frederick J. Streng
*Edited by Sallie B. King and
Paul O. Ingram*

Buddhist theology
Critical reflections by contemporary
Buddhist scholars
*Edited by Roger R. Jackson and
John J. Makransky*

The Glorious Deeds of Purna
A translation and study of the
Purnavadana
Joel Tatelman

Early Buddhism – A New Approach
The I of the Beholder
Sue Hamilton

Contemporary Buddhist Ethics
Edited by Damien Keown

Innovative Buddhist Women
Swimming against the stream
Edited by Karma Lekshe Tsomo

Teaching Buddhism in the West
From the wheel to the web
*Edited by V. S. Hori, R. P. Hayes and
J. M. Shields*

Empty Vision
Metaphor and visionary imagery in
Mahayana Buddhism
David L. McMahan

**Self, Reality and Reason in Tibetan
Philosophy**
Tsongkhapa's quest for the middle
way
Thupten Jinpa

In Defense of Dharma
Just-war ideology in Buddhist
Sri Lanka
Tessa J. Bartholomeusz

Buddhist Phenomenology
A philosophical investigation of
Yogacara Buddhism and the
Ch'eng Wei-shih Lun
Dan Lusthaus

**Religious Motivation and the
Origins of Buddhism**
A social-psychological exploration of
the origins of a world religion
Torkel Brekke

**Developments in Australian
Buddhism**
Facets of the diamond
Michelle Spuler

Women in Pali Buddhism
Walking the spiritual paths in mutual
dependence
Pascale Engelmajer

Tibetan Buddhism in Diaspora
Cultural re-signification in practice
and institutions
Ana Cristina O. Lopes

The following titles are published in association with the *Oxford Centre for Buddhist Studies*

 Oxford Centre for Buddhist Studies
a project of The Society for the Wider Understanding of the Buddhist Tradition

The *Oxford Centre for Buddhist Studies* conducts and promotes rigorous teaching and research into all forms of the Buddhist tradition.

Early Buddhist Metaphysics
The making of a philosophical
tradition
Noa Ronkin

**Mipham's Dialectics and the
Debates on Emptiness**
To be, not to be or neither
Karma Phuntsho

How Buddhism Began
The conditioned genesis of the early
teachings
Richard F. Gombrich

Buddhist Meditation
An anthology of texts from the Pāli
Canon
Sarah Shaw

**Remaking Buddhism for Medieval
Nepal**
The fifteenth-century reformation of
Newar Buddhism
Will Tuladhar-Douglas

**Metaphor and Literalism in
Buddhism**
The doctrinal history of Nirvana
Soonil Hwang

The Biographies of Rechungpa
The evolution of a Tibetan
hagiography
Peter Alan Roberts

The Origin of Buddhist Meditation
Alexander Wynne

Tibetan Buddhism in Diaspora
Cultural re-signification in practice and institutions

Ana Cristina O. Lopes

Routledge
Taylor & Francis Group

LONDON AND NEW YORK

First published 2015
by Routledge
2 Park Square, Milton Park, Abingdon, Oxon OX14 4RN

and by Routledge
711 Third Avenue, New York, NY 10017

Routledge is an imprint of the Taylor & Francis Group, an informa business

British Library Cataloguing in Publication Data
A catalogue record for this book is available from the British Library

Library of Congress Cataloging in Publication Data
Lopes, Ana Cristina, author.
Tibetan Buddhism in diaspora : cultural re-signification in practice and
institutions / Ana Cristina Lopes.
   pages cm. – (Routledge critical studies in Buddhism)
   Includes bibliographical references and index.
   1. Buddhism–Tibet Region–History–20th century. 2. Buddhism–Tibet
   Region–History–21st century. 3. Tibetan diaspora. 4. Tibet Autonomous
   Region (China)–History. I. Title.
   BQ7590.L67 2014
   294.3'92309045–dc23   2014023399

ISBN: 978-0-415-71911-7 (hbk)
ISBN: 978-1-315-73814-7 (ebk)

Typeset in Times New Roman
by Wearset Ltd, Boldon, Tyne and Wear

Printed and bound in the United States of America by Publishers Graphics,
LLC on sustainably sourced paper.

To my parents, with love

Contents

Acknowledgments

First and foremost, I would to express my eternal gratitude to my dear doctoral advisor, Professor Maria Lucia Montes. With her keen talent for revealing the beauty in all things, Maria Lucia kindled in me the passion for knowledge and guided me with brilliance throughout every phase of my doctoral research. I would also like to express my heartfelt appreciation for Professor Robert Thurman, who advised me during my MA degree in Religious Studies at Columbia University, and introduced me with his rare eloquence and charisma to the endlessly fascinating world of Tibetan Buddhism.

I would like to convey my gratitude to FAPESP (Fundação de Amparo à Pesquisa do Estado de São Paulo) for their financial support during my doctoral years, and later, during the post-doctoral research period.

I would also like to thank all those who so generous participated in my fieldwork: Segyu Rinpoche, who granted me crucial interviews, and who received me several times at his center in California; Gen Kelsang Tsultrim, who enabled my fieldwork research at Manjushri Institute in England; Lama Gangchen Rinpoche, who opened his center in Italy to me; and also his secretary, Cosy Back, for helping me with bureaucratic issues. I would also like to thank Lama Caroline and Lama Kalden Rinpoche, for long hours of interviews that proved to be crucial for my research, and my friend Ely Inoue, who followed the development of this research from the very beginning.

My deepest appreciation goes to Professors John Cowart Dawsey, Peter Fry, Emerson Giumbelli and Vagner Gonçalves da Silva, who served on the board of examiners that evaluated this work when it was initially presented as a doctoral dissertation at the Graduate Program in Social Anthropology of the University of São Paulo. I would also like to thank Professors José Guilherme Cantor Magnani, Josidelth Gomes Consorte, Paula Montero and Oliveiros Ferreira, who participated in the qualifying examination related to this work. The incisive comments and suggestions given by these professors greatly contributed to the first version of this book.

I would like to express my enormous gratitude to my colleagues at Napedra (Center for Anthropology, Performance and Drama) at the University of São Paulo, and especially to Professor John Cowart Dawsey, who in the last few years has offered me innumerable and precious opportunities to discuss my research, and to André Kees-Schouten, who provided me with crucial insights about the work of Walter Benjamin.

I would like to thank Professor Janet Gyatso, for sponsoring me as a visiting scholar at the Center for the Study of World Religions (CSWR) at Harvard University, and Professors Diana Taylor and Deborah Kapchan, for sponsoring me at the Department of Performance Studies at New York University. The research done at these institutions was crucial for updating and improving upon my initial research.

Furthermore, I would like to convey my appreciation to Professor Robert Barnett, who through stimulating conversations provided me with important insights on the current political situation in Tibet.

In addition, I would like to thank the editorial team of the Routledge series Critical Studies in Buddhism – Dorothea Schaefter, Jillian Morrison, Rebecca Lawrence and, especially, the series editor, Professor Stephen Berkwitz, whose insightful comments and suggestions were invaluable to the final result of this work.

My special thanks goes to Professor Gabriela dos Reis Sampaio, my dear friend and colleague, who helped me both with her kind support and her careful reading of this book during its final phase of preparation. Also at this crucial moment, my esteemed friend Clarita Maia generously helped me with communication logistics. I express here my sincere gratitude for her key assistance. Furthermore, my heartfelt appreciation goes to Marcia Binder-Schmidt, Dr. Shireen Patell and Dr. Isabelle Onians for their careful reading of selected chapters of this work.

I would like to thank Affonso Parga Nina, for his encouragement during the doctoral years of this research.

Also, I would like to thank my mother(-in-law), Susan Gentry, for her loving support and for giving me shelter during the concluding phase of the redaction of this work.

Last, but by no means least, I would like to profusely thank Professor James Gentry, my ultimate colleague, friend and love, whose meticulous reading of this work improved it in multiple respects, from its language to the richness in references and insights on Tibetan Buddhism. Over the years, James has generously shared his deep knowledge of Tibetan Buddhism with me, dramatically changing my understanding of this religion.

Introduction

This existence of ours is as transient as autumn clouds.
To watch the birth and death of beings
is like looking at the movements of a dance.
A lifetime is like a flash of lightning in the sky,
Rushing by, like a torrent down a steep mountain.

Buddha Shakyamuni, in the words of Sogyal Rinpoche (1992: 25)

This is a study on impermanence, the transience of all existing elements, the certainty of death, the movements of a dance. An essential part of life, impermanence is a source of suffering for those who persist in ignoring it. For those who understand it, however, impermanence represents the gates of freedom. No Buddhist teaching would make sense without the realization that all things, having arisen, disappear. No Buddhist tradition would make sense if it were not also subject to the same laws of impermanence and change that govern all the rest.

This is a study on the malleability of a particular Buddhist tradition, on its adaptability in new contexts. The imperialist ambitions of China, which invaded Tibet in the late 1940s, have sparked the spectacular spread of Tibetan Buddhism worldwide, and especially in western countries. On this side of the planet, the signs of impermanence are more evident than ever, laid bare by the transience of modern life. Modernity pours us into a "maelstrom," as Marshall Berman puts it in his famous essay. A maelstrom "of perpetual disintegration and renewal, of struggle and contradiction, of ambiguity and anguish. To be modern is to be part of a universe in which, as Marx said, 'all that is solid melts into air'" (Berman 1982: 15).

The mastery over technology and its ramifications and consequences for the lives of billions of individuals permeate every aspect of what we call modernity. The industrialization shaping the global landscape, emptying the fields and often causing the uncontrollable growth of cities; scientific advancement of knowledge drastically altering our conception of the universe, its origins, and our place in it; and the development of mass media that obliterates geographical distances are just a few examples of the widespread effects of technological progress on the planet. Nothing could seem more distant, at least at first sight, from the modernity that surrounds our western world than the baroque features and, in fact, the archaic materiality of Tibetan Buddhism. In the centuries before the Chinese invasion, Tibet lived relatively isolated from the rest of the world. Few westerners dared penetrate the country's capital, Lhasa, also known as the "Forbidden City," because foreigners were seldom welcome. In stark contrast to the West, technical progress would not reach the Tibetan plateau until Chinese invaders took it by force.

If the mastery over technology is largely the "engine" that engenders changes at a breakneck pace in the modern world, we could point to the deeper understanding of the impermanence of all things cherished by Buddhists as an important factor that can directly contribute to the great adaptability of monks and lamas in this context. Parallel to the role played by technology in modern societies, this deep understanding provides an internal dynamism to Buddhism that is expressed externally in the manifold configurations that this religious tradition has assumed over two and a half millennia, and more recently, in its intense encounter with the West. Indeed, despite past indifference to what was happening in the rest of the planet, Tibetan spiritual teachers, lay and monastic, would navigate the busy modern setting with great ease already in the mid-1960s. Within two decades, a significant (to say the least) expansion of Tibetan Buddhism would take place first in Europe, North America and neighboring countries in Asia, before reaching more peripheral areas, such as Latin America and Australia.

The research presented in this book reflects an analytic movement that was sparked in one of these peripheral locations and gradually came to encompass the international Tibetan Buddhist circuit in a multi-sited ethnographic project – the exact opposite path of that taken by the lamas. At the outset of this investigation, the "field" was circumscribed to the Shi De Choe Tsog Dharma Center founded in 1987 in the city of São Paulo by Lama Gangchen Rinpoche (b. 1941), a Tibetan lama living in Italy until the present day.[1] Two of the most important "characters" of this book – Lama Gangchen and a Brazilian lama, Lama Shakya (b. 1950) – were involved with this center. Another Brazilian lama, Lama Michel (b. 1981), a disciple of Lama Gangchen, also played a major role in this initial phase.

There are many different kinds of so-called "lamas" among religious specialists active in Tibetan Buddhism. The three lamas present in the initial phase of this project perhaps represent the most classic paradigm: the so-called "reincarnate lama." The case of Lama Michel, for example, was similar to the cases of other western boys who were recognized when still children as reincarnations of Tibetan lamas. After being identified by Lama Gangchen, who was himself a representative of a long lineage of reincarnate lamas, Lama Michel moved to India, where he studied for many years in Sera-me Monastery. Lama Michel thus had the opportunity to immerse himself from a young age in Tibetan culture. However, the same cannot be said for Lama Shakya. This lama was "discovered" when he was already 30 years old, after he had already become fully immersed in Afro-Brazilian religions. Hence, his insertion in the world of Tibetan

Buddhism was much more complex. As an observer of this process, my research therefore became driven by an interest to understand the complicated dynamics of "cultural re-signification" pertaining to the multiple adjustments that this lama had to make in order to integrate his native spiritual inheritance into his new religious status.

During the initial years of research, I closely followed Lama Shakya, Lama Gangchen and Lama Michel. Since these lamas did not have a permanent residence, in their walkabouts around the world they "showed" me new features of Tibetan Buddhism and new contexts in which representatives of this tradition coursed. Gradually, the contemporary Tibetan Buddhist tradition unfolded itself before my eyes as a complex network of networks that connected lamas, monks, western disciples and university professors through extensive international circuits. At the core of this network was the figure of the Dalai Lama, complicated by his dual political and religious attributes. Refracted through the lens of this central character, the combination of politics and religion emerged for me as one of the principal characteristics of Tibetan Buddhist institutions. At the *Tibetan Freedom Concert* that took place in the summer of 1996 in San Francisco, for instance, I had the opportunity to directly observe in the most unexpected arrangements the intimate rapport of these two aspects of Tibetan Buddhism. The association of rock stars with the Tibetan cause and their direct influence over young people on this issue, the presence of monks and nuns – and, in particular, Palden Gyatso, who had been in prison in Tibet for 30 years[2] – pointed to the futility of separating politics and religion in the case of Tibetan Buddhism.

During that same summer in California, on the occasion of an Avalokiteshvara initiation presided over by the Fourteenth Dalai Lama, Tenzin Gyatso, in Pasadena, Los Angeles, this link between politics and religion became even more evident. By the time this initiation took place, I had had the opportunity to do fieldwork in many dharma centers in San Francisco, and more importantly, in Lama Shakya's center in Sebastopol, California. Almost all of the people that I encountered in those first months of research in California were in Pasadena for this event. Moreover, others that I would encounter later, such as Professor Robert Thurman and other professors, also took part in the initiation. In addition, innumerable popular stars like Richard Gere, Steven Seagal and Adam Yauch, the late lead singer of the Beastie Boys, lent the event an atmosphere which was in a sense very similar to the *Tibetan Freedom Concert*. Pasadena had certainly become a veritable pop Buddhist Mecca that summer.

Lama Shakya too was present, along with a good portion of his American disciples. It was in this context that for the first time he confided in me his hesitations about having his name associated with Lama Gangchen's. Up to then, I believed that Lama Gangchen was one of Lama Shakya's main supporters. After all, Lama Shakya's entrance into the Tibetan Buddhist world had begun at the dharma center founded by Lama Gangchen in São Paulo, Brazil. I soon discovered that the tension expressed by Lama Shakya was related to a crisis engendered by the Dalai Lama's decision to advise against the propitiation of a Tibetan

Buddhist protector.[3] According to the Tibetan leader, this protector was nothing more than a mundane god who would promote sectarian conflict among the members of the Tibetan community in exile. Lama Gangchen, one of the few lamas that insisted on propitiating this protector overtly, was considered an enemy of the Dalai Lama and also of the Tibetan cause.

In the context of the event led by the Dalai Lama, Lama Shakya and Lama Gangchen revealed themselves in a new light, one very different from the setting of their dharma center in São Paulo. New sides of these lamas and their relationships with the controversy surrounding the aforementioned protector would also emerge in 1999, when I met them along with Lama Michel in Nepal. The trajectories of these lamas retraced in the preliminary lines of my research induced me to attempt to understand the fragmentation and dispersion of Tibetan Buddhist traditions in the diaspora context, especially in light of the impossibility of detaching politics from religion. Indeed, the diaspora process and its consequences in the political field represent the very core of the complex issues related to the insertion of Tibetan Buddhism into new contexts within the modern world.

The above issue suggested to me that Tibetan Buddhist traditions have acquired new functions in the diaspora context. Taken from its original context and exposed to an intense process of cultural fragmentation, Tibetan Buddhism, and Tibetan culture as a whole, has gained new meanings. In the words of the Brazilian anthropologist Manuela Carneiro da Cunha (1986), outside its original context, any culture is transformed primarily into an instrument that enables communication with new conversation partners. Thus, for a culture to be successful in this task it is necessary to select among its elements the items that will best facilitate meaningful dialogue, since, as Cunha says, "one does not take all their belongings to the diaspora" (Cunha 1986: 101). In the context of the diaspora, Tibet's Buddhist heritage became through a process of "condensation" – both politically and religiously – a synopsis of Tibetan culture, its most visible face and the main negotiation token for Tibetans. In other words, Tibetan Buddhism turned into an identity-defining diacritical feature[4] for Tibetans in the diaspora.

Before the Chinese invasion and the subsequent exile of Tibetans throughout the world, the dissemination of Tibetan Buddhism was primarily limited to Tibet and its immediate neighbors – Nepal, Bhutan, Mongolia, China and so forth. Once the process of Tibet's occupation had begun, transmitting Buddhist teachings became a matter of survival for many lamas who sought asylum in Asian countries and the West. Then, in a second stage, this made possible a concentration of power in the hands of some of these lamas, which enabled them to act with considerable independence from the mainstream institutions of Tibetan Buddhism.

The diaspora and the reorganization of Tibetan Buddhist institutions in exile represents the direct consequence of both the destruction of the Tibetan state headed by the Dalai Lama, and the dismantlement of Tibetan Buddhist religious organizations, which were precipitated by the Chinese invasion and the propagation of a policy of terror in Tibet. The specters of these institutions continue to exist outside their original contexts and become activated in new settings. Thus, underlying the spread of Tibetan Buddhism in the world, there are "de-institutionalized" and "de-territorialized" projects of political power and religious organization, which, among several other consequences, has engendered the gradual "autonomization" of lamas and lineages inside the religious field of Tibetan Buddhism.

The institutions of Tibetan Buddhism are, in this new context, refracted on a broken mirror, reflecting in a fragmented way an infinite number of representations. Here, James Clifford's considerations about what he calls "ethnographic surrealism" (Clifford 1988: 117–51) are apropos. His usage of the term "surrealism" goes beyond its habitual meanings to describe "an aesthetics that values fragments, curious collections, unexpected juxtapositions – that work to provoke the manifestation of extraordinary realities drawn from the domains of the erotic, the exotic and the unconscious" (ibid.: 118). In a larger sense, and according to the orientation related to the cultural order proposed by Clifford, I was compelled by the extreme situation of the dispersion of Tibetan Buddhism in the world today to adopt as the main issues of my study the fragmentation and juxtaposition of cultural values. In a certain sense, its insertion into the modern world did more than bring Tibetan Buddhism into a new context. The main effect was to trigger some of the logics pertaining to modernity – and more specifically, the tendency toward fragmentation and confrontation with other cultural realities – within the core of this religious tradition. This work is an exploration of that process of transformation, as provoked by the new elements that now permeate Tibetan Buddhism.

I believe it is precisely in terms of the encounter with modernity and the assimilation by Tibetan Buddhism of some of modernity's most fundamental elements that we should understand the process of transformation or cultural re-signification currently experienced by this religious tradition. It is crucial therefore to go back to Marshall Sahlins's comments about the relationship between history and structure:

> In action and in the world – technically, in acts of reference – the cultural categories acquire new functional values. Burdened with the world, the cultural meanings are thus altered. It follows that the relationship between categories changes: the structure is transformed.
>
> (Sahlins 1987 [1985]: 138)

In the case of Tibetan Buddhism, we should take into consideration that the transformations experienced by this tradition, albeit dramatic, are happening in accordance with the internal logic (or logics) of pre-Chinese invasion Tibetan culture and religion, which should be understood as the subjacent structure that confers meanings to the historical process, or to its interpretations. Hence, if contact with the West certainly has the effect of transforming Tibetan Buddhist institutions, and Tibetan culture as whole in the diaspora, this happens within parameters that are determined largely by cultural categories that already existed in Tibet.

On the other hand, to understand the diaspora situation it is necessary to transpose the theory developed by Sahlins in *Islands of History* to a more global context, which is not accomplished without investing the theory with new dimensions and implications. Clifford Geertz gives us a good indication about how to determine the parameters within which Sahlins's reflections could be applied to the case of Tibetan Buddhism, by developing, and in a certain sense enlarging, his concept of the "interpretation of cultures" as "thick description." As he puts it:

> [I]n answering this question [about what the accounts of the senses of self-hood can tell us in relation to the native's point of view in Java, Bali and Morocco], it is necessary, I think, first to notice the characteristic intellectual movement, the inward conceptual rhythm, in each of these analyses, and indeed in all similar analyses, including those of Malinowski – namely, a continuous dialectical tacking between the most local of local detail and the most global of global structure in such a way as to bring them into simultaneous view.
>
> (Geertz 1983: 69)

Here, Geertz is talking about the process of understanding, which in his view pertains to anthropological knowledge in general, as interpretation that must work along hierarchically stratified levels of meanings, allowing for the distinctions between winking, blinking and a satirist rehearsing in front of a mirror. Yet, today perhaps it is necessary to understand the relationship between the "local" and the "global" introduced in *Local Knowledge* in a much more literal sense.

Indeed, in many ways, the Tibetan diaspora and the transformation of its religious traditions can be best understood through an analysis that takes into consideration the reciprocal influences established in the dialectic of events of local meanings and the global, planetary context in which traditions are reflected and transmuted. In this sense, the "most local" detail in the peculiar religious trajectory of Lama Shakya, for example, is capable of shedding new light on "more global" processes, which are related to logics that govern the transformations experienced by Tibetan Buddhism as a whole. In the same vein, the political context in which the Dalai Lama approves or disapproves of certain ritual practices, as in the case of the controversial protector deity mentioned above, can help clarify the relationship between a Tibetan lama like Lama Gangchen and a Brazilian lama in a distant dharma center in São Paulo. It is when analyzing the global-local dynamics of the Tibetan diaspora that the image of a Tibetan Buddhist transnational religious field comes into focus. As we will see throughout this study, even if this field's ties are rather loose due to a lack of centralized institutional support, there is a sense of cohesion capable of imposing certain limitations or even complications to the activities of "autonomized" lamas around the world.

Finally, it would not be possible to conclude this introduction without broaching a few issues related to the narrative structure in which this study is presented. It is first necessary to consider the object of this research, Tibetan Buddhism, and the problem that determines its approach, the dynamics of culture, or its process of transformation and re-signification, in the context of the diaspora and the Tibetan government in exile's[5] agenda to achieve some level of self-governance for Tibetans in Tibet, if not complete autonomy from China. The contemporary Tibetan exile situation, with its fragmentation and dispersion, requires an analytical approach that is capable of articulating the "local" and the "global" in a non-metaphorical sense, meaning, ethnographic descriptions of micro-level case studies and their contextualization within political and religious dynamics carried out on a global scale. Without a doubt, this is a big challenge. Nonetheless, I believe that the method through which I approach this object of study should be in accordance with the moment in which we live today, taking into consideration that certain factors – like the interdependence between societies and the mutual consciousness of cultures that confront each other across multiple registers of the globalization process – ask for new forms of sensibility and, at the same time, new styles of ethnographic writing (Marcus and Fischer 1986).

It was the so-called postmodern turn in anthropology (Clifford 1988; Clifford and Marcus 1986; Marcus 1998; Taussig 1987, 1992) that in recent times has called attention to the issue of representation, emphasizing not only some of its traditionally hidden dimensions (like power relations that permeate the social construction of representation), but also the issue of how to represent research findings by means of ethnographic writing. Perhaps Tibetan Buddhism represents, in this sense, an exemplary case, in which the issue of representation should constitute a focal point of theoretical reflection. This is not only because of the impossibility of ignoring power issues in the construction of its meanings today in the diaspora, but also because of the dispersion and fragmentation that this religious tradition embodies, creating an almost infinite multiplicity of representations that supposedly translate its meanings in the present world.

Geertz's concept of "interpretation," according to which it is not possible to separate analysis from ethnographic (thick) description (Geertz 1973: 3–30) is a first crucial reference for the narrative structure of the present book. At the same time, following Michael Taussig's example, I have tried to bring forth through an extensive reading of documentary, primary and secondary literary materials, other perspectives to which I could not have had immediate access by means of fieldwork research alone. These include newspapers, official documents, secondary scholarship, and Tibetan language narrative and ritual literature, among other sources. I have thus endeavored to realize what George Marcus calls an "ethnography of complex connections," through which it is possible to produce one narrative that is, at the same time, macro and micro and none of them in particular (Marcus 1998: 50). In this way, I have sought to articulate some of the different viewpoints by means of which Tibetan Buddhism is represented and consequently culturally re-signified.

In order to accurately convey the plurality of representations that in new contexts express the multiple forms of Tibetan Buddhism, transformed anew into a "synthesis" of Tibetan culture in the diaspora, it is crucial to adopt a narrative style that reflects a plurality of viewpoints. In general terms, the structuring principle of this work's narrative style is based on the montage technique, in which the ideational elements of the image "remain unreconciled, rather than fusing into one harmonizing perspective" (Buck-Morss 1989: 67). In this regard, I follow in the footsteps of Walter Benjamin, who was convinced of the necessity of a visual logic, not a linear logic, affirming that it was essential to build concepts in images, "according to the cognitive principles of montage" (ibid.: 218). In this Benjaminian spirit, the narrative structure of this book was designed as a mandala, a kind of graphic representation in which all the parts relate to one another and to the whole, seeking thus bring to light the unexpected connections that arise from the montage principle.

In the same vein, the sequence of the chapters makes reference to what can be called the "Science of Death," one of the most central and well-known aspects of Tibetan culture. Over the centuries, Tibetans have explored the nature of death, developing a series of death-related teachings and practices that are at the very core of Tibetan Buddhism. These teachings maintain that the existence of sentient beings is divided into three stages: death, bardo (intermediate stage) and rebirth. I have organized the chapters of the present work in accordance with these three stages, with the belief that this arrangement is capable of communicating an important feature of the Tibetan worldview.

Part I, Death, presents two chapters that deal with the processes of destruction and creation. In Chapter 1, *Echoes of terror from the top of the world*, I discuss how a politics of terror was established throughout Tibet during and after the Chinese invasion. I argue there that this gradually produced a space in which Tibetan culture was, in a certain sense, torn apart, a "space of death," as the other face of a civilizing project (the communist one) that intended, at least theoretically, to improve the lives of the Tibetan people. In Chapter 2, *The power of compassion*, I go back in time to analyze the bases upon which the government of the Dalai Lamas and its symbolic apparatus were built. Established in 1642 by the Fifth Dalai Lama, Ngawang Lobsang Gyatso (1617–82), this government endured until the Chinese communists little by little dismantled its old power structures.

Part II, Bardo, features Chapter 3, *Buddhist encounters in the diaspora*, which sets the stage for the ethnographic portion of the book. In this chapter, I discuss the formation of the transnational religious field of Tibetan Buddhism in the diaspora, emphasizing both the refashioning of the Fourteenth Dalai Lama's identity and the creation of "dialogue zones" along with its implications for the process of re-signifying this religion in new contexts.

Part III, Rebirth, comprises three chapters that discuss the re-signification of Tibetan Buddhism, on the bases of ethnographic research done in several locations around the globe. Chapter 4, *A confluence of spiritual universes*, explores the insertion of three lamas – Lama Gangchen Rinpoche, Lama Shakya Zangpo (a.k.a. Segyu Rinpoche) and Geshe Kelsang Gyatso (b. 1931) – into the transnational religious field of Tibetan Buddhism. Through the practice of healing, the reinvention of ritual, and the creation of study programs, these lamas, with a missionary spirit of their own, helped ensure a rebirth of Tibetan Buddhism in the diaspora, revealing in their actions the dynamic process of the cultural "resignification" of this religion in open exchange with western cultures. Chapter 5, *Etiquette, fantastic tales and the construction of sacred space*, is mainly concerned with the constitution of power relations through the symbolic construction of the sacred in Brazil and other parts of the world, where Lama Gangchen Rinpoche, Segyu Rinpoche and Geshe Kelsang Gyatso are active. Chapter 6, *The divine theater of Kalachakra*, demonstrates how the state myths and rituals, and the power held by the Dalai Lama as king of Tibet were not completely lost through the destruction of the governmental structure brought about by the Chinese invasion of the country. In this chapter, I show how by staging the Kalachakra ritual the Dalai Lama keeps the symbolic power of the former Tibetan state alive, using means similar to those utilized in the past, such as recourse to the spectacle.

The final part, Once more death... returns once again to the beginning of the sequence, but rather than complete it, opens the field to further meanings. Chapter 7, *Spiritual politics*, discusses the controversy around the decision made by the Dalai Lama to advise against the propitiation of a protector deity of the Gelug School of Tibetan Buddhism, Dorje Shugden. In the context of diaspora, previously existing conflicts around the figure of Dorje Shugden gained new dimensions. In the face of the fragmentation of Tibetan culture, new political alliances were formed, giving birth to a conflicting situation, which, although rooted in a traditional setting, acquired different meanings. In analyzing the controversy around the protector Dorje Shugden, I shed light on the realignment of forces within the transnational religious field of Tibetan Buddhism.

Notes

1 The research presented in this book has as its point of departure my Ph.D. dissertation in anthropology at the University of São Paulo. This study was released in Brazil in 2006 by the publishing house of the University of São Paulo under the title *Ventos da Impermanência: um Estudo sobre a Ressignificação do Budismo Tibetano no Contexto da Diáspora*. Over the years, and especially when I was a visiting scholar at Columbia, Harvard and New York Universities, I had the opportunity to update and improve upon this foundational material, particularly through gaining access to primary literature in the Tibetan language and deepening my knowledge of relevant secondary literature. The current study is the fruit of research done during this time abroad, combined with the ethnographic work conducted in the context of my Ph.D. research.

2 In the following year, Palden Gyatso released his autobiography in the United States and the United Kingdom under two different titles: *The Autobiography of a Tibetan Monk* (1997a) and *Fire Under the Snow: Testimony of a Tibetan Prisoner* (1997b). In it, Palden Gyatso reports in detail the invasion of Tibet and his suffering in Chinese prisons. As we will see in the first chapter of this book, for Palden Gyatso and many other Tibetans the publication of autobiographies became an important instrument of resistance against the Chinese occupation of Tibet. Before traveling to the United

States, Palden Gyatso was politically active in Tibet, inside and outside Chinese prisons. The report about human rights in Tibet published by Asia Watch in 1988 cites his name. According to the report, Palden Gyatso distributed pamphlets promoting Tibetan independence and shared with others his hopes that the Dalai Lama would return to Tibet (Asia Watch Committee 1988: 37).

3 The so-called "dharma protectors" have a fundamental role in Tibetan Buddhism. In René De Nebesky-Wojkowitz's words,

> to protect the Buddhist religion and its institutions against adversaries, as well as to preserve the integrity of its teachings is a task assigned, in accordance with precepts common to the various sects of Tibetan Buddhism, to an important group of deities, best known under the name *chos skyong* (Skt. *Dharmapāla, Dvārapāla*), "protectors of the religious law".
>
> (Nebesky-Wojkowitz 1993: 3)

4 Another important reference in the study of ethnic groups and their permanence across boundaries is, of course, Fredrik Barth's celebrated introduction to the book *Ethnic Groups and Boundaries* (1969). In it, Barth discusses, among other things, the essential role played by "individual actors" in determining which features are significant in the process of marking ethnic differences. In his words,

> The features that are taken into account are not the sum of "objective" differences, but only those which the actors themselves regard as significant. Not only do ecologic variations mark and exaggerate differences; some cultural features are used by the actors as signals and emblems of differences, others are ignored, and in some relationships radical differences are played down and denied. The cultural contents of ethnic dichotomies would seem analytically to be of two orders: (i) overt signals or signs – the diacritical features that people look for and exhibit to show identity, often such features as dress, language, house-form, or general style of life, and (ii) basic value orientations: the standards of morality and excellence by which performance is judged.
>
> (Barth 1969: 14)

5 The official name of the Tibetan government in exile is the Central Tibetan Administration (CTA). However, to clearly distinguish this political apparatus from contemporaneous power structures in occupied Tibet proper, throughout this work I refer to the India-based governing body using the more commonly known phrase Tibetan government in exile. Moreover, I believe that the term "government in exile" conveys better one of the main premises of the Central Tibetan Administration, which is to be a continuation of the independent government of Tibet.

Part I
Death

1 Echoes of terror from the top of the world

Nowadays I avail myself of this primary distinction concerning all aesthetic values: in every case I ask, "Is it hunger or superabundance that have become creative here?" At first glance, a different distinction may appear more advisable – it's far more noticeable – namely, the question of whether the creation was caused by a desire for fixing, for immortalizing, for being, *or rather by a desire for destruction, for change, for novelty, for future, for* becoming.

Friedrich Nietzsche, *The Gay Science* (2001 [1882]: 235)

I start with terror and, most probably, its echoes will be heard throughout this work. In its abstract, aseptic, rational form, terror can very well be understood as one necessary step towards civilization, a stage that leads to a blank sheet on which the most beautiful projects of society can be sketched. In practice, terror tears apart, but also leaves its imprint, often becoming an invisible and creative bond, the birdlime connecting, in a fragile arrangement, fragments of fragments, impressions of totality already dissolved. In the case of the Chinese occupation of Tibet, terror was born from the clash between two worldviews predominantly incompatible with each other, if not completely contradictory.

I start my account by the report of an encounter that happened almost 30 years after the Chinese People's Liberation Army (PLA) marched triumphantly through Tibetan territory, announcing the revolution to come. We are in August of 1979, in the eastern Tibetan village of Tashikhiel, where a crowd of 6,000 people gathered little by little.[1] Hours earlier the local population had received the news of the imminent visit of a fact-finding delegation sent by the Fourteenth Dalai Lama himself. More than 20 years had passed since the Tibetan spiritual and secular leader had fled Tibet to take refuge in India, and since then Tibetans had been deprived of any contact with the Dalai Lama or members of his family. The delegation that would visit Tashikiel was led precisely by the Dalai Lama's brother, Lobsang Samten.

As they approached the village, the delegation members became increasingly surprised by what was there to greet them. In Lobsang Samten's words, "it was unbelievable. Everywhere, people were shouting, throwing scarves, apples, flowers" (Avedon 1994: 333). The presence of the Dalai Lama's brother among the members of the delegation transformed the fact-finding mission into a religious ceremony. "They were dying to see us," reported Lobsang Samten. "They climbed on the roofs and pushed inside, stretching out their hands to touch us." Meanwhile, the Chinese officials screamed, trying to protect the delegation: "Don't go out! Don't go out! They'll kill you! They'll kill you!" (ibid.).

The Chinese officials had no doubt that the superiority of the communist system was already totally assimilated by Tibetans after more than 20 years of occupation, and several reeducation sessions. They firmly believed that the lives of the fact-finding delegation members were at risk since they represented everything bad that existed in the Tibet of the past: "Feudalism," "the poison of religion," and the "oppression of the people."[2] However, the scenes of devotion and commotion witnessed by them in Tashikiel would happen again and again wherever the delegation went, gaining colossal dimensions in the capital city of Lhasa.

Tibetans cried profusely as they reported the details of what had become of their lives in the past decades. Everyone had a story of death and torture in their family to tell. Monasteries had been destroyed; lamas and monks had been executed or put in prison. Similar stories would be told and retold in all the villages and towns the delegation visited. The Chinese officials seemed surprised with what they saw. Mr. Kao, a senior official in the Nationalities Affairs Commission that accompanied the mission, confided to Lobsang Samten:

> "You are the representative of the Dalai Lama," he shouted, "and people are trying to get blessings even from you. What will happen if the Dalai Lama himself came? We cannot control it. We cannot be responsible. These people are just crazy!"
>
> (Ibid.)

The sincere surprise of Mr. Kao in the face of the strong display of Tibetan devotion is, in a certain way, the portrait of many decades of Chinese occupation in Tibet. Since the Chinese communists crossed the Tibetan border with the aim to integrate Tibet into their political project, they were constantly confronted by the unconditional faith of Tibetans in their religion and especially in the figure of the Dalai Lama. Convinced of the superiority of the communist system, the Chinese officials clearly had a hard time understanding the attachment of Tibetans to their "backward and feudal" religion. The conflict of almost opposite worldviews, ways of life, codes of conduct and so forth engendered in Tibet a situation that, even with the passing of decades, has proven itself to be in many senses untenable. The recent cases of Tibetans setting their bodies on fire in order to protest against the conditions of life under Chinese rule represents perhaps the most extreme outcome of the politics of terror and oppression perpetrated by the People's Republic of China (PRC) against some minorities in their territory.[3] Symbolic transgression, death and destruction have been among the weapons used by the Chinese to sever the connection between Tibetans and their own sense of cultural identity and history.

Histories of Sino-Tibetan relations

It could indeed be said that different views of history are at the very core of the clash between Tibetan and Chinese worldviews. Chinese claims over Tibet go back to the thirteenth century.[4] According to the Chinese version of history, it was during that time that Tibet became an integral part of Chinese territory. This argument is based on the Mongol conquest of both regions. In general terms, Tibetans and Chinese agree that the crucial encounter in 1247 between the Tibetan spiritual master Sakya Pandita (1182–1251) and the powerful Mongol prince Goden Khan (d. 1253), the grandson of Genghis Khan (d. 1227), marked the beginning of important changes in the power structures of Tibet. The Government White Papers, a historical account prepared by the Information Office of the State Council of the PRC in English,[5] describes this encounter as an instance in which the "terms for Tibetan submission to the Mongols" was decided. It then explains that

> the regime of the Mongol Khanate changed its title to Yuan in 1271 and unified the whole of China in 1279, establishing a central government, which, following the Han (206 BC – AD 220) and Tang (618–907) dynasties, achieved great unification of various regions and races within the domain of China.

The traditional Tibetan historiographical approach to the matter emphasizes, on its side, the religious aspects of Sakya–Mongol relations, pointing out the essence of Tibetan political theory vis-à-vis the country's neighbors. According to this interpretation of the historical facts, the kind of relationship established between Mongols – and later the Yuan dynasty (1271–1368) – and Tibetans did not involve the direct interference of foreign forces in the internal affairs of Tibet, even though it did imply the payment of tributes to the suzerain state, and so forth. Tsepon Wangchuk Deden Shakabpa (1907–89), the finance minister and senior diplomatic representative of the Dalai Lama in India during the first years of the Chinese occupation, writes in his massive historical treatise *One Hundred Thousand Moons* that after conquering most of Tibet, Goden Khan "needed a good lama who knew how to teach the essential path of Buddhism in Hor and Mongolia" (Shakabpa 2010: 209). He then asked the Hor Golden Calligrapher,[6] an office of the Mongolian Empire akin to an envoy, to send a letter to Sakya Pandita, who had the reputation of being one of the most accomplished Tibetan Buddhist teachers of his time, summoning him to a meeting.

Shakabpa, who was encouraged by the Fourteenth Dalai Lama himself to write his treatise on Tibetan history,[7] identifies in this encounter (and the circumstances leading up to it) the beginnings of the so-called "preceptor–patron relationship" (Tib. *mchod gnas dang yon bdag*) with the Mongols. Briefly stated, this relationship implies that the lama act as a teacher to a powerful leader, who offers in return protection and patronage. In Shakabpa's narrative, which is based primarily on Tibetan sources, Sakya Pandita is said to have healed Goden Khan of leprosy and to have further impressed the Mongol warrior with his ability to unmask a ruse created to test his powers (ibid.: 212–13). According to this version of history, the particular kind of relationship established between Sakya Pandita and Goden Khan would be repeated and strengthened by the Tibetan lama's nephew, Phagpa Chögyal (1235–80), and the next important Mongol leader, Kublai Khan (1215–94).

The discussion around the Sakya–Mongol partnership sets the stage for the central argument of *One Hundred Thousand Moons*. In the words of Derek Maher, who translated and annotated the English edition of the book, it is the preceptor–patron relationship that Shakabpa "sees as animating the rest of Tibetan history" (ibid.: 199). This is a crucial point for the appreciation of differences in the Tibetan and Chinese historical interpretations. Without necessarily denying the particulars of the Chinese arguments connected to their "ownership of Tibet," as it is stated in the White Papers, Tibetans assert their independent status through expounding historical facts on the basis of the preceptor–patron relationship, i.e., seeing them mainly through the lenses of religion.

The Ming dynasty (1368–1644) succeeded the Yuan, becoming the "first native Chinese dynasty to control all of China since the T'ang" (Smith 1996: 101). In the White Papers document it is asserted, "The central government of the Ming Dynasty retained most of the titles and ranks of official positions instituted during the Yuan Dynasty." This claim and others associated with it, such as the conferral of titles to lamas, are directly contested by Shakabpa right at the beginning of Chapter 5 of *One Hundred Thousand Moons*, which discusses the religious and political developments from the middle of the fourteenth century to the beginning of the seventeenth century (Shakabpa 2010: 249). Western scholars tend to agree with Shakabpa that Tibet experienced during this period a situation of total independence in relation to Chinese imperial forces. In a paper that seeks to clarify some of the contradictions between Tibetan and Chinese positions, historian Elliot Sperling is categorical: "Bluntly put, there was no Ming political authority over Tibet – no ordinances, laws, taxes, etc., imposed inside Tibet by the Ming" (Sperling 2004: 27).[8]

Matters became more complicated during the ruling period of the Qing (1644–1911), the dynasty that succeeded the Ming. Like the Yuan dynasty, the Qing also had a foreign origin, more specifically Manchu. Despite this fact, as historian Jonathan Spence puts it, "While some descendants of the Ming ruling house fought on with tenacity, most Chinese accepted the new rulers because the Manchus promised – with only a few exceptions – to uphold China's traditional beliefs and social structures" (Spence 1990: 4). The PRC Government White Papers lead us to believe that the involvement of the Qing dynasty in Tibet's affairs came in the first years of the new rule:

> When the Qing Dynasty replaced the Ming Dynasty in 1644, it further strengthened administration over Tibet. In 1653 and 1713, the Qing emperors granted honorific titles to the 5th Dalai Lama and the 5th Bainqen Lama [i.e., the Fifth Panchen Lama], henceforth officially establishing the titles of the Dalai Lama and the Bainqen Erdeni and their political and religious status in Tibet.

Tibetan and western historiographies present this period in a more complicated light. As we will see in more detail in the following chapter, the Fifth Dalai Lama Ngawang Lobsang Gyatso (1617–82) came to power in 1642 with the help of Gushri Khan (b. 1582),[9] leader of the Qoshot Mongols, establishing the Ganden Podrang government,[10] which lasted until the Chinese invasion of Tibet in 1950. After the war led by Gushri Khan, vast segments of Tibetan territory were unified and brought under the rule of the new government. During the time of the Fifth Dalai Lama and his powerful Mongol protectors, there seemed to be a reasonable degree of independence on the Tibetan side in relation to the Manchu court, even if a certain level of ceremonial subordination was present.

Things gradually became more complicated with the weakening of Qoshot Mongol leaders and the consequent rise of external threats. In 1718, Chinese imperial troops had to intervene in Tibet in order to expel Jungar Mongol invaders. After successfully completing the task, the emperor installed a provisional military government in Lhasa (Petech 1950: 62), subsequently establishing the norms for a Chinese protectorate. The grip of the Manchu court over Tibet became stronger than ever after the Gorkha invasion of Tibet in 1792, when the Ganden Podrang government pleaded for Chinese military help once more. In 1793, the Qing court promulgated the "Regulations for Resolving Tibetan Matters" (Sperling 2004: 13), a document with 29 articles that, according to the White Papers and other Chinese documents, was created "to better govern Tibet."

The presence of representatives of the Manchu emperor in the Tibetan court known as "ambans," or "high commissioners," from this time on represents perhaps the most damaging fact against the argument for Tibet's full autonomy during that time. The "Regulations for Resolving Tibetan Matters" elevated the rank of these representatives to a "level equal to that of Chinese provincial governors" (ibid.: 13). The extent of power of the ambans in Tibetan affairs varied over time, but in general terms they served as intermediaries between the Ganden Podrang government and the Manchu emperor. The institution of the so-called "Golden Urn," which at least in theory granted the Manchu emperor the final word in the process of recognizing important Tibetan lamas, such as the Dalai Lama and the Panchen Lama, represented yet another serious interference in Tibetan affairs.[11] Notwithstanding Shakabpa's assertion that the Golden Urn was "either not used, or a pretense was made of having used it" (*apud* Sperling 2004: 21), the fact remains that some authority – albeit purely ceremonial – was granted to the emperor in a very crucial terrain, creating in this way a precedent that has engendered serious consequences even in recent times, as I will discuss in greater detail below.

In the same vein, another important matter that emerged during the Qing era is directly connected to the figure of the Panchen Lama – called "Bainqen Erdeni" in the Chinese document – the second most important lama in the political hierarchy of the Gelug School. In 1728, the Manchus presented the Fifth Panchen Lama, Lobsang Yeshe (1663–1737), with an imperial edict establishing his secular power over "gTsaṅ [Tsang] and Western Tibet as far as Kailasa

[Mount Kailash]," which marked, according to historian Luciano Petech, the creation of "his political importance as some sort of balance against that of the Dalai Lama" (Petech 1950: 139). Partly due to this historical event, the Chinese communists would later develop a very close relationship with the Tenth Panchen Lama, Chökyi Gyaltsen (1938–89), attempting to transform him into their most important Tibetan ally in their occupation of Tibet.

With the collapse of the Qing dynasty and the subsequent establishment of the Republic of China (1912–49), it is generally agreed among Tibetan and western scholars that Tibet became a de facto independent territory. The Chinese official position, however, is that the "continuous rule over Tibet" was effective also during this period. In the words of historian Tsering Shakya, however, "When the Qing regime collapsed in 1911, the Tibetans severed all ties with China, expelled the Amban and his military escort and declared independence, thus ending nearly two centuries of Qing authority in the region" (Shakya 2009: 100). The situation of civil war that erupted in China around that time made it possible for the small Tibetan army to push the Chinese forces back to Dartsedo, an important town at the border of the two territories. The Thirteenth Dalai Lama, Thubten Gyatso (1876–1933), believed nevertheless that a political solution should eventually be sought. The Tibetan leader decided then to ask Great Britain to mediate the negotiations. At that time, Great Britain represented the only connection between Tibet and the West.[12]

A certain level of ambivalence, nevertheless, characterized Anglo-Tibetan relations. On the one hand, they were determined by British India's commercial need to gain access to the Himalayan region, and the Tibetan determination to prevent that from happening. While on the other hand, the British represented an important counterbalance to Chinese ambitions for Tibetan territory, as British commercial interests in Tibet caused Great Britain to delegitimize Chinese claims over the country. In the face of the imminent Chinese threat, the Thirteenth Dalai Lama and his government would then appeal to British India. Coordinated by Sir Henry McMahon, representative of British India, the Simla Convention was held between 1913 and 1914 as an attempt to solve the crisis between Tibet and China. Through this convention, and with British support, the Thirteenth Dalai Lama tried to reaffirm Tibet's autonomy from China. The Chinese, however, not agreeing with the terms of the accord, decided not to sign it. Tibet and Great Britain nevertheless signed it, thus creating the only international document that recognized Tibetan autonomy.[13]

Civilization, terror and storytelling

Whatever the legal status of Tibet vis-à-vis China has been over the years, it is undeniable that the level of encroachment between the two countries increased dramatically during the communist era. Tibet was then also included in a civilizing impetus that for centuries had marked the interactions between Chinese[14] rulers and diverse ethnic groups living inside and along the periphery of their territory. Given the profound influence China had throughout Central Asia, the

Confucianist project promoted by the Han emperors of the Ming dynasty and later by the Manchu emperors of the Qing dynasty is perhaps the most remarkable example of this kind of civilizing project. In a certain way, the communist project represents a continuation of the Confucianist project.

Chinese communist rule was founded on the establishment of a superior–inferior relationship among the many ethnic groups inside what came to be known as the People's Republic of China. Between 1956 and 1958, an ethnographic and linguistic survey on a national scale was conducted with the goal of identifying the minority groups in China (Wu 1990: 2). The Chinese communists "classified the population within China's political borders into 56 *minzu*, or 'nationalities,' so that every citizen of the People's Republic of China is defined as belonging to a group that is more civilized or less so" (Harrell 1995: 9). Tibet was classified in the third level, as a feudal society. This scale, presented in a "scientific" language and based on Friedrich Engels' interpretation of Lewis Morgan's writings, would supposedly be able to determine how much each of the minority groups had to progress in order "to catch up with the civilizers" (ibid.). In accordance with the premises of the communists, all minorities should be considered equal, and the "civilizing center" should not be explicitly Han, thereby avoiding a situation where the majority ethnicity occupies a privileged position. In practice, however, the prejudice against minorities and the notion that Chinese of Han origin were ahead in an "evolutionary historical scale" brought the communist project very close to the Confucianist project (ibid.: 22–7).

It can perhaps be said that the Chinese communists created with this classification a kind of cosmology, an ordered worldview that they tried to impose upon minority groups. Among the fundamental elements of this cosmology, the ideas of a civilizing center, an established order and a possible path towards progress occupy privileged position. However, as Walter Benjamin rightly affirms, there is "no document of civilization which is not at the same time a document of barbarism" (*apud* Taussig 1992: 14). The communist project is no exception to this maxim, and the politics of terror fits its underlying civilizing ideology in different ways. Soon after the Chinese communist revolution triumphed, the barbaric aspects of its civilizing project emerged, as the government implemented practices of terror that became part of the daily life of some of the populations included in the vast territory of the PRC. Tibetans in particular suffered the prolonged effects of the communist politics of terror. This is so largely because the Chinese have never culturally assimilated Tibetans, as is the case for most minority groups inside the PRC. In an important insight, Elliot Sperling states this quite well, pointing to the crux of the matter concerning Chinese claims that Tibetans are just one more minority group among many others inside China:

> In the case of Tibet, where the historical memory encompasses a sense of nationhood and a knowledge of a time when Tibetans presided over a Tibetan state, administered by a Tibetan bureaucracy using Tibetan-language administrative documents and tools, the persistence of tensions is not surprising. The category of "national minority" ultimately reduces

Tibetans to a par with a variety of other groups, many numbering just tens of thousands or fewer, and having no similar national history or consciousness.

(Sperling 2004: 29–30)

In the face of this undeniable sense of Tibetan history and nationhood, one of the biggest challenges for the Chinese was to immediately replace the Tibetan worldview with a communist, materialistic worldview. In order to accomplish this, practices of symbolic transgression and violence were established. Gradually, these practices of transgression and violence created a space in which Tibetan culture would be torn apart, a space of death that can be described as the other face of the communist civilizing project, which, at least in theory, aimed at bettering the lives of Tibetans.

It would not be long before echoes of the politics of terror born from the communist civilizing project in Tibet were heard across the world through the voices of exiled Tibetans who fled their country in tens of thousands over the last 50 years. As soon as 1959, the International Commission of Jurists published a report on the Tibet question, discussing, among other things, the violation of human rights in Tibet upon the basis of interviews conducted with exiled Tibetans (International Commission of Jurists 1959). Amnesty International, International Campaign for Tibet, Tibet Information Network and other organizations also interviewed exiled Tibetans, producing a number of reports to denounce human rights abuses in their country of origin.

Side by side with these humanitarian reports, the Tibetan diaspora has also brought about another very particular kind of account to describe communist policies of oppression in Tibet: autobiographies. Tibet has a long and robust tradition of producing first person written accounts of life stories.[15] In the past, these autobiographies were mainly written by religious figures, lamas in particular, who sought to inspire disciples with the detailed narration of their own spiritual paths. The Chinese invasion and the subsequent escape of Tibetans into exile changed this pattern. Now, side by side with autobiographies by these highly regarded religious figures stand accounts by simple monks, ordinary people and aristocrats, some of whom have served as officials in the pre-invasion Tibetan government.[16] All these works have in common a highly political tone born from the direct experiences lived by the authors under Chinese rule and in the exile context.

These autobiographical lines started to be written in the space of death, which I referenced above. They constitute a direct response to the state-sponsored violence Tibetans have suffered since the invasion of their country. In the face of the extreme conditions experienced under the new political regime (and also in the face of the strong, official Chinese propaganda inside the PRC), autobiographical writing can be seen as an important instrument in reaffirming Tibetan individual identities and history. As anthropologist Michael Jackson writes in the *Politics of Storytelling*, "To reconstitute events in a story is no longer to live those events in passivity, but to actively rework them, both in dialogue with others and within one's own imagination" (Jackson 2002: 15). In the case of Tibetan refugees, these autobiographies, which were mostly written in English (sometimes with the help of sympathizers with the Tibetan cause), represent, among other things, an important means to establish a dialogue with westerners, gathering in this way allies in the struggle to secure Tibet's autonomy from Chinese rule.

It comes as no surprise, then, that a number of these autobiographies were born from the direct appeal of the Fourteenth Dalai Lama himself, who requested that Tibetans newly coming into exile commit to writing their stories of hardship under Chinese rule. In his efforts to bring the attention of the world to the Tibetan cause, the Dalai Lama realized very early on in his exile the power of first person narratives. In 1962, a mere three years after he escaped to India, he published his first autobiography under the suggestive title, *My Land and My People* (Tenzin Gyatso 1962). In it, his own personal tragedy is presented as the tragedy of Tibet and the Tibetan people. In 1990, the Dalai Lama would release a second autobiography, this time entitled *Freedom in Exile* (Tenzin Gyatso 1990), detailing further his personal story and also including in the narrative the first decades of his exile.

If for a national leader like the Dalai Lama, expanding the boundaries of his own private experience to epitomize the suffering of his nation can be seen as the rule, a similar movement from private to public can also be detected in the other autobiographies under discussion here. Such a movement is perfectly captured by Hannah Arendt's argument that "storytelling is a strategy for transforming private into public meanings" (Jackson 2002: 14–15). In the case of Tibet, the "private meanings" described in these autobiographical works are derived from collective, and hence public, adversities. The movement from private to public works then as a kind of humanizing, private "lens," bringing into focus experiences of suffering that had been publically shared from the outset. In the endless confrontations between "official versions" of the "facts" about Tibet, autobiographies, and, for that matter, first person testimonies collected by international organizations, emerge as powerful records of the Tibetan experience under Chinese communist rule. The political strength of first person accounts can be measured in part by their potential to shield their authors from accusations of propaganda. It is noteworthy in this regard, for example, that Buddhist studies scholar John Powers, in his book *History as Propaganda: Tibetan Exiles versus the People's Republic of China* (2004), leaves autobiographies out of his quite indiscriminate characterization of Tibetan, Chinese and western works on the history of Tibet as propaganda.

Historian Melvyn Goldstein, who in a number of works (e.g., 1990, 1989, 1971) has been quite zealous in presenting a picture of old Tibet that brings to light the social injustices that existed in the pre-occupation period,[17] seems to clearly recognize the power of first person narratives when he states:

> The literature on modern Tibet has been monopolized by the voices of monks, lamas, and aristocrats, i.e., people who dominated the traditional semifeudal society and generally opposed modernization and change. They

present the conflict in stark black-and-white images – good Tibetans against malevolent Chinese communists – and have come to represent the face of Tibetan nationalism in Western literature.

(Goldstein *et al.* 2004: xiii)

In order, then, to bring a different perspective to the discussion of the Tibet issue, Goldstein (with the help of English professor Siebenschuh) put forth, in a first person narrative, the life stories of two Tibetans sympathetic to Chinese communism. In *The Struggle for a Modern Tibet: The Autobiography of Tashi Tsering* (Goldstein *et al.*1997), the story of a "Tibetan nationalist with a burning desire to reform and modernize the old society," as he is described on the back cover of the book, is told in the first person by the American professors. In a second book, *A Tibetan Revolutionary: The Political Life and Times of Bapa Phüntso Wangye* (Goldstein *et al.* 2004), the authors tell the fascinating story of Phüntso Wangye (1922–2014), a Tibetan revolutionary who played an important part in the Chinese occupation of Tibet, and then spent 18 years in solitary confinement in a Chinese prison in Beijing.[18]

In what follows, I describe the invasion and the first decades of occupation, taking a cross-section of these autobiographies as my basis. My goal in using these first person accounts is to investigate the style and content with which they describe how Chinese rule dismantled the old power structures of Tibet. I perforce focus my efforts on the accounts of lamas, government leaders, and their associates, and to a lesser extent, the accounts of other Tibetans from different positions, who were all eyewitnesses to those events. As a response of sorts to Goldstein's critical remarks about the "face of Tibetan nationalism in Western literature," I include, side-by-side, the accounts of both sympathizers and detractors of the communist Chinese civilizing project. And although my narrative gives stronger voice to lamas and leaders than to common Tibetans, it is through the perspective of traditional Tibet's powerbrokers that we stand to learn most about how China dismantled old Tibet's power structures. And as we shall see from the complexity of their accounts, the concerns of Tibet's traditional leadership find deep resonance in the cares and concerns of most Tibetans and cannot simply be written off as the complaints of the losing party.

Invasion

Lhasa, summer of 1950. One day before the beginning of the traditional Opera Festival in the Tibetan capital, the young Fourteenth Dalai Lama was preparing to go to bed when he felt the earth shake under his feet. Minutes later he heard a crash in the distance. He ran outside with a few servants. As they looked up into the sky, they heard another crash, and then another. The Dalai Lama estimated that a total of 30 to 40 explosions occurred that night. At first he assumed that the crashes and tremors were caused by a military test being conducted by the Tibetan army. Later he would learn it was a natural phenomenon that was witnessed "throughout the length and breadth of Tibet," as far as Chamdo, about

400 miles to the east, and Sakya, 300 miles to the southwest. The Tibetan leader interpreted the strange occurrence as an omen, "a portent of the terrible things to come" (Tenzin Gyatso 1990: 50–1).

Two days later, Tathag Rinpoche, the Dalai Lama's regent, received a message describing a fatal Chinese communist raid on a Tibetan post in Chamdo. Tibetan areas outside the control of the Ganden Podrang government had already been suffering from incursions perpetrated by Chinese soldiers since the previous year. They were getting closer. In October, two months after the strange phenomenon happened in the sky of Tibet, the worst fears of the young Tibetan leader came true. "News reached Lhasa that an army of 80,000 soldiers of the PLA had crossed the Drichu river east of Chamdo" (ibid.: 52).[19] The Dalai Lama and officials of the Tibetan government knew from the outset that Lhasa would soon fall. They realized that the Tibetan army would not have the capacity to resist the Chinese offensive.

Despite efforts made by the Thirteenth Dalai Lama to reorganize the Tibetan army, almost no measures in this direction were taken after his death in 1933. When the Chinese came in 1950, the Fourteenth Dalai Lama tells us, Tibet was almost totally unprotected. The country's army had 8,500 troops, and only "fifty pieces of artillery of various kinds" – 250 mortars and about 200 machine guns (Tenzin Gyatso 1962: 80). In a meeting of the Tibetan National Assembly, it was agreed that Tibet did not have the means to repel the PLA forces, and that the better course of action would be to contact countries and request their assistance. Four delegations were appointed to visit Britain, the United States, India and Nepal. Before the delegations left Lhasa, telegrams were sent to these four governments, explaining the situation and announcing the intention to send delegations. However, the plan did not bear fruit. In the words of the Dalai Lama:

> The replies to these telegrams were terribly disheartening. The British gov-
> ernment expressed their deepest sympathy for the people of Tibet, and
> regretted that owing to Tibet's geographical positions, since India had been
> granted independence, they could not offer help. The government of the
> United States also replied in the same sense and declined to receive our del-
> egation. The Indian government also made it clear they would not give us
> military help, and advised us not to offer any armed resistance, but to open
> negotiations for a peaceful settlement on the basis of the Simla agreement
> of 1914.
>
> (Ibid.: 81–2)

The decision to bring the case to the United Nations that same year was also futile (Tenzin Gyatso 1962: 84; 1990: 53). The Tibetan government was paying the price for a policy of virtual diplomatic isolation. At this dramatic moment in Tibetan history, the government decided after consulting high lamas and oracles that the Dalai Lama, who was only 16 years old at the time, should assume his role as secular leader of Tibet. Not long after he was conferred full powers in a traditional ceremony, members of the National Assembly in Lhasa, out of concern for the Dalai Lama's safety, convinced him to escape in disguise to Yadong, a town near the border with India.

After invading Chamdo, the Chinese summoned the Tibetan government to send a delegation to Beijing in order to "discuss the terms of a peaceful liberation of Tibet." The Tibetan government eventually agreed to send a five-person delegation. Ngabo Ngawang Jigme (1910–2009), the newly appointed governor-general of Chamdo and a minister of the Tibetan central government, who was being held captive by the Chinese after the capitulation of his province, joined the delegation and acted as its head. After a little more than a month of negotiations in Beijing, an agreement was reached. The so-called "Seventeen-Point Agreement for the Peaceful Liberation of Tibet" was signed on May 23, 1951, against the backdrop of the threat of a massive military invasion if some crucial demands made by the Chinese were not met.

Phüntso Wangye took part in the negotiations on the Chinese side. In his autobiography, he reports, "the first big argument occurred over the issue of sending PLA troops into Tibet." The Chinese insisted on the necessity of sending troops "in order to drive the foreign imperialist forces out and then secure and defend the national borders." The Tibetan delegation, of course, objected, arguing that there were no foreign imperialistic forces in Tibet. In Phüntso Wangye's words:

> Arguments went back and forth, but in reality, the movement of the troops into Tibet was a foregone conclusion. The central government [i.e., the Chinese government] was committed to troops being stationed there. The Tibetan delegation argued long and hard but finally, under the threat of the discussions collapsing and the PLA attacking, conceded.
>
> (Goldstein *et al.* 2004: 146)

The issue of the movement of troops into Tibet and the "defense" of the Tibetan territory against foreign forces were indeed among the main topics of the Seventeen-Point Agreement. In its first clause, Tibetans were summoned to unite in order to expel the "aggressive imperialistic forces" from Tibet.[20] "The Tibetan people shall return to the big family of the Motherland, the People's Republic of China," it also said. The second clause stated furthermore that the "local government of Tibet" should "actively assist the PLA to enter Tibet and consolidate the national defenses." The fourth clause of the document asserted that "the central authorities" would not "alter the existing political system in Tibet," and the fourteenth clause stipulated that all external affairs of Tibet would be the responsibility of the central government in Beijing.

In many ways, this agreement represented the demise of Tibet as an independent nation-state. From his exile in Yadong, the Dalai Lama heard on Radio Beijing a statement read by Ngabo about the newly signed agreement. Although the Dalai Lama was quite distressed by the news, he realized that there was nothing he could do but comply with the Chinese imposition. "The terms," he said,

> were much worse than we anticipated [...] Yet we were helpless. Without friends there was nothing we could do but acquiesce, submit to the Chinese dictates in spite of our strong opposition, and swallow our resentment. We could only hope that the Chinese would keep their side of this forced, one-sided bargain.
>
> (Tenzin Gyatso 1962: 89)

Also among the signatories of the agreement was the Tenth Panchen Lama. As I briefly mentioned above, in the eighteenth century the Qing emperor is said to have invested the Fifth Panchen Lama with temporal powers over Western Tibet and Tsang. A close relationship between successive Chinese rulers and representatives of this reincarnation line and their entourages continued to develop over the centuries. In the first half of the twentieth century, the Ninth Panchen Lama, Lobsang Chökyi Nyima (1883–1937), fled from Tibet to China due to disputes with the Ganden Podrang government over taxation and political issues.[21] He died while in exile in Qinghai province, without having a chance to see his native land again. A new incarnation was found in a Tibetan area inside China by his followers, but officials in Lhasa refused to recognize the boy as legitimate (Goldstein *et al.* 2004: 147).

Traditionally, the Dalai Lamas and the Panchen Lamas have the final word in the recognition of each other's reincarnations. Hence, when the Panchen Lama took part in the initial discussions around the Seventeen-Point Agreement he had no authority in the eyes of the representatives of the Tibetan government. The Chinese government decided then to coerce the Dalai Lama to recognize the Tenth Panchen Lama. In the words of Phüntso Wangye:

> The Central Committee had decided they had to force the Tibetan government to accept this boy as the Panchen Lama and allow him to return to Tashilhunpo. But agreement did not come easily, as the Tibetan delegation flatly declared that they had no authority to recognize a lama, let alone the reincarnation of the Panchen Lama. That was the prerogative of the Dalai Lama. The Chinese delegation countered by saying that talks could not go forward without settling this issue. At that point Ngabö [as the head of the Tibetan delegation] sent a telegram to the Dalai Lama in Yadong, who replied (by telegram) that he accepted the boy as the Tenth Panchen Lama.
>
> (Ibid.: 148)

The resolution of the pending dispute surrounding the recognition of the Tenth Panchen Lama under Chinese pressure was by no means a marginal occurrence. It foreshadowed, among other things, the Chinese practice of intervening in religious matters that would soon become current in Tibet. More than that, however, the effort to ensure the Panchen Lama's official recognition and the consequent winning over of his entourage was advantageous for the Chinese communist political agenda in multiple ways. The more obvious way was the possibility of grooming from a young age a strategic collaborator. The historical proximity between the Panchen Lamas and Chinese rulers seemed to represent the promise of a successful outcome in that domain. However, as we shall see later in this chapter, this was not to be the case.

Just as flowing water, avoiding the heights and hastening to the lowlands

In the first years of the occupation, there was still some meaning to the word "peaceful" in the idea of "peaceful liberation of Tibet" propagated to this day by the Chinese communists. In effect, according to numerous accounts by Tibetans and Chinese alike, Chinese soldiers were initially very cordial to the local populations in Tibet. They paid for food and other supplies without bargaining, built hospitals and roads at a fast pace and established schools for people from all social strata. It is said that during that time a popular song could be heard in the streets of Lhasa:

> Communist Chinese, as kind as parents;
> Showering a limitless rain of silver coins.
> (Dewatshang 1997: 91)

Phüntso Wangye, who became the main Tibetan cadre in the Chinese Communist Party between 1951 and 1958, was sent to Lhasa with the specific goals of "winning the Tibetan upper classes over to the new Chinese policies" and "maintaining good relations between the Tibetans and the Chinese" (Goldstein *et al.* 2004: 136). He explains, "the soldiers were instructed not to take anything forcibly from the people and to respect symbols of the indigenous nationality, culture and religion" (ibid.). The idea was not to disrupt the lives and culture of people through the observation of strict discipline. Following his advice, the PLA also brought food from China in order to prevent hungry soldiers from acting in any unruly fashion.[22]

The Chinese communists expected to win the hearts and minds of Tibetans by exposing them to the benefits that a socialist regime could bring to their country, hence the haste in establishing essential services to the population. Mao believed that the socialist transformation should happen slowly in Tibet, with the gradual and voluntary adhesion of the local people. Moreover, self-rule was the promise that motivated nationalist Tibetans sympathetic with communist ideals to cooperate with the Chinese – this was precisely the case of Phüntso Wangye. Notwithstanding this general orientation of respect and fairness, the seeds of conflict had been present since the beginning of occupation. In Tibet, the distance between theory and practice was accentuated by all kinds of different expectations on both sides. Underscoring such conflicting expectations were very distinct senses of history and identity, as discussed above, that could not be overcome or obliterated simply by general directives.

The official ban on the word "man-ze" (barbarian) – the common Chinese word to refer to Tibetans – for example, would certainly not be enough to eradicate an ingrained sense of superiority nurtured over the centuries by the Han in relation to ethnically distinct populations that lived in and around the Chinese territory. Phüntso Wangye views this kind of attitude as a legacy from the Guomindang period. "Even though the party declared that all nationalities should be treated equally," he says, "there are many remnants of the Guomindang attitude of Han superiority – what we call in communist jargon 'Great Han Chauvinism' [ch. *da Hanzu zhuyi*]" (ibid.: 171). Whatever the case may have been, the fact remains that despite promises of self-determination and so forth, this sense of Han cultural and racial superiority directly tinted the first years of cohabitation on many levels. This determined a predicament of Tibetan subordination to the Chinese in power structures that can still be observed to this day.

During the first years of the occupation, the so-called "United Front policy" was set in place. In few words, this policy consisted of an alliance between the Chinese communists and the ruling classes in Tibetan areas (and in other minority areas in China). Its aim was to strengthen the consolidation of Chinese sovereignty in the region. In apparent consistency with the Seventeen-Point Agreement clause safeguarding the "existing political system in Tibet," a few old power structures were left in place. This was the case with the government headed by the Dalai Lama and the Kashag – the highest Tibetan executive office – which continued to function, albeit considerably weakened. Concurrently, additional structures were also created reflecting the influence of newly forged allegiances between Tibetan authorities and the Chinese communists.

The Preparatory Committee for the Autonomous Region of Tibet (PCART) was established in 1956, having the Dalai Lama as its Chairman, and the Panchen Lama together with a Chinese general, Zhang Guohua, as the Vice-Chairmen. In practice, Zhang Guohua was in charge of administrating affairs on a day-to-day basis. As historian Tsering Shakya comments, "The function of the PCART was defined as an authoritative body for consultation and planning during the transitional period before the establishment of the Autonomous Region of Tibet" (Shakya 1999: 125). And he further contends that,

> The new organization gave Panchen Rinpoche the same status and power as the Dalai Lama in Lhasa. Unprecedented authority was thus conferred on Panchen Rinpoche and his estate. It gave him the right to appoint his own people to the PCART.
>
> (Ibid.: 128)

This state of affairs greatly upset members of the Tibetan government, but they did not have enough political force to change the situation.

Beyond the high spheres of Tibetan power represented in particular by the figures of the Dalai Lama and the Panchen Lama, the Chinese communists would use the authority of other lamas, especially the so-called "tulkus" (Tib. *sprul sku*), or reincarnate lamas, and traditional leaders to establish a firm foothold in Tibet. According to Chen Jingbo, director of the United Front Department of the Tibetan Work Committee when the PCART was established,

> a large number of individuals from the local upper classes were appointed to various posts under the Committee [i.e., the PCART]. At the time, there were about 6,000 people that belonged to middle and upper classes (including major clan chiefs) in the whole region [...].
>
> (Lixiong 2009: 44)

In many senses, the cooptation of these lamas and traditional leaders was key for the success of the Chinese occupation of the country. And this is so not only because some of them had political authority or influence in local areas, but also because they were among the few Tibetans with a high degree of education, and hence capable of assuming administrative tasks. In line with the Chinese strategy of promoting a smooth transformation in Tibet, the cooptation of lamas and leaders occurred, especially in Central Tibet, through invitations and payment of salaries.

Jamyang Sakya tells us in her autobiography, for example, how Chinese officials tried to coopt her husband Dagchen Rinpoche, a high lama belonging to the Sakya School, and herself to work with them in the first transitional years.

> Many nobles and some lamas now were taking salaries from the Chinese in payment for appearances at meetings which were mainly propaganda-oriented. The Chinese could see my husband's influence with Sakya followers and hoped to use him to get their views across to the people, so it was natural that they attempt to pressure him.
>
> (Sakya and Emery 1990: 218)

During a dinner party at the Chinese government headquarters, they were informed that the Chinese communists had already paid him the equivalent of a two-month salary, and that the money was waiting for him at the home of the Sakya representative in Lhasa (ibid.: 218–19). They protested that they had not done any work, but the Chinese would not accept the money back. Later, it was Jamyang's turn to be "invited" to head the propaganda organization called "Women's Group of Western Tibet," which had the goal of promoting Chinese culture (ibid.: 243).

There is something quite revealing about the Chinese insistence that Dagchen Rinpoche accept the salaries for which he had not yet worked. As a matter of fact, such conduct brings to light an essential trait of the strategy of forcefully absorbing into the party as many influential people as possible, while at the same time giving a sense of continuity with the old hierarchies. Money is indeed a powerful binding substance. It requires active participation on two ends: the act of giving and the act of receiving. Even when not received willingly, money once spent consolidates bonds. Much like the cases of the Dalai Lama and the Panchen Lama, who also received salaries from the Party, the absorption of other lamas and nobles through these means represented in practice the corrosion of traditional power structures from their very core.

In the same vein, the clear impossibility to refuse party "invitations" shows not only that these were not "invitations" in the strict sense of the term, but also that they were supposed to accomplish other ends by being put forward as such. From the reactions to these "invitations," the Chinese communists hoped to identify "revolutionary" or "reactionary" tendencies among the authorities they were seeking to coopt. This was part of a larger plan to radically redefine Tibetan society in terms of the class struggle model. For that to be accomplished it was necessary to gather as much information about the local populations as possible, and that was sometimes done with the unsuspecting help of the local population throughout Tibet. Ama Adhe, a Khampa woman who organized an underground movement to give support to the Khampa guerrillas in the first years of the occupation,[23] recounts in her autobiography, for example, that the Chinese communists in their frequent visits to her family house tried to get from her father, a local authority himself, this kind of information. In her words:

> [T]he Chinese had identified the most respected and influential Tibetans, the authorities of the society, the wealthy families, the beggars, the monks, and the abbots of the monasteries. Their main purpose in spending time with us had been to discern these things. They had effectively noted the wealth of the monasteries, how much livestock they possessed, and what types of statuary they contained. They also collected information regarding the individual wealth of all the families in the Karze region [in eastern Tibet].
>
> (Tapontsang 1997: 48–9)

Similarly, Aten, a Khampa man who was initially trained in Beijing to become an administrator for his region, but later became the leader of one of the Tibetan resistance groups, relates in his autobiography that he was directly instructed to "try and locate those who are intimately associated with the people, who possess the power to alter public opinion and who have the trust of the people." He was told moreover that it was "also important to know how much gold, silver and cash each family has" (Norbu 1986 [1979]: 84). The information about familial and monastic wealth would later be used in the confiscations of private property in the name of socialism. For now, I would like to emphasize here the effort to create a database for the sake of classifying the population. This kind of information would be employed not long after to frame the attacks on influential figures as part of class struggle processes.

Indeed, sooner than later, the lamas and traditional lay leaders who refused to cooperate were classified as "serf-owners" and became the main targets of violent programs of reeducation promoted by the Chinese authorities. The intensity of these attacks was greater at first in the areas that were not considered by the Chinese to be part of the so-called "Tibetan Autonomous Region (TAR)," i.e., the eastern regions of Kham and Amdo.[24] While the Chinese tried as much as possible not to directly interfere in the lives of Tibetans in the central and western regions of the Tibetan plateau that would later become the TAR, the situation was quite different in the eastern regions. In eastern Tibet, the strategy was much more invasive, leading to a number of bloody conflicts and the prompt disorganization of social life.

Violation of sacred spaces in Tibet

From the mid-1950s on, the Chinese had to face the growing resistance of Tibetans against the occupation of their territory. It was precisely in Kham and Amdo that the main foci of popular rebellion were concentrated. The attempt to introduce the so-called "democratic reforms" in Kham in 1955 triggered a widespread insurgence in the region. Considered to be a crucial and necessary stage in the transition to socialism, the imposition of such reforms consisted, among other things, in the redistribution of land and the classification of the heterogeneous Tibetan population into social classes following the Marxist model of class struggle. In the particular case of Kham, another factor aggravated the state of affairs. As Warren Smith explains, "One reason for this was that reforms included confiscation of weapons, which were a part of the normal attire of the Khampas" (Smith 2008: 38). Khampas are indeed known for their love of guns. And there had been "a great influx of guns into Kham and Amdo" after World War II and the Civil War in China (Shakya 1999: 138). The Chinese were not very successful in their campaign to compel the Khampas to forfeit their weapons voluntarily, and when they tried to put the democratic reforms into practice, they met with the fierce and armed resistance of the population. "Kanding Rebellion" was the name given by the Chinese to a series of non-coordinated insurgencies that emerged in response to the attempts to introduce collectivization of lands and so forth in the region. When the cadres came to the villages to enforce the democratic reforms, "they were attacked and, in many instances, killed by the villagers" (ibid.: 139).

The counter-offensive of PLA troops forced fighters, and villagers in general, to take refuge in two important monasteries of the Kham region, Changtreng Sampheling and Lithang. The PLA response transformed these religious institutions into arenas for some of the bloodiest episodes in the history of the Chinese occupation of Tibet. In the words of Tsering Shakya:

> By the end of February 1956, the 3,000 monks in Changtreng Sampheling had taken in thousands of villagers. Some were refugees from other parts of Kham; others had come to defend the monastery. At first the PLA troops laid siege to the monastery and an aeroplane dropped leaflets urging the monks and people to surrender. Although the monastery was well fortified, the Tibetans did not have any defence against Chinese mortar attacks. The PLA troops did not storm the monastery, which would have caused heavy casualities on the Chinese side, but called in a single plane which bombed

the monastery. The Khampas had no choice but to surrender. The monastery was in ruins and hundreds of monks and laymen were killed.

(Shakya 1999: 140)

Tsering Shakya tells us further that news of the destruction of this particular monastery spread quickly throughout eastern Tibet. A militia was soon organized to defend the monastery of Lithang by a "young" and "charismatic" leader, Yonru-Pon Sonam Wangyal. "On the second day of Tibetan New Year (the end of February) 1956, as Yonru-Pon rode towards the monastery, his group was ambushed by the PLA troops and Yonru-Pon was killed" (ibid.: 141). The population of Lithang rose in revolt and attacked all the PLA encampments in the area. The rebels then took refuge in the local monastery, which was surrounded by PLA troops for many weeks. The episode culminated in the bombing of the monastery and the killing of thousands of villagers. In his autobiography, the Fourteenth Dalai Lama expresses his sorrow upon hearing the news of the bombardment:

No matter how successful the resistance was, the Chinese would overcome it in the end by sheer force of number and superior fire-power. But I could not have predicted the aerial bombing of the monastery at Lithang in Kham. When I heard of it, I cried. I could not believe that human beings were capable of such cruelty to each other.

The bombardment was followed by the merciless torture and execution of women and children whose fathers and husbands had joined the resistance movement and, incredibly, by the disgusting abuse of monks and nuns. After arrest, these simple religious people were forced – in public – to break their vows of celibacy with one another and even to kill people.

(Tenzin Gyatso 1990: 110)

The destruction of monasteries due to their use as safe havens by insurgents and the subsequent violence directed against monks and nuns indicate a connection between Tibetan Buddhism and the nationalistic resistance against the Chinese. By that time, the Chinese communists had already realized that the strong faith of Tibetans in their religion would be the biggest obstacle to the assimilation of Tibet and the institution of socialist reforms. It should come as no surprise then that attacks against Buddhism would from then on be systematized through the establishment of the so-called "thamzing," or "struggle sessions," in which the people were supposed to denounce their "oppressors." Important lamas, abbots, and prominent monks were targeted as reactionaries for various reasons and submitted to beatings, public humiliation and transgressive practices in the name of "reeducation processes." Ama Adhe reports in her autobiography the violent treatment to which one of the lamas from her region was submitted in 1955:

One day, all the townspeople were called to attend a *thamzing* session. Several villagers and a lama had been arrested. To our horror, the first lama in our town to be humiliated was our family's special lama, Kharnang Kusho. One of the female soldiers walked over to where the prisoners were standing. The beggars were told to observe how she dealt with the lama and then they were to do the same. Kharnang Kusho was forced to kneel, and the soldier knelt on his legs behind him. She then took a rope and put it in his mouth, as one would do to a horse, and jerked his head backward. She poured urine on his face, trying to force him to drink it. When he refused, she just spilled it on his face.

(Tapontsang 1997: 67)

The choice of reincarnate lamas as a major target in the "struggle sessions" had very precise objectives in the logic of the "politics of terror," which came to dominate the Chinese occupation of Tibet. In fact, the so-called "institution of reincarnate lamas" represents one of the most essential traits of Tibetan Buddhism. Beginning from the twelfth century, the tradition of searching for reincarnations of deceased lamas swiftly came to occupy a privileged place both in the internal politics of monasteries and in the politics of state in Tibet.[25] The reincarnate lama is considered to be an emanation of a revered past master, and sometimes of a bodhisattva, or a Buddha. By attacking these reincarnate lamas the Chinese were killing two birds with a single stone. They were fighting what they believed to be one of the main foci of "feudal power" and, at the same time, questioning the spiritual power that lamas were supposed to have, showing Tibetans the "powerlessness" and "fallaciousness" of their religion.

Given the central role that lamas played in Tibetan society, it is easy to imagine the emotional impact that Tibetans experienced when witnessing the aggression they endured, being beaten up and put into contact with impure substances such as urine and feces. For the Chinese communists, however, it was not enough to make the people passively observe those violent spectacles. The "reeducation process" required also that the Tibetan people take part in it, directly humiliating, beating and even killing lamas. In the words of the aforementioned Khampa fighter Aten:

These "struggles" were diabolically cruel criticism meetings where children were made to accuse their parents of imaginary crimes; where farmers were made to denounce and beat up landlords; where pupils were made to degrade their teachers; where every shred of dignity in a person was torn to pieces by his people, his children and his loved ones. Old lamas were made to have sex with prostitutes in public. And often the accused was beaten, spat and urinated upon. Every act of degradation was heaped upon him – and it killed him in more ways than one. When someone was through in a *thamzing* session, no one ever spoke of him again. He was no martyr for the people, because the people had killed him. His death lay in the hands of those who should have honoured and remembered him; but in their guilt, the people tried to forget him and the shameful part they had played in his degradation.

(Norbu 1986 [1979]: 133–4)

The kind of violence present in these meetings is close in its general structure and consequences to a rite of passage. The systematic practice of forcing Tibetans to commit transgressive acts against lamas and sacred objects was a clear attempt to cause a complete rupture with the old Tibetan way of life, old power structures and, in particular, with Buddhism.

A turning point: the 1959 uprising and its consequences

The implementation of democratic reforms in the eastern regions of the country and the armed resistance it brought about generated a great influx of refugees into Lhasa. Atrocious stories of looting, torture, death and destruction were now circulating in the capital, infusing its superficially calm atmosphere with fear and suspicion. In *Freedom in Exile*, the Fourteenth Dalai Lama reveals that, "some of the stories they brought with them were so horrifying that I did not believe them for many years." It was only after the publication in 1959 of the report "by the International Commission of Jurists that I fully accepted what I had heard: crucifixion, vivisection, disemboweling and dismembering of the victims was commonplace. So too were beheading, burning, beating to death and burying alive [...]" (Tenzin Gyatso 1990: 124).

The growing tension between Tibetans and Chinese in the capital reached its apex when General Chiang Chin-wu invited the Dalai Lama to attend a theater presentation scheduled to take place in the Chinese military headquarters on March 10, 1959. The commander of the Dalai Lama's bodyguard was instructed to drop the "usual formality and ceremony" of the Tibetan leader's visits. The Chinese insisted that no Tibetan soldiers accompany him, "only two or three unarmed bodyguards if absolutely necessary, adding that they wanted the whole affair to be conducted in absolute secrecy" (ibid.: 132). The imposition of such unusual conditions led Tibetans to believe that the Dalai Lama's life was in danger. Fearing the worst, thousands of people surrounded the Norbulingka Palace, where the Dalai Lama was residing, and decided to prevent their secular and spiritual leader from attending the presentation.

Tubten Khétsun, a Tibetan government official who was an eyewitness of the events, tells in his autobiography that on March 10, "cabinet ministers, chiefs of palace staff, chief secretaries, chamberlains and officers of the bodyguard regiment came out to address the crowd," telling them to return to their homes. "A delegation of sixty representatives was then summoned inside the gate." There they were told that the Dalai Lama "had decided not to accept the invitation" (Khétsun 2008: 27–8). The crowds, nevertheless, did not disperse.

The Dalai Lama sent three of his most senior ministers to meet with General Tan Kuan-sen and explain his decision not to attend the event. The outcome of this meeting was not favorable. In the words of the Dalai Lama:

> [The Chinese general and other senior officers] harangued the Tibetans for several hours about the treachery of the "imperialist rebels," adding the accusation that the Tibetan Government had been secretly organising

agitation against the Chinese authorities. Furthermore, it had defied the orders of the Chinese and refused to disarm the "rebels" in Lhasa. They could now expect drastic measures to be taken to crush this opposition.

(Tenzin Gyatso 1990: 133)

The Dalai Lama realized that the Chinese were issuing an ultimatum. About a meeting held later that same day outside of the Norbulingka Palace, he said "seventy junior government officials, together with the remaining popular leaders and members of my personal bodyguard, held a meeting [...] and endorsed a declaration denouncing the Seventeen-Point 'Agreement', adding that Tibet no longer recognised Chinese authority" (ibid.: 134). Little by little a pro-independence movement took shape. Popular leaders were elected and meetings were held around the capital.

A few days went by and tensions only grew. The Chinese were clearly preparing to bring more reinforcements and a confrontation seemed inevitable. The Dalai Lama consulted the State Oracle Nechung[26] twice about the course of action to be taken, and the response was invariably to stay in place. On March 16, the Dalai Lama received a letter from General Tan, explaining that they were planning to attack the crowds and the Norbulingka. He wanted a map of the palace, indicating where the Dalai Lama was going to be, "so that the artillerymen could be briefed to aim off whichever building I marked" (ibid.: 135). On the 17th, the Dalai Lama consulted the Nechung Oracle again. This time around, the Dalai Lama reports, "he shouted, 'Go! Go! Tonight!'" (ibid.: 136). After giving precise directions about the route to be taken, the medium collapsed. At this very moment, "as if to reinforce the oracle's instructions, two mortar shells exploded in the marsh outside the northern gate of the Jewel Park" (ibid.). In the evening of that very day, the Dalai Lama, his family members, some of his closest advisers and bodyguards put on commoner clothes and in disguise went through the crowds. After a journey through the Himalayas that lasted for more than a month, they reached their destiny in India. Following the Dalai Lama, 80,000 Tibetans also escaped the country (Barnett 2009: 6).

On March 20, the Chinese began bombing Norbulingka. "[S]till thinking that the Dalai Lama was inside," they instigated "an attack on all the Tibetans' fortified positions. Within three days the fighting in Lhasa was over, Chinese superiority in organization and weaponry having enabled them to crush Tibetan resistance" (Smith 1996: 447). Martial law was then imposed and the Tibetan government dissolved. The Chinese propagate to this day the idea that members of the upper classes of the Tibetan population were the ones who instigated the uprising in order to maintain their old privileges. The article, "The Victory of Democratic Reforms in Tibet," published in the March 1960 edition of the *Peking Review* (a Maoist journal published in English) stated:

This reactionary clique had hoped to stage their rebellion under the cloak of nationalism; they wanted to conceal the true nature of their aim which was to preserve the interests of the reactionary serf-owning class. Events have shown that this rebellion and its quelling was definitely not a "national war" but a class war, a war instigated by a handful of arch-reactionary feudal serf-owners to oppose the Communist Party's leading the broad masses of the serfs to stand up; it was an uncompromising class war.

(apud Smith 1996: 456)

In response to the Tibetan counter-revolutionary resistance, the Chinese communists decided to abandon the United Front policy, instigating instead class struggle. Simply put, the aim now was to directly attack the local elite. Also in retaliation to the uprising, it was decided that democratic reforms should immediately be implemented in the TAR. It comes as no surprise that among the favorite targets of the democratic reforms were the monastic institutions, which effectively represented the greatest landowners in Tibet and were therefore perceived as foci of resistance. Not only was the land that belonged to these monasteries expropriated, but the monasteries themselves were also destroyed. Tens of thousands of monks were arrested, expelled or executed in accordance with the intensity with which they resisted (International Campaign for Tibet 1990: 7–10). In this regard, it is interesting to note that even the official documents of the Communist Party attest that the resistance to the democratic reforms gained the contours of a mass movement in some areas, even before they became generalized in the Tibetan territory. The communists interpreted such resistance once more as an attempt on the part of reactionary upper class individuals to maintain their privileges. In the words of Chang-Chih-I, deputy director of the Chinese Communist Party United Front Work Department:

[This] small number of blind, reactionary figures of the upper classes is making use of national and religious banners; posing as guardians of the nation and the religion, they have tricked a part of the masses. This activity, which is opposed to reform, has thus, to a certain extent, taken on a mass nature in some areas.

(apud Smith 1996: 395)

Along with the democratic reforms and the official classification of the population into social classes came the intensification of thamzing. Not even the junior tutor of the Dalai Lama, Trijang Rinpoche (1901–81), escaped the ordeal of the struggle sessions. According to Tubten Khétsun:

[The Chinese] incited people against him by staging a special display of illicit items and arranging for a couple of [former] junior attendants to claim that these things had been found in his Lhasa residence (*Khri byang bla brang*). They obliged members of the families that had been his main sponsors, like Rampa and Kashöpa, to lead the denunciation, and they emphatically claimed at numerous public rallies that Kyapjé Dorjé-chang [i.e., Trijang Rinpoche] was an immoral person.[...] Even more cruelly, the remaining [senior] members of the monastic communities of Séra and

Drépung and the upper and lower tantric colleges who had been inducted into an organization called Buddhist Association (*Chos tshogs*) were especially forced and harassed into denouncing and rejecting Kyapjé Rinpoché, and many of those who had received his teachings and initiations and refused to denounce him were imprisoned.

(Khétsun 2008: 140–1)

Tubten Khétsun's report indicates how the Chinese communists used thamzing as a powerful instrument to sever Tibetan society's ties of solidarity, directly choosing the "denouncers" from among the people who were most deeply connected with the victim. In the new reality engendered by the generalized practice of thamzing, the society as a whole was pit against itself.

Together with the targeting of lamas, abbots and other religious figures in the context of thamzing, during the 1960s other forms of attack on religious beliefs and the ritual violation of the sacred became part of day-to-day reality for the people of Tibet. For example, under the excuse of promoting better hygiene, the Chinese obliged Tibetans to kill dogs and flies, which represented a clear affront to the Buddhist ideal of refraining from harming sentient beings. To cite Tubten Khétsun once more,

as a campaign for the eradication of insects said to "cause disease and damage productivity," both the Buddhist Association people and the ordinary citizens were required to kill one hundred flies per day and as many mice and sparrows as they could, and present the corpses to their group leader every evening to be checked.

(Ibid.: 142)

The generalized attack on Tibetan religious sensibilities and other acts of violence committed against the Tibetan population after the 1959 uprising led the Panchen Lama to write a lengthy document, criticizing the Chinese Communist Party policy in Tibet. In it, the Tibetan religious leader detailed his findings about the situation in Tibet from inspection tours he undertook in 1961 and 1962. As we will see next, the writing of what became known as the "70,000-Character Petition" engendered severe consequences for the Panchen Lama. Such consequences constitute a clear portrait of Chinese suspicions concerning what, precisely, was perceived as a "nationalist" affront in the period after the 1959 uprising.

"The big rock" and his "poisoned arrow"

Not long after the suppression of the popular uprising of 1959, the Communist Party made the Panchen Lama the Acting Chairman of the PCART, a position previously held by the Dalai Lama. He was also soon to become Vice-Chairman of the Chinese People's Political Consultative Conference, which elevated him to "the rank of a national leader" (Barnett 1997: x). Hence, in 1962, when he presented his petition to senior leaders of the Communist Party, the Panchen Lama was the highest-ranking religious leader in Tibet, despite being only 24 years old. The trust conferred on his figure by the Chinese communists was clearly still quite solid. Very few, be they on the Chinese side or even on the side of the Tibetan government in exile, could imagine that he would be responsible for the most incisive document of criticism directed against the Communist Party to date. In the words of Robert Barnett, who together with the Tibet Information Network was responsible for bringing this document to public attention for the first time:[27]

> Indeed, no other document exists in China, as far as we know, in which a senior official attacks so explicitly and in such detail the policies and practices of Chairman Mao. The Party itself ruled that the Petition exceeded, in its criticism of the Party, that other famous internal critique of Mao Zedong, the 10,000 character letter which led to the downfall of Peng Dehuai in 1959.
>
> (Ibid.: ix)

The strength of the document, it could be said, derived from the care with which the Panchen Lama wove sincere and well-informed data about the catastrophic situation in Tibetan areas post-1959 with an astute perception of Chinese expectations about Tibet, not asking for more than what was stipulated in the minority policies dictated by the Party and the general constitutional guarantees in China. An example of the skillfulness of the Panchen Lama in his wording of the document can be discerned in the manner in which he addressed the controversial issue of the uniqueness of Tibetans inside China. In a very direct and bold statement in the petition, the Panchen Lama clearly differentiates Tibetans from other minorities, making a case for the need of special treatment:

> [A]lthough Tibet has been under the jurisdiction of the motherland for several hundred years, because methods of rule and ways of managing its internal affairs are different from those of other minorities within [*neidi*] the motherland, most of the people in all strata strongly perceive themselves as Tibetan, and only have a weak perception of the motherland; they have an urgent desire for the Party Central Committee to give Tibet special care, and the situation is complicated. Tibet has long boundary lines with foreign countries; imperialists and Indian reactionaries are incessantly scheming to split Tibet from the motherland; they cooperate with Tibetan reactionaries who have fled the country and gone abroad, they make many plans, work night and day, and they have done and are doing many bad things.
>
> (Panchen Lama 1997: 63)

The tactic of "enveloping" the crux of the question, in this case the different perception Tibetans have of their own cultural-historical identity, within the heavy ideological parlance of the Chinese Communist Party characterizes the style that the Panchen Lama imparted to the document as a whole. Despite the daring nature of the petition, when the Panchen Lama presented it to the premier Zhou Enlai in May 1962, he received a favorable response at first. The premier took the document seriously, admonishing the generals Zhang Guohua and Zhang Jingwu, the highest ranked Chinese rulers in Tibet, to critically evaluate their work in the region in light of what was said in the petition. As Robert Barnett suggests in his preface to the English publication of the document, "In theory, its appearance [the petition's] was a vindication of the United Front System, set up by the Chinese Communist Party so that representatives of non-Chinese nationalities or non-Party sectors of society could express their views and criticise policy" (Barnett 1997: xvi). If the first reactions to the petition were positive, Mao Zedong would later qualify it as "a poisoned arrow aimed at the Party by reactionary feudal overlords" (ibid.: xvii). The Panchen Lama was clearly not fulfilling his destiny as Beijing's most important Tibetan ally, or at least not in the way it was envisioned by certain Chinese leaders of the time.

The Panchen Lama became, in the words of General Zhang Guohua, a "big rock on the road to socialism" (Avedon 1994: 274). In September 1964, he was submitted to thamzing during the Seventh Meeting of the PCART. For 50 days during this meeting he was criticized, beaten and humiliated. In his own monastery, Tashilhunpo, similar meetings were held, denouncing his activities. Arjia Rinpoche, a high-ranking lama who lived under communist rule for more than 46 years and was a protégé of the Panchen Lama, describes the emotional impact caused by this particular reeducation campaign:

> The political campaigns of the 1960s were not created by cadres and positivists, but rather by their leaders. Our tormentors at Tashi Lhunpo were just loyally implementing the plans and commands of their superiors. But what a horrendous crime we were forced to commit! Everyday we had to criticize and denounce the Panchen Lama, our teacher, in violation of everything we stood for. I felt debased by this, but in my fear I also felt I had no choice. Monks who refused to go along were tortured, sent to prison camps, and even killed. We didn't dare to discuss our feelings amongst ourselves, for betrayal was all too common. Day after day, our torment grew.
>
> (Arjia Rinpoche 2010: 71–2)

Between 1964 and 1966, the Panchen Lama was put under house arrest. In August 1966, at the beginning of the Cultural Revolution, he was taken to the Xiannongtan sports stadium in Beijing and once again submitted to thamzing, but this time in front of thousands of people. Alternating between prison and house arrest, he would only be released in 1978, after Deng Xiaoping came to power.

Destruction and (re)creation[28]

With the figures of the Dalai Lama and the Panchen Lama out of the picture, the destructive power of the Cultural Revolution[29] (1966–76) penetrated Tibet, almost completely erasing, at least temporarily, any trace of Tibetan religious life that still persisted after the democratic reforms. In reality, years before the advent of the Cultural Revolution, "most monasteries had been closed down and most monks had been forcibly defrocked" (Barnett 2009: 9). During the Cultural Revolution, even exceptions to the restrictions placed on religious life, as was the case of Arjia Rinpoche due to the protection of the Panchen Lama, suffered radical transformations in their lifestyle. In the monastery of Kumbum, Arjia Rinpoche witnessed transformations in the daily routine of the monks, and in their organization and function inside the monastery. There, even before the beginning of the revolution, all the monks had to wear civilian clothes, and Arjia Rinpoche and others were put to work in the fields as "peasant monks." After returning from a visit home that coincided with the unleashing of the revolution in his region, Arjia Rinpoche noted:

> [...] [W]e saw that in the short time we had been away the internal divisions caused by the Cultural Revolution had now fully invaded our monastery. Ngawang Jimba, who had been the administrator of religious reform at the monastery since 1958, led one group of positivist monks. Lobsang Rabgyal headed up another, claiming that Ngawang Jimba, having been longtime director of the Democratic Management Committee of Kumbum Monastery, was part of the ruling class. Uneasy about the accusation, Ngawang Jimba directed his followers to burn sutras and smash Buddha statues in an attempt to demonstrate his loyalty to the revolution.
>
> (Arjia Rinpoche 2010: 81–2)

This was, of course, just the beginning of the wave of destruction that would sweep across the whole of China during those tumultuous years. In the monastery of Kumbum, as in other monasteries in Tibet, the material destruction of religious objects was almost complete. Once more, Arjia Rinpoche was a direct witness to dramatic scenes in his monastery:

> One cloudy autumn day, while we were harvesting green peas in the field, we heard a voice come over the loudspeaker demanding that we attend a meeting. We sensed that something terrible was about to happen. When we arrived at the courtyard, we saw that a crowd had gathered, including hundreds of college students; where they had come from, we did not know. They began a political study session, but the meeting was chaotic, and they began to argue among themselves. [...]
>
> The Red Guards swarmed into the Maitreya Hall next door and began to toss bundles of ancient sutras into the courtyard from the second floor of the Buddha Hall. They lit a fire, and soon the monastery was filled with the thick smoke of burning books. Some monks lost control and began to wail. Others stood motionless. Still others joined in the destruction of the sutras, spurring on the students. Panic and rage were everywhere, like demons unleashed.
>
> (Ibid.: 82–3)

Similar scenes of destruction would happen all throughout the territories of the PRC. In these difficult years, Arjia Rinpoche mainly worked in the fields, as a "peasant monk," receiving religious instructions only scarcely and secretly from his gurus. With the death of Mao Zedong in 1976 and the consequent fall of his immediate followers known as the "Gang of Four," Deng Xiaoping came to power as the paramount leader of the Communist Party and the state. Deng pursued new external and internal strategies to deal with the Tibet issue as part of a more generalized liberal policy. Externally, talks were resumed with the Dalai Lama seeking his return to the country. Such talks resulted in the decision to send to Tibet fact-finding delegations, like the one headed by Lobsang Samten, the Dalai Lama's brother, and cited at the beginning of this chapter. Internally, the strategy adopted had two main components, as Melvyn Goldstein explains:

> (1) an ethnic dimension – making the Tibet Autonomous Region more Tibetan in overall character by fostering a revitalization of Tibetan culture and religion, including more extensive use of Tibetan language, and by withdrawing large numbers of Chinese cadre and replacing them with Tibetans; and (2) an economic dimension – rapidly improving the standard of living of individual Tibetans by temporarily eliminating taxes and "below-market" quota sales, and developing infrastructure to allow Tibet to grow economically in the years ahead.
>
> (Goldstein 1997: 65–6)

In 1979, when he received the news that monks were allowed to wear robes and practice religion again, Arjia Rinpoche and other fellow lamas and monks expressed suspicion at first (Arjia Rinpoche 2010: 117–18). Even if the sudden liberalization was part of preparations for the arrival of a delegation sent by the Dalai Lama, as Arjia Rinpoche would learn later, the changes, nevertheless, were there to stay: it seemed that religious life was to be revitalized and reorganized by the Communist Party. After he graduated from the newly created Department of Tibetan Studies at Qinghai University for Nationalities, Arjia Rinpoche took a job as a clerk in a liaison office of the Buddhist Association of China in Xining, where he acted "as a bridge between the Tibetan religious community and the government." He accepted the position, despite feeling "uncomfortable" with the past "atrocities" committed by the communist government against Tibetan monasteries. He "rationalized it" by telling himself that he "was able to serve Tibetans, Mongolians and other Buddhists in this way" (ibid.: 128). It did not take long for him to realize that his position "was nothing more than a window dresser." Through his work, he made suggestions that were invariably "ignored by the Party, where all real power laid" (ibid.: 129). In the early 1980s, Arjia Rinpoche became a member of the board of the Buddhist Association in China and the Vice-Chairman of its Qinghai branch. His steps were carefully watched while holding these high positions. As he explains, "Chinese religious organizations, although technically not affiliated with the government, are allowed to function only within strict limits set by the authorities." At his office in Qinghai, he continues, "a Party secretary was always present to keep an eye on rinpoches and other non-party members" (ibid.: 142).

Despite the restrictions, much progress was made in relation to the period of the Cultural Revolution. Now, he had the chance to work closely and even travel abroad with the Panchen Lama, who had been released from prison in 1978. Committed to the preservation of Tibetan language and culture, the Panchen Lama, who was rehabilitated in the early 1980s, took several important steps in this direction. In 1987, he established the High-Level Tibetan Buddhism College of China in Beijing, "to help offset three decades of systematic destruction of Tibetan Buddhism by the Communists" (ibid.: 148). According to Arjia Rinpoche, the college "was only a beginning. The Panchen Lama also began to prepare to develop other institutions, including schools that would offer language programs in Tibetan regions where Chinese was the only language taught in schools" (ibid.: 149). The Panchen Lama, nevertheless, died quite suddenly in 1989, before his projects could come to full fruition. The circumstances involving the search for his incarnation,[30] which became an international human rights issue, showed the world that the Chinese "good will" towards religious liberalization was limited in scope.

Arjia Rinpoche was once again an important eyewitness to the events that eventually lead to the christening of one of the youngest martyrs in the recent history of the world: the boy recognized as the reincarnation of the Tenth Panchen Lama through the joint efforts of the Dalai Lama and a search team in Tibet. The Chinese government itself invited the Dalai Lama to participate in the search for the new incarnation, but he would have had to come to China, so he declined. Innovatively, the search team was composed of a political division, which consisted of "important figures from the central and provincial governments," and a religious division, which was headed by Gyayak Rinpoche, the main guru of Arjia Rinpoche, and Chadrel Rinpoche (ibid.: 166). Arjia Rinpoche himself was also part of the search team. Nonetheless, for a series of reasons, chief among which was the death of Gayak Rinpoche in 1990, Chadrel Rinpoche ended up being the main person in charge of searching for the reincarnation. Secretly, he was in communication with the Dalai Lama. When a final decision was finally made in May 1995, the Dalai Lama announced in Dharamsala that the Eleventh Panchen Lama had been recognized. Arjia Rinpoche reports that he was stunned by the news of the public announcement: "My immediate fear was that the Chinese government would not accept his decision and would put itself at odds with Tibetan tradition" (ibid.: 197). The fears of Arjia Rinpoche were well founded. After the announcement, the Chinese government took the boy and his family to an undisclosed location; their destiny remains unknown to this day.

The events that followed the disappearance of the recognized Panchen Lama would have a profound impact on the relationship between the Chinese government and Tibetan Buddhist proponents. Learning of the secret contact between Chadrel Rinpoche and the Dalai Lama, the Chinese government decided to directly control the selection of the Eleventh Panchen Lama. Arjia Rinpoche tried to escape the political pressure he was sure to suffer, but shying away from it was not an option at this point. Initially, he and other high lamas were forced to travel to Beijing to record a TV broadcast, expressing "their" thoughts about the government agenda to solve the issue by eliminating the candidate chosen by the Dalai Lama, denouncing Chadrel Rinpoche and mandating a Golden Urn ceremony. As Arjia Rinpoche states, "everyone spoke against the Dalai Lama and in favor of the government decision. To my shame, I was no exception" (ibid.: 202–3). The lamas were later offered a banquet and some money for their participation. Back in Kumbum Monastery, Arjia Rinpoche soon received the news that he was to participate in the search team to find a new Panchen Lama.

When the time came to take part in the Golden Urn ceremony, he and other lamas tried to feign illness in order to be excused, but they were informed that the "best doctors" would be accompanying them and that "for this event, everybody must be present" (ibid.: 204). As soon as he arrived in Lhasa, Arjia Rinpoche noted the oppressive atmosphere in the city, which was flooded with PLA soldiers. The ceremony happened in the middle of the night, even though the next day it was announced on TV that it had happened at 10 o'clock in the morning. Bumi Rinpoche, the Ganden Tripa, or throne-holder of Ganden Monastery, and leader of the Gelug School appointed by the Chinese government, had the function of drawing the lots. Arjia Rinpoche thought it was odd that instead of shaking the lots, the Ganden Tripa "passed his hand quickly over the lots and pulled one out." Watching the ceremony later on TV, Arjia Rinpoche had the impression that the "ivory lot selected by Bumi Rinpoche stood slightly above the others" (ibid.: 206), but he would only know the whole truth about the ceremony a few days later.

Ye Xiaowen, who was part of the State Administration for Religious Affairs of the PRC, told him in a casual tone: "When we made our selection we left nothing to chance. In the silk pouches of the ivory pieces we put a bit of cotton at the bottom of one of them, so it would be a little higher than the others and the right candidate would be chosen" (ibid.: 207). A campaign to denounce the Dalai Lama was then promoted (Shakya 2009: 206). Being "invited" by the government to serve as tutor for the Chinese Panchen Lama was the last straw; Arjia Rinpoche abruptly made the decision to escape.

Concluding remarks

Over the years following the Chinese invasion, the Tibetan sense of historical and national identity has gained new characteristics. In the past, internal political divisions marked what could be termed a wider "Tibetan ethnographic area"[31] within and beyond the sphere of Lhasa's direct control, and there existed language and custom barriers between and among people from Central Tibet, Western Tibet, Kham and Amdo, to cite only the main regions. Even though such barriers still persist to a considerable degree today inside the PRC and even in exile, the suffering and oppression perpetrated by foreign rule brought Tibetans together and strengthened their sense of trans-regional identity. A new awareness of what it is to be Tibetan was born from the terror and oppression of occupation. This new sensibility was cemented together, by among other things, the reports of atrocities circulated by exile Tibetans who have been fleeing their country in the tens of thousands over the last five decades. As we have seen, underlying those reports is the continual attack on Tibetan Buddhism inside Tibet.

In the face of such attacks, the nature of the alliance between religion and politics that has always characterized Tibetan Buddhism has been deeply redefined. On the one hand, the Chinese have profoundly disorganized and manipulated Tibetan Buddhism in attempts to make political use of its leaders and institutions. The issue surrounding Chinese control of the recognition of lamas, as in the case of the Panchen Lama, represents the most significant illustration of the effort to use Tibetan Buddhism for political ends and the consequences of such endeavors for the integrity of the tradition and its holders. On the other hand, the way Tibetans relate to their religion has also changed. Partly because it has been the main target of Chinese oppression, Buddhism has become the primary fuel for Tibetan resistance (inside and outside Tibet).[32] In the diaspora context, with the intense dissemination of Tibetan Buddhism in the wake of lamas and monastic figures persecuted by the regime, this tradition's new role as a stronghold of resistance has become even more accentuated, constituting the basis upon which the Tibetan struggle for autonomy is being built.

Notes

1 The account of this episode is based on the interview given by Lobsang Samten, head of the delegation and brother of the Dalai Lama, to John Avedon for his book *In Exile from the Land of Snows* (1994).

2 Püntsog Wangye, a Tibetan revolutionary who has played a pivotal role in the Communist invasion and rule over Tibet, gives in his autobiography his own testimony of the surprise that the visit caused among the Chinese officials. In his words,

> This was the first Tibetan exile delegation to visit Tibetan areas, and the government wanted to ensure they had a positive experience. It sent instructions to the areas they would visit, instructing the leadership to carefully inform the local people and cadres to give the delegates a warm welcome. (The United Front Work Department believed that the Tibetan masses were still very bitter about the old society, and feared they might treat the exile delegates rudely as class enemies and separatists.) In Lhasa, the local officials went so far as to hold neighborhood meetings warning the people not to throw stones or spit at the delegates.
>
> (Goldstein *et al.* 2004: 279)

Püntsog Wangye concludes a few pages later: "Everything that happened made it painfully obvious how little the government was in touch with Tibetans' real feelings. The delegation's experience showed vividly that the government had in a sense been fooled by its own propaganda" (ibid.: 284).

3 For more on the recent self-immolations in Tibet, see the report on the topic prepared by the International Campaign for Tibet (December 2012).

4 Over the last 60 years, a lot of ink has been spilt over the subject of the political status of Tibet vis-à-vis China. Tibetan, Chinese and western scholars have produced compelling historical accounts that tend to emphasize one or another side of the argument,

engendering a very complex picture of Sino-Tibetan relations over the last eight centuries (e.g., Sperling 2004; Shakya 1999; Tucci 1999; Snellgrove and Richardson 1995; Goldstein 1989; Petech 1990, 1950; Shakabpa 1967, 2010; Ahmad 1970). It would be futile at this point to try to contribute with yet another approach to this complicated issue. In the short space of this section, I intend solely to present in very general lines the crucial points of contention.

5 All the passages from the White Papers are cited from the Chinese government's official website (www.china.org.cn/e-white/tibet/). One of the criteria in my decision to use this document as an illustration of the PRC's official view of history stems from its accessibility to all those interested in this issue, a crucial aspect considering that the present work is concerned primarily with the diaspora context.

6 It is interesting to note here that Shakabpa emphasizes in his book that the Golden Calligrapher along with government debt collectors were the only Mongolian authorities stationed in Tibet (Shakabpa 2010: 209).

7 Shakabpa's historiographical project actually had a few different "incarnations" over the years. In the 1960s, pressed by the Dalai Lama's request and by the urgency of the moment, Shakabpa decided to first publish a shorter version of the book in English, which was entitled *Tibet: A Political History* (1967). In his words, "since foreigners did not understand Tibet's status, I saw the great importance of publishing my political history as it was at the time" (Shakabpa 2010: xliii). Shakabpa took a temporary leave of his functions in Delhi in 1963 to spend some time at Yale University, where he translated his book, and with the assistance of Turrell Wylie, professor at Washington State University, put it in "the customary form" (ibid.: xliii–xliv). A considerably more comprehensive version of Shakabpa's historiographical project would be completed a few years later and published in Tibetan in 1976, in Kalimpong, India (Shakabpa 1976). The English translation of this last work was released in 2010 under the title *One Hundred Thousand Moons*.

8 Even though my general aim here is to show in a very schematic way the two sides of the historical issue, I will also sporadically rely on the work of western historians for the sake of clarifying a few points throughout this section.

9 Ganden Podrang was initially the name given to the Dalai Lama's estate at the monastery of Drepung, in Lhasa. After the Fifth Dalai Lama came to power in 1642, his government also became known as "Ganden Podrang" (*see* for instance Shakabpa 2010: 327, fn. a).

10 For more on this important period of Tibetan history see, for instance, Chapter 7 of *One Hundred Thousand Moons* (Shakabpa 2010: 293–379).

11 For more information on the use of the Golden Urn, see Sperling (2012).

12 In 1903, the British sent an expeditionary force to Lhasa in order to secure its commercial ties with the Tibetan government. Led by Colonel Francis Younghusband (1863–1942), the mission culminated with the British imposition of a commercial treaty known as the "Convention of Lhasa," which was signed by the Thirteenth Dalai Lama's regent – the Tibetan leader having fled to Mongolia just before the mission arrived in Lhasa.

> The convention imposed a heavy indemnity on the Tibetans; it allowed a permanent British diplomatic and commercial presence at Gyantse, including the right of a British representative there to visit Lhasa whenever it was considered necessary for him to do so.
>
> (Addy 1994: 18)

Later, due to international pressure, the British decided to attenuate the terms of the treaty, reducing in particular the indemnity that the Tibetans should pay.

13 Shakabpa discusses the Simla convention in detail in the sixteenth chapter of *One Hundred Thousand Moons*, "Proof of Tibet's Enduring Independence" (2010: 759–81). For more on the British in Tibet, see also Wendy Palace (2005).

14 The concept of "Chinese" is a fairly complex one. Among the ethnic groups living within People's Republic of China territory, the Han ethnic group represents more than 90 per cent of the total population. In a certain sense, the Han embody what is generally understood by "Chinese." Nevertheless, among the many minority groups in China, some are practically indistinct from the Han. Such is the case with the Manchu ethnic group, which ruled over the Han majority during the Qing Empire (1644–1911). Even though the Manchus had a different ethnic origin they were culturally assimilated by the Han majority in such an extensive way that today it is almost impossible to differentiate a Manchu from a Han. It is furthermore important to note that during the Qing period, the supporting philosophy of the Empire was Confucianist, hence of Han origin.

15 For an insightful discussion of the culture of autobiographical writing in Tibet, see Janet Gyatso (1998).

16 A few examples of these autobiographies with political overtones written by lamas and lay people are: Trungpa (2003 [1977]); Geshe Lhundub Sopa and Donnelly (2012); Sakya and Emery (1990); Taklha (2001); Yangchen and Mackenzie (2007 [2006]); Norbu (1986 [1979]); Harrer and Norbu (1986 [1960]); Ani Panchen and Donnelley (2000); Tulku Yeshi Rinpoche (2012); Arjia Rinpoche (2010); Khétsun (2008); Dewatshang (1997); Palden Gyatso (1997a, 1997b).

17 For a critical discussion about Goldstein approach, see Norbu (2004 [1992]).

18 This book was translated from English to Tibetan by Chung Tsering, and published in 2006 by Tibet Times, a publishing house situated in Dharamsala, India. Today, this Tibetan version of the book can be amply found throughout the Tibetan language bookstores in Tibetan exile communities.

19 Some sources speak of 40,000 soldiers. See for example Shakya (2009: 101).

20 The idea of "aggressive imperialistic forces" threatening Tibet is ludicrous in the face of the actual number of westerners stationed in Tibet at the time: not more than a dozen. The Dalai Lama states in his autobiography, *My Land and My People* that in his knowledge there were only six Europeans in Tibet in 1948:

> Three of them, one missionary and two radio operators, were British. The other three were two Austrians and one White Russian, all of whom had been refugees from British internment camps in India during the war. None of them had anything to do with military matters.
>
> (Tenzin Gyatso 1962: 80)

In his other biography, the Dalai Lama revises this number slightly to include a few more foreigners that were present in the Tibetan capital while he was growing up (Tenzin Gyatso 1990: 37–8).

21 For more on the life of the Ninth Panchen Lama, see Jagou (2011).

22 However, the mass influx of Chinese troops, in Phüntso Wangye's own account, "led to serious inflation, and shortages of foodstuffs and fuel" as soon as the beginning of 1952 (Goldstein *et al.* 2004: 173).

23 In 1958, Ama Adhe was arrested and spent the next 27 years in prison (Tapontsang 1997).

24 For more on the geopolitical division of Tibetan territory under Chinese rule, see Barnett and Schwartz (2008: xix).

25 For an extensive study on the polity powers of incarnate lamas, see Michael (1982).

26 For a detailed study of the origins and institutionalization of the Nechung cult during the time of the Fifth Dalai Lama, see Christopher Bell (2013). For a discussion of the role of Nechung in the diaspora context, see Urmila Nair (2010).

27 Robert Barnett tells us that the Communist Party still to this day considers the document highly confidential. A copy of the document "emerged in an envelope delivered" to the Tibet Information Network (TIN) in London in October of 1996. And after 11 months of work, which involved three translation teams, the TIN came up with a translation and published it in 1997 (personal communication, 2013).

28 This particular section of the chapter was composed mainly based on the important testimony of Arjia Rinpoche, given in his autobiography, *Surviving the Dragon* (2010). Arjia Rinpoche's account of the events that ravaged Tibet during the Cultural Revolution and later is particularly invaluable due to his unique position as a high lama who grew up under communist rule and who came to occupy important positions in Buddhist associations and in the government. In 1998, Arjia Rinpoche escaped to exile, bringing to the public previously unknown details about the communist grip on Tibetan Buddhism.

29 For a discussion of the Cultural Revolution in Tibet, see Goldstein, Jiao and Lhundrup (2009).

30 For a critical study on the artistic, literary and media products produced in the PRC to commemorate the selection of the reincarnation of the Tenth Panchen Lama, see Barnett (2008b). For a well-informed journalistic take on the circumstances involving the search for the reincarnation of the Tenth Panchen Lama, see Hilton (1999).

31 In the words of Robert Barnett:

> This "ethnographic" Tibet, as [Hugh] Richardson termed it, includes the northeastern area of the plateau sometimes called Amdo by Tibetans, which lies mainly within China's Qinghai province and southern Gansu, and the eastern area known in Tibetan as Kham, much of which now lies within western Sichuan and the northern tip of Yunnan.
>
> (Barnett 2008a: xix)

32 The many demonstrations, peaceful and violent, staged by monks and nuns over the last decades have shown that, in a certain sense, the Chinese have succeeded in politicizing Tibetan social life. (What Chinese leaders could not have predicted was that this politicization process would turn against them.) Buddhism in Tibet has always been intimately entangled with politics, and has certainly been one of the main diacritical marks of Tibetan identity. The Chinese attacks on this tradition on the one hand, and their attempts to raise the conscience of monks and nuns (along with the lay population) on the other could arguably be seen as factors that contributed to the organization of nationalistic demonstrations against the PRC's rule in Tibet. However, instead of finding their inspiration in communist ideology, monks and nuns have adopted the principles of democracy and human rights promoted since the 1960s by the Dalai Lama within the context of his government in exile (Schwartz 1994: 126–7). For a detailed account of the participation of monks and nuns in the nationalistic demonstrations that took place in Tibet as part of the emergence of a non-violent nationalistic movement during the 1980s, see Schwartz (1994).

2 The power of compassion

North of Vajrasana in the east, there is a place called "Tibet." It has sky pillars of high mountains; turquoise mandalas of lowland lakes; crystal stupas of white snow; golden stupas of yellow meadows; medicinal incenses of delicious fragrances; gold flowers of brilliant hues; and turquoise flowers of exquisite summers. Oh, protector of the Land of Snow Mountains, Avalokiteshvara, in that place is your field, and in that field are your disciples!

A passage from the *Kadam Legbam,* as cited by the Fifth Dalai Lama[1]

Ngawang Lobsang Gyatso, the Fifth Dalai Lama, came to power in 1642, marking the consolidation of a process that gradually placed Buddhism at the center of Tibetan life. With the help of Gushri Khan, leader of the Qosot Mongols, the Fifth Dalai Lama subjugated local warlords and finally defeated the king of the western region of Tsang, Karma Tankyong Wangpo (1606–42), who also precariously ruled over Central Tibet. The Great Fifth, as the Fifth Dalai Lama was also known, created in this way the conditions for the reestablishment of a centralized government in Tibet, and also for the concentration of public resources into the hands of religious institutions (in particular Gelug institutions), a crucial factor for the spectacular development of Buddhism in this country.

The political project inaugurated by the Great Fifth and his associates endured for more than 300 years until its dissolution was brought about by the brutal Chinese occupation. The coup de grâce on this unique type of government occurred when the current representative of the Dalai Lama incarnation line, the Fourteenth Dalai Lama, fled Tibet to become in exile one of the most renowned religious figures in the world. As we will see in Chapter 6, the status of the Dalai Lama as the king of Tibet and the rituals and myths of the state did not completely disappear with the Chinese destruction of Tibetan power structures. In effect, many of the elements that were previously associated with the state continued to have a central importance in the diaspora, but in this context they acquired new meanings and configurations.

The persistence of these elements in a completely new context can be directly traced to the nature of the Tibetan state itself. It is essential for the argument developed in this book, then, to investigate the bases upon which the government of the Dalai Lamas and its symbolic apparatus were built. From the outset, it could be said that one of the main characteristics of this government was a strong concern with the ritualization of its activities. A clear example of this dynamic was the creation of festivals and ceremonies at the time of the Fifth Dalai Lama. This effectively transformed the year in the capital city of Lhasa into a succession of commemorative rituals.[2] In a similar vein, the palace where the Dalai Lama resided, the Potala, and the governmental organization as a whole were conceived as mandalas, which in the context of Tibetan Buddhism can be succinctly described as the prime organizing principle of ritual space.

In view of the overwhelming presence of the mandala concept in these power-related structures, the notion of "Galactic Polity" can offer an insightful first approach to the nature of the government established by the Fifth Dalai Lama. Stanley Tambiah developed the idea of "Galactic Polity" in relation to Thevaradin states in Southeast Asia (1976; 1985).[3] In the words of Tambiah, the term "Galactic Polity" derives from the concept of mandala – "a core (*manda*) and a container or enclosing element (*la*)" (Tambiah 1976: 102). In this model, Tambiah invokes the image of a kingdom, a prototype of the cosmos, in which there is a governing center with less important replicas gravitating around it. The center serves as an exemplar capable of providing a paradigm of civilization.[4] What interests us here in relation to this model is the centrality of performance in the kinds of governmental structures in question. This prominent role of performance is a point that has also been beautifully illustrated by the concept of "Theatre State," which was put forth by Clifford Geertz in *Negara* (1980) to describe the nineteenth-century Balinese state. Both the "Galactic Polity" and "Theatre State" models underline the idea of a central government that does not directly administer the peripheral regions, thus leaving to expressive forms, such as the spectacle and the court ceremonial, a good part of the activities of governance. Although the precise degree to which the central government in Lhasa exercised direct control over its surrounding territories is a matter of considerable debate,[5] it is simply the direct correspondence in Tibet between performance and the act of governing that interests us here.

However, to better understand the mechanisms at work in the establishment of the Ganden Podrang government, as the Dalai Lama's government came to be known, it is necessary to take this idea of performance a step further. Following the ideas put forth by sociologist Erving Goffman in his classic work, *The Presentation of the Self in Everyday Life* (1959), I believe it is important to investigate the establishment of the Dalai Lama government in terms of the presentation of one particular self, the Fifth Dalai Lama's, which, when closely scrutinized, reveals a consistent effort to at once internalize and publicize symbols directly relevant to statecraft in Tibet. Foundational for the Ganden Podrang government was precisely the role that the Great Fifth himself played in the creation of rituals and a state cosmology through his writings, decrees and so forth. Interwoven with these elements was his concern with building his own public image, or his political persona, and an associated mythic-historical context, as the stage on which he would act as ruler of the new polity.

The work of British historian Peter Burke on the "fabrication of the public image" of Louis XIV and its "place in the collective imagination" (Burke 1994: 1) constitutes a fundamental theoretical inspiration for this chapter. The main focus of Burke's study is the images of Louis XIV, such as statues, paintings, coins and so forth, created during the king's lifetime. In a similar vein, the center of my investigation in this chapter gravitates to images, but in the more figurative sense of the term, i.e., images built from the Fifth Dalai Lama's own writings. Like many of the "visual images" of Louis XIV discussed in Burke's work, the Fifth Dalai Lama's "textual images" have an essential role not only in the construction, or fabrication, of the public image of the Fifth Dalai Lama, but also in the construction of the personas of all the Dalai Lamas that followed him, as well as those that came before.

The Fifth Dalai Lama was a prolific writer. His *Collected Works* (Tib. *gsung 'bum*) comprises more than 25 volumes, with writings that range from historical, biographical, and autobiographical narratives to meditation manuals, behavioral guides, edicts, personal correspondences, monastery regulations, law codes, and much more (Ngawang Lobsang Gyatso 1991–5a). His historical, autobiographical and biographical writings are particularly revealing about his efforts to create a historical and mythological framework that would serve as a symbolic foundation for the new state power. When taking into consideration the impressive volume of his works, it would be fair to say that the Fifth Dalai Lama saw in the activity of writing a substantial aspect of being a ruler.

In 1643, the very next year after coming into power, the Fifth Dalai Lama directly took up the task of writing an official history of Tibet. Composed at the request of Gushri Khan, *The Song of the Spring Queen* (Ngawang Lobsang Gyatso 1991–5b) had a direct influence not only on the Tibetan imaginary, but also on western academic understandings of Tibetan history.[6] As Peter Burke puts it in relation to Louis XIV's rule, "The best evidence for the government's preoccupation with posterity is surely the effort put into finding suitable authors for an official history of the reign" (Burke 1994: 153). If this statement is clearly true for *The Song of the Spring Queen*, two other works written by the Great Fifth in the following few years can also be said to reflect this concern with posterity. I am referring here to the biographies of his two predecessors, the Third Dalai Lama, Sonam Gyatso (1543–88) (Ngawang Lobsang Gyatso 1991–5c), and the Fourth Dalai Lama, Yonten Gyatso (1589–1616) (Ngawang Lobsang Gyatso 1991–5d), written respectively in 1646 and 1652. Finally, two other works authored by the Fifth Dalai Lama deserve to be singled out here: his "outer" autobiography,[7] entitled *Fine Silk Cloth* (Ngawang Lobsang Gyatso 1991–5e), and his "secret" autobiography, *The Sealed One* (Ngawang Lobsang Gyatso 1972).

All the works mentioned above played a crucial role in the creation of the Fifth Dalai Lama's own public image.[8] Among other elements, they brought together paradigmatic figures of the Tibetan mythic and historical domains, relating them to the lineage of the Dalai Lamas in ways that would be concomitantly activated and reinforced through the performance of rituals, festivals and the creation of artistic objects and architecture. But before proceeding to a discussion of the fabrication of the Fifth Dalai Lama's image and the symbolic apparatus of the Ganden Podrang government per se, I will first present a brief historical background detailing the emergence of the lineage of the Dalai Lamas and the ascension of the Fifth Dalai Lama as the religious and secular leader of Tibet.[9]

I Historical background

The rise of the Dalai Lama lineage

In the centuries preceding the Fifth Dalai Lama's birth, Tibet was immersed in conflicts that encompassed the religious, social, economic and political fields. Different political groups were fighting among themselves for control over land and resources. These forces were divided primarily between local aristocracies ruling over the regions of Central Tibet and Tsang. In intimate connection with them, religious groups led by charismatic lamas played a decisive role in this volatile scene.

In the fourteenth century, Tsongkhapa (1357–1419), the founding figure of the Gelug School, emerged in this setting as a major player. Through the patronage of powerful individuals connected to the Phagmodru rulers of Central Tibet, Tsongkhapa instituted the Monlam Chenmo, or Great Prayer Festival in 1409, and also founded Ganden monastery on the outskirts of Lhasa, that same year. Also supported by the patronage of the Phagmodru, one of Tsongkhapa's disciples, Jamyang Choje (1379–1449), founded in Lhasa the monasteries of Drepung (1416) and Sera (1419) (Shakabpa 1967: 85). The establishment of the Monlam Festival and these three Gelug monasteries – which from an early time housed thousands of monks – represented important steps towards the ascension to power orchestrated by the Fifth Dalai Lama and his associates.

One of the most renowned students of Tsongkhapa was Gendun Drubpa (1391–1474), who would be known posthumously as the First Dalai Lama. One of his most notable accomplishments was the foundation of Tashilhunpo monastery in Shigatse, Tsang, where the Kagyu School already had a firm basis of support. Tashilhunpo rapidly became an important Gelug center and represented an effective way to extend the influence of the nascent Gelug School to the Tsang area. In 1475, a year after the death of Gendun Drubpa, a boy was recognized as his reincarnation at Tanag Segme in the region of Tsang (Shakabpa 1967: 91). Gendun Gyatso (1475–1542), as this reincarnation came to be called, was reputed to be an accomplished contemplative responsible for building many large and small monasteries. In particular, he founded in 1509 the monastery of Chokhorgyal, 90 miles to the southeast of Lhasa (ibid.). Gendun Gyatso extended the sphere of influence of the Gelug School well beyond Shigatse and Lhasa through extensive travels and the creation of a network of powerful disciples who sponsored his institutional activities (Maher 2007: 263). His authority within the Gelug School can be measured by the fact that, in different periods, he served as abbot of both Tashilhunpo and Drepung monasteries. The residence he built for himself in Drepung, Ganden Podrang, would inspire the name of the government established by his later successor, the Fifth Dalai Lama (Shakabpa 2010: 294). Finally, it should be noted that Gendun Gyatso, by becoming the abbot of Drepung, shifted the base of operations of the Dalai Lamas to the Lhasa area. As we will see shortly, this move was a consequential maneuver for the appropriation of important symbols connected to this city, much along the same lines as the earlier foundation there of the three massive Gelug monasteries and the Monlam Chenmo festival.

The first two Dalai Lamas played pivotal roles in the Gelug School's ascension to power. Gendun Drubpa and Gendun Gyatso acquired great reputation during their lifetimes for their spiritual and scholarly accomplishments, as well as for founding important monasteries in the regions of Central Tibet and Tsang. And it was precisely this combination of personal and institutional renown that constituted a mark of a politically important lama. It meant, among other things, that both lamas were major players in the patron-priest relationship style of doing politics in Tibet. With the third incarnation of the linage of the Dalai Lamas, Sonam Gyatso, the entanglement between religion and politics became even more conspicuous. The progressive strengthening of the Gelug School promoted in part by the first two Dalai Lamas would take an important turn with the encounter in 1587 between Sonam Gyatso and Altan Khan, leader of the Tümed Mongols. This meeting would prove to be a factor leading to the establishment of the government of the Dalai Lamas.

Like his predecessors, Sonam Gyatso was reputed for being a great spiritual master and scholar. Moreover, as Sørensen and Hazod have shown in *Rulers of the Celestial Plain*, multiple literary sources describe Sonam Gyatso as the "Virupa of Tibet," associating his efforts to prevent floods in the most sacred temple in Lhasa, the Jokhang, with the Indian saint Virupa's "fabled exploits in controlling the water" (Sørensen and Hazod 2007: 527). As early as 1562, Sonam Gyatso undertook the initiative to prevent floods in the Jokhang area on two fronts: he both conducted flood-averting rituals and helped with the maintenance of dikes. That particular year, Lhasa suffered from extensive rainfalls, and the waters of the Kyichu River violently ruptured the stone dikes and flooded the city (Shakabpa 1967: 92). In the next year, Sonam Gyatso instructed monks of three important Gelug monasteries around the Lhasa area – Sera, Drepung and Gawadong – to repair the dikes that protected Lhasa and the Jokhang on the last day of the Monlam Chenmo festival (Sørensen and Hazod 2007: 527; Shakabpa 1967: 92).

In their book, Sørensen and Hazod document in detail the central place in the political environment of medieval Tibet reserved for the protection of the Jokhang temple in Lhasa against floods. As I will discuss below, the vital importance of this kind of endeavor evidently did not escape the Fifth Dalai Lama, who in his narrative of Sonam Gyatso's life would, for example, highlight this master's past lives as some of the key lamas that were renowned as protectors of the sacred temple against flood. For now, it suffices to have in mind that Sonam Gyatso's activities as the protector of Lhasa and the Jokhang played a particularly key role in paving the way for the ascension to power of the Dalai Lama lineage.

Around the middle of the sixteenth century, the balance of power tipped from Central Tibet to Tsang with the gradual ascension of the governor of Tsang, Zhingshakpa Tseten Dorje (b. sixteenth century), as trans-regional force, a shift that eventually led to the emergence of the Tsang dynasty. The rise of the Tsang dynasty favored in general terms the Kagyu School. The Gelug School tried to compensate for the disadvantage through seeking the patronage of Mongol leaders. The prestige of Sonam Gyatso led Altan Khan, leader of the Tümed Mongols, to invite him to Mongolia, inaugurating an alliance that had profound implications for the authority of the Dalai Lama incarnation line.

The traditional accounts report that Altan Khan was extremely impressed by Sonam Gyatso when they met in 1578. He gave the Tibetan lama the title of "Dalai," which means "ocean," implying that he was an ocean of learning and wisdom. Since then, he and his successors (and retrospectively, his predecessors) would be known as the Dalai Lamas. Sonam Gyatso, on his end, conferred upon Altan Khan the title of Dharmarāja, or in Tibetan, "Chokyi Gyalpo" (Tib. *chos kyi rgyal po*) (Shakabpa 1967: 95; 2010: 301; Tucci 1949: 47–8). Sometimes translated as "religious king," Chokyi Gyalpo should perhaps be more accurately rendered as "the king who rules in accordance with dharma." The impulse to civilize the Mongols through Buddhism is implied in this title.[10] The meeting between Sonam Gyatso and Altan Khan evoked other paradigmatic encounters between Tibetans and Mongols, i.e., that of Sakya Pandita and Goden Khan, and maybe even more strongly, that of Phagpa Chögyal and Kublai Khan (c.f. Chapter 1). Even if Altan Khan lacked the authority to confer any temporal jurisdiction on Sonam Gyatso, as had been the case with Kublai Khan and the Sakya hierarch, the reenactment of these symbolically charged historical events strengthened the political power of the Gelug School,[11] and provoked the suspicion of the Tsang kings.

The relationship between Gelug hierarchs and Mongol leaders would be deepened when the next reincarnation of the Dalai Lama was discovered within Altan Khan's own family. Roughly two years after Sonam Gyatso passed away in 1588, a search party concluded, based on reports about children born during this period and consultations with oracles, that the great-grandson of Altan Khan was the reincarnation of Sonam Gyatso (Shakabpa 1967: 96; 2010: 305; Tucci 1949: 50). The Fourth Dalai Lama, Yonten Gyatso, did not live long, He passed away at the end of 1616 at the age of 28 "under mysterious circumstances," which were probably "an outcome of anti-Mongol sentiments" present in certain circles (Sørensen and Hazod 2007: 537). His greatest accomplishment was undoubtedly the political strengthening of the Gelug School by means of his family ties to Altan Khan. The impact that bringing Mongol blood into the increasingly powerful Dalai Lama line had for both the Gelug School and the descendants of Altan Khan did not escape the Tsang kings, who would later put a ban on the recognition of the next incarnation (ibid.), the Fifth Dalai Lama.

The traditional enmity between Central Tibet and Tsang, and to some extent between the Gelug and Kagyu schools, seems to have reached a critical point around that time. The growing presence of Mongols in the political machinations of the period had the clear effect of adding fuel to the fire.

A monk seizes political power

It was amidst this tumultuous background that a fifth representative of the Dalai Lama lineage would be found, this time in a family connected to the famous Zahor royal line. Due to the unstable political situation that had become the rule on the Tibetan plateau, Sonam Chöpel (1595–1658), who had been the main attendant of the Fourth Dalai Lama, secretly dispatched parties to different locations to look for the new incarnation (Shakabpa 1967: 101). In 1619, he received information that a child showing "exceptional signs" (ibid.) was born to an aristocratic family in the castle of Tagtse, the old seat of the Phagmodru dynasty. The child's paternal ancestors had served the Phagmodru rulers, whose power dwindled in the first half of the fifteenth century when the Rinpung dynasty ascended, shifted the concentration of power back to Tsang and thus provided the conditions for the eventual rise of the Tsang kings after the middle of the sixteenth century.

Shortly after the birth of the Fifth Dalai Lama, his father Dudül Dorje (*c.* seventeenth century) – or Dudül Rabten as he was also known – became involved in a plot against the Tsang king, resulting in his arrest at Samdrubtse Castle, the headquarters of the Tsang dynasty. He would remain there until his death in 1626, without ever seeing his son again (Karmay 2002: 68). The events that let to the arrest of the Dalai Lama's father occurred in 1618, which was a particularly turbulent year that became known in the literature as the "Earth-Horse Year Warfare" (Sørensen and Hazod 2007: 537). It was at this time that Central Tibet and Tsang directly engaged in bloody battles, which were often presented in the Tibetan historiographical literature as skirmishes between representatives of the Gelug and Kagyu schools.

While the Fifth Dalai Lama was growing up, the conflicts did not recede. In the beginning of the 1630s, Gelug hierarchs decided to seek the support of Mongol groups that had recently converted to Buddhism. Representatives of the three great Gelug seats in the region of Central Tibet – Sera, Drepung and Ganden – were sent to make contact with Mongol leaders in the border regions of Tibet (Shakabpa 1967: 103). This was a tactic that would ultimately lead to the conquest of political power by the Gelug School. Among these representatives was Sonam Chöpel (1595–1658), who was also responsible for the discovery of the Fifth Dalai Lama. Historians are unanimous in identifying him as the main architect of the Gelug ascension to power (*see* for example Shakabpa 1967, 2010; Tucci 1949; Karmay 2002; Schaeffer 2005). Having been the main attendant of the Fourth Dalai Lama, Sonam Chöpel certainly was in a particularly privileged position to negotiate alliances with the Mongols. Sonam Chöpel figures in the Fifth Dalai Lama's writings as the great mediator between the lama and Gushri Khan, the young leader of the Qosot Mongols who eventually decided to help the Dalai Lama and the Gelug school defeat their enemies inside and outside Tibet.

Gushri Khan's conquest of Tibet was gradual, even if relatively fast. After defeating Tsang loyalists and other enemies of the Gelug School between 1637 and 1641, he engaged in a one-year battle against the king of Tsang, Karma Tankyong Wangpo, the most powerful ruler of the time. As soon as he took control of the Tsang region, Gushri Khan sent for the Fifth Dalai Lama. This happened at the beginning of the third month of the Water-Horse year (1642). Led by Gushri Khan, Sonam Chöpel and others, a welcoming party composed of a large number of monks and lay people went to greet the Dalai Lama at Dechen, between Lhasa and Shigatse. There Gushri Khan presented the Dalai Lama with Phagpa Chögyal's "agate bell, an offering object fashioned from emerald, and other treasures that were famed throughout Mongolia. He also offered the Dalai Lama the thirteen provinces of Tibet. He gave whatever was to his left and to his right" (Shakabpa 2010: 346–7). A few weeks later, in a more formal ceremony carried out in the great audience hall of Samdrubtse Castle, the Dalai Lama was "raised up on the high golden fearless snow lion throne, where he was invested with the leadership." Gushri Khan and Sonam Chöpel "were seated on two thrones that were lower by one-fifth than the throne of the supreme sovereign" (ibid.: 347).

Once more, the so-called "chö-yön relation," or "secular protector–spiritual preceptor relationship," was enacted between a Tibetan hierarch and a Mongol leader in a formal ceremony. However, unlike the symbolic nature of the agreement between Altan Khan and Sonam Gyatso, or even the relatively short-lived Sakya rule born from the pact between Kublai Khan and Phagpa Chögyal, the Dalai Lama and the Gelug School would be able to establish a long-term governmental structure and politically unify an important part of the Tibetan cultural territory. This meant, among other things, that the new state was able to expand its sphere of influence well beyond the area that for almost a century had been under the jurisdiction of the Tsang kings.

II History, myth and text

A palace for the bodhisattva king

Soon after the Mongol–Gelug alliance's seizure of power, the Fifth Dalai Lama, Sonam Chöpel and Gushri Khan decided in a meeting to build what would become one of the main symbols of the new Tibetan government: the Potala Palace[12] (Shakabpa 2010: 350). Erected over the ruins of a palace built by the imperial period king Songtsen Gampo on the Red Mountain (Tib. *dmar po ri*) of Lhasa, the Potala Palace was named after the earthly mountain abode of Avalokiteshvara, the so-called "bodhisattva of compassion."[13] Basing his account on the Great Fifth's autobiography, Shakabpa relates:

> Having come to an agreement on the plans, the Dalai Lama, Sönam Chöpel, and Gushri Khan rode out to the site on the twenty-eighth day of the third

month of 1645. The retired [Zurchen] Künkhyen Chöying Rangdrol drew the geomantic lines pacifying the earth spirits with his own hand. The ceremonial horn of the Conqueror Tsongkhapa from Ganden Monastery and the ceremonial horns of Lhajik Dīpaṃkara Atīśa and Sakya Paṇḍita were brought out and sounded in all directions.

On the twenty-ninth day of the third month, the ritual dance that tames the earth was performed. The image of Avalokiteśvara that had been used by King Songtsen Gampo in his practice had previously been given to Tumé Chechen Taiji by Kyishö Depa Apel as a reward for his military alliance. It was kept in Mongolia at that time. Yet, on the twenty-second day of the fourth month, it was effortlessly brought to the site and conveyed in a religious procession through the magical powers of Gushri Khan's queen, Dalai Kunji (Sunji).

(Ibid.: 350–1)

This concise description of the first steps taken in the construction of the Potala Palace is a small illustration of the kinds of processes involved in the creation of a symbolic apparatus for the nascent government. A profusion of important symbols of power is activated first in the rituals, then in the Fifth Dalai Lama's autobiography, and finally in Shakabpa's modern work of historiography, coming to us in the present day. These written mediations, instead of weakening the potency of the seminal events – i.e., the rituals – infuse them with new layers of significance. As we will come to see, this movement from ritual to text and from text to ritual would be repeated over and over again in a variety of settings.

Let us focus then on the process of the embodiment and assimilation of symbols, a dynamic that constitutes the core of the Fifth Dalai Lama's project of power, and is clearly present in the short passage cited above. Invoked through objects, and in between the lines of the rituals themselves, six figures emerge. They are historical, semi-mythical and mythical characters that occupied a privileged place in the establishment of a centralized power in seventeenth-century Tibet. Two of them have already been introduced in the present work. First, we have Sakya Pandita, who was responsible for establishing the foundational chö-yön relationship with a Mongol leader – a relationship that had as its final consequence the Mongol conferral of secular power over the 13 myriarchies of Tibet to Phagpa Chögyal. As we have just seen, this seminal moment was reenacted in a structurally similar ceremony involving the Fifth Dalai Lama, Gushri Khan and Sonam Chöpel. Second, we have Tsongkhapa, who, because of being the founding figure of the Gelug School, has an evident symbolic import for the Dalai Lama's project of power. Furthermore, as we shall see later in this chapter, the Monlam Chenmo Festival in Lhasa created by Tsongkhapa and the three massive Gelug monasteries around Lhasa, which are directly connected to this lama's activities, also played an essential role in the establishment of the new power.

For now, I will direct my attention to the other characters invoked in the ceremony described above: Avalokiteshvara, Songsten Gampo (d. 650),

Padmasambhava (eighth century) and Atisha Dipamkara (b. 972/982). These figures were arguably the most directly relevant for the creation of the public image of the Fifth Dalai Lama and the symbolic apparatus of the state. It stands to reason, then, that they serve as a focal point in *The Rulers of the Celestial Plain*, a magisterial study of the disputes over symbols in the district in which Lhasa is situated, Kyishö, between the thirteenth and sixteenth centuries (Sørensen and Hazod 2007). The emphasis of Sørensen and Hazod's book falls on both the ideological and actual battles fought over the potent symbols present in the city, which under the Fifth Dalai Lama's government would once more become the capital of Tibet. The revival of the geo-political centrality of Lhasa, as they and others have exhaustively shown (*see* especially Kapstein 2000), is directly connected with the enduring legacy of the cult of Avalokiteshvara and the related glorification of king Songtsen Gampo. As one of the three dharma kings held responsible for bringing Buddhism to Tibet, Songtsen Gampo began to be worshipped starting from the eleventh century as an emanation of the bodhisattva Avalokiteshvara. The Potala Palace, named after the abode of Avalokiteshvara on earth and built on the ruins of the king's old citadel, thus became one of the most potent symbols of the new government.

Another detail in the description of the rituals to consecrate the construction grounds should be noted here: the presence of the famous Nyingma lama Zurchen Chöying Rangdrol (1604–69) as the officiant of the ceremony. This indicates, among other things, the close proximity of the Fifth Dalai Lama with the Nyingma School. Since his childhood years, the Fifth Dalai Lama studied with masters from the Nyingma School. This proximity with the oldest order of Tibetan Buddhism strongly influenced him on both the personal and political levels. According to the historian Phillipe Cornu, already in 1636, he received from the Nyingma master Khöntön Paljor Lhündrup (1561–1637) extensive teachings on Dzogchen[14] that deeply influenced him (Cornu 2002: 35). After Khöntön Paljor Lhündrup's death, Zurchen Chöying Rangdrol played an especially important role in the religious life of the Dalai Lama, transmitting to him many tantric teachings. On many occasions, this Nyingma master was sought by his illustrious disciple for spiritual protection (Tenzin Gyatso and Cutler 2000: 229).[15] The contact with Nyingma masters had, moreover, the important effect of intensifying the Fifth Dalai Lama's mystical visions, which, as we will see, played an important part in the creation and sedimentation of the symbolic apparatus of the state.[16]

Having all of this in mind, it is easy to see how the description of rituals marking the beginning of the construction of the Potala Palace can be said to epitomize an almost perfect synthesis of the processes and elements involved in the Fifth Dalai Lama's project of power. Indeed, it captures the essence of this project by indicating how the Dalai Lama and his associates ventured to bring about a new centralized government through the assimilation of symbolic modalities prevalent in the Tibetan imaginary of the time. As I hope to show, it was through recourse to literary production, performance and aesthetic forms, such as architecture, that this was accomplished. In this regard, it is important to note also that the explicit purpose of the rituals briefly described above, namely the consecration of the ground where the palace was to be built, points first to the seminal moment of establishing the foundations of the new government, and then to the power-oriented generative force emanating from the figures invoked therein. With this short description of these rituals as my point of departure, I wish to discuss next some of the mechanisms involved in this process of creating a new government.

The bodhisattva, the king and the luminary: Avalokiteshvara, Songtsen Gampo and Atisha

A good start for us here would be to relate the figures invoked in the ritual above to the way they are depicted in *The Song of the Spring Queen*,[17] the history of Tibet written by the Fifth Dalai Lama just a year after he ascended to power. This work is particularly illuminating for us because it offers a preliminary template for the Fifth Dalai Lama's own vision of power and his place in history. Indeed, even though there is no direct mention of his own personal history in the text, references are made to his connections with an Indian family of noble origin, the Zahor family. More importantly, Avalokiteshvara, the bodhisattva of compassion with whom the Dalai Lama's line is associated,[18] figures in the narrative as a major character with a special relationship to Tibet. The composition of this history at the early date of 1643 indicates, among other things, a conscious effort to rapidly establish symbolic foundations for the new government. As Sørensen and Hazod (2007) have illustrated,[19] the main symbols that would support the Dalai Lama's government were coveted by multiple groups, not least by the Kagyu School representatives, who can arguably be acknowledged as the main adversaries of the Dalai Lama and the Gelug School in the religio-political domain. Just like the Dalai Lamas, for instance, the holders of the main Kagyu reincarnation line, the Karmapas, were also considered to be emanations of Avalokiteshvara. The Karmapas, nevertheless, had precedence in this domain, since they were the first to propagate this association, and, for that matter, the reincarnation institution as a whole in Tibet. In any case, these symbols were the objects of fierce dispute, hence there was a certain sense of urgency in taking a hold of them.

In this respect, *The Song of the Spring Queen* can be read as a means to assimilate these symbols into a genealogical rationale of power that would ultimately lead to Gushri Khan (and consequently to the Fifth Dalai Lama, even though not directly stated as such in the work).[20] The way this genealogy of power is presented in *The Song of the Spring Queen* conveys a sense of history, which is naturally very different from the one found in modern works of historiography. Concerning this, the particular conjunction between myth and history expressed in *The Song of the Spring Queen* should be discussed in light of the emergence in Tibet of a distinct body of literature, the so-called "Treasures" (Tib. *gter ma*), from the eleventh century on.[21] In this literary genre, the frontiers between history and myth, in the western sense of these concepts, are typically blurred. This is directly reflected in the work of history written by the Fifth Dalai Lama, since some of its main sources stem from works belonging to the Treasure tradition. The Avalokiteshvara cult and the glorification of king Songtsen Gampo, which figure as major topics in *The Song of the Spring Queen*, have their origins in two sets of texts belonging to the Treasure literature genre, the eleventh century *Kachen Kakholma* (Tib. *bKa' chems ka khol ma*) and the twelfth century *Mani Kabum* (Tib. *Maṇi bka' 'bum*) (Sørensen and Hazod 2007: 464). The authorship of the *Kachen Kakholma* is attributed to Songtsen Gampo himself and that of the *Mani Kabum* to Padmasambhava, the Indian tantric master who came to Tibet through the invitation of another dharma king, Trisong Detsen (742–800).

Following the logic underlying the "Treasure literature," their authors are said to have hidden these compilations, envisioning their future discovery by trusted disciples (or their reincarnations). The *Mani Kabum* was discovered by the important Treasure-revealer (Tib. *gter ston*) Nyang-rel Nyima Oser (1124–92), a Nyingma lama who, as we shall shortly see, would be included in the list of previous reincarnations of the Dalai Lamas. The traditional attribution of the *Kachen Kakholma*'s discovery to Atisha Dipamkara has been the focus of some debate, and is usually considered a religious "fabrication." That discussion interests us less here than the fact that Atisha's role in this discovery and his importance for the dissemination of the Avalokiteshvara cult is strongly asserted by traditional accounts and, with particular relevance for us here, by the Fifth Dalai Lama himself.

In *The Song of the Spring Queen*, for example, the Great Fifth describes the *Kachen Kakholma* as one of "the religious texts of the Great Compassionate One [Avalokiteshvara]," which was "recovered by Dipaṅkara Śrījñāna [Atisha], the great scholar fully versed in the five branches of learning, from the north side of the 'leafy pillar' (in the Jo-KHaṅ of Lhasa)" (Ahmad 1995: 8–9). Directly citing the *Kachen Kakholma* and the *Mani Kabum* as his sources, the Fifth Dalai Lama puts forth the origin myth of Tibetans as the descendants of "the son of the union between a monkey and a rock-dwelling demoness" (ibid.: 9). The monkey was in reality an emanation of Avalokiteshvara. From their union,

> six children came into being [...]. The father's line consisted of quick-witted ones, who had great compassion and were clever inside. The mother's line consisted of red-faced ones, who longed for sinful actions and were (living) corpses. Growing from these, in course of time, Tibet became a kingdom of human beings.
>
> (Ibid.: 9–10)

Here and throughout *The Song of the Spring Queen*, the Fifth Dalai Lama emphasizes the special relationship between Avalokiteshvara and the Tibetan people. Referring to another important Treasure source, namely the *Thang yig* (Tib. *Thang yig*), a seminal biography of Padmasambhava, and to the *Kadam Legbam* (Tib. *bKa' gdams glegs bam*), a collection of teachings and stories of

Atisha and his disciples, the Fifth Dalai Lama introduces the coming of Songsten Gampo by invoking prophecies in those texts that predict the birth of a "prince" who will bring happiness to the "lordless" land of Tibet (ibid.: 17). Then, in a particularly revealing passage, the Fifth Dalai Lama tells two parallel stories connected to the Potala Palace, one of divine nature and the other more directly connected to past events in Tibet, thus clearly showing that the lines between these realities are not so sharply defined in his history.

When Songtsen Gampo was 13 years old, the Dalai Lama tells us, his father enthroned him as a "mighty wheel-turning king" on his own "fearless lion-throne." At that moment, so goes the text, the Victor, i.e., Avalokiteshvara,[22] had a thought: "Would that I were a consecrated (king) in order to do good to the people of Tibet!" (ibid.). The text, which seems to have been written in purposely ambiguous language, goes on to describe how, "at the time he thought this, the glorious Samantabhadra washed his body with a precious pitcher filled with water of divine nectar." Amitabha touched the "head of the king," and through that consecrated him. It seems that "king" here could refer to Songtsen Gampo, and on some level it surely does, but the sequence of the text opens up the field of possible interpretations: "Countless incarnations, difficult to describe, came forth and endless wonderful signs [...] appeared. Having built his palace on the peak of the hill of Potala, he dwelt there" (ibid.). Kings of the four directions, "deprived of their powers," came to pay their respects. They saw miraculous manifestations of buddhas and bodhisattvas, such as self-arisen "six syllables" – i.e., OM MAṆI PADME HUM[23] – and self-arisen images of Avalokiteshvara, Tara and Hayagriva appear on rocks around the palace. Then, "Through the skill of the fingers of Nepalese sculptors of sacred images, the shrines of the body and speech (of the three divinities named above) were carved out, just as they appeared" (ibid.: 17–18).

The interplay between the divine and the mundane continues, when finally, "in course of time, the king, together with his retinue," came to the Potala. "He built a high and awe-inspiring palace [...] as delightful as the palace of gods descended on earth" (ibid.: 18). The Fifth Dalai Lama then goes on to talk more directly about the "earthly accomplishments" of Songtsen Gampo. In such a way, he expresses the transcendental nature of Songtsen Gampo, playing with markers of time and place in his narration of two stories of the Potala Palace's construction. A third story of the Potala Palace's construction, I must add, was about to be "written" right then and there by the Fifth Dalai Lama himself.

It seems important at this point in the discussion of *The Song of the Spring Queen* to call attention to the danger of anachronistically reading these lines – and for that matter the totality of mechanisms involved in the creation of a symbolic apparatus for nascent government – simply as a means of legitimation, or better yet, as a kind of self-conscious propaganda. Legitimacy was undoubtedly acquired through writing and other means (architecture, ritual and so forth), but one should also read a text like *The Song of the Spring Queen* as an expression of devotion towards, among others, Avalokiteshvara. In the same way, the grandiose Potala Palace of our times should also be appreciated as an expression of the glory of Avalokiteshvara/Dalai Lama. The Fifth Dalai Lama, by his superimposition in the passage above of two stories of the construction of the Potala Palace (and implicitly a third one, his own), points more to a particular vision of reality than to a cynical and self-conscious project of power. A similar warning presented by Peter Burke in relation to the differences between European mentalities of the past and the present can help clarify this point. Invoking Lucien Lévy-Bruhl's notion of "mystical reality," Burke explains how in the pre-enlightenment European mentality, the connection between a king and Hercules, for example, was much more than a "metaphor saying that he is strong." The correspondence was more direct, as "if the aura of the demigod rubbed off on him." In Burke's words:

> These analogies were treated not as human constructions but as objective parallels. Political arguments assumed their reality, claiming for example that the commandment "Honour thy Father and thy Mother" forbade resistance to kings. We might therefore speak of "mystical mentality", noting similarities with the concept of "mystical participation" put forward in the twentieth century by the French philosopher-anthropologist Lucien Lévy-Bruhl, but avoiding his term "primitive". The word "mystical" was used by Lévy-Bruhl to refer to non-observable connections or identifications, like the identification made by one tribe between twins and birds.
>
> (Burke 1992: 127–8)

In the case of the "tantric Buddhist mentality" prevalent in Tibet, this direct correspondence between the divine and the human is strongly present, as the example of the direct association between lamas and bodhisattvas makes clear. There is no reason to doubt that the Dalai Lama thought of himself as an emanation of Avalokiteshvara. Similarly, there is no reason to doubt that he also believed that the Karmapa was as well a manifestation of the same bodhisattva. Hence, I believe that we should see the effort around building a symbolic apparatus for the state through the expressive forms of writing, architecture, ritual and so forth as a means to express the "glory" of the Dalai Lama/Avalokiteshvara and the Fifth Dalai Lama's vision of his and this bodhisattva's special relationship to Tibet. The legitimacy that derives from these undertakings should be understood within the framework of this expression and affirmation of the glory of Avalokiteshvara in the person of the Dalai Lama.

The association between the Dalai Lamas and Songtsen Gampo through the belief in their incarnational continuity should also be understood within this same frame of analysis. Songtsen Gampo came to be known through Treasure literature as the dharma king who created the conditions for the first successful transmission of Buddhism to Tibet. As the Fifth Dalai Lama tells us in *The Song of the Spring Queen*, Songtsen Gampo sponsored the creation of a script for the Tibetan language. "In order to look after his people," the exalted Lord Lokeshvara, "in the guise of the lord of men [i.e., Songtsen Gampo]," dispelled the darkness, "with the sun of knowledge." He considered that a script "would be the basis of all virtues" (Ahmad 1995: 18). Songtsen Gampo sent one of his "ministers," Thonmi Sambhota, to India in order to learn a script. In India, Thonmi Sambhota learned "364 kinds of writing"; later, in Tibet, he supplicated Manjushrighosa,[24] and from the "field of his mind," now "moistened by the rain of [...] compassion, [...] arose the stalk of the changes in the arrangement of the forms of Tibetan letters" (ibid.: 19).

Another important aspect of Songtsen Gampo's life in the Tibetan popular imaginary, and which is narrated in *The Song of the Spring Queen*, is his marriage to two foreign princesses: the Nepalese Tritsun and the Chinese Kung-chu (ibid.: 23). Versed in geomancy, Kung-chu "saw Tibet in the form of a demoness[25] lying on her back" (ibid.: 35). Through further examination, Kung-chu drew a more complete picture of the geomantic aspects of the land of Tibet (ibid.: 36). Seeing to the "inauspicious examination of the land," the king and his two wives performed rituals in the surrounding areas. "In order to suppress the signs" that appeared in the rituals and the "limbs and little fingers of the demoness" (ibid.: 37), they built many temples all over the land, both through ordinary means and more exalted ones, such as the king "revealing emanations of himself" to build the temples (ibid.: 38–40). It was then that the most important temple in Tibet, known today as the Jokhang Temple, but referred to in *The Song of the Spring Queen* as the Trulnang (Tib. *'Phrul snang*), or self-arisen temple, was built in Lhasa. It houses the most important Buddha statue in Tibet, and is said to be located at the heart of the demoness.[26]

The king and the tantric master: Trisong Detsen and Padmasambhava

Trisong Detsen is the next great "dharma king" occupying an important place in the Tibetan imaginary. Under his rule, the Tibetan Empire attained the apex of its territorial expansion (Beckwith 1987). The reference to this figure in *The Song of the Spring Queen* interests us here in two respects. The first one has to do with Trisong Detsen's invitation of the Indian scholar Shantarakshita (b. eighth century) to Tibet to promote the dissemination of Buddhism. Particularly relevant for us is the connection that is made in the text between the Fifth Dalai Lama's royal family origins and that of Shantarakshita's. In the Dalai Lama's words,

> Having been born in the high-caste royal family of Za-Hor, (Śāntarakshita) was the highest of all the learned of men who had drawn hitherward, with arrows of the five branches of learning, the traditions of the Buddhist religion, both in its noumenal and phenomenal forms.
>
> (Ahmad 1995: 53)

As the Dalai Lama tells us further in *The Song of the Spring Queen*, because Shantarakshita "expounded the doctrines to the king," when in Tibet, the "gods and demons" of the land became enraged, and "threw a thunderbolt" on the

Potala Palace. "The harvest was ruined and an epidemic ravaged both men and beasts." Shantarakshita then explains to the king that, despite the efforts made by his ancestor, i.e., Songtsen Gampo, to build temples and so forth, "the gods and demons" had not been subdued. Due to that, kings had faced obstacles in the past and the Buddhist religion did not blossom to its full potency. "In order to subdue these lands fearsomely," Shantarakshita spoke of a master called Padmasambhava, who came from Odiyana, in India (in today's Pakistan), and was extremely versed in mantras. "If he," the scholar said, "is invited, the pure white wishes of the king's heart will all be fulfilled" (ibid.: 54).

The king sent his messengers with an invitation. Even before they arrived at their destination, Padmasambhava manifested to them his miraculous powers. "The Ācārya [i.e., the Master] knew that the messengers would be tired and fatigued." Through magical means, he met them when they were on their way. "He showed endless magical feats, performed by himself, such as making a river flow upwards, so that the messengers were filled with firm and unchanging devotion (towards him)" (ibid.: 54–5). Hence, amidst a profusion of miraculous displays, Padmasambhava made his entrance into Tibet. Soon after his arrival, together with Trisong Detsen, his ministers and Shantarakshita, Padmasambhava became involved in the construction of a monastery, Samye, in the place where the old kings had been buried, Chongye in the Yarlung Valley. Padmasambhava bound the eight classes of spirits to a pledge, making possible in this way the building of the monastery. He "had the buildings raised by men during the day and by gods and demons during the night" (ibid.: 57).

When Samye was finally built, 12 Sarvastivadin[27] monks were invited to Tibet, and Shantarakshita was appointed abbot. In the new monastery, the Dalai Lama tells us, the first Tibetan monks were ordained. There, those "who had the gift of wisdom were taught the art of translation. The difficulties connected with the many problems of Sanskrit grammar were solved." Hence, "three precious scriptures of the Sarvāstivādins, namely the *Vinaya*, the *Sūtras*, and the *Abhidharma*," and the "lower tantras," and other works were translated. Trisong Detsen also sent translators to India. Such was the case for the "great translator" Vairochana (b. eighth century), and the monk Namkha Nyingpo (b. eighth century) (ibid.: 62). Additionally, the famous Indian scholar Vimalamitra (b. eighth century) was also invited to Tibet. Through all of these deeds, it was possible to quell the "obstructions" that the Bön religion,[28] because of being "widespread in this (land of) Tibet," had imposed on the "triumph" of Buddhism: "the translators of the time destroyed all doctrines of the Bon with their clear logic." Padmasambhava also "translated many *sādhanas* of the true and secret Vajrayāna *tantras*." These functioned to provide "*karma*-ridden persons with (an object of) prayer and to ripen (the actions of) and release (from Saṁsāra) the many lords and subjects (of Tibet)" (ibid.: 63).

This portrait of Trisong Detsen's kingdom traces the origins of some of Tibetan Buddhism's main features. Indeed, the complex combination of monasticism, scholarship and extensive translations, on the one side, and mastery over local deities, gods, demons and forces of nature in general, on the other, seems to constitute the core of this religious tradition.[29] It is revealing to observe in relation to Trisong Detsen and his deeds a point that actually surfaces in many passages of *The Song of the Spring Queen*, namely, the way Buddhism is depicted as playing a civilizing role in Tibet. In the era of this second great "dharma king," this is clearly inferred from the coming of great scholars and the training of translators that were able to diffuse the doctrine by means of high learning, and perhaps even more importantly, through the institution of monasticism in the country. In this regard, there is a clear parallel between the process of "taming" local gods and spirits that summarizes the foundational activities of Padmasambhava and the process of "taming" Tibetans by means of the Buddhist doctrine.

It is not difficult to see in the person of the Fifth Dalai Lama a combination of the paradigmatic roles of king, monk-scholar and tantric master played respectively by Trisong Detsen, Shantarakshita and Padmasambhava, at this seminal moment of Tibetan Buddhist history. It is not by chance then that a little further in the text, these three characters reappear in the section pertaining to the royal family line of the Fifth Dalai Lama, the Zahor family (ibid.: 165–73). There, the Fifth Dalai Lama traces his ascendency directly to the paradigmatic patron of Buddhism, king Ashoka (*c.*268 BCE), mentioning also king Indrabhuti, who is presented as his grandson and "the king of Zahor," a devotee of "mantra." The son of Indrabhuti's son, king Tsuglag Dzin, so the Dalai Lama's account goes, "breathed the profound teachings and instructions of the great Ācarya (Padmasambhava). He had three children called Dharmarāja; the great abbot, (Śāntarakshita); and the princess, Mandārava" (ibid.: 165). According to traditional accounts, Mandārava became the consort of Padmasambhava, or as the Dalai Lama says in *The Song of the Spring Queen*, "the head of all the knowledge-bestowing sky-wanderers (*jñāna-ḍākinīs*)" (ibid.).

Perhaps the most revealing aspect of the connection between the kingdom of Trisong Detsen and the Zahor family is the explanation of how the Fifth Dalai Lama's family migrated to Tibet. Indeed, in this section of the text, the Dalai Lama retells the story of how Padmasambhava, Shantarakshita and king Trisong Detsen invited Pehar (or Pekar – both spellings are present in *The Song of the Spring Queen*) to come to Tibet to be the guardian of Samye monastery. Together with Pehar, king Dharmapala, who is said to be the son of the aforementioned king Dharmaraja, was also invited. "Thus the gods and the humans came (from Za-Hor) to Tibet." In Tibet, king Dharmapala, the Dalai Lama tells us, became Trisong Detsen's lama. "He took a member of the sky-wanderers' family, one called Pho-Yon-bZa', to wife [sic] and had two sons (called) dPal-Gyi rDo-rJe and Rin-Cen rDo-rJe" (ibid.: 166). These are the first Tibetan ancestors of the Fifth Dalai Lama. In the next few pages, the Great Fifth unfolds the genealogy of his family in Tibet, which came to be called the "Chongye family" after the place they settled on the plateau.

In view of what has been discussed so far, it is possible to say that one of the most prominent outcomes of *The Song of the Spring Queen* is the delineation of indirect connections between the Fifth Dalai Lama and central figures of the Tibetan imperial past, and, ultimately, Avalokiteshvara. In this regard, it is important to note here that the association between the Dalai Lama line and the bodhisattva Avalokiteshvara was not a creation of the Fifth Dalai Lama. As Ishihama Yumiko shows in her insightful article about the dissemination of the belief in the Dalai Lama as a manifestation of Avalokiteshvara, reference is already made to such associations in the biography of the First Dalai Lama, composed in 1494 (Ishihama 1993: 45). Among other things, this well-established connection between the Dalai Lama line of incarnations and Avalokiteshvara explains why we can think of *The Song of the Spring Queen* as an important text in the creation of the Fifth Dalai Lama's own public image, even if no explicit reference is made to his figure. Moreover, and perhaps more importantly, having this in mind, we can read *The Song of the Spring Queen* as a means of providing the association between the Dalai Lamas and Avalokiteshvara with a political dimension through its embedment within a historical framework.

Indeed, in light of the genealogical sense of history that characterizes *The Song of the Spring Queen*, it seems fair to say that the superimposition of this political dimension onto the connection Dalai Lama/Avalokiteshvara represented an essential step towards the establishment of a new form of political succession in Tibet, i.e., political succession by incarnation. In between the lines of *The Song of the Spring Queen*, the Fifth Dalai Lama emerges as an ideal first representative of this new form of succession. As an embodiment of Avalokiteshvara and Songtsen Gampo, and as the holder of royal connections that go back to Ashoka, the Dalai Lama embodies two important aspects that define kingship in accordance with the Tibetan view of history, namely the direct identification between the kings of the past and divine figures, and affiliation with a dynastic succession that originates in India.

History, biography and autobiography

The genealogical sense of history present in *The Song of the Spring Queen* is also in a certain sense expressed in the biographical and autobiographical works composed by the Fifth Dalai Lama. Hence, also relevant for our discussion of the creation of a new kind of political succession – and the creation of the Great Fifth's public image – are the biographies of the Third Dalai Lama, Sonam Gyatso, and the Fourth Dalai Lama, Yonten Gyatso. As I mentioned above, the Great Fifth himself also composed these two works during the first years of his government, more specifically, in 1646 and 1652, respectively.[30] In these biographical accounts – which from the Tibetan Buddhist point of view could also be considered autobiographical accounts since its protagonists are past incarnations of the author – a similar movement from myth to history and from general history to personal history is set in motion. As an illustration, it is worth perusing a short passage from *The Chariot of the Ocean of Accomplishments*, the biography of Sonam Gyatso, the Third Dalai Lama (Ngawang Lobsang Gyatso 1991–5b).

At the very beginning of the text, Avalokiteshvara is introduced as the special protector of Tibet. In a citation there from the *Kadam Legbam*, Avalokiteshvara is said to declare, "In general, I am the protector of all sentient beings; in particular, I rule amidst the snowy mountains" (ibid.: 35). Then, reproducing a trajectory similar to the one found in *The Song of the Spring Queen*, the Dalai Lama goes on to mention the names of important Tibetan kings of the past, such as Lhathothori, Songtsen Gampo and Trisong Detsen. He introduces these kings by saying, "In particular, because in the peripheral kingdom of Tibet itself, initially no taming was done by way of a spiritual friend, or a commoner, the kings of Tibet were construed as authorities" (ibid.). What is implied in this passage is that the kings acted not only as promoters of the religion, but also as its direct propagators, as "tamers" of beings – a role that was to be even more explicitly embodied by the Dalai Lamas themselves.

In my view, the flow of the text (and of history) from Avalokiteshvara to these kings indicates less that all of them are direct emanations of this bodhisattva, than that they are the manifestation of his designs for Tibet.[31] Or phrasing it differently, this movement suggests that the unfolding of Tibetan history itself could be interpreted as a manifestation of Avalokiteshvara. In the case of *The Chariot of the Ocean of Accomplishments*, this flow of history is presented in stages until it merges with the personal story of Sonam Gyatso. Along the way, other historical figures present in the Tibetan imaginary are assimilated into the narrative, and consequently to Sonam Gyatso's biographical record. The following passage is particularly illustrative of this assimilatory impetus:

> Since [Avalokiteshvara] displayed infinite incarnations, such as Kache Gonpa [*c.*11th c.], Sachen Kunnying [1092–1158], Lama Zhang [1123/1121–93] protector of beings, the Sovereign Nyang Nyima Ozer [1124–92], Lhaje Gewa Bum [*c.*1200–50] and so forth; furthermore, because great bodhisattvas who are situated on the bhumis are sure to manifest infinite emanations at the same time, one should not doubt that they emerge at the same time, and that [the same] bodhisattva exists in other records of births and so forth, just as ten million reflections emerge from a single moon disc.
>
> (Ibid.: 37)

Even without discussing in depth the significance of the characters cited above, it is possible to discern in this excerpt three important aspects in the project of the creation of the public image of the Fifth Dalai Lama. First, once again we have the identification between the Dalai Lamas and Avalokiteshvara, but this time the association is made directly in a biographical account of one of the Great Fifth's previous incarnations. Second, some of these characters, such as Lama Zhang, Nyang-rel Nyima Oser and Lhaje Gewa Bum, played important roles related to public policies in Lhasa. More specifically, they protected the Jokhang temple against floods (Sørensen and Hazod 2007). As we saw earlier in this chapter, Sonam Gyatso himself became known as the "Virupa of Tibet" due to his efforts to protect the Jokhang. Finally, the figures cited in this short passage belong to different schools of Tibetan Buddhism, namely, Kagyu, Nyingma and Sakya. We could say then that the reference to these figures here reflects, among other things, the Fifth Dalai Lama's concern with presenting his predecessor – and hence himself – as a trans-sectarian leader. In this vein, it is important to draw attention to the fact that, even though the Fifth Dalai Lama represented in many senses the most refined "political product" of the Gelug School, his political project of power could only be successfully implemented because of his capacity to transcend the boundaries of his own tradition, asserting in this way a trans-sectarian identity.

This trans-sectarian tendency is even more evident in the Fifth Dalai Lama's so-called "secret autobiography" (Tib. *gsang ba'i rnam-thar*). More specifically, in this text we find the same "triangle" that has in its vertices the notion of protection, in its more transcendental sense represented by the figure of the bodhisattva Avalokiteshvara, along with the notions of public works projects and trans-sectarianism. Such notions – transcendental protection, public works and trans-sectarianism – with which the Fifth Dalai Lama associated Sonam Gyatso and, in his secret autobiography, himself, can be thought of as essential elements of the nascent state power. Entitled *The Sealed One* (Tib. *rGya can*), this text – a detailed account of his mystical visions – expresses quite eloquently the interplay between these three notions through their embedment in visionary narratives involving mythical and semi-mythical figures of the imperial period in Tibet. Here, Avalokiteshvara can once more be seen as the embodiment of the notion of transcendental protection, while the figures of Songtsen Gampo and Padmasambhava embody both the notion of political power/public service and, because of being more directly connected to the Nyingma School, trans-sectarianism. In his visions, the Fifth Dalai Lama not only interacts with these three mythical and semi-mythical characters, but also frequently has the experience of directly becoming them.

It would be in the intimacy of his mystical contemplations that, in a movement that ran parallel to the material establishment of the centralized state in Tibet, the Great Fifth immersed himself in a process of internalizing some of the elements of his public image. As the brief analysis of some of his other writings has shown thus far, Avalokiteshvara, Songtsen Gampo and Padmasambhava are precisely some of the main figures that contributed to the creation of this image. As an illustration, I will quote here a passage from the secret autobiography in which these characters appear in a series of visions that the Dalai Lama had in the context of a retreat in 1660, when he was 44 years old.

In the afternoon, I brought out two images of Padmasambhava [...]. I recited the seven-line supplication many times. My ordinary perception ceased. At first, while Padmasambhava in the form of Zahorma radiated very brightly, some white dakinis[32] were playing hand drums and bells and dancing. In a state of love, together with them, I too went on the rainbow arc.

In the middle of an extremely vast plain that I had never seen before, there was a red mountain; on its top there was a palace with Chinese eaves and features such as precious pillars inside. At its center, on top of a jeweled throne sat Karmaguru,[33] the vidyadhara[34] of enlightened activities. Just when I thought that I was arriving before him, light radiated from his heart and struck me, by which a lucid image of Karmaguru emerged. At that time, also from the navel of Karmaguru fire blazed forth and the tips of the flames struck me. Intense flames leapt everywhere striking my body. My body became exhilarated with the sensation of great bliss. At that moment, initially it blazed on the surface of my body, and then it entered me gradually and blazed up to the crown of my head. Then, my body burned like the feather of a bird would. Within that state, I manifested as Karmaguru, as though I could be touched and seen.

The central deity blessed me by placing on the crown of my head a black *torma*,[35] transparent like crystal, inside of which were seated an assembly of deities. [...] Then the central deity said as follows:

> "Son, your troubling obstacles were pacified by this. Do the wrathful Karmaguru practice for seven days! Do not chase fame and reputation!"

Just after he said that, a white girl led me back and the vision vanished. I then supplicated Avalokiteshvara, at which time I experienced a boy standing with a blue topknot and a white cotton skirt, his right hand in the gesture of giving protection, his left hand holding a crystal staff, coming before me urgently. He said the following:

> "Listen! There will come nine beings possessing the signs of being spirits who can bring Tibet to ruin. [...] They will come in the fire, water and wood element years. If you restore the temples of the Tibetan kings of the past, it will help."

Then he changed into the form of the dharma king Songtsen Gampo with a white lotus in his right hand, and his left extended toward his knee. He was standing in royal ease with his two queens. The dharma king gave advice about the government and then dissolved into the heart of Lokeshvara.

(Ngawang Lobsang Gyatso 1972: 124–8)

This vision is only one of many instances in which the Dalai Lama interacts with these three particular characters in his mystical experiences. In this passage, as in others in the text, the sense of mystical interaction is often combined with more pragmatic actions, such as the utterance of prophecies related to the destiny of the kingdom, and the dispensation of political and administrative advice. In this sense, it becomes clear in the short passage cited above that "multiple orientations towards reality" (Tambiah 1990: 84–110) coexist in the view of power expressed in *The Sealed One*. Moreover, due to the performative quality of this text, the interplay mentioned above between the notions of transcendental protection, political power/public service and trans-sectarianism acquires new dimensions. This performative quality can be detected most readily in the visual imagery of the text, which approximates the visual arts in its vividness, and in the transformations that are described in this imagery. Furthermore, this performative quality is also clearly expressed by the unfolding of the intangible matter of these visions in state rituals, architecture, and decisions about what policies should be adopted by the government.

We know, for example, that temples from the imperial period were restored after the Dalai Lama received in a vision advice from Tangtong Gyalpo (1361/65–486) (Karmay 1988b: 46), a renaissance-type figure, who among many other accomplishments, is known for the construction of iron bridges throughout Tibet and the invention of Tibetan opera.[36] As if to assert the imagistic nature of the vivid descriptions given by the Fifth Dalai Lama, the aforementioned Sangye Gyatso, the fifth regent of the Great Fifth, commissioned 23 thangkas portraying some of the visions of *The Sealed One* (ibid.: 24). Moreover, Ishihama has drawn attention to a list of initiations and mantra recitation authorizations connected to Avalokiteshvara that the Fifth Dalai Lama gave between 1652 and 1653. These were conferred after an episode described in *The Sealed One* in which the Great Fifth appeared to the aforementioned Zurchen Chöying Rangdrol as Cittavishramana, a form of Avalokiteshvara (Ishihama 1993: 49–52). Another revealing instance of the performative unfolding of the secret visions is the so-called "*Gold Manuscript*," a compilation of texts containing a summarized version of *The Sealed One*, along with illustrations of some of the figures connected with the visions, and drawings of associated ritual elements and implements. With the creation of *The Gold Manuscript*, the Fifth Dalai Lama's written descriptions of the visions, now beautifully illustrated in gold and colored ink against a black background, became art objects in and of themselves.[37]

Through these and other expressive means, the symbols that the Fifth Dalai Lama invoked in his writings contributed toward fashioning the public image of himself and his government. As we have seen, most of these symbols, which were referenced in his historical, biographical and autobiographical writings revolve around figures from the Tibetan Empire. These figures represented first and foremost the prevalent "images" of power in the Tibetan imaginary of the Great Fifth's time. In this sense, we can detect here a movement from public (the Tibetan imaginary) to private (personal take on history, biographies and visions), and back to public (expressive forms). I believe it is this movement that undergirds the Fifth Dalai Lama's project of power. Perhaps nothing expresses this movement better than the sequence of ceremonies that marked the calendar in the capital of Tibet, Lhasa.

III Politics as spectacle

Lhasa, as we have seen, housed some of the most potent symbols of the Tibetan Empire. In the centuries before the advent of the Ganden Podrang government, control of Lhasa was therefore a constant source of contention between multiple political and religious groups. It comes as no surprise then that one of the direct (and necessary) outcomes of the establishment of a new centralized power was the reinforcement of the connection between this city and Tibet's glorious imperial past.[38] It was indeed a substantial part of the Great Fifth's project of power to revive the geo-political centrality of Lhasa. Certainly the most visible and perennial illustration of this idea was the replacement of the old ruins of Songtsen Gampo's palace on the Red Hill with the imposing Potala Palace, the most distinctive mark of the new government. The so-called "White Palace" part of the edification was completed in 1649, whereas the "Red Palace" was only finished a few decades later, in 1694, after the Dalai Lama's death.

Against the backdrop of this palace, and also inside and around the Jokhang Temple, the oldest and most sacred temple in Tibet, ceremonies promoted by the state were enacted throughout the year. These ceremonies directly contributed toward making visible the imperial associations of Lhasa. Hugh Richardson, who as a representative of the British Government of India,[39] witnessed these events many times, explains that the origin of most of these ceremonies "lies in the remote past, but they have been rearranged and elaborated at different times, especially in the seventeenth century during the rule of the Great Fifth Dalai Lama and his equally great regent Sangye Gyatso[40]" (Richardson 1993: 7).

These ceremonies activated many of the symbols and historical connections directly pertaining to the formative moment of the Ganden Podrang government discussed so far. For instance, we have in the first month, "three successive events of a military character introduced by the Fifth Dalai Lama in recognition of the services of the Mongol chieftain Gushri Khan in defeating his opponents and establishing him in power in 1642" (ibid.: 30). In the second month, the Fifth Dalai Lama himself was the object to be commemorated in the Great Assembly of Worship (Tib. *Tshogs mchod chen po*), a ceremony instituted by the regent Sangye Gyatso after the death of the Tibetan leader (ibid.: 60). In the sixth month of the year, the festival of Universal Incense Offering (Tib. *'Dzam gling spyi bsangs*) commemorates "the preparation for the founding of the Samye Monastery when Padmasambhava subjugated the gods, *nagas* (serpent spirits) and local deities and made them protectors of the Buddhist faith" (ibid.: 94).

In addition to the permanent reminder of Songtsen Gampo and his kingdom provided by the Potala Palace, the dharma king is also present in many of the ceremonies, as was the case, for instance, in the ceremony that celebrates the First Turning of the Wheel of the Dharma, or the first sermon uttered by Buddha Shakyamuni in Sarnath, India (ibid.: 96). The association of the commemoration of this first paradigmatic Buddhist teaching with Songtsen Gampo is in itself an illuminating detail. It indicates, among other things, the interweaving of his roles as king and teacher mentioned above.

Richardson also mentions at least two occasions on which the visions of the Dalai Lama were invoked in official ceremonies promoted by the government. The first ceremony under consideration here is called "The King's New Year" (Tib. *Rgyal po lo gsar*) and takes place on the second day of the Tibetan New

Year. Contrasting this with the ceremony of the previous day, "The Lama's New Year" (Tib. *Bla ma lo gsar*), brings to light a dual view of power that, as we will see briefly, characterizes the Ganden Podrang government. Furthermore, since the Dalai Lama figures in both ceremonies as the main character, these public spectacles also indicate how both religious and secular power directly emanate from him in this dual conception of government.

Going back to the festivities of "The King's New Year," Richardson tells us that in his first public appearance that day, the Dalai Lama is followed by a procession of 13 officials in outfits that were supposed to resemble those worn at the court during Tibetan imperial times. "They were arrayed in robes of precious old brocade or flowered silk and had small conical yellow silk caps on their heads except for one who had a tall wide-brimmed hat in Mongolian style, topped by a peacock feather" (ibid.: 15–16). Richardson further informs us that they also wore "ornaments of unusual size," which "were seized by the Fifth Dalai Lama from the palace at Nedong, from the effete Phamodru family" (ibid.: 16). In this setting, pregnant with political symbols, a masked dance is performed representing different deities and spirits who appeared to the Fifth Dalai Lama in a vision. The figures depicted by the masks[41] interest us here less than the fact that this vision is reenacted in the context of a ceremony that directly celebrates the Dalai Lama's secular power and its continuity with the Tibetan Empire. This indicates, among other things, the fundamental connection between the Fifth Dalai Lama's personal visions and the formation of the Ganden Podrang government.

The second ceremony connected to the visions also makes direct reference to imperial times. Entitled "The Yellow Procession of Worship"[42] (Tib. *Tshogs mchod ser sbreng*), an allusion to the color of the robes and hats of monks in the procession, this ceremony was instituted by the regent Sangye Gyatso as part of the funeral service of the Fifth Dalai Lama. It included a public recitation of his secret autobiography (Sangye Gyatso 1973: f.571a.2), and would henceforth become an annual commemoration of the Great Fifth's life and legacy. This particular ceremony centers around the parading of ancient sacred objects that were housed in a treasury "in the north-west corner of the first floor of the Jokhang" (Richardson 1993: 74). As we have seen, the Jokhang is said to be the first temple built in Tibet, marking the introduction of Buddhism into the country during the reign of Songtsen Gampo. The configuration of this particular ceremony can help us trace connections that illuminate the general lines of the Fifth Dalai Lama's project of power. Thus, it is worth citing passages of Richardson's description of the Yellow Procession as he witnessed it in the middle of the last century.

Early in the morning, Richardson tells us, "monks chosen by their teachers from several colleges of the great monasteries assemble at the Jokhang, having washed themselves well and wearing their best robes [and] yellow hats." Each of these monks is then given a banner or one of the sacred objects, which include "images, small paintings, portable shrines, books, mandalas, polished mirrors said to repel dust, incense burners, holy water ewers and bowls, silver-mounted conch shells, musical instruments and many more" (ibid.). Then, describes Richardson:

When the sun lights up the summit of Gyamberi, the mountain overlooking Drepung – the usual time signal for most ceremonial events – the procession sets out round the Barkor [the circuit surrounding the Jokhang]. It is headed by the master of ceremonies with a stick of incense, followed by a number of learned teachers in robes of fine wool, brocade waistcoats and yellow hats, each proceeded by a bare-headed monk carrying a large yellow, red and blue, fringed, umbrella. Then comes a line of monks in yellow hats each carrying a similar umbrella – there are about twenty or more of them; then a similar number with tall cylindrical banners of bright brocade; then many parties of dancers in all sorts of different dress and masks, and musicians playing long trumpets manned by two monks, cymbals, oboes, horns, and drums of all shapes and sizes.

(Ibid.: 74–6)

After completing the Barkor circuit, the procession goes around the Lingkor, the outer circuit of the city, before winding its way towards an open space at the west end of the so-called "Shö precinct," in front of the Potala Palace.

As soon as the leaders of the procession reach the stone pillar opposite the main entrance to the Shö the boom of long horns from the roof of the Potala gives the signal for hauling up the Köku – "The Silk Image" – a great appliqué banner which covers the lower face of the Potala for a space of some 75 by 40 feet.

(Ibid.: 77)

Both banners depict Buddha Shakyamuni surrounded by deities and bodhisattvas. Richardson goes on to describe a series of events, including the ceremonial trance of the so-called "state oracle" – Nechung – and a variety of dances that take place against the background of the Potala and the banners. He highlights in particular the myriad of dresses, hats, masks, hand implements, and so forth, which infuse the performances with great magnificence. In his words, "there is an ever-changing pattern of colour and movement: bright umbrellas blowing in the breeze, the rich dresses of the dancers and of officials in their ceremonial robes" (ibid.). In the early afternoon, the procession leaves out of the Shö to undertake again the Barkor circuit. Then, he adds:

The Dalai Lama's live elephant arrives with beautiful silk and brocade trappings. It kneels and salutes the presence of the Dalai Lama and marches off followed by a fine horse with gilded caparison carrying a gold Wheel of Dharma on its back – both are symbols of universal sovereignty.

(Ibid.: 80–1)

The way the visions are represented in the ceremonies described above, and especially in the Yellow Procession, calls for a discussion about what exactly is being enacted and conveyed in these settings. What seems to be emphasized in both ceremonies is less the direct reenactment of the visions as they came to the Fifth Dalai Lama, and more the sense of transcendental connection that such visions create between the Ganden Podrang government and the imperial past. In this regard, it should be made clear that the point here is not exactly the communication of information, or even meaning, but first and foremost the eloquent (because mystical) expression of the glory of the imperial past in the present. Among other things, the two ceremonies associated with the visions described above can be said to make public the sense of intimate relationship between the Dalai Lama and the figures of the imperial past appearing in *The Sealed One* through a combination of the art of citation and sensorial enjoyments.[43]

Historian Paul Veyne can help us better understand this last idea when he defends the thesis that images should be understood as description and not as a language. "Their descriptive power makes them appropriate to show, if not to give information in the exact meaning of the word" (Veyne 1988: 9). Veyne is primarily speaking here about works of art, but he also extends his discussion to ceremonials (ibid.: 13). His main argument in the article, as far as I can tell, is that both pleasure and excess of meaning represent the crux of the matter when it comes to understanding the difference between expression and the communication of propositional information.

Arguing against, for example, the commonsensical notion that "sculpted or painted decoration of churches" are the "catechism of the illiterate," he affirms that the churches' imagery "was for pleasure rather than instruction" (ibid.). This is an important distinction that might be applied not only to the two ceremonies associated with the visions, but to the totality of ceremonies staged throughout the year by the Ganden Podrang government. Important as well is the idea that works of art can sometimes present an excess of meaning hardly graspable by their viewers. In this regard, Veyne's rejection of the general approach of historians to the Trajan Column (and its profusion of reliefs, which are invisible to the naked eye) as a work of imperial propaganda is crucial for us here. For Veyne, the

> Column expresses the glory of Trajan, just as the heavens (which it is useless to itemize star by star) express the glory of Jahweh. In both cases there have to be far too many stars and far too many sculpted scenes. *The expression of a superiority is only undoubted when it is excessive.*
>
> (Ibid.: 3, my italics)

As we have seen, the Yellow Procession is paradigmatic in both the senses of being enjoyable[44] and excessive in its profusion of symbols, music, dances and entertainment. It presents a particularly rich illustration of the idea of expressing superiority through excess, a dynamic that underlines the interplay of writing and performance in the Fifth Dalai Lama's project of power.

As I have already indicated, the writings of the Great Fifth are extensive, including a diversity of topics that go well beyond what has been addressed here.

I believe that one of the effects of producing such a massive corpus of writings was to create a culture around the nascent government that, even if not directly assimilated in its original format by the population at large, informed what was seen in festivals and other forms of aesthetic expression. Hence, even if the public did not know (nor most of the time even see) each object being carried in the Yellow Procession, or understand the meaning of the dances, or recognize which mask represented which deity, or even have awareness of which visions exactly were being invoked in the festivities, there was a general sense that these objects were associated with the Tibetan Empire, and that a vision of the Great Fifth were an important part of the ceremony.

In view of the disjunction between the impossibility of grasping the totality of the Yellow Procession's symbols and the possibility of grasping its general implications, the sense of excess that this contrast produces seems to be pointing to the allegorical nature of the festival. The Yellow Procession, in effect, emerges as an allegory for the appropriation of Tibetan imperial symbols by the Fifth Dalai Lama and the Gelug School. As an allegorical performance, it also represents a means for the continued appropriation of these same symbols. The connection with the Fifth Dalai Lama's visions (and especially with his writings about them) transforms this sense of appropriation into a "private matter," the "fabrication" of a particular king and his dynasty.

One important element in this ceremony that necessarily underscores the sequence of festivals as a whole is the overwhelming predominance of Gelug monks with their yellow and maroon robes coloring the scene. As Richardson comments on the etymology of the Tibetan word for "procession" in Yellow Procession, "the word *sbreng-ba* is used of things happening or joined together in sequence as in the flow of a river or the beads of a rosary (*phreng-ba*) [...]" (Richardson 1993: 74). It is as "a rosary surrounding the Potala," he observes, that many Tibetans see this possession. In this regard, it should be noted that the encirclement of the Jokhang and then all of Lhasa by a yellow string of monks mirrors in an essential sense the closing of borders of tantric rituals such as drubchens (Tib. *sgrub chen*), or "great accomplishment" rites, in which the officiators circumambulate the grounds of the ceremony, performing particular rites at the cardinal points. In the case of the Yellow Procession, the ritual grounds corresponded precisely to the "sacred, or pacified, mandala-shaped protective zone circumscribing the Jo-khang *sanctum* – that early on was proclaimed and would indeed become regarded as the centre of the Tibetan realm" (Sørensen and Hazod 2007: 8).

The ritual encirclement of the Lhasa "mandala-zone" in the Yellow Procession could also be seen as a yearly re-enactment of a more concrete encirclement of the same area that transpired in the fifteenth century. Here I am referring to the construction of the three massive Gelug monasteries of Ganden, Sera and Drepung around Lhasa. The immense presence of the Gelug School in Lhasa and its immediate surroundings was certainly one of the main factors that paved the way for the imposition of the rule of the Fifth Dalai Lama in Central Tibet and Tsang. Besides the heightened material presence in the region, it is important to have in mind what this massive monastic presence of the Gelug School represented in terms of the gradual appropriation of Lhasa and its symbols. Sørensen and Hazod consider, for instance, the construction of these monasteries and the institution of the Monlam Chenmo festival that preceded it as "strategic." They claim that this was as much a part of the fixation upon Lhasa to become regarded as the "national centre of the Tibetan religious and historical universe" as were the armed conflicts over supremacy in Lhasa that transpired between the fourteenth and seventeenth centuries (ibid.: 9).

In this sense, the festival founded by Tsongkhapa in the fifteenth century can be said to have laid the first foundation stone of the Ganden Podrang government. Not only did it contribute in conjunction with the massive Gelug monastic presence to bring the Gelug School fully into the scene. In its spectacular ritualistic dimensions it was also, in and of itself, the germ of the Ganden Podrang government. It is not by chance then that the Monlam Chenmo was the most popular of all Tibetan festivities, attracting every year until the Chinese invasion thousands of pilgrims from all the regions of the immense and loosely connected Tibetan territory. It celebrated (and still does in a more limited way) the "Great Miracle at Sravasti when the Buddha defeated the heretics and preached the dharma" (ibid.: 27). Following the timeline of the account of the miracle contest, the festival started with the new moon and reached its climax in the full moon. In these settings, the Dalai Lamas did not act only in their role as sovereign, or only as the highest symbol of the sacred; they surely acted in both capacities simultaneously. Additionally, they also played the fundamental role of acting as the direct teachers of their subjects, when on those occasions they would give sermons to the monastic community.[45]

The monk as prince

In a certain sense, each time the Dalai Lama played the role of spiritual master, he came closer to the simple monk or lama. This perception helps us understand that the construction of the status of monks, Gelug monks in particular, constituted in itself an important foundation on which the state was established. Indeed, the "fabrication" of the figure of the Dalai Lama through the combination of his roles as bodhisattva, sovereign and monk did not function solely to present him as the main public face of the power of the new state. The amalgamation of these roles in the figure of the Dalai Lama had in addition the important effect of raising the monastic "class" to the level of nobility. I am applying here, in a reverse sense, the "doctrine of the exemplary center" put forth by both Tambiah (1976) and Geertz (1980). On the one hand, like Southeast Asian and Balinese kings, the Dalai Lama – due to his high political and spiritual status – represented a Buddhist ideal to be followed and even copied. In this sense, he molded the world around him. On the other hand, the fact that the Tibetan sovereign was also a monk made it so that, in a mirror effect, monks also came to be seen as nobles and power holders. Having in mind this dialectical relationship is a first step toward understanding the tendencies of centralization and devolvement, rigid control and fluidity, which impregnate in a paradoxical and complementary way the notion of hierarchy in the Tibetan context.

The Dalai Lama and other important lamas were certainly seen as superior beings, or at least as ahead on the spiritual path. Nevertheless, there also existed a belief in the potential of all beings to reach the same level. I am well aware that this kind of reasoning is tainted by a good dose of theory. In practice, the average Tibetan would tend to see the Dalai Lama as a divine figure. In any case, the notion of a hierarchy that is at once highly centralized and fluid seems to find support in the fact that in relative terms – within and beyond the Gelug School – the Dalai Lamas are not necessarily seen as the apex of the spiritual hierarchy, or at the very least, they are not alone in this position. Other lamas of the Gelug School itself can also be considered in spiritual terms just as important as the Dalai Lama. Furthermore, it is essential to highlight here the fact that each school had its own spiritual hierarchy, which was more often than not totally separate from the hierarchy of the state. In a certain way, the task of creating a consensus around the figure of the Dalai Lama as sovereign of the country seemed to require in this context a continuous effort.

Concern with the ritualization of the state's political activities as a whole – and in particular, the spatial and conceptual structuring of the government based upon the mandala rubric – represents in my opinion a direct consequence of the effort to symbolically construct power in the Dalai Lama state. A mandala can be alternately defined as a sacred space created for the realization of rituals, a symbolic representation of the universe, or even a model for the universe. In Tibet, from the place where the Dalai Lama resided all the way up to the governmental organization, all aspects connected to the state had been structurally conceived as mandalas.[46] The division of the governmental functions between two wings, the secular and the monastic, was also conceived in accordance with this fundamental structure. The sacred aspect, represented by the figure of the Dalai Lama and other high lamas, constituted the center around which the secular aspects of government administration gravitated.

Hence, the effect of the "ennoblement" of the monastic class discussed above can be said to have been directly reflected in the ritualized balance between secular and religious forces in the state apparatus, a balance that was certainly one of the main traits of the Ganden Podrang government. The so-called "dual system of government" adopted by the Fifth Dalai Lama distributed official positions between monks and aristocrat officials (Carrasco 1959; Michael 1982; French 1995). Among other things, such a system considerably increased the prestige of monks and monastic institutions, and represented an efficacious way to absorb and control aristocratic power.[47] The monasteries – and in particular the Gelug monasteries – controlled at least forty per cent of all the territory under the jurisdiction of the Ganden Podrang government and absorbed nearly the totality of resources that in the past were invested in military affairs (Michael 1982: 157). A consequence of the economic power that monasteries now possessed was the fact that the "monastic career" represented in the new political context an important avenue for the civil service and, consequently, a possibility of social ascension. "Young monks who showed promise – from families of all social levels – were chosen, trained, and tested for government service" (French 1995: 46). The three large Gelug monasteries of the Lhasa region – Sera, Drepung and Ganden – constituted the main recruitment centers.

The mandala of power

There is a general consensus that the Ganden Podrang government ruled the vast stretches of territory under its jurisdiction through a small bureaucracy at all times (Carrasco 1959; Michael 1982; French 1995; Samuel 1993) in a kind of federation system. In this administrative arrangement, the reduced number of officials necessarily limited the scope of action. In practice, that meant that only the most complex or pressing affairs would be brought to the attention of central government officials. Consequently, the majority of the affairs were taken care of locally by the leaders of each region, or by the land administrators, in the case of monastic and aristocratic lands. In this regard, the conceptual organization of the state based on the mandala matrix, side by side with the creation of elaborate and exuberant state ceremonies, seemed to have as one of its functions to keep cohesive this loose sphere of power. The mandala is a crucial element in tantric Buddhism, representing ultimately the foundation on which tantric initiations are realized. The idea of the reconstruction or recreation of the world is key for the understanding of the usage of the mandala concept in this context.

Indeed, one of the ways in which the Ganden Podrang government was presented had to do with the ideal of transforming and controlling the environment through ritual. The creation of a "pure land," a Buddhist paradise, where everything leads to dharma, is clearly invoked here. In effect, the Tibetan system of government could be understood, at a certain level, as a continuous tantric ritual, an attempt to transform ordinary reality into a "pure" environment. In this regard, it should be recalled that mandalas are three-dimensional representations of deities' palaces. In the case of the Tibetan state, the "simulation" of a "pure land" engendered by conceiving of the state as a mandala-like structure has in its center not a celestial deity, but the figure of the Dalai Lama, the personification of king Songtsen Gampo and Avalokiteshvara as two faces of the same divine plan of power. Hence, if ultimately the ideal of the state was to reproduce, even imperfectly, the conditions of a pure land, in a more immediate sense this state was also presented, through the same magical expedients, as a recreation of the Tibetan Empire. However, instead of a court of kings, queens, princes, noblemen and women, we have the figures of monks reenacting this glorious time of the Tibetan past.

Notes

1 This citation can be found in *The Chariot of the Ocean of Accomplishments*, the biography of the Third Dalai Lama written by Fifth Dalai Lama (Ngawang Lobsang Gyatso 1991–5c: 4a–4b).

2 For a detailed description of the rituals promoted by the Tibetan state before the Chinese invasion, see Richardson (1993).

3 In *Civilized Shamans* (1993), the anthropologist Geoffrey Samuel, a direct student of Stanley Tambiah, suggested the concept of "Galactic Polity" as a suitable model to approach the Tibetan state of the Dalai Lamas (61–3).

4 For a full discussion of this concept, see Chapters Seven and Eight in *World Conqueror and World Renouncer* (Tambiah 1976).

5 The real reach of this government vis-à-vis other important political units, such as Tashilhunpo, in Shigatse, and the Sakya estate, has been a topic of a heated debate among western scholars. Robert Ekvall and C.W. Cassinelli (1969) defended that these smaller estates were de facto autonomous entities, whereas Melvyn Goldstein (1971) supported the thesis that those units were in fact subordinate to the Ganden Podrang government. In *Civilized Shamans* (1993), Geoffrey Samuel presents the general lines of this debate (55–61).

6 As Benjamin Bogin astutely observes, "The *Song of the Queen of Spring* has commanded our view of Tibetan history in much the same way as the Potala commands the cityscape of Lhasa" (Bogin 2006: 7).

7 In Tibetan literature there are three kinds of autobiography: the secret autobiography, which describes visionary and mystical experiences of a master; the inner autobiography, which records the teachings received by a master; and finally the outer autobiography, which is closest to the western literary genre of biography and autobiography.

8 Of course these were not the only works that contributed to the creation of the public image of the Fifth Dalai Lama. In particular, his last regent, Sangye Gyatso (1653–1705), wrote extensively about the Fifth Dalai Lama's life, the symbols associated with him, and the ways to commemorate his legacy. For more on the role of Sangye Gyatso in the creation of the symbolic apparatus of the Ganden Podrang government, see Schaeffer (2006).

9 Once more, I rely for my narrative mostly upon Tsepon Shakabpa who, 300 years after *The Song of the Spring Queen* was composed, wrote another influential, but very different kind of official history of Tibet. In the first chapter of the present work we saw that Shakabpa, who held political and diplomatic positions in the Tibetan government during the first years of the Chinese occupation, was instigated by the Fourteenth Dalai Lama himself to write a treatise on Tibetan history.

10 See Ahmad (1970: 145–6) for a discussion of the secular implications of the conferral of such titles. According to Ahmad, the Dalai Lama "giving titles and seals to Mongolian Khans [...] seemed to have had the effect of formalizing the Khan's accession to the Khanate [i.e., to power]" (146).

11 Altan Khan also expected to have a political gain from this encounter. This is clear, for instance, by the prominent place occupied by Buddhism in the *Jewel Translucent Sutra*, a Mongolian document that recounts the history of Altan Khan and his descendants. For a translation and study of this text, see Johan Elverskog's *Jewel Translucent Sutra* (2003).

12 For a discussion about the symbolic centrality of the Potala Palace for the Dalai Lamas, see Chayet (2003).

13 According to Tibetan and Indian Buddhist historiographical traditions, Potala is the name of a mountain said to be located to the southeast of contemporary Sri Lanka where Avalokiteshvara resides (Lobsang Thrinley 2002: 1273).

14 Considered to be the pinnacle of the tantric teachings of the Nyingma School, Dzogchen, or the Great Perfection, is not practiced by any schools among the *sarma* or "new translation" schools of Tibetan Buddhism – Gelug, Sakya and Kagyu. Only the Bön tradition holds its own separate lineage for these teachings.

15 In addition to these masters, the Fifth Dalai Lama had connections with a number of other illustrious masters of the Nyingma School. Among them, Terdak Lingpa

Gyurme Dorje (1611–62) should be singled out as especially significant for the Great Fifth's association with the Nyingma School. It was from this treasure revealer that the Great Fifth received many of the Nyingma School's most important ritual cycles. For more details on this and other aspects the Fifth Dalai Lama's Nyingma connections, see Ehrhard (2012).

16 In his foreword to the book *Secret Visions of the Fifth Dalai Lama*, the Fourteenth Dalai Lama explains that the teachings contained in his secret autobiography (and reproduced and translated in that volume) belong to the Nyingma School. In his words: "Within the classification of the Ancient (*Nying-ma*) and New (*gSar-ma*) translations, which are distinguished according to the period in which they were done in Tibet, the Extremely Secret Teachings are classified as a cycle belonging to the Ancient translations" (Karmay 1988b).

17 I base my analysis here mostly on the translation of *The Song of the Spring Queen* put forth by Zahiruddin Ahmad (1995), but I also consult the original in Tibetan.

18 For an insightful discussion about the belief in the Dalai Lama as a manifestation of Avalokiteshvara and the dissemination of this belief, see Ishihama (1993).

19 See especially Appendix II "Control over the lHa-sa Maṇḍala Zone," pp. 401–552.

20 As the colophon of the work states,

> The Song of the Queen of Spring, celebrating the Prince of the Age of Fulfilment [Gushri Khan] and speaking, principally, of the kings and ministers, who (descended) from heaven to rule on earth; who honoured, with honour than which there was no higher, the precious teaching of the son of Śuddhodana; and who held firmly to (seeking) refuge in the Three Holy Jewels, in this land surrounded by snowy mountains.
>
> (Ahmad 1995: iv)

21 For more information about the terma tradition, see Janet Gyatso (1986, 1993, 1994, 1996 and 1998) and Tulku Thondup (1986).

22 In Tibetan, "victor," *rgyal ba*, is an epithet for Buddha. Ahmad interprets it as referring to "The Buddha" (Ahmad 1995: 17), without saying more. In the context of the text, it seems to me that *rgyal ba*, in its most transcendental rendering, i.e., the Cosmic Buddha principle, might be a direct reference to Avalokiteshvara.

23 This is the mantra of the bodhisattva Avalokiteshvara.

24 Another name for Manjushri, the bodhisattva of wisdom.

25 For more on the so-called "Supine Demoness," see Gyatso (1987) and Mills (2007).

26 For more on this association between the location of the Jokhang and the heart of the supine demoness, see Sørensen and Hazod (2007: 452–53).

27 This is one of only two ancient schools of Buddhism about which there is substantial knowledge today, the other one being the Theravadin (Gethin 1998: 48).

28 The so-called Bön School is practiced by a minority in Tibet. Despite several similarities with Tibetan Buddhism, including aspects of doctrine, ritual, meditation practices, monastic life and even clear mutual influences, the two religions have maintained a long-standing rivalry. According to its followers, the Bönpos, Tönpa Sherab, who was enlightened from birth, founded the Bön School in lands to the west of Tibet. Its followers also say that Tibetans practiced the Bön School long before the arrival of Buddhism. For more on Bön, see Snellgrove (1967), Kværne (1995) and Martin (2001).

29 In *Civilized Shamans* (1993), Geoffrey Samuel talks precisely about these features, dividing them into the analytical categories of Clerical Buddhism and Shamanic Buddhism, respectively.

30 The decision to compose the biographies of these two lamas (and not of the first two Dalai Lamas) seems to be connected to, among other things, the close relationship between these two figures and the Mongols. In this regard, it is interesting to also recall here that Gushri Khan was the one who commissioned *The Song of the Spring*

Queen. In this seminal moment of the establishment of the Ganden Podrang government, the need for strengthening the ties between the Gelug School and the Mongols by means of literary production seems clear enough through these examples.

31 Hence, I disagree with Ishihama's reading of the same passage cited above as indicating that Trisong Detsen, for example, is an emanation of Avalokiteshvara (Ishihama 1993: 46). In the Treasure literature that emerged from the eleventh century on, there is a clear "division of labor" between the three so-called "dharma kings." Songtsen Gampo is said to be an emanation of Avalokiteshvara, Trisong Detsen of Manjushri, and Relpachen, the last great "dharma king," of Vajrapani. Moreover, in the biography of Sonam Gytaso, the Fifth Dalai Lama seems to embrace the view that Trisong Detsen is an emanation of Manjushri when he cites *The Genealogy of Divine Kings* (Tib. *Lha'i rgyal po'i skyes rabs*), saying, "Manjuvajra [i.e., Manjushri], [you should] go there! Great hero, go to Tibet! Trisong Detsen, become Tibet's lord!" (Ngawang Lobsang Gyatso 1991–5b: 36).

32 Dakini (Skt. *ḍākinī*) generally refers to female deities who are considered to be embodiments of wisdom that teach and inspire tantric practitioners.

33 The deity Karmaguru is a wrathful manifestation of Padmasambhava.

34 Literally, vidyadhara (Skt. *vidyādhara*) means "holder of spells," or "holder of knowledge," and generally refers to someone who has reached refined levels of attainment, including complete enlightenment, through the practice of Buddhist tantra. In the context of the vision, the term is used more specifically to refer to Karmaguru's status as an enlightened being.

35 Torma (Tib. *gtor ma*) is a ritual oblation cake made of flour, butter and other ingredients utilized in Tibetan Buddhist tantric rituals for a broad range of purposes.

36 Tangtong Gyalpo himself was considered to be an emanation of Avalokiteshvara. For more on this figure, see Stearns (2007).

37 The performative quality of this manuscript can be assessed by the fact that it became the centerpiece of an exhibition at the Musée Guimet in Paris in 2002. For more on this exhibition, see its catalogue (Karmay 2002).

38 For a discussion of the importance of Lhasa in the seventeenth century, see Pommaret (2003).

39 Richardson, a British diplomat fluent in Tibetan, spent nine years in Lhasa, between 1936 and 1950, as representative of the British Government of India. He bases his account of state ceremonies in Lhasa on his own experience of these ceremonies and on accounts by other western and Tibetan observers and scholars (Richardson 1993: 7–8).

40 For more on how Sangye Gyatso directly contributed to the creation of ceremonies connected to the Ganden Podrang, see Schaeffer (2006).

41 According to Richardson,

> they included the benevolent figures of Tshangpa, Gyachin and Namtösé (Brahma, Indra and Vaishravana); Chenmizang the Guardian King of the West, the mountain deity Chamo Zangmo, several *driza* "perfume eaters" playing lutes, woodwinds and drums; Nöjin demons; Trülbum charnelhouse ghosts; *mi* and *mimayin*; a garuda and a peacock.
>
> (Richardson 1993: 18)

One possible interpretation for the reenactment of this particular vision in the context of the King's New Year's ceremony is the reinforcement of a certain hierarchical view of the world, in which the Hindu gods are put into the service of the Buddhist doctrine to tame the spiritual world.

42 In *Ceremonies of the Lhasa Year*, Richardson renders the name of this ceremony as "Golden Procession." I disagree with this rendering, since *ser* means yellow and not golden (which in Tibetan is *gser*). Besides, the color yellow seems to be a direct reference to the color of the monks' robes.

43 The extent to which the precise content of *The Sealed One* was known to the public is of course impossible to establish here. However, even if very few people had direct access to the text, it seems fair to assume that there was at least some general knowledge about some of its elements. In *Apparitions of the Self*, Janet Gyatso speaks of a small, but unquestionable readership of secret autobiographies such as *The Sealed One*, which included trusted disciples, fellow teachers and key patrons (1998: 7). Through their oral teachings, lamas to this day commonly spread the visionary experience of yogis they read about in books. Furthermore, some of these visions are also shared through rituals, which contain more formalized versions of the original visionary experience. Finally, the yearly repetition of the ceremonies in question certainly contributed toward spreading a general knowledge about its contents. In these ceremonies, the objects, masks and ancient sacred articles can be said to function as indexes pointing back to the Fifth Dalai Lama's mystical experiences.

44 Richardson himself describes the *Yellow Procession* as a "particularly brilliant and enjoyable festival" (Richardson 1993: 81).

45 The long sermons of the Dalai Lamas were in some cases documented. Glenn Mullin published, for example, some of the sermons given by the Thirteenth Dalai Lama in the festival of 1929 (Mullin 1988).

46 For more on the organization of the Ganden Podrang government in terms of the mandala model, see French (1995).

47 One of the most visible transformations in the social domain was connected to the change of status among aristocratic families. While retaining part of their privileges, those families had a good part of their land confiscated by the state (Carrasco 1959; Michael 1982; French 1995). The power they held in the past, which was based on land propriety and their own military force, was considerably restricted and an important portion of it was transferred to the government. Nevertheless, these families still had their part to play in the new government.

> A few of these families developed into an upper class of official nobility: they maintained their estates through many generations, accumulating landholdings in exchange for providing as public servants one or more sons per generation, who were sent to secular schools and internships at secular offices.
>
> (French 1995: 47)

As a result of this system, the Fifth Dalai Lama forged alliances with the traditional noble families – certainly his potential enemies – eliminating, at the same time, their autonomous authority (Michael 1982: 45–6).

Part II
Bardo

3   Buddhist encounters in the diaspora

Dalai Lama means different things to different people. To some it means that I am a living Buddha, the earthly manifestation of Avalokiteshvara, Bodhisattva of Compassion. To others it means that I am a 'god-king'. During the late 1950s it meant I was a Vice-President of the Steering Committee of the People's Republic of China. Then when I escaped into exile, I was called a counterrevolutionary and a parasite. But none of these are my ideas. To me 'Dalai Lama' is a title that signifies the office I hold. I myself am just a human being, and incidentally a Tibetan, who chooses to be a Buddhist monk.

Tenzin Gyatso, The Fourteenth Dalai Lama, *Freedom in Exile*

On the evening of March 17, 1959, against the burbling background noise of a large crowd stationed outside his residency, the Dalai Lama divested himself of his royal attire and crossed the gates of Norbulingka Palace, the summer residency of the Dalai Lamas. Disguised in the clothes of a simple soldier, the Tibetan leader went out in the company of close relatives, attendants and a few servants. Perhaps he did not imagine at that moment that he would leave behind his royal garments not only during the difficult journey to his exile in India, but most probably forever. In exile, the Dalai Lama would say later, it made no sense to wear silk and brocades, gold and turquoise; he would become from that point forth "a simple Buddhist monk." More than 50 years after that night, the metamorphosis of the Dalai Lama can be perceived in the diversity of roles he plays in different, and sometimes unexpected, contexts. Although the Tibetan leader left his royal adornments in Tibet, his monastic robes would raise him to a highly prominent position throughout the four quarters of the planet, a position which very few monks, Buddhist or not (simple or not), could even dream of occupying.

Over the last few decades, the Dalai Lama has become one of the world's most celebrated spiritual leaders. In western countries, his conferences and initiations sometimes attract 15,000 people; in Asia, his audience can easily reach a total of 300,000 people. Among his most illustrious followers are Hollywood stars, such as Richard Gere and Goldie Hawn, and pop celebrities, like the late lead singer of the Beastie Boys, Adam Yauch. The history of his life has been the subject of two massive Hollywood productions: Martin Scorcese's *Kundun*

(1997), an adaptation of the Dalai Lama's first autobiography; and Jean-Jacques Arnaud's *Seven Years in Tibet* (1997), based on the homonymous book by Heinrich Harrer, an Austrian deserter, played by Brad Pitt, who went to Tibet to escape World War II.

The Dalai Lama's books, published in all the main languages of the world, are international bestsellers. In the context of interfaith dialogue, the Dalai Lama has become a high profile figure, taking part in countless conferences with other spiritual leaders. In 1994, for example, he was the first non-Christian to be invited to lead the John Main Catholic Seminar, where he introduced Buddhist interpretations of the gospels. The seminar was registered in the book entitled, *The Good Heart* (1996). It is important to stress, moreover, that the Dalai Lama's scope of activities extends well beyond the strictly religious sphere. Since the end of the 1970s, the Dalai Lama has been taking part in conferences with western scientists, psychologists and the like, debating with them topics as diverse as theoretical physics, cosmology, cognitive science, the healing power of emotions, the death process, dreams, sleep and more (e.g., Tenzin Gyatso *et al.* 1991; Goleman 1997; Varela 1997; Zajonc 2005). If in the past Tibetan Buddhism was considered a degenerate form of Buddhism, today an article that has the collaboration of the Dalai Lama can even be published in a renowned scientific journal such as *Nature*. Such was the case of the research conducted by Herbert Benson, then chair of the Department of Behavioral Medicine at Harvard Medical School, on the physiological effects produced by the advanced practice of meditation of Tibetan yogis (Benson 1982).

Finally, it is essential is this regard to call attention to the Dalai Lama's position as a champion of world peace. This is a role that led to him being awarded the Nobel Peace Prize in 1989, the same year that the world watched with stupefaction the Tiananmen Square massacre in Beijing. The Tibetan leader has received such enormous prestige in this domain that it would be difficult to imagine any important forum on the topic of world peace, be it religious or not, that does not include his presence or make reference to his work.

In many senses, the transformation undergone by the Dalai Lama – from religious and secular leader of a relatively isolated country to one of the most renowned religious figures in the world – can only be understood when contextualized within the broader phenomenon of the Tibetan diaspora. Over the last 50 years, the world has witnessed the spectacular dissemination of Tibetan Buddhism, a religion that, until very recently, figured in the western imagination as a mystical sect of lamas living in a magical universe. Indeed, before the diaspora, Tibetan Buddhism was mainly known in the West through the so-called *Tibetan Book of the Dead* (Evans-Wentz 2000 [1927]), or through works that portrayed it in a mystical or even fantastical way – as for example the novel by James Hilton, *Lost Horizon* (1960 [1933]), or the controversial autobiography of T. Lobsang Rampa, *The Third Eye* (1956).[1] Today, hundreds of "flesh and bone" lamas travel around the world, founding dharma centers dedicated to the practice and study of Tibetan Buddhism. In the publishing market, dozens of titles explaining the principles, philosophy and history of that religion are launched annually. In universities, American universities in particular, chairs of Tibetan Buddhist studies are being created. Finally, the number of western followers of that religion is well beyond hundreds of thousands and continues to grow.

The planetary renown of the Dalai Lama (certainly something unimaginable 50 years ago), along with the spectacular dissemination of Tibetan Buddhism, seem to be a direct consequence of the globalization process that we can observe in the world today. Following David Harvey (1989) and Anthony Giddens (1990), the globalization process can be succinctly described as a radical reorganization of time and space, in which there is an intensification of global interconnectedness, cultural interchange, mobility and so forth. As we will see throughout the remaining chapters of this work, the life and activities not only of the Dalai Lama, but of other exile lamas too, strongly inflect the effects of globalization. As I briefly mentioned in the introduction to this work, constant travel, the creation of Buddhist centers in multiple countries, and a strong presence on the Internet and in the publishing market characterize the interaction of Tibetan lamas with their disciples around the globe.

As a result of this intensive, globalized activity, a transnational religious field has formed over the years bringing together lamas, Tibetan Buddhist practitioners, the Dalai Lama's wider circle of admirers and Tibetan refugees, among others. This field, which was constituted initially by the global interest sparked in Tibetan Buddhism, has strong political overtones due to the centrality that the Dalai Lama occupies within it and the fragile political situation of Tibet and Tibetans. Owing to the unique circumstance of Tibetan Buddhism in the contemporary diaspora context, the use of the concept of "field" in the context of this work requires some qualifications in relation to previous formulations. The transnational religious field of Tibetan Buddhism involves the formation of a "network of objective relations between different positions [occupied by agents]" (Bourdieu 1993: 30) that is defined, first and foremost, by its global and fragmentary characteristics. So, what we have here is not a circumscribed field with well-delimited borders, or borders that correspond to those of a specific society, but rather, one in which the distribution of power among "occupants, agents, and institutions" (Bourdieu *apud* Wacquant 1989: 52) takes place across different nations, giving rise to very particular ways of conducting politics within the religious sphere.

Faced with the political practices found in the Tibetan Buddhist transnational religious field, we should, along with Arjun Appadurai, "make an effort to think ourselves beyond the nation" (1996b: 40). In a number of works (1996a; 1996b; 2001), Appadurai has elaborated upon the idea that we live in a post-national political world marked by disjunctures in "the links among space, place, citizenship and nationhood" (1996b: 48). In this highly fragmented scenario, Appadurai singles out media and migration as two key agents in the complex process of globalization we witness in the world today, highlighting their powers of disaggregation and reaggregation of human groups. Media and migration are, according to him, responsible for the promotion of the "work of imagination" as a major and "constitutive feature of modern subjectivity" (1996a: 3). Expanding upon Benedict Anderson's well-known *Imagined Communities* (2006 [1983]), Appadurai discusses how "electronic capitalism can have similar, and even more powerful effects" than print capitalism in terms of representing an "important way in which groups who have never been in face-to-face contact can begin to think of themselves as Indonesian or Indian or Malaysian." According to Appadurai, this is so because "they do not work only at the level of the nation-state" (ibid.: 8). He goes on to say:

> Collective experiences of the mass media, especially film and video, can create sodalities of worship and charisma, such as those that formed regionally around the Indian female deity Santoshi Ma in the seventies and eighties and transnationally around Ayatolla Khomeini in roughly the same period. [...]
>
> [Sodalities] are communities in themselves but always potentially communities for themselves, capable of moving from shared imagination to collective action. Most important [...] these sodalities are often transnational, even postnational, and they frequently operate beyond the boundaries of the nation. These mass-mediated sodalities have the additional complexity that, in them, diverse local experiences of taste, pleasure, and politics can crisscross with one another, thus creating the possibility of convergences in translocal social action that would otherwise be hard to imagine.
>
> (Ibid.: 8)

I believe that the Tibetan Buddhist transnational religious field, "powered" by the imagined communal ties it creates among people from around the world, constitutes a very particular case pertaining to the more general phenomenon of the formation of transnational sodalities. The field at issue does not exactly constitute a cohesive community, or sodality, but rather a network of communities that is formed, however, following the same dynamics as the constitution of transnational sodalities to which Appadurai is referring. To discuss the singularity of the Tibetan case, let us contrast some of the reasons for its exceptionality with ideas advanced in Arjun Appadurai's work *Modernity at Large*.

First, there is the ethnic and cultural heterogeneity of the members belonging to the Tibetan Buddhist transnational religious field. Mass migration, one of the diacritics of globalization mentioned by Appadurai as a major force in the "work of imagination" of our times, certainly plays a role in the configuration of this field. Nevertheless, mass migration is relatively less important for the kind of phenomenon under discussion here than it is in contexts in which the ethnic component has a strong cohesive power. In the Tibetan case, what we observe is a myriad of transnational and translocal communities of different dimensions that were formed around *displaced* lamas through the resettlement of Tibetan refugees, and that are connected to one another through a number of distinct channels.

This point leads us to the second reason for the exceptionality of the Tibetan case: the fundamental role played by charismatic lamas in the creation of multiple sodalities, which together produce a broader multi-cored network. In this sense, the Tibetan case is slightly at odds with Appadurai's general argument about how, in our current "postelectronic world," imagination has broken away from "the special expressive space of art, myth and ritual" to become part of "the quotidian mental work of ordinary people in many societies." In this new scenario, he maintains, "it is no longer a matter of specially endowed, charismatic individuals, injecting the imagination where it does not belong" (Appadurai 1996a: 5). I do agree that this "emancipation" of imagination, and its expression especially in electronic media, constitutes an essential element in the process itself of *imagining*, if not a community per se, at least a strong affiliation to a greater Tibetan Buddhist sphere. In a similar way, however, charismatic lamas bearing their sense of affiliation to traditional lineages and schools, along with their disciples around the world, also play a fundamental part in this process.

Among these lamas, there is, of course, the figure of the Dalai Lama. Nevertheless, his position is so singular that it constitutes in itself a third reason for the exceptionality of the Tibetan Buddhist transnational religious field in the global context. Today the Dalai Lama is the exiled political leader with the highest profile in the world (to the desperation of the Chinese government). Furthermore, the Dalai Lama is not like most political leaders. His status as sacred king of the mythical Tibet had its place in the western imagination well before the Chinese invasion and the consequent Tibetan diaspora. As I have briefly mentioned, in the years following his exile, the Dalai Lama has brilliantly reinvented his own identity, mobilizing a great deal of his political power to become one of the most important voices today in defense of world peace and global ethics. More than anyone, then, the Tibetan leader is capable of activating the imagination in relation to Tibetan Buddhism, providing the Tibetan Buddhist transnational religious field with a sense of cohesion that brings it close to the idea of a community, or sodality.

To a certain extent, and in large part due to the centrality of the Dalai Lama, the current field can be considered an expansion of the traditional religious field of Tibetan Buddhism to a planetary setting. Vestiges of traditional institutions – centers, monasteries, teaching institutions and so forth – can be easily traced in the diaspora. At the same time, it is also possible to witness these institutions undergoing a profound process of re-signification in their new global contexts. As we will see throughout this work, the results of this process of re-signification are far from uniform, but carry at their core something characteristically current: the survival of the archaic in modern forms (Benjamin 1999). In the following pages I will discuss the formation of the transnational religious field of Tibetan Buddhism, taking some exemplary cases as my point of departure. In so doing, I will attempt to identify some of the dialogue zones that made it possible for a religion that was previously circumscribed to a very delimited territory to conquer the world.

I Two formative movements of the field

From the Indian village to the global village (outward)

The Dalai Lama's escape in 1959 and the consequent hardening of the Chinese communist regime in Tibet spurred a mass flux of Tibetans into exile. Since the beginning of the 1960s, Tibetan refugee settlements have formed primarily in India, Nepal, and Bhutan. After briefly establishing himself in Mussoorie, in the north of India, the Dalai Lama moved to Dharamsala, further north (Tenzin Gyatso 1990: 158). In this old British hill station, situated at 4,780 feet, the Tibetan government in exile was instituted. It would not take long before Europeans and Americans, in part propelled by countercultural ideals prevalent in their societies, visited the settlements in these Asian countries and had direct encounters with Tibetan lamas. Such access was something that until then was the privilege of only a few adventurers who dared to cross the Himalayas and enter Tibet, often clandestinely.

As a result of these encounters – real "ground zeros" of the Tibetan diaspora – the first nuclei of Tibetan Buddhism in the West were formed. As an illustration, it is worth mentioning here the case of the French filmmaker Arnaud Desjardins, a case that is seminal and paradigmatic at the same time. Desjardins went to India in 1966 to film a documentary about Tibetan Buddhism. "Upon returning to France," Stephen Batchelor tells us,

> Desjardins showed the rushes of his film to friends and spoke excitedly of the lamas he had encountered. This prompted a small stream of men and women to travel to Darjeeling, who formed a circle of Europeans disciples around Kangyur Rinpoche in India and established the nucleus of a Tibetan Buddhist group in France.
>
> (Batchelor 1994: 69)

Kangyur Rinpoche (1898–1975) was an important lama connected with the Rime tradition[2] of Tibetan Buddhism. Even though Kangyur Rinpoche died in 1975, without being able to visit Europe, his legacy is still alive to this day. In 1980, the Association du Centre d'Études de Chanteloube, in Dordogne, France, was created under the guidance of two of the greatest contemporary Nyingma lamas, Dudjom Rinpoche (1904–87) and Dilgo Khyentse Rinpoche (1910–91). These two lamas visited Chanteloube for the first time in the 1970s at the request of Kangyur Rinpoche. Today, the sons of Kangyur Rinpoche, Jigme Khyentse Rinpoche (b. 1963) and Pema Wangyal Rinpoche (b. 1947), are at the forefront of a series of activities connected to the preservation and expansion of Tibetan Buddhist spiritual culture, including the Association du Centre d'Études de Chanteloube and the Padmakara translation group.[3]

Parallel and similar stories transpired throughout the 1960s and 1970s (and still happen to this day), engendering a proliferation of centers and other kinds of organizations connected to Tibetan Buddhism in the West, and in Asian localities where this tradition did not exist before, or had only minor and limited representation, such as Hong Kong, Taiwan and Malaysia, to name a few. Some of the lamas that now have disciples in multiple countries around the world continue to reside in Nepal and India, where they originally settled; others ended up moving abroad, in particular, to Europe or North America. In the majority of cases, owing to the heterogeneous and global make up of their groups of students, international travel became the norm in the life of these Tibetans, who ironically lived before in a country renowned most for its isolation. If the extremely long distances were something new, the practice of inviting lamas to teach, and paying for their expenses and teachings, goes all the way back to ancient India and was ubiquitous in Tibet. It is not by chance, then, that these lamas naturally developed a closer connection with wealthier countries, where they found the resources to continue their activities of teaching the dharma. It would only be later that lamas started to travel to poorer countries, such as those of South America.

The dynamic exchange between Tibetans lamas and, in particular, western disciples had the important indirect effect of gradually inserting, through more than one channel, the Tibetan political cause into the political discourse of the main countries in the world. In the first and most difficult years of exile, the prestige of the Dalai Lama (and of the Tibetan exile community) was, in the best of estimates, neutral among western countries. In general terms, world powers cultivated an attitude of indifference in relation to the Tibet issue. This was in many senses a continuation of the western attitude about the Chinese invasion and subsequent violations of human rights in Tibet. As anthropologist Rinzin Thargyal puts it, Tibetans refugees "felt in the 1960s and 1970s that they were treated as political 'lepers' by the international community" (Thargyal 1993: 30).

New political winds in the Tibetan community in exile (inward)

Contact with the western ideals of democracy, especially in their Indian incarnation, would have a profound impact on the political organization of the Tibetan community in exile. Already in 1961, for example, the Dalai Lama promulgated a "Constitution for the Future of Tibet" based on the modern principles of democracy. According to the Tibetan leader, even though the constitution was generally well received by Tibetans, "the provision, which stipulated that if circumstances demanded the power of the Dalai Lama could be taken away according to the Constitution" had "to be revised" due to strong opposition among the people (Shiromany 1998: 277). Two years later, a more detailed draft of the constitution was announced. Among other things, it abolished the "bipolar system of appointing monk and lay officials to each position" (ibid.), which as we have seen was established during the Fifth Dalai Lama's rule. However, because the constitution reflected, according to the Dalai Lama, "circumstances prevailing at that time," it still ensured the "ultimate authority of the government to the Dalai Lama." In the Dalai Lama's words, "Naturally, I was not satisfied with this clause – I felt this constitution fell far short of my conception of a genuine democracy" (ibid.). The Tibetan leader would have to wait almost four decades to see his political wishes completely come true.

In 1990, a new step in this direction was taken, when the Dalai Lama instituted a committee to draft a new constitution.[4] In order to elicit feedback and suggestions, the Committee "widely circulated" a draft of the so-called "Charter for the Tibetans-in-Exile." The Committee then submitted a final draft for the approval of the Dalai Lama. In July 1991, the Eleventh Assembly of Tibetan People's Deputies officially approved the Charter. Among the main innovations of the Charter was the separation between the three branches of the government: the judiciary, the legislative and the executive. Despite the advances achieved by the Charter in terms of the modernization of the government and the universalization of democratic ideals, it still determined that "the executive power of the Tibetan Administration shall be vested in His Holiness the Dalai Lama, and shall be exercised by Him, either directly or through officers subordinate to Him."[5] In 2001, the first direct election to Kalon Tripa, "Prime Minister," took place. A high-ranking lama, Samdhong Rinpoche (b. 1939) was elected. Despite being the head of the Kashag (Cabinet), which was "the highest executive division of the government," the Kalon Tripa nonetheless remained subordinate to the Dalai Lama. Another ten years would go by before the Dalai Lama could definitively renounce his secular powers.

In the session of the Tibetan Parliament in Exile beginning on March 14, 2011, the Dalai Lama announced his decision to relinquish his formal authority to the elected Kalon Tripa. In an eloquent speech[6] encapsulating 15 centuries of Tibetan history, the Dalai Lama talked about the dharma kings, the period of political fragmentation, the establishment of the Ganden Podrang government, the difficulties faced by his predecessor, the Thirteenth Dalai Lama, to modernize Tibet, and finally the steps he himself had taken to establish democracy among the Tibetan community in exile. He concluded his speech by urging the members of parliament to take all the necessary steps in that "very session" to bring the Charter in conformity with "the framework of a democratic system in which the political leadership is elected by the people for a specific term." In a public address a few days later, the Dalai Lama explained his decision to the exile community in Dharamsala, pointing out in particular his unique position to end what the Fifth Dalai Lama had started almost four centuries before:

> It started during the time of the fifth Dalai Lama under different circumstances and the influence of the Mongol chieftain Gushri Khan. The system has brought many benefits since then. But now as we are in the twenty-first century, sooner or later the time for change is imminent. But if the change comes under the pressure of another person, then it will be a disgrace to the former Dalai Lamas. Since the fifth Dalai Lama, Ngawang Lobsang Gyatso, the Dalai Lamas have assumed both spiritual and temporal rule over Tibet. As I am the fourteenth in the line of that institution, it is most appropriate if I on my own initiative, happily and with pride, end the dual authority of the Dalai Lama. Nobody except me can make this decision and I have made the final decision. The leadership democratically elected by the Tibetan people

should take over the complete political responsibilities of Tibet. Some kind of a vestige of the dual system will remain if I am vested with the political authority in the Charter. This should change and now seems to be the time to do it.

(www.dalailama.com/messages/retirement/retirement-remarks)

Shortly after the Dalai Lama delivered this speech, the Tibetan community in exile elected Lobsang Sangay as the new Kalon Tripa.[7] Lobsang Sangay (b. 1968), a holder of a Ph.D. from Harvard Law School, became the first layperson to occupy the highest position in the political structure that is a continuation of the government established by the Fifth Dalai Lama. Sangay's election thus completed the transitional period towards the establishment of a fully democratic system among Tibetans in exile.

This new approach of openness towards the world, and especially the western world, was behind an important transformation of the status of Tibetans in the political sphere. Tibetans learned with the Chinese invasion that the political isolation of their country was in fact incompatible with the modern world. The process of gradual democratization,[8] and also of secularization, of the Tibetan government in exile seems to be a direct response to the Chinese accusation that their political system was feudal and exploited the masses in Tibet. However, more than that, this process is also a direct fruit of contact with the international community and an "entry visa" into this community.

By leaving behind his "royal adornments" and adopting democratic principles, the Dalai Lama clearly aligned himself and his government with western governments, among others. This positioning, moreover, has amplified his possibilities of dialogue in the political arena. By gradually forsaking his temporal powers, it is the Dalai Lama's role as a (now worldly) religious leader that has come to the forefront. From this new position, the Dalai Lama has been able to better situate himself in the political arena, thus beginning to erase the image of "political lepers" that previously stigmatized Tibetan refugees.

II Dialogue zones

The rise in the global interest in Tibetan Buddhism, particularly among westerners, can only be explained by bringing several elements into account. Nonetheless, the aspect common to the discourses of many lamas (and Buddhist religious specialists in general) in their interactions with westerners, and certainly one of the main factors that differentiates Buddhism from other religious traditions, is the emphasis on meditation practice.[9] The keyword here is "technique," or better yet, in the terms of Daniel Goleman, author of the bestseller *Emotional Intelligence*, the "articulation of the technique." (Tenzin Gyatso *et al.* 1991: 106). A general conception has dawned in the West that meditation practices, as techniques distilled and systematized from the experiences of Buddhist practitioners, are powerful instruments for the transformation of the mind, or in other words, for self-cultivation and self-transformation. If meditation can be understood in this way as foundational to the dissemination of this traditional throughout the West, in this and other contexts different elements that are more or less emphasized by proponents of Tibetan Buddhism have also come to play defining roles in this process.

Essential to this discussion is the notion of *contrast culture* developed by the Brazilian anthropologist Manuela Carneiro da Cunha (1986). First, it should be stated that if Tibetan Buddhism emerges as the main "channel of communication" – in the sense of a privileged "language" – for the dialogue with the West, it happens to the detriment of other aspects of Tibetan culture(s), which in this process of "reduction" are left out or deemphasized. This same process can also be identified in relation to Buddhism itself. Indeed, some aspects of this tradition were emphasized, or accentuated, more than others in the contact with the West. In the present chapter, I seek to identify some of the different dialogue zones that were born from this process of "cultural accentuation," without having the ambition of exhausting the subject.

A first criterion adopted here in my choice of dialogue zones to be discussed comes from my observations of the Dalai Lama's activities in the context of diaspora. The central position that the Tibetan leader occupies in the transnational religious field of Tibetan Buddhism has transformed him into a privileged agent both in the opening of new dialogue zones and in the exploration and expansion of zones previously opened by other lamas, or by practitioners of other Buddhist traditions. In effect, the Dalai Lama tends to have an intense presence in most domains connected to Tibetan Buddhism in the world today. Moreover, I would say that some niches opened by the Dalai Lama represent a preferential sphere of activity for other lamas.

The first zone to be analyzed is connected to the issue of world peace, a domain in which, as we briefly saw above, the Dalai Lama occupies a privileged position. Partially related to the topic of world peace – especially in terms of the Dalai Lama's activities – are Buddhist engagements with environmental issues. This is the second dialogue zone to be explored in this chapter. Third, I discuss the general lines of dialogue between Tibetan Buddhism and the West in relation to different kinds of scientific practices. Finally, the last zone to be addressed concerns the academic tradition of Tibetan Buddhism. Over the years, several institutions and programs related to the study of the Buddhist teachings have been created inside and outside universities. The Dalai Lama has also played an important role in this domain, sometimes directly influencing the creation of some of these institutions and programs.

Buddhism and world peace

Just after the Dalai Lama received the Nobel Peace Prize, a publication dedicated to an examination of the Buddhist approach to non-violence was released. *Inner Peace, World Peace* (1992), as it was titled, was the fruit of collaboration between some of the top scholars in the field of Buddhist studies

at the time, along with social activists connected to Buddhism. Clearly reflecting certain ideas present in the western imaginary, the first paragraph of the introduction straightforwardly asserted the long association between Buddhism and the notions of peace and non-violence, putting forth that "no major war has been fought in the name of Buddhism," and that only "few crusades or inquisitions" have been recorded by history (Kraft 1992: 1). In sheer contrast with *Inner Peace* (and sometimes with a clear sensationalistic penchant), some more recent publications have been directed at showing the exact opposite: that Buddhism in all its forms and at all times has had intensive engagements with violence that are often ignored by western scholarship (Zimmermann 2006; Jerryson and Juergensmeyer 2010; Dalton 2011; Tikhonov and Brekke 2013).

In his introduction to *Buddhism and Violence* (2013), for example, Tikhonov dates the "common (mis)perception" that "Buddhism is somewhat more 'peaceful' than the rest of local and global religions" back to the "nineteenth century introduction of Buddhism to Europe by modernist intellectuals searching for a 'rational,' 'philosophical' religion compatible with the best traditions of Enlightenment." A little later, he states that the collection of articles he is introducing intends precisely to clarify this misconception by showing that "Buddhism possesses its own logic of 'permissible violence' fully comparable with that of Christian 'just war' theories, which still seem, by the way, to define the views of most mainstream churches on the matters of war and peace" (Tikhonov and Brekke 2013: 9–10). In my opinion, there is a great danger in equating traditions in such a way. If the nineteenth-century perception of Buddhism as purely philosophical and rational was rectified later by more accurate scholarship, which presented this tradition in fuller complexity, this later correction did not obliterate the existence of Buddhist philosophical and rationalistic tendencies. One can argue, in this regard, that the highly developed fields of Buddhist philosophical studies in Europe and the United States give testament to the overwhelming existence of such tendencies.

In a similar vein, if Buddhism was received in the West with a special emphasis on peace and non-violence, this is due less to the ignorance of historical or doctrinal facets of this tradition than to the availability of an extensive repertoire related to these ideas in Buddhist doctrines and sensible symbols. It was, after all, Buddhism's multiple possibilities of expressing non-violent ideas[10] that led avant-garde American poets, such as Gary Snyder and Allen Ginsberg, for example, to protest against the Vietnam War by doing meditation and reciting sutras, or chanting mantras (Büyükokutan 2011: 625). The Vietnam War also brought to the spotlight powerful images of peaceful monks protesting against the conflict. The Vietnamese monk Thich Nhat Hanh, who gained international recognition for his efforts to put an end to the Vietnam War, was nominated for the Nobel Peace Prize in 1967. Another Vietnamese monk, Thich Quang Duc, also became an icon of the Buddhist defense of world peace, when in 1963 he made a radical decision to protest against the persecution of Buddhists by the South Vietnamese government headed by Ngo Dinh Diem. In a book marked by a confessional tone and a political take on Buddhism, the Columbia University professor Robert Thurman tells how he was haunted by the image of Thich Quang Duc's self-immolation:

> smiling cheerfully at some video camerapersons, he calmly approached a chosen site, sat down in mediation posture, doused himself with gasoline, and was suffused with roaring frames. He did not recoil in either pain or terror, and all the while a slight smile spread across his lips. After fully fifty seconds of blackening, sizzling, charring consumption by the flames, his body lost structural integrity and imploded. He had remained unmoved from the peace he knew.
>
> (Thurman 1998: 11)

The Dalai Lama follows in the footsteps of these Buddhist monks, having become today one of the most important global leaders in defense of world peace. Indeed, it is this role that has provided the greatest visibility to the Tibetan leader. Moreover, through his high-profile defense of principles that concern humanity as a whole, such as peace, tolerance, justice and so forth, the Dalai Lama has also succeeded in positioning the Tibetan cause on a universal level, transforming the fight for the autonomy of Tibet into a (generalized) fight for a more equitable and peaceful existence in an ode to non-violence that echoes the seminal words of Mahatma Gandhi.[11] At the same time that his position as a world peace champion was gradually consolidated, the Dalai Lama attenuated the terms of his claims over Tibet in the 1970s. In 1999, for example, in his annual speech commemorating the Lhasa Uprising of 1959, the Tibetan leader expressed these views:

> It is with this realization that in the early seventies I discussed and decided with my senior officials the main points of my "Middle Way Approach." Consequently, I opted for a resolution of the Tibet issue, which does not call for the independence of Tibet or its separation from China. I firmly believe that it is possible to find a political solution that ensures the basic rights and freedoms of the Tibetan people within the framework of the People's Republic of China. My primary concern is the survival and preservation of Tibet's unique spiritual heritage, which is based on compassion and non-violence. And, I believe it is worthwhile and beneficial to preserve this heritage since it continues to remain relevant in our present-day world.
>
> (www.dalailama.com/messages/tibet/10th-march-archive/1999)[12]

Based on this and several other messages posted on his official website, (www.dalailama.com/messages), it is clear that the Dalai Lama's adoption of the "Middle Way Approach" means, among other things, that the Tibetan cause could be firmly grounded in the domain of the universal struggle for human rights. In a message commemorating the 60th anniversary of the Declaration of

Human Rights, for example, after discussing the issue of human rights abuses in China, the Dalai Lama declares,

> There is a great and growing desire for change in the world; change that ushers in a renewed commitment to ethical and spiritual values, that resolves conflicts peaceably, employing dialogue and non-violence, that upholds human rights and human dignity as well as human responsibility.
> (www.dalailama.com/messages/world-peace/human-rights-democracy-and-freedom)

The promotion of ethical and spiritual values as a way to change the world constitutes the subject matter of two of the Dalai Lama's books, the bestselling *Ethics for the New Millennium* (1999), and the recently released *Beyond Religion*[13] (2011). These two publications share the feature of not making explicit references to Buddhism, while at the same time, being totally in agreement with the religion's basic precepts. In them, the Dalai Lama's teachings are presented as a kind of universal wisdom, which is attuned more to the general idea of peace than to specifically religious concepts. In *Ethics for the New Millennium*, the Dalai Lama directly addresses this idea, when he states,

> My concern in this book is to try to reach beyond the formal boundaries of my faith. I want to show that there are indeed some universal ethical principles which could help to achieve the happiness we all aspire to.
> (Tenzin Gyatso 1999: 22)

The Dalai Lama's posture in this regard points to another important domain of his activities in the West: the dialogue (particularly via the idea of world peace) with other religious leaders. In many ways, both books could be said to be a fruit of this kind of dialogue. In this regard, it is important to highlight here the diplomatic policy of the Tibetan leader in relation to other religious traditions. In another passage of *Ethics for the New Millennium*, for instance, the Dalai Lama reiterates his trans-religious tendencies, making clear at the same time his resolution to not seek the conversion of westerners (at least, not explicitly).

> It is doubtful whether globally even a billion are what I would call dedicated religious practitioners, that is to say, people who try, on a daily basis, faithfully to follow the principles and precepts of their faith. The rest remain, in this sense, non-practicing. Those who are dedicated practitioners meanwhile follow a multiplicity of religious paths. From this it becomes clear that, given our diversity, no single religion satisfies all humanity. We may also conclude that we humans can live quite well without recourse to religious faith.
>
> These may seem unusual statements, coming as they do from a religious figure. I am, however, Tibetan before I am Dalai Lama, and I am human before I am Tibetan. So while as Dalai Lama I have a special responsibility

toward furthering interreligious harmony, as human being I have a much larger responsibility toward the whole human family – which indeed we all have. And since the majority does not practice religion, I am concerned to try to find a way to serve all humanity without appealing to religious faith.

(Ibid.: 20)

In *Beyond Religion*, which presents a further elaboration of the ideas in *Ethics for the New Millennium*, the Dalai Lama invites readers to come to their "own understanding of the importance of inner values. For it is these inner values which are the source of both an ethically harmonious world and the individual peace of mind, confidence, and happiness we all seek." Although, he continues, "all the world's major religions can do and promote inner values," the reality of the world today "is that grounding ethics in religion is no longer adequate. This is why," he concludes, "the time has come to find a way of thinking that is beyond religion" (Tenzin Gyatso 2011: xv). Thanks to his skillfulness in incorporating the Tibetan cause into his activities in the humanistic domain, and in maintaining a friendly relationship with other religious traditions,[14] the Dalai Lama has occupied over the last decades a high-profile position in the worldly political arena. If in the 1950s, when the Chinese occupation began, Tibetans did not get the support of any government to fight off the invaders, today, despite constant threats of retaliation from China, the Dalai Lama is received, with state honors or not, by the leaders of the main countries in the world. The fact that the frequency of these visits substantially increased after the Dalai Lama received the Nobel Peace Prize is a clear sign that the strengthening of his image as world peace champion is one of his main assets in the fight for Tibetan autonomy.

A cursory analysis of the list of world leaders with whom the Dalai Lama has met since he went into exile provides us a glimpse into the dimensions of this award's political importance. According to this list, which is posted on the official website of the Dalai Lama (www.dalailama.com/biography/dignitaries-met), during the years preceding 1989, the year he was awarded the Nobel Peace Prize, the Dalai Lama met almost exclusively with Asian heads of state. The main exceptions to this pattern were Erskine Childers, president of Ireland, (along with some of his ministers), who met with the Dalai Lama in 1973;[15] Jacques Chirac, then prime minister of France, and Rudolf Kirchschlaeger, president of Austria, who met with the Tibetan leader in 1986; and Carlos Salinas de Gotari, president of Mexico, who met with the Dalai Lama in 1989 just before the Tibetan leader received the prize. This state of affairs changed drastically after 1989. Since then, the Dalai Lama has been constantly received by the heads of state of the major European countries, Canada, Africa, and South America, as well as all the American presidents throughout the last 25 years – President Bill Clinton, for example, met with the Tibetan leader on five separate occasions.

In sum, among all the roles the Dalai Lama has played in the context of his exile, the one of world peace champion has certainly marked him the most, expanding the scope of his activities well beyond Tibetan Buddhist circles. However, to be clear, the Tibetan leader is not the only lama to stroll along the world peace road. Following a quite different path, which has its origins in (personal and planetary) healing practices, Lama Gangchen Rinpoche, the Gelug lama mentioned in the introduction, also built an image for himself as a world peace advocate. Although the path leading up to this position differs from the Tibetan leader's, the role that Lama Gangchen has fashioned for himself is quite close to the international role of world peace champion that the Dalai Lama has been cultivating over the last few decades. For instance, as we will see in greater detail below, Lama Gangchen has formed strong connections with the United Nations, a terrain of difficult access for the Dalai Lama due to Chinese pressure. Similarly, over the last decade, Geshe Kelsang Gyatso (b. 1931), another important character featuring in the present study, has also begun to associate his activities with the idea of world peace. In particular, the temples connected to his tradition, The New Kadampa Tradition, are now said to be dedicated to "world peace" (kadampa.org/en/centers/international-temples-project).

Buddhism and the environment

In June 1992, along with a 108 heads of state and 30,000 other participants, the Dalai Lama took part in the United Nations Conference on the Environment and Development, also known as Earth Summit, or Rio Summit. The conference held in Rio de Janeiro, Brazil, "marked the beginning of a continuing dialogue between the rich and poor nations over the management of the planet" (Pickering and Owen 1997 [1994]: 672). Certainly the most important conference of this kind up to then, the Earth Summit reached three major agreements:

> Agenda 21, a global plan of action to promote sustainable development; the Rio Declaration on Environment and Development, a series of principles defining the rights and responsibilities of States; and the Statement of Forest Principles, a set of principles to underpin the sustainable management of forests worldwide.
>
> (www.un.org/en/development/devagenda/sustainable.shtml)

That the Dalai Lama was invited to take part in the Earth Summit seems to be clearly related to his own activities as world peace champion. This is reflected, for example, in the address he gave on that occasion, entitled, "Universal Responsibility and the Global Environment" (www.dalailama.com/messages/environment/global-environment). One of the major topics broached by the Dalai Lama in that address had to do with the importance of demilitarization for the preservation of the environment. In his words, "Demilitarization will free great human resources for protection of the environment, relief of poverty, and sustainable human development." Significantly, through his address the Dalai Lama was able to introduce to the heads of state and tens of thousands of other participants present at the event his own vision for Tibet as a peaceful and ecological sanctuary:

I have always envisioned the future of my own country, Tibet, to be founded on this basis. Tibet would be a neutral, demilitarized sanctuary where weapons are forbidden and the people live in harmony with nature; This is not merely a dream – it is precisely the way Tibetans tried to live for over a thousand years before our Country was tragically invaded. In Tibet, wildlife was protected in accordance with Buddhist principles. In the seventeenth century, we began enacting decrees to protect the environment and so we may have been one of the first nations to have difficulty enforcing environmental regulations! However, mainly our environment was protected by our beliefs, which were instilled in us as children.

(Ibid.)

Through inserting the Tibetan cause into the agenda of environmentalism, the Dalai Lama adds one more dimension to the Tibetan fight for autonomy, while at the same time engaging in an important and highly politicized field of activity that brings together scientists, world leaders, Buddhists, and other sympathizers with this tradition concerned with environmental issues like climate change, pollution, deforestation and so forth.[16] This is, in fact, a prime dialogue zone previously opened by representatives of other Buddhist traditions.[17] Once more, it was Thich Nhat Hanh who played a seminal role in this domain. The Vietnamese monk proposed the notion of "Engaged Buddhism" in the 1950s, when he first published in a Vietnamese newspaper a series of articles about Buddhism in the realms of education, economics, politics and so forth. The efforts made by Buddhist practitioners to protect the environment are also part of this tradition of engaged Buddhism. As he explains in a talk given in Hanoi, in 2008:

Engaged Buddhism is the kind of wisdom that responds to anything that happens in the here and the now – global warming, climate change, the destruction of the ecosystem, the lack of communication, war, conflict, suicide, divorce. As a mindfulness practitioner, we have to be aware of what is going on in our body, our feelings, our emotions, and our environment.

(Nhat Hanh 2008b: 6)

Thich Nhat Hanh has published a number of books and articles on the topic of Buddhism and the environment[18] and has been a central presence in forums discussing such issues. Moreover, Thai monks have also been particularly active in this arena over the years. A particularly visible example of Thai involvement is the monastic movement to protect forests by "ordaining" trees. As anthropologist Susan Darlington explains,

Since the late 1980s a small number of monks have performed these rituals in which they consecrate a tree and the surrounding forest to bring attention to environmental problems, especially concerning the forests and the water, that make life difficult for Thai villagers, and by implication for the nation as a whole.

(Darlington 2012: 4)

The engagements between Thai monks and nature are not something new. The long involvement with environmental issues of two Thai monks, Buddhadāsa and Dhammapiṭaka, through their writings, for example, is the topic of an article by the Buddhist Studies scholar Donald Swearer (Swearer 1997: 21–44). In Japan too, where the notion of Buddha nature is sometimes extended to plants and minerals, there are many examples of interplay between Buddhism and ecology.[19]

In recent years, the Seventeenth Karmapa, Ogyen Trinley Dorje (b. 1985), has also become a major participant in the Buddhist conversation over environmental issues. In an article published in 2011, for instance, he invokes his nomad background to establish his intimate connection with wildlife in Tibet. He explains that later, when he "grew up and began studying Buddhist philosophy and teachings," he discovered a great "harmony between Buddhism and the environment movement." In his words, "The emphasis on biological diversity, including ecosystems – in particular, the understanding that animate and inanimate beings are parts of a whole – resonates very closely with Buddhism's emphasis on interdependence" (Ogyen Trinley Dorje 2011: 1094). In 2009, the Karmapa created the Khoryug association, together with the website www.khoryug.com. As the page explains, Khoryug (Tib. *khor yug*) means environment in Tibetan and is the short version of the association's name: Rangjung Khoryug Sungkyob Tsokpa. Khoryug constitutes a network of Tibetan Buddhist monasteries and nunneries that are committed "to help protect the Himalayan region from environmental degradation." On the occasion of the creation of Khoryug, the Karmapa defended, "In order to save the Himalayas and Tibet from the threats of deforestation, climate change, and pollution, we have to be full of courage and believe whole heartedly that this endeavor is winnable. The alternative is unthinkable" (www.khoryug.com/history/). Hence, just like the Dalai Lama, the Karmapa expands the commitment to Tibetan autonomy to the more general struggle connected to environmental issues. The activities of the Karmapa in this domain have the additional feature of directly engaging the monastic community connected to his school, the Karma Kagyu, in actions to preserve the environment.

As we will see in detail below, Lama Gangchen is another lama who has a strong presence in the Buddhist involvement with environmental issues. In this regard, it is noteworthy that Lama Gangchen grounded his pro-environment activities in two very different domains. First, he created a spiritual practice connected with these issues, taking the engagement between Buddhism and Ecology to yet another sphere. Second, his defense of the environment, as well as that of world peace, represents a crucial field of activity of The Lama Gangchen World Peace Foundation (LGWPF), his United Nations-affiliated nongovernmental organization. This lama's articulation of environmental issues on these two levels of activities will be a major topic in Chapter 5 of the present study.

Buddhism and the sciences

When Orgyen, the monk-protagonist of the movie *The Cup* (1999), tries to explain to two Tibetan refugees freshly arrived in India why the World Cup matches happen in the middle of the night, he soon gives up. "You are Tibetan. You would never understand!" he says with impatience. The director of the movie, the lama Dzongsar Khyentse Rinpoche, plays with the incredible fact that Tibetans believed that the Earth was flat up until the Chinese invasion. This past indifference to science and technology (in the most conventional sense of these terms) is in sharp contrast with the dialogue over science that has been established over the last few decades between western scientists and scholars, and Tibetan Buddhists.

The scientific collaboration initiated in 1979 between the Dalai Lama and the aforementioned Herbert Benson led to a research project that can be described as a landmark in the exchange between Tibetans and western scientists in the diaspora context. The Tibetan leader arranged for advanced practitioners of the so-called "Tum-mo yoga" (Tib. *gtum mo*) to be evaluated by "Dr. Benson's sophisticated equipment" (Tenzin Gyatso 1990: 210) when in meditation in hermitages in the Indian locations of Ladakh, Dharamsala and Sikkim. In his autobiography, *Freedom in Exile*, the Dalai Lama explains that the decision to collaborate with the Harvard professor was not made without hesitation. In his words:

> I knew that many Tibetans were uneasy about the idea. They felt that the practices in question should be kept confidential because they derive from secret doctrines. Against this consideration I set the possibility that the results of such an investigation might benefit not only science but also religious practitioners and could therefore be of some general benefit to humankind.
>
> (Ibid.)

Among other things, the dialogue with scientists undertaken by the Dalai Lama represented a powerful way to show the world a different facet of a tradition that, arguably more than any other Buddhist tradition, had been stigmatized as corrupt and archaic. This dialogue, moreover, can also be construed as a response to accusations of backwardness advanced by the Chinese in relation to Tibet and Tibetan Buddhism. In the chapter of *Freedom in Exile* entitled, "Magic and Mystery," for example, the Dalai Lama discusses a series of topics – ranging from oracles and rebirth to the Tibetan medical system and the Buddhist notion of non-duality between mind and matter – that in his view could directly contribute to scientific knowledge. While cautioning his readers about the possible dangers of submitting spiritual beliefs to science,[20] the Tibetan leader questions the Chinese view of Tibetans as a retrograde people:

> I am well aware, however, of the danger of tying spiritual belief to any scientific system. For whilst Buddhism continues to be relevant two and a half millennia after its inception, the absolutes of science tend to have a

relatively short life. This is not to say that I consider things like the oracle and the ability of monks to survive nights spent out in freezing conditions to be evidence of magical powers. Yet I cannot agree with our Chinese brothers and sisters, who hold that Tibetan acceptance of these phenomena is evidence of our backwardness and barbarity. Even from the most rigorous scientific viewpoint, this is not an objective attitude.

(Ibid.: 220)

The Dalai Lama's initial hesitation gave way to an increase in the frequency of these encounters with scientists, which led eventually to their institutionalization in the context of the so-called Mind and Life Institute. Initiated in the 1980s, the Mind and Life conferences are certainly the most important and perennial series of encounters between science and Buddhism. Here, the Dalai Lama once again figures in as the main Buddhist interlocutor. As Alan Wallace explains, "the Mind and Life dialogues between His Holiness the Dalai Lama and western scientists were brought to life through a collaboration between R. Adam Engle, a North American businessman, and Dr. Francisco J. Varela, a Chilean-born neuroscientist living and working in Paris" (Wallace 2003: 417). The first Mind and Life conference took place in Dharamsala, India, in 1987. This event brought together the Dalai Lama and specialists in the area of neurobiology from some of the most important research centers in the world to discuss the cognitive sciences in particular. The results of the dialogues were published under the title *Gentle Bridges: Conversations with the Dalai Lama on the Sciences of Mind* (Hayward and Varela 1992).

Since then other conferences have been organized. The discussions were frequently published as books, which were often translated into other languages. The second Mind and Life conference took place in 1989 in Newport Beach, California, and focused on neuroscience and the relationship between mind and body. The dialogue was published as *Consciousness at the Crossroads: Conversations with the Dalai Lama on Brain Science and Buddhism* (Houshmand, Livingston and Wallace 1999). In some cases, such dialogues could be seen as the scientific sequel to particular facets of the encounter between Tibetan Buddhism and the West. In the third Mind and Life conference, for example, which happened in Dharamsala, with the aforementioned Daniel Goleman as coordinator, discussions were focused on the relationships between health and emotional experience. Published under the title *Healing Emotions: Conversations with the Dalai Lama on Mindfulness, Emotions, and Health* (Goleman 1997), this and other conferences in the Mind and Life series touch upon the topic of healing, which, as we shall see in the chapters ahead, is also quite central to other lamas involved in the transmission of Tibetan Buddhism to the West. As I briefly mentioned above, for example, the topic of healing is important for Lama Gangchen, who developed it in relation to other domains, such as world peace and the environment. Furthermore, healing also occupies an important place in the practices of Lama Shakya (who would later be known as Segyu Rinpoche), yet another lama featured in this study. In his case, however, the practice of healing is directly connected to his background in Afro-Brazilian spiritualist traditions. The diverse roles of these two lamas as healers will be explored in greater depth in the chapters ahead.

Another theme that is central to the transmission of Tibetan Buddhism in the western context was the focus of the fourth encounter of the series that took place once more in Dharamsala, in 1992, with Francisco Varela as scientific coordinator. This encounter addressed the topics of sleep, dreams, and the process of dying. The dialogues of this third dialogue were published as *Sleeping, Dreaming, and Dying: An Exploration of Consciousness with the Dalai Lama* (Varela 1997). Since the publication of the *Tibetan Book of the Dead* in 1927, the Tibetan understanding of the dying process has had a privileged place in the western imaginary – something that can be discerned for example from the impact of Timothy Leary's psychedelic experiences with *The Tibetan Book of the Dead* (Leary *et al.* 1992 [1964]). The diaspora brought to the scene concrete examples of the exceptional mastery exhibited by Tibetan lamas at the moment of death. With witnesses that include western disciples, doctors and sometimes even police officers, great masters such as Dudjom Rinpoche, Lama Yeshe and Chagdud Rinpoche remained in a meditative state known as Thugdam (Tib. *thugs dam*) for several days after all their vital functions had ceased. The gap between the moment in which, according to western scientific knowledge, death occurs, and the moment in which the consciousness of these masters leaves their bodies and their mediation ceases, cannot yet be explained within the parameters of modern western medicine. It is in this "obscure" interval between life and death, and also, why not, between death and what is beyond it, that there is quite an unexpected possibility of "dialogue" between science and the tradition of Tibetan Buddhism.

It would be remiss at this juncture not to mention what is surely the best selling publication about Tibetan Buddhism to date: *The Tibetan Book of Living and Dying* by Sogyal Rinpoche (1992), which sold millions of copies and was published in more than 50 different countries. According to Sogyal Rinpoche, his goal with this book was to "explain and expand the *Tibetan Book of the Dead*, to cover not only death but life as well, and to fill out in detail the whole teaching of which the *Tibetan Book of the Dead* is only a part" (Sogyal Rinpoche 1992: 11). One of the main outcomes of *The Tibetan Book of Living and Dying* is the Spiritual Care Programme, a "non-denominational outreach programme that offers training and care in the arenas of both living and dying." As it is further explained in this organization's website, its basic orientation comes from "understandings drawn from the Buddhist tradition, particularly from *The Tibetan Book of Living and Dying* by Sogyal Rinpoche," with an approach that is nevertheless "not religious" and that "completely supports each person to draw from their own inner resources" (www.spcare.org/en/about/who-we-are). In brief, Sogyal Rinpoche's book can be seen as a way of inserting Tibetan Buddhist ideas about death and dying into the hospice care movement, which was strengthened in the 1970s by the work of pioneers such as Elizabeth Kübler-Ross and Raymond Moody, who are both referenced in the book (Sogyal Rinpoche 1992: 10).

Back to the Mind and Life, the conferences promoted by this institute have continued to take place over the years, exploring a variety of topics around which Buddhism and science are thought to converge. For instance, the new physics and cosmology were the subjects of the sixth encounter of the series that took place in Dharmasala in 1997 with Arthur Zajonc (Amherst University) as scientific coordinator. This sixth Mind and Life dialogue was published as *The New Physics and Cosmology: Dialogues with the Dalai Lama* (Zajonc 2004). In 2011, a new topic, Ecology, was included in the discussions,[21] reflecting once more a current trend in the dialogue between Buddhism and the West.

Also worth mentioning is that, despite its wide range of topics, the Mind and Life series of conferences with the Dalai Lama is clearly grounded in the cognitive sciences. As Alan Wallace comments in the preface of *Buddhism and Science*, "among all the natural sciences this [i.e., the cognitive sciences] is the field that most directly pertains to Buddhism, which holds the understanding of the mind and its relation to the rest of the world to be of paramount importance" (Wallace 2003: xv). This affinity with the cognitive sciences is directly reflected in the dynamic interchange between Buddhism and western psychotherapy that has been going on since the 1950s. The book *Zen-Buddhism and Psychoanalysis*, published in 1960 by Erich Fromm, D.T. Suzuki and Richard de Martino, was an important landmark in this domain. This book was born from the exchanges between the accomplished Japanese scholar and Zen master Daisetz T. Suzuki and western scholars in 1957, "when Erich Fromm invited Suzuki and a group of colleagues to his home in Cuernavaca, Mexico for a one-week intensive seminar on the applicability of Zen Buddhism to psychology and psychotherapy" (Bankart 2004: 54). It is not possible to discuss in the limited space of this chapter the many reasons behind the affinity between Buddhism and the so-called "sciences of the mind," as reflected in the history of the dialogue between these "two cultural institutions" (Safran 2003). For the purposes of this study, it suffices to summarily remark that such an affinity is founded upon the systematic analysis of human behavior and the mapping of the mechanisms involved in the workings of the mind, which are at the core of Buddhist doctrine and practice.

Conscious of the possibilities of dialogue about the convergence of Buddhist and psychoanalytical concepts, some lamas saw in this niche an important channel of communication with the West. This was precisely the case of Tarthang Tulku (b. 1935), a lama belonging to the Nyingma School of Tibetan Buddhism, who founded the Nyingma Institute in 1973 in response to the demands of psychologists and other mental health professionals with an interest in deepening their knowledge of Buddhism. Based in Berkeley, California, the institute has as its main purpose

to provide a new channel for integrating the teachings of Eastern and Western approaches – to bring these traditional understandings of awareness within reach of modern psychological investigation and to communicate these methods as a basis for a more meaningful approach to life.

(Tarthang Tulku 1989 [1975]: xi)

One of the Tibetan lamas who most strongly emphasized the integration of Buddhist insights with western psychology was Chögyam Trungpa Rinpoche (1939–87). Unlike many lamas active in the West during the early years of its encounter with Buddhism, Chögyam Trungpa had intensive contact with western culture from an early age. He moved to England in 1963, where at Oxford he studied "among other subjects, comparative religion and philosophy" (Trungpa 2003a [1977]: 262). In 1970, Chögyam Trungpa relocated to the United States and very rapidly gathered a large number of students around him. In 1974, the Tibetan lama founded in Boulder, Colorado the Naropa Institute, which later became Naropa University, a liberal arts college with the ambition of bringing together Buddhism and western models of secular education. As the introduction to his collected works states, "contemplative psychology was one of the areas of study from the beginning" (Gimian 2003: xxii). In a famous article entitled, "The Meeting of Buddhist and Western Psychology," Chögyam Trungpa explains the basis of his educational philosophy as the combination of theory and practice:

> In the training of a psychotherapist, theoretical and experiential training should be properly balanced. We combine these two elements in our Naropa Institute psychology program: one begins with a taste of meditation, than applies oneself to study, then experiences meditation more fully, then does more intensive study, and so forth. This kind of approach actually has an interesting effect: it enhances one's appreciation of what one is doing. The experience of one's own mind whets the appetite for further study. And the study increases one's interest in observing ones own mental process through meditation.
>
> (Trungpa 2003b [1982]: 541)[22]

Naropa University had as its basis the model of the monastic University of Nalanda, which flourished in India between the fifth and twelfth centuries. As the University's website explains, "contemporaries knew Nalanda for its joining of intellect and intuition, and for the atmosphere of mutual appreciation and respect among different contemplative traditions. This has become the ongoing inspiration for the development of Naropa University" (www.naropa.edu/about-naropa/history/roots.php).

The academic tradition of Tibetan Buddhism

In a movement that lasted from the mid-seventh century to the twelfth century, thousands of Tibetans undertook the perilous journey across the Himalayas to study in India with some of the major Buddhist masters of their times. Largely patronized by kings and powerful local lords, these intellectual "adventurers" put together the greatest work of compilation and translation of Buddhist texts still extant today – many of the texts originally written in Pali or Sanskrit that were lost with the decline of Buddhism in India, for example, are preserved only in their Tibetan versions. Hence, a remarkable intellectual effervescence marked the introduction of Buddhism into Tibet. This scholarly trend of Tibetan Buddhism represented an important avenue of contact with the West, an avenue that had been inaugurated by European travelers – religious and lay – who, in a movement in many ways analogous to what took place centuries before in Tibet, ventured to Asian countries and learned about Buddhism from renowned masters. The travel histories of the French scholar and adventurer Alexandra David-Neel constitute in this context an exemplary case. The spectacular dissemination of Tibetan Buddhism triggered by the Chinese occupation of Tibet represented a turning point in this movement. Tibetan scholars, who before had lived mostly in isolated Tibet, would become far more accessible in the diaspora.

In this new context, one of the most prominent characteristics related to the process of Tibetan Buddhism's dissemination throughout the world is the swift insertion of certain lamas into the western academic field. The styles of insertion were different in each case. We have seen, for example, how Chögyam Trungpa came to the West and founded what would become the first Buddhist university in the United States. Other lamas became professors at western universities. A very early example is Namkhai Norbu Rinpoche (b. 1938), a holder of both the Nyingma tradition of Tibetan Buddhism, and the allegedly pre-Buddhist Bön tradition. In 1960, the great orientalist Giuseppe Tucci met him in Sikkim, where the Tibetan lama had taken refuge after the Chinese invasion. Tucci invited Namkhai Norbu to work with him in his institute in Rome (Istituto Italiano per il Medio ed Estremo Oriente – IsMEO). After working there for two years, Namkhai Norbu transferred to the University of Naples, "L'Orientale," in 1965, where he became professor of Tibetan and Mongol linguistics (Batchelor 1994: 76–7).

Geshe Lhundup Sopa (1923–2014), or simply Geshe Sopa, is another paradigmatic case of a highly educated Tibetan who was absorbed by a western academic institution. Geshe Sopa went into exile in 1959 and in 1962 received the title of geshe with highest distinction (Tib. *lha rams pa*).[23] Not long after, at the request of the Dalai Lama, he moved to the United States in the company of three of his pupils. In 1967, Professor Richard Robinson, who had initiated a pioneering Buddhist studies program at the University of Wisconsin, invited Geshe Sopa to join the faculty. As the geshe writes in his autobiography, Richard Robinson "had decided that the Tibetan language was important" for the program he had created in the University of Wisconsin. "There were many texts preserved in Tibetan for which the Sanskrit text had been lost, so Robinson decided to find a traditional Tibetan scholar to teach the classical Tibetan language" (Geshe Lhundup Sopa and Donnelly 2012: 268). Eventually, Geshe Sopa would become the first Tibetan to be tenured at an American university. Together with Richard Robinson, Geshe Sopa trained many of the first generation of Buddhist scholars and translators in the United States, such as Jeffrey Hopkins, José Cabezón and John Makransky, among several others.

The graduates from Wisconsin's Buddhist studies program "filled many of the positions in Buddhist Studies that opened at American colleges and universities during the late 1960s and early 1970s" (Lopez 1998a: 159). The Tibetan diaspora played an unequivocal role in the creation of a field of studies directly pertaining to Tibetan Buddhism in North America. If the origins of Buddhist studies can be traced back to the first half of the nineteenth century, and the founding figure of Eugene Burnouf (Goméz 1995: 193; Cabezón 1995: 233), the study of Tibetan Buddhism in the academic context was established definitively only after the diaspora. The new field of Tibetan Buddhist studies was defined in large part by the personal religious commitment to the tradition of some of the field's leading figures. Such is the case, for instance, with pioneering scholars like Jeffrey Hopkins, who created at the University of Virginia the most comprehensive program of Tibetan Buddhist studies in North America; and Robert Thurman, who came to occupy the first endowed chair of Tibetan Buddhism in the United States, the Jey Tsong Khapa Chair in Indo-Tibetan Studies, at the Religion Department of Columbia University.

In *Prisoners of Shangri-la*,[24] Donald Lopez, a former student of Jeffrey Hopkins, underlines the influential role that Geshe Wangyal (1901–83), a Mongolian monk who settled in the United States in the 1950s, played at that seminal moment. In 1955, Geshe Wangyal founded the first Tibetan Buddhist monastery in the United States, the Lamaist Buddhist Monastery of America, in Freewood Acres, New Jersey (Lopez 1998a: 42). In 1963, both Robert Thurman and Jeffrey Hopkins left Harvard University to live at the Monastery under his tutelage. Geshe Wangyal accompanied Robert Thurman to India, where in 1965 the Dalai Lama himself ordained him as a Tibetan Buddhist monk. He thus became the first westerner to be ordained in this tradition. Later, "Geshe Wangyal would encourage him to return to Harvard, where he completed his B.A. and Ph.D." (ibid.: 164). Hopkins, for his part, stayed for ten years with Geshe Wangyal, and then "enrolled in the graduate program in Buddhist Studies at the University of Wisconsin, where he and Robinson established Tibet House, a place for students of Tibetan Buddhism to study with visiting refugee Tibetan lamas" (ibid.). The kind of dynamic interaction between western scholars and Tibetan lamas exemplified by the life stories of Thurman and Hopkins, and the institution of Tibet House can perhaps be construed as one of the most defining characteristics of the development of the field of Tibetan Buddhist studies in North America.

A direct and more structural fruit of the intense interaction between Tibetan lamas and western scholars can be detected in the fact that Jeffrey Hopkins initially "derived the graduate program in Buddhist Studies from the model of the Gelug monastic curriculum" (ibid.: 168). Later, especially after David Germano assumed direction of the program, it would be totally reformulated, but it is interesting to note here its "embryonic connections" with Tibetan scholarship. Outside of the universities, there are also cases of Gelug lamas who designed programs for westerners that more or less corresponded to the monastic academic curriculum. As an illustration of a center that directly followed the scholastic lines of the Gelug School, we have the Tharpa Choeling Center of Higher Tibetan Studies, founded in Switzerland in 1977 by Geshe Rabten (1921–86). It was the Dalai Lama himself who asked Geshe Rabten to teach Buddhism to westerners in Dharamsala (Batchelor 1994: 198). In 1974, at the invitation of

Anne Ansermet, who in the future would become one of his main sponsors, Geshe Rabten visited Europe for the first time. The following year, Geshe Rabten was chosen by the Dalai Lama to serve as abbot of Rikon Institute, a monastery also founded in Switzerland with the primary aim of attending to the needs of the local Tibetan community.[25] Soon, due to the great interest shown by westerners in learning more about Tibetan Buddhism, Geshe Rabten decided to create Tharpa Choeling (which was renamed Rabten Choeling after his death).

According to Gonsar Rinpoche (b. 1949), the current director of Rabten Choeling, Geshe Rabten conceived the center's curriculum specifically with westerners in mind. In his words,

> there was the necessity of a place where westerners could study Tibetan Buddhism, and in particular the Gelugpa tradition, in an authentic way, a little bit like in the way we studied in the monasteries, but it was not identical. It would be impossible to follow the same kind of studies.[26]

Besides the traditional topics of philosophical and dialectical studies, Geshe Rabten also included in the curriculum the teachings of Lamrim and Lojong, which are more directly connected to spiritual practices. Some of the greatest specialists in Tibetan Buddhist studies, such as Georges Dreyfus and Alan Wallace, were monks that went through the Tharpa Choeling program.

The study programs created by Geshe Kelsang Gyatso constitute another important case in point. In 1979, accepting an invitation from Lama Thubten Yeshe, Geshe Kelsang assumed direction of the Manjushri Institute, a center in Ulverston, England, connected to the Foundation for the Preservation of the Mahayana Tradition (FPMT).[27] Shortly thereafter, a series of conflicts emerged between Geshe Kelsang and the directorship of the FPMT, which culminated in the detachment of the Manjushri Institute from the Foundation. As we will see in detail in Chapter 4, Geshe Kelsang then went on to establish the New Kadampa Tradition and a series of study programs associated with it.

III A field in continuous reconfiguration

This brief analysis of the dynamics involved in the constitution of the Tibetan Buddhist religious field shows that a diversity of dialogue zones have been in play since the beginning of the Tibetan diaspora. It shows, furthermore, that the formation of such zones, or specialized niches of activities, was not a random, or totally novel endeavor, but followed patterns that existed before the diaspora and that were at times specific to the school or lineage to which the lamas in charge belonged. In the diaspora context, the activities of Tibetan lamas were essentially re-signified, in accordance to the cultural logics that they encountered abroad, and in light of the repertoire of traditional concepts and practices available to them.

Specialization in particular niches became in some cases the condition for lamas to have a global sphere of influence. As we will see in the chapters ahead, such has certainly been the case with Lama Gangchen Rinpoche and Geshe Kelsang Gytaso. The Tibetan diaspora, with the new dynamics and forces of influence it has brought about, has helped these lamas to expand their field of activities into new and previously unimaginable directions. In this regard, it is important to note that the cases of Lama Gangchen and Geshe Kelsang, with the global reach of their influence, do not constitute exceptions. Lamas who in Tibet had scopes of activity sometimes limited to specific localities, in general a village or a monastery bearing their name, now have responsibility over tens, and sometimes hundreds of centers scattered around the world. This state of affairs has given certain lamas a considerable degree of autonomy within the Tibetan Buddhist religious field relative to the pre-diaspora situation.

The diaspora has been advantageous for the concentration of power in the hands of the Dalai Lama, since a greater cohesion (and even a greater consistency) between Tibet's diverse and competing factions has been deemed necessary to more successfully carry on the fight for Tibetan autonomy. In this way, the political consensus around his figure has in some respects grown outside of Tibet (even if, without a country to govern, his powers acquired a different nature). In the religious field, the Dalai Lama has become to the international public the main representative of Tibetan Buddhism as whole – which was not the case in pre-occupation Tibet. In fact, traditionally the spiritual authority of the Dalai Lama lineage pertained to only one of the four main schools of Tibetan Buddhism, the Gelug School. Even though there has always been a great reverence in relation to his figure, the Dalai Lamas, in principle, tended not to interfere in the internal affairs of the other schools.[28]

The prominent role that the Dalai Lama plays in the main dialogue zones that were created in the diaspora, or better yet, his ubiquitous presence in these zones, has the effect of imbuing the internal dynamics of the transnational religious field of Tibetan Buddhism with a highly political component. It seems that the Dalai Lama became a privileged interlocutor in these domains precisely due to his political authority. Inversely, it could also be argued that his pervasive insertion in the transnational religious field and the new global role he has come to occupy have had a direct impact on the very nature of this political authority.

A public speech that the Dalai Lama gave to further explain his retirement as secular leader of the Tibetans in exile, and the consequent end of Ganden Podrang rule, beautifully illustrates this double movement, and clearly shows the lucidity of the Dalai Lama in relation to the new roles he has assumed in the diaspora context. It was March 19, 2011, just a few days after he publicly announced for the first time his decision to retire. Perhaps moved by the many phone calls he received from Tibetans in Tibet expressing their sense of worry and abandonment, the Dalai Lama detailed further the kind of role he envisioned for himself after his retirement. It is particularly apropos, then, to conclude this chapter with a lengthy excerpt from this speech:

So now is the right time to end the dual system of governance established during the fifth Dalai Lama and retain the kind of unanimity and recognition gained by the first four Dalai Lamas in the spiritual domain. Particularly, the third Dalai Lama received the honorific title of an ecumenical master with yellow hat. So like them I will continue to take spiritual responsibilities for the remaining part of my life.

Personally, I have been working for the promotion of moral values and religious harmony in the world. These are proving quite beneficial. Moreover, I receive many invitations from different schools and universities around the world. They are not asking me to come to preach on Buddhism as such, but to teach how to promote inner happiness and Buddhist science to which many people take interest and love to listen. So when the present Dalai Lama is in such a position, it would be a matter of great pride if the 400-year-old rule of Dalai Lama as both the spiritual and temporal authority gracefully comes to an end. No one else except me can decide to end something started by the fifth Dalai Lama and my decision is final.

Recently, I received telephone calls from Tibetans inside Tibet saying they are extremely worried and feel abandoned as I am retiring. There is absolutely no need to worry. After taking retirement, I will continue to lead Tibet in spiritual affairs like the first four Dalai Lamas. Like the second Dalai Lama Gedun Gyatso, who founded the Gaden Phodrang institution and led Tibet spiritually with unanimous mandate, I will also retain that kind of spiritual leadership for the rest of my life. [...]

If such a Dalai Lama with a unanimous mandate to lead spiritual affairs abdicates the political authority, it will help sustain our exile administration and make it more progressive and robust. Similarly, the international community, who support the Tibetan cause, will commend the Dalai Lama's sincerity for the complete democratization of the Tibetan polity. It will raise our prestige in the world. On the hand other, it will fully expose the falsehood and lies of the Chinese government that there is no Tibet problem except the issue of the Dalai Lama's personal rights. The Tibetan people inside Tibet should not feel discouraged because I have made this remarkable decision by taking in consideration the benefit of the Tibetan people in the long run. The Tibetan administration in exile will be more stable and progressive. Contrary to the system of the Chinese Communist's authoritarian rule in Tibet, our small community in exile has been able to establish a complete modern democratic system.

(www.dalailama.com/messages/retirement/retirement-remarks).

Notes

1 For more on the western imagination about Tibet, see Lopez (1998a), Schell (2000), Neuhaus (2012) and the article "Western Views of the Dalai Lamas" by Martin Brauen (2005b).

2 Rime was a nonsectarian movement led by Jamyang Khyentse Wangpo (1820–92), Jamgon Kongtrul Lodro Thaye (1813–89/90), and Chogyur Lingpa (1829–70), among others. These three important nineteenth-century figures traveled throughout eastern Tibet collecting oral instructions and initiations of Tibetan Buddhist traditions that

risked extinction, compiling these teachings together into collections. For an excellent summary of this movement and its seminal figures, see E. Gene Smith, *Among Tibetan Texts* (2001: 225–72).

3 For more on the activities of this particular group, see its website, www.songtsen. org/F/intro/index.php.

4 The information in this paragraph is drawn from the official website of the Tibetan government in exile, www.tibet.net.

5 The Charter can be found on the official website of the government in exile, www. tibetjustice.org/materials/tibet/tibet6.html.

6 This speech is posted on the Dalai Lama's official website, under the following address: www.dalailama.com/messages/retirement/message-to-14th-assembly.

7 The title Kalon Tripa was officially amended in September 2012 to Sikyong (Tib. *srid skyong*), rendered as "political leader" by the official page of the government in exile, (tibet.net/2012/09/20/parliament-amends-kalon-tripa-to-sikyong/). Lobsang Sangay is therefore known now as the "Sikyong."

8 For a more detailed account of the process of democratization among Tibetans in exile, see Frechette (2007).

9 In the last decades, for instance, some branches of the Catholic Church have been incentivizing the creation of Christian meditation movements, a tendency that seems to reflect, at least in part, a concern about the loss of followers to Buddhism. An example of this kind of movement is the World Community for Christian Meditation, currently under the direction of the Benedictine monk Dom Laurence Freeman.

10 For a deeper exploration of the Buddhist repertoire of ideas related to peace and non-violence, see the work cited above (Kraft 1992).

11 In his autobiography, *My Land and My People*, which was published in 1962, the Dalai Lama already associates his struggle for Tibet's independence and his own political positioning with the work of Mahatma Gandhi. In his words,

> I am a steadfast follower of the doctrine of non-violence which was first preached by Lord Buddha, whose divine wisdom is absolute and infallible, and was practised in our own time by the Indian saint and leader Mahatma Gandhi. So from the very beginning I was strongly opposed to any resort to arms as a means of regaining our freedom.
>
> (Tenzin Gyatso 1962: 6)

12 In many senses, this proposal of "autonomy" for Tibet is very close to the program created by Deng Xiaoping for Hong Kong after the British protectorate was returned to China. The so-called "One country, two systems" program was established in Hong Kong when the ex-British colony was integrated within China in July 1997. While the Dalai Lama's claims seem at first glance quite reasonable and viable, the distance that separates Hong Kong from Tibet in economic, cultural and social terms seems to point to a different reality (at least for now). First, the Chinese government has had real economic interest in not altering the social, economic and political landscapes of Hong Kong. In fact, all of China's efforts in the economic domain go in the direction of opening their economy to the world market. In this context, Hong Kong plays an essential role as one of China's financial capitals, capable of providing the necessary infrastructure for business deals with countries all over the world. Tibet, on the other hand, represents exactly the opposite portrait of Hong Kong's economical dynamism. Tibet is a remote region of China. And although Tibet is rich in natural resources, it has an underdeveloped economy with a relatively minor specialized labor force. If China's prominent position in the world market is a guarantee that the Chinese government will not implement radical changes in Hong Kong, the same condition represents in obstacle to the dream of Tibetan autonomy. On the global economic stage, dependence on China prevents many governments from protesting against the atrocities perpetrated in Tibet.

13 In January 2012, I had the opportunity to witness the official presentation to the public of *Beyond Religion* by the actor Richard Gere in a formal ceremony that took place during the event "Kalachakra for World Peace" held by the Dalai Lama in Bodhgaya.

14 In his autobiography, *Freedom in Exile*, for example, the Dalai Lama declares, "Whenever I go abroad, I try to contact as many other religious practitioners as possible, with a view to fostering inter-faith dialogue" (Tenzin Gyatso 1990: 201).

15 Also in 1973, the Dalai Lama had an encounter with Pope Paul VI, who despite not being a head of state per se, deserves also to be singled out here on account of his high-profile position in the global religio-political sphere.

16 By saying this I do not mean that the Dalai Lama is acting solely out of political concerns. On the contrary, the Tibetan leader's brilliance consists precisely in embracing causes that are important for the world and for Tibet, without ever loosing sight of his primary responsibility in relation to the Tibetan people. In this sense, I would like to distance my point of view from that of Ian Harris, who in a series of articles (Harris 1997, 1995a; 1995b; 1994; 1991) has criticized the supporters of a Buddhist environmental ethic for distorting Buddhist history and doctrinal elements in order to make them compatible with contemporary environmental ideals. In his words,

> in their praiseworthy desire to embrace such a 'high profile' cause, or to put it more negatively, in their inability to check the influence of a significant element of modern globalized discourse, Buddhist environmentalists may be guilty of a *sacrificium intellectus* very much out of line with the critical spirit that has played such a major role in Buddhism from the time of the Buddha himself down to the modern period.
>
> (Harris 1997: 378)

It is not my intention here to directly discuss the contents of Harris's well-informed articles. I feel compelled, however, to question the general impetus of his articles, which is to determine the compatibility (or lack thereof) between Buddhism and environmental issues. Is it really the role of the scholar to be normative in such a way? If followers of Buddhist traditions, be they the Dalai Lama or a western practitioner, see in the doctrine points that can be applied to the defense of the environment, is it really fair to dismiss their claims? It seems to me that the whole issue of "authenticity," when stated in the terms proposed by Harris, is mistaken. I firmly believe it is not the role of the scholar, for that matter, to decide upon what is authentic or inauthentic within a tradition. Otherwise, we risk loosing sight of the dynamism of the traditions we study.

17 For more on Buddhism and the environment, see Badiner (1990). For a detailed bibliography on the topic, see the article by Duncan Ryūken Williams in the volume *Buddhism and Ecology* (Tucker and Williams 1997).

18 For recent examples, see Nhat Hanh (2013a; 2013b; 2008a; 2008b).

19 For more on the engagement between Japanese Buddhists and the environment, see the articles by Paul O. Ingran, Steve Odin and Graham Parkes in the volume, *Buddhism and Ecology* (Tucker and Williams 1997).

20 In a recent book (2010), Donald Lopez also advises against the risks of trying to make Buddhism compatible with science. Lopez's main premise in *Buddhism and Science: A Guide for the Perplexed* is that in order for such compatibility to be established, "Buddhism must be severely restricted, eliminating much of what has been deemed essential, whatever that might be, to the exalted monks and ordinary laypeople who have gone for refuge to the Buddha over the course of more than two thousand years" (Lopez 2010: xiii). However, it is not very clear to me exactly what Lopez really has in mind when he talks about making Buddhism compatible with science. How exactly would a dialogue between Buddhism and science concretely restrict Buddhism as a religious tradition? Or better yet, having in mind the intensification of this dialogue over the last few decades, what evidence do we have that this sort of restriction is

happening? Is it really possible, for example, that the findings of Herbert Benson's research on Tum-mo yoga would transform this spiritual practice solely into "a technique for raising one's body temperature" (ibid.: 212), as Lopez suggests? In fact, aside from vague conjectures, Lopez does not offer any concrete example of "restrictions" to Buddhism due to its engagements with the scientific field. His book, moreover, is unjustifiably selective, almost completely ignoring the recent developments in the dialogue between Buddhism and science promoted by the Dalai Lama, and the well-established intellectual exchanges between Buddhism and the cognitive sciences. Perhaps too eager to fit his work into the postcolonial trend sweeping across the American academy over the last two decades, Lopez grounds his discussion in the assertion that "for more than 150 years, the claims for the compatibility of Buddhism and Science have remained remarkably similar, both in their content and in their rhetorical form" (ibid.: xii). Despite a few good insights, then, Lopez's publication suffers from the lack of a deeper intellectual engagement with the subject matter that would take into account the maturation of the dialogue between Buddhism and science, especially over the last few decades.

21 The video of this conference can be watched on the following Internet address: www. mindandlife.org/dialogues/past-conferences/ml23/.

22 For more on Chögyam Trungpa Rinpoche's approach to the relationship between Buddhism and western psychology, see his collection of writings on the topic, *The Sanity We Are Born With: A Buddhist Approach to Psychology* (Trungpa 2005).

23 The information about Geshe Sopa was mainly obtained from the website of Deer Park Buddhist Center (www.deerparkcenter.org/NewFiles/sopa.html), a center this lama founded in 1975, and from the Foundation for the Preservation of the Mahayana Tradition (FPMT)'s page (fpmt.org/teachers/lineage-lamas/sopa/). For more on this lama's life, see his autobiography (Geshe Lhundup Sopa and Donnelly 2012).

24 For an inclusive survey of the formation of the "field of Tibetan Buddhist studies" in the United States, see Chapter 6 of *Prisoners of Shangri-la* (Lopez 1998a).

25 The connection between Switzerland and Tibet is also the connection between the Alps and the Himalayas. The two Swiss brothers, Henry and Jacques Kuhn, who helped Tibetans relocate in their country, were alpinists and it was during a trip to Nepal that they became aware of the Tibetan case. In the words of Jacques Kuhn,

> A Swiss man who lived in Nepal and was doing research for a Swiss university and for the UN was there when Tibetan refugees came over the Himalayas by tens of thousands. And he was concerned because Nepal was very poor. He went to the king first – he knew him very well, because he had had many conferences with him. And he said: "We have to do everything that we can to help those Tibetans by sending most of them further to India, because the living standards are better in India than in Nepal." Then he flew over to Switzerland [...] He made a proposal to the Swiss government to take refugees into Switzerland to help Nepal and that was accepted. Already in 1961, thousands of Tibetans could come into Switzerland. That is a funny thing that our small country here, in the center of Europe, has 2,500 Tibetans, this is more than [the number of Tibetans in] Europe altogether. [...] And so we have a factory down here, and by that time my brother and me were ruling the factory. So we decided to help, and we built 50 apartments. [...] So we got the first group in 1963: 27 Tibetans. For two years everything went well, but then we realized that things were not going the way we would like them to go. The younger generation was fascinated with the new way of life: electricity, the water coming out in the house, cars and motorcycles. The old generation, on its turn, was very conservative, and it is like that up to now. There was a kind of separation within the families. We did not like that at all. The younger generation worked eight hours a day, but afterwards they did not know what to do; they did not have many contacts, so they drank and did things

like that. We saw very ugly pictures and we were afraid. My brother and myself, because we have invited them in a way to our place, we felt responsible for them.

(Personal communication, 2002)

They decided then to ask for an audience with the Dalai Lama; the Rikon Institute was born from this encounter.

26 Personal communication, 2002.

27 In 1975, Lama Thubten Yeshe (1935–84), one of the most active lamas in the West, created the FPMT with the goal of connecting all the centers founded by his disciples around the world.

28 There are, of course, many exceptions to this "rule." One could cite here, for example, the case of the enthronement of the current Sakya Trinzin, the head of the Sakya School of Tibetan Buddhism. Since the two families that alternate in providing a successor for this role were in dispute, the Dalai Lama was called to intervene and his decision was final (Sakya and Emery 1990: 109–21). Moreover, Tibetan history is full of accounts of the Ganden Podrang government forcibly transforming other sects' monasteries into Gelug institutions (*see* for instance Shakabpa 2010: 353). Despite the exceptions listed here (and many others besides), it seems safe enough to assume that the consensus around the figure of the Dalai Lama grew in the extreme situation of the diaspora. Finally, the controversy around the selection of the new Karmapa and the fact that the Dalai Lama played in the diaspora a decisive role in tipping the balance to the side of the so-called "Tai Situ Karmapa," Ogyen Trinley Dorje (b. 1985), in detriment of the "Shamar Karmapa," Trinley Thaye Dorje (b. 1983), could arguably be seen as an illustration of the expansion of the scope of the Dalai Lama's influence. For more on this controversy, see the statement given by anthropologist Geoffrey Samuel to the High Court of New Zealand, submitted as part of a court case: www.scribd.com/doc/138857011/Affirm-Geoffrey-Samuel.

Part III
Rebirth

4   A confluence of spiritual universes[1]

You are a physician skilled in healing,
Who dispenses the elixir of happiness.
Through the path of the previous victorious ones, you eradicate all illnesses of
*   beings,*
The lingering symptoms of false belief, affliction, and ignorance that has
*   accumulated!*
For this reason, you are the sublime physician and guide who courses upon the
*   earth.*

Lalitavistara sūtra[2]

I Healing

One of the most common analogies employed in Buddhism describes the Dharma as a powerful medicine, which the Buddha, a skilled physician, dispenses to cure sentient beings of their ailments, ignorance and afflictions. This analogy unfolds on many levels. In Mahayana Buddhist texts the notion of "healing" is understood from three different points of view: (1) illness is cured through healing agents (herbs and food), surgery and other physical methods; (2) there are spiritual causes and cures of diseases; and (3) curing illness is a metaphor for spiritual growth, in which the Buddha is seen as the Supreme Physician (Birnbaum 1989: 3). Often the various layers of meaning with which the notion of healing can be apprehended in Buddhism are superimposed and inextricable. This seems to be particularly true with regard to Tibetan Buddhism, which incorporated medicinal practices from India and elsewhere[3] and developed them to a considerable extent along indigenous lines.

In this vein, Tibetan lamas are frequently seen by their disciples as doctors. And indeed, sometimes they are actual doctors. This is the case of Lama Gangchen, who at the age of 13 started to study and practice medicine and related subjects such as anatomy, physiology and the composition and interaction of various medicinal substances (Gangchen 2001 [1991]: 15).[4] Recognized as coming from an incarnation line of healing lamas, Lama Gangchen surpassed his role as a formal doctor. According to his biography, he performed so-called miraculous cures from early on. Even the tight monitoring of the

Chinese, who forced him to work in the fields from the 1960s onwards, did not stop him from curing people. This resulted in him spending two years doing forced labor in prison, an exhausting physical effort that left him seriously ill. It became evident that it would be wise for him to flee Tibet.

During his exile in India he completed his education in the Gelug monastic curriculum, where the Dalai Lama and his two main tutors, Ling Rinpoche (1903–1983) and the aforementioned Trijang Rinpoche (c.f. Chapter 1), were his preceptors. Meanwhile, he continued to heal people. His fame crossed borders and in the 1970s the king of Sikkim "called him to come and cure his mother who was suffering from an illness in the eyes considered by doctors to be incurable" (ibid.: 17). According to his biography, Lama Gangchen managed once again to perform an improbable cure.

Naturally, therefore, when he first arrived in the West in 1981, more specifically to the Greek island of Lesbos, with only a few words of English, his main form of communication was the gift of healing. He founded his first center in the West, Karuna Choetsok, on the island of Lesbos with the help of an Italian woman he had cured of cancer. In 1983, he was once again invited by other Italians to return to Europe for another "healing tour." In 1985 he received a more binding invitation: a wealthy "sponsor of the Dharma" was his host in the Italian city of Gubbio, not far from Assisi, where he lived for about two years.

This is when he met Claudio Cipullo, an Italian who was then just over 30 years old and had been a monk in the Tibetan Buddhist tradition for over ten years. He was a direct disciple of Lama Yeshe (1935–84), but had also studied Buddhist philosophy and tantra at the Tharpa Choeling Center of Higher Tibetan Studies, Geshe Rabten's institution in Switzerland. Claudio met Lama Gangchen just before Lama Yeshe died. He recalls that after the death of his master, it was natural for him to become closer to Lama Gangchen: "I started working as a translator for him from Tibetan to Italian, English, French, Spanish and Portuguese. For five years, from 1985 to 1990, I went round the world with Gangchen Rinpoche." They visited countries where Lama Gangchen had opened centers and on those journeys new centers were established. Individual cures were the seeds for the building of new public spaces through which Lama Gangchen would create a network of international disciples. In Brazil it was a similar story. One of the first Lama Gangchen centers, Shi De Choe Tsog Dharma Center, was inaugurated in 1987. Isabel Villares Lenz Cesar, the center's founder, said that people initially contacted the center in search of a cure.

I don't know how, but a journalist from the newspaper *Folha* [*de S. Paulo*] discovered that he [Lama Gangchen] was coming and pestered me for more information. The fact is that the news that Rinpoche was coming ended up on the front page of the *Folha*. There were more than 500 people at the conference that Rinpoche gave. And every single day more than one hundred people would turn up at my house, where he was staying, all hoping to be cured [...]. I thought to myself "Jesus Christ has come down here and is performing miracles." I saw that by blowing and lightly spitting he cured many people. There was a girl that arrived with a tumor on her groin that was very swollen; she couldn't even sit down. She was really desperate as she was allergic to anesthetic and could not have an operation. Rinpoche treated her and a week later she came back with a bunch of flowers to thank him and said that the tumor was growing smaller day-by-day.

Lama Gangchen was different from many other lamas, such as Lama Yeshe and Lama Zopa, who had already been active in the West for some time. He did not teach very much. In fact, he hardly ever spoke. His older disciples relate that he only transmitted one mantra, the Buddha Shakymuni mantra: "Om Muni Muni Shakya Muni Maha Muniye Soha." Lama Gangchen explained that this was a healing mantra and he advised his disciples that its recitation should be accompanied by visualizations in which negative emotions such as jealousy, anger and envy, and negativities in the body, speech and mind are imagined as a black light that we expel when we breathe out.[5]

Mônica Benvenuti, his first Brazilian pupil, tells that Lama Gangchen arrived in the West at a time of transition, as some important lamas such as Lama Yeshe and Geshe Rabten had recently died. According to Mônica, Lama Gangchen "was the right lama for his times. There had been a lot of theory, a lot of teaching here and there. Rinpoche simply put into practice, into action, the famous Dharma." Lama Gangchen's style, geared towards practice, often translated into concrete changes in the lives of his pupils. Mônica herself made very significant decisions in her life by following Lama Gangchen's practical advice. At the beginning of the 1990s, for example, he suggested that she move to Milan, where, thanks to the donation of a building by an Italian disciple, Franco Ceccarelli, the first dharma center in Italy was established, Kunpen Lama Gangchen. For some years Mônica and other disciples lived with Lama Gangchen in the center itself. When Lama Gangchen moved to his new center in the Lake Maggiore region, an hour and a half away from Milan, Mônica was one of the first to buy an apartment in the area. In 2002, she divided her life between Milan, where she lived with her husband and worked in the Kunpen Lama Gangchen shop selling Dharma articles, and the Albagnano Healing Meditation Center, where she spent the weekends.[6]

José-María Arocena, a Spanish disciple who spent a large part of his time in Albagnano, told me a similar story of transformation, which involved personal healing as a result of his meeting with Lama Gangchen:

> This was how I met Lama Gangchen; there was a sort of energetic contact, because he did not offer teachings, only pills, the Shakyamuni mantra and the four limitless thoughts.[7] And, in group sessions, the White Tara[8] practice. "The 'pujas'[9] can fix it," he used to say. With time I came to understand why he said this. I did not believe that it was something magical. With Lama Gangchen, we would get on a bus and he would always start the puja. We would get into a car and he would start the puja. I started to connect with a type of energy I did not understand. For me, it was something new,

for what had always attracted me to Buddhism was mental control, the taming of the mind, controlling phenomena, learning how to control emotions, but I had not experienced this magical aspect until I got to know Lama Gangchen.

José-María met Lama Gangchen in 1989, in Spain, when he was recovering from some emotional problems caused by a relationship that had ended badly. He relates how he decided to help the Lama with his consultations:

> I was doing nothing out of the ordinary. I stayed outside and explained to those that went in and out how they had to take their medicine. But I noticed that they all came out with a radiant smile. They all went in weighed down by illness and then they came out quite changed.

José-María says that when he was helping Lama Gangchen he used to get up at six in the morning and get home after 11 in the evening.

> It was like this for a whole week, but I felt an incredible energy. But the most impressive thing was when I saw that woman [*his ex-girlfriend*] on one of those days, it was as if everything had disappeared, all the affection I had for her, I had changed!

He realized that he was cured of his emotional problems. After this experience, José-María, despite his physical limitations – about ten years earlier, when he was only 26 years old, a car accident had left him paralyzed from the waist down – decided to follow Lama Gangchen in his travels and assist him in his activities.

This story of Lama Gangchen's meeting with José-María provides us with considerable insight into the lama's insertion in the West. José María perceived his contact with Lama Gangchen as a new type of healing. Here we are not just talking about physical illnesses, but more specifically, ailments of a purely emotional nature. Lama Gangchen's treatment of emotional problems comes close to the traditional Buddhist idea of curing illness as a metaphor for teaching the path towards enlightenment. This emotional aspect, when combined with his role as physical healer, reveals how Lama Gangchen's initial encounters with his disciples were often structured. As Gabriella Ferro, a young (though longstanding) Italian pupil tells us: "he started as a healing lama, he visited his patients, blessed and cured them. Through the healing of the body many embarked on a spiritual cure. Many of his disciples had once been his patients."

In José-María's pilgrimages in the company of Lama Gangchen – he travelled with the lama for several months across Europe and later visited Asian countries such as Indonesia and Nepal – this pupil began to recognize another of Lama Gangchen's peculiarities: "travelling becomes a type of teaching in itself" (and also a form of healing). Much like the case of José-María, a number of other disciples gradually gathered around Lama Gangchen, particularly in his center in

Milan, and started to visit with the lama some important places of pilgrimage and countries where the lama had founded dharma centers. His first long trip took place in 1987, when Lama Gangchen returned to Tibet for the first time since his departure. Though the trip was improvised (often they did not know where they would spend the night), some important seeds were sown, such as the future reconstruction of Gangchen Monastery, which had been destroyed during the Cultural Revolution. This trip also presented the opportunity for an ever-growing group of disciples to return to Tibet each year.

Gabriella, who had been living and travelling with Lama Gangchen since the beginning of the 1990s, when she was only 21 years old, believes that there are two aspects to travelling as a form of practice:

> First of all, it is the practice of accumulating merit, since we always go to places of pilgrimage, such as Borobudur, Tibet or Nepal. He realized that people were interested in Buddhism and decided to take them directly to these places.

Gabriella emphasizes the possibility of being blessed, and consequently, even healed, during a visit to a sacred place.

> Very often I noticed the difference in a person at the beginning and the end of a trip. I remember a particular occasion when a young English man came to Borobudur. They had given him two months to live. He had had a brain operation; he had a tumor. He is still alive, and after this trip to Borobudur [1998] he had an incredible recovery. Of course it wasn't only the trip, there were a number of other factors, even karmic and mental predispositions. In any case, going to sacred places is something that Buddhists – and even Christians – have always done.

Another of his disciples, the artist Leonardo Ceglie, or Duccio as he is known, who has lived with him since the mid-1980s – first in Milan and then in Albagnano – sees the pilgrimages as the core of the lama's "way of teaching." "Instead of explaining how life is in Indonesia and the differences between one particular place and another, he takes you there and a sort of knowledge derives from this experience." He continues:

> You start to think about how we live in the world. You understand that it is different there, because it is hotter or it is colder. You start to think about things in a different way, you open your mind. You learn that you can sleep on the street or in a hotel costing US$400. In short, you understand where the differences lie or perhaps that there are no differences. In other words, you *become another person*. When the historic Buddha, for example, was around, he used to walk through the forest with his disciples, from city to city. He covered a very large area. Today Rinpoche uses an airplane. It is very easy. It becomes easier to learn.

In Duccio's terms, these trips represent, among other things, a direct form of getting in touch with the "other," and as a result, the development of the capacity to see one's own identity in more relative terms. It would seem that this disciple saw in this capacity a certain affinity with the Buddhist teaching of selflessness, i.e., the absence of any inherently permanent, unitary and independent nature in all things.

It is worth pointing out another aspect raised by Gabriella with regard to these trips. She claims that Lama Gangchen is able to "energetically revitalize" the places he visits: "For example, in China there are so many sacred places, though many have been 'abandoned' for a very long time. When he goes to these places, he revitalizes them." The significance of these trips, which include the characteristics described above, and their relationship with Lama Gangchen's understanding of healing would only become clear to his disciples later, during what could be called the second phase of his stay in the West.

Body, speech and mind

Lama Gangchen often says that during the first ten years of his stay in the West he gave his "body" to his disciples, in the next ten years he gave his "speech" and finally, during the next ten years, he will give his "mind." The allusion here is to the body, speech and mind of Buddha, his three enlightened aspects, or even the three bodies of Buddha: *nirmanakaya*, *sambhogakaya* and *dharmakaya*.[10] This is a fundamental symbolic representation in Mahayana and tantric (Vajrayana) Buddhism. In the case of Lama Gangchen, his disciples understand this "offering of the body" as the practice of miraculously curing illnesses, especially those of a physical nature. Gradually, Lama Gangchen abandoned this more direct practice to stress other aspects of the notion of healing. In fact, in many ways, his gift would be "expanded," leading to new and unexpected developments.

After almost ten years of few utterances, Lama Gangchen started to transmit more complex teachings to his pupils. His first book, *Self-Healing I*, was originally published in Brazil in 1991. It was the transcription of a workshop, which Lama Gangchen conducted in the Shi De Choe Tsog Dharma Center in April 1990. In the book, the idea of self-healing, central to all his teaching, is expressed in written form for the first time. Along general lines, Lama Gangchen identifies the causes of our diseases in terms of internal factors, thus pointing to the possibility of cure through self-transformation. The way in which this notion of self-healing is presented is geared for a contemporary audience. Lama Gangchen uses practical examples, such as addiction caused by cigarettes, alcohol or coffee, to develop his theory about our "internal enemies and friends." He explains in simple and direct language our relationship with cigarettes:

> In our mind, we will always think of cigarettes as our friends, we think that they help us. This happens because our mind is very close to this object. We think: "Ah, a friend must be very close and an enemy must be far away."

For example, when we buy a packet of cigarettes, we place them close to our bodies, often inside a pocket, near our heart; if it were possible, we would make a hole and place them inside our heart.

(Gangchen 2001 [1991]: 47)

It is important to point out, however, that while Lama Gangchen uses examples taken directly from daily life in the West, his proposed method of "internal healing" is firmly rooted in more traditional teachings – a balance between the "modern" and the "traditional," something which the Tibetan lama, without doubt, has always sought. When he first started expressing his teachings in words, it was obvious that he was concerned with ensuring that Buddhist methods were presented according to parameters that were easy to understand for the "modern" public with which he was now in contact. It was necessary to "teach our mind" that cigarettes were harmful, that they were our real enemy. It was necessary to overcome this "negative mental habit" and listen to our bodies.

When we suck on a cigarette we feel more energy, but then we start to cough. This tells us that our body is suffering. Coughing is a reaction to the harm we are causing, as if our bodies were saying: "This is harming me, this is harming me".

(Ibid.: 12)

This shows that for Lama Gangchen the different levels of healing as they are understood within Buddhism cannot be separated from one another. In fact, as we will see, we can "read" the development of Lama Gangchen's activities in the West in terms of the growing transparency of this inextricability. In any case, what we can deduce from Lama Gangchen's work is that healing is not something that comes from outside: "taming of the mind," one of the most fundamental goals of Buddhist practice, can lead not only to our "definitive healing," or enlightenment, but also to the cure of physical (and mental) diseases.

The publication of another book, *Self-Healing II*, in 1993 – first in Brazil and subsequently in Europe, both in English and Italian – represents an important milestone in the history of the insertion of Lama Gangchen in the West. In this book, the idea of "self-healing," which up to that point had been dealt with in general terms, takes on new and more specific meanings. In *Self-Healing II*, "Ngalso tantric self-healing" is presented for the first time. It is a spiritual practice which brings together western melodies, mantras, mudras, visualization and concentration on internal chakras, the aim being to "help us realise and heal the subtle energies of body and mind, as well as teaching us how to use these energies in the right way" (Gangchen 1997 [1993]: 23).

This is undoubtedly an innovative tantric ritual. While it is certainly true that its principles are strongly rooted in traditional tantric knowledge, this knowledge was "distilled" into a new format so that the final result was different, at least in appearance, from previous Tibetan Buddhist practices of Lama Gangchen's tradition.[11] It cannot be over-emphasized what the creation of this new Tibetan

Buddhist practice signified. Lama Gangchen did not want to break with his gurus, or with the tradition to which he belonged,[12] the Gelug tradition. However, by formulating a ritual that was not only new – this would have been relatively common – but innovative in its format and general conception, as well as being for the benefit of western people, he was moving towards giving his spiritual activities a certain autonomy within the Tibetan Buddhist network. To be sure, the value of his "tantric self-healing" was corroborated by representatives of the Gelug School, but he circulated it only among his followers, outside more traditional Gelug circuits.

If Lama Gangchen was gradually declaring some sort of independence in relation to the traditionalism of his original school, he was also extending its range of activities in the West. Thus, perhaps one of the most important aspects of *Self-Healing II* was a certain missionary spirit with which he presented his spiritual activity. Lama Gangchen called himself and other pioneering lamas active in the West "Lama Marco Polos." As he says: "Marco Polo was the pioneer who brought eastern culture to the west in the thirteenth century – now 'Lama Marco Polos' are giving us the messages of Lord Buddha's healing methods, the Five Supreme Healers and the Shambala Kingdom" (ibid.: 41).

Shambhala

This missionary spirit is directly expressed in the structure of Lama Gangchen's "tantric self-healing." This practice was formulated primarily in relation to a prophesy which predicts that in around 300 years there will be a battle between enlightened warriors of a mythical kingdom called Shambhala and the materialist forces which will then dominate the planet. According to the vast literature related to the Kalachakra tantric system,[13] the kingdom of Shambhala exists in the world but is hidden behind an invisible barrier. In Shambhala, "enlightened kings" oversee the most secret Buddhist teachings, preserving them for the moment when "all truth in the outside world is lost in the war and the lust for power and wealth" (Bernbaum 2001 [1980]: 4). This is the time when, according to the prophecy, the future king of Shambhala will command his army of enlightened warriors against the forces of evil. Victory will bring about a "golden age" for humanity and the world will finally be transformed into "a place of peace and plenty" (ibid.).

Lama Gangchen, therefore, urges his disciples to prepare themselves for the "ultimate Shambala war." In his words:

> The ultimate Shambhala war can be understood as the final "healing crisis" of our world. The present rise of pure spiritual and life energy, can be understood as the initial stages of self-healing for the severely unbalanced energies and elements of our world, our society and our self. We must relax these dependently arising sufferings by healing our outer, inner and secret worlds on the gross, subtle and very subtle levels.
>
> (Gangchen 1997 [1993]: 37)

It is no exaggeration to say that Lama Gangchen has been organizing, in many senses, his spiritual practice and the activities in his dharma centers on the basis of preparing his disciples and adepts for this confrontation, which, as his books explain, should be understood on different levels. Lama Gangchen particularly stresses the allegorical nature of the Shambhala war, describing it as a battle between negative and positive forces on the so-called "outer, inner and secret levels." He states:

> The outer Shambala war, the warlords and army, is an allegory for the inner and secret Shambala wars, through which we can transcend our negative emotions and attitudes. It symbolises the strengthening of our inner self-healing power and the development of our inner Rigden Guru, our enlightened consciousness. The warriors symbolize the wisdom with which we need to slay the enemies of our 84,000 ignorances, negative minds, mental poisons, egoism and other disturbed and distorted states of consciousness.
>
> (Ibid.: 38)

The "inner enemies" Lama Gangchen talks about in *Self-Healing I* are dealt with more "technically" here, expressed in Buddhist terminology. Buddhism identifies 84,000 types of mental obscurations, which emanate from five primary afflictions: lack of knowledge, attachment, anger, pride and envy. Lama Gangchen identifies these as "our worst enemies" and warns that all suffering emanates from them, including diseases, wars, disasters, hunger and so on. Thus, gradually the Tibetan lama is building the idea that not only do we have the ability to change our lives, but also the external conditions that surround us. In this way, Lama Gangchen presents the Shambhala war as the final opportunity for healing, not only of "our minds and bodies," but also society, the environment, the planet and even the cosmos itself.

Underlying Lama Gangchen's vision is the idea of the interlinking of macrocosm and microcosm, a notion that would be further refined in his future publications and would gain new meanings through his activities in the West. The Tibetan lama bases himself on the *Kalachakra Tantra* to develop the notion that the universe and our bodies are directly related. In his book *Making Peace with the Environment*, first published in Italy in 1995, Lama Gangchen develops this idea in greater detail. He explains in this book that according to the *Kalachakra Tantra* we have in our bodies and minds the same elements and energies that are found in the outer environment. His "self-healing of the environment" practice is based on the idea that by working with the elements and energies in our internal environment on an energetic level it is possible to positively influence the elements and energies of the outer environment. As Lama Gangchen explains further:

> Inside our body we have the five elements of space, wind, fire, water and earth as well as consciousness. These elements and consciousness are also to be found in the outer world. In this book I explain how to work on the

subtle energy streams or the "winds" of the elements by using concentration, mudras, visualizations and mantric keys. In this way we can unblock and purify the elemental energies of: EH the space element, LAM the earth element, YAM the wind element, BAM the water element and RAM the fire element. Purifying the subtle flow of energies in our inner environment (the body) and the outer environment (the universe) increases the health of our body, purifies the five consciousnesses, heals the environment, and cosmos and many other negative social manifestations of elemental imbalance.

(Gangchen 1996: 27–8)

The same idea expressed in the practice of "tantric self-healing," the integration of micro and macrocosms, is directly applied here to the outer environment in order to "heal" and purify it through tantric ritual. The notion of healing is now not only applied to the universe as a whole, but more significantly, this wider understanding becomes the only possible alternative. In fact, our health, Lama Gangchen says, is directly linked to the outer environment. According to the lama, in order to heal ourselves we need to heal the universe.[14] In a presentation entitled "The importance of the Amazon in Healing the Inner and Outer Environment," which he gave in São Paulo in 2001, Lama Gangchen clearly expressed this idea. According to the lama, we should not consider the environmental question as merely a "world problem," external to ourselves.

In fact, the environment is totally linked to our health, since nowadays medicine cannot fully cure us. Doctors are doing their best but there are so many new illnesses emerging that they do not know how to help. They learn at university that this or that disease can be treated with a particular medication, but what is happening today is totally disorientating. Medicine is not working; it does not provide the answers. A doctor cannot get a picture using medical examinations to provide advice on how to treat a particular disease. What they do not understand is the relationship between causes and conditions. This is very difficult for them. So, why do we become ill? Because our environment is polluted, our day-to-day lives are turned upside down; everything is different. Our bodies, our minds and our emotions, everything is different.

Furthermore, according to Lama Gangchen, the whole Earth is intoxicated, full of poison, and this ends up affecting us both collectively and individually. It is therefore necessary to become aware that our food comes from the Earth and that this food is becoming increasingly intoxicated because we pollute the soil we cultivate. "This food," he claims, "satisfies our hunger to a point, but it is actually poisoning us." In his opinion, our illnesses are, in most cases, "side effects" of the toxic chemicals we are ingesting. It is interesting to note that as well as proposing a spiritual practice to "heal the environment," Lama Gangchen suggests here (and in other places, as we will see later) that an effort should be made to bring about a collective awareness of the problems of the world, an educational project or "non-formal education," as he calls it. This project, in a way, has become the background for all of Lama Gangchen activities, and has gone much further than just a question of environmental or personal health, encompassing life as a whole.

As José-María, who works with Lama Gangchen in non-formal educational projects in various places around the world, particularly in Europe, explains:

> Non-formal education has to start even before birth, when a woman is pregnant, that is, the relationship between the woman and her fetus, and the husband and his wife and child that is about to be born. It is necessary to establish a very special relationship with the being that is about to be born. Otherwise, the fetus is born scared and embodies all this fear. The first years of a child's upbringing are also important. How do we have a relationship with children without violence, without aggression? When they become adolescents, is there a type of education to control certain emotions, for example, the passion a fifteen-year-old boy feels? How do we work with and control these emotions? When someone is ill, how do we educate him or her to deal with illness, to live with illness? When someone dear to us passes away, how do we deal with the subject of death? This is non-formal education. We have to nurture this in order to arrive at a blueprint on how to live better.

In fact, we can already detect this same zeal to nurture a "non-formal education" in *Self-Healing I* when Lama Gangchen warns of the problems (and "false friendship") with smoking, coffee and alcohol. From this we can deduce that the notion of the need in the world today for a type of education that is not acquired at university, or at any other conventional teaching establishment, derives from Lama Gangchen's observations of the western way of life and his attempt to put Buddhist teachings into practice there. One of Lama Gangchen's main concerns, therefore, is the creation of spaces where "information," as he puts it, can be transmitted. Spiritual practice certainly represents a way of attaining this type of knowledge. Lama Gangchen, however, would not limit the reach of his activities to his groups of disciples. Rather, he would extend these to other areas not necessarily related to the religious sphere.

A movement toward institutionalization

Right from the beginning, Lama Gangchen's activities in the West were extremely diversified, encompassing many areas. When in 1992 the lama founded Lama Gangchen World Peace Foundation (LGWPF),[15] a non-governmental organization that would bring together all of his activities, his students saw this as a formalization of the humanitarian work he had already been engaged in for some years. As his English student Sharon Dawson comments with respect to Help in Action, the humanitarian branch of LGWPF created at the same time as the Foundation:

I would like to think that Help in Action started a long time ago, when Lama Gangchen was still living in India. Older Tibetans say that Lama Gangchen is a pure lama, not only because he is pure [in the spiritual sense], but because he is the only lama that would go to people's houses with presents, such as a bag of rice – generally when a lama visits you, you are the one that has to offer him something.

In her apartment – which also serves as the headquarters of Help in Action and Peace Publications, the publishing house of the Lama Gangchen group – Sharon, who also works as a volunteer with Help in Action, describes how Lama Gangchen used to borrow money to help people and then borrow more money to pay for the loans he had taken out. Help in Action, she claims, started in this way with only two families. In 2002, financial assistance was provided to more than 2,000 families.

Help in Action assists Tibetan, Indian and Nepalese families in their countries of origin in areas such as health, education and infrastructure. The organization receives donations, and volunteers, mainly Lama Gangchen's pupils, carry out the work. In 1999, for example, Lama Gangchen travelled with 50 people from the West to work on the reconstruction of his monastery in the small village that bears his name. Around US$300,000 was raised for the Gangchen Village Project, which also involved the creation of health and education services throughout the area. Through LGWPF, Lama Gangchen also took Tibetan monks to Europe. They went on tours constructing sand mandalas and raising funds for their respective monasteries. In Kathmandu, as well as directly helping some families through a system of "long-distance" adoption, Help in Action was instrumental in the establishment of a health center, the Healing Center, where Lama Gangchen implemented an inverse approach to the one he had adopted in the West. In the words of Isthar Adler, a Swiss woman who represents LGWPF on behalf of Lama Gangchen at the UN:

We provide a sort of exchange, offering western doctors the opportunity to spend time in Asia delivering health provision to the local population while learning from them about the types of problems they have. Of course, these doctors decided to go to Nepal as they were attracted by this culture; they could have gone to Africa, for example. They will seek to learn more about the local culture, about local medicine. Thus, we have created a space where it is possible to also learn about the natural medicine practiced in the Himalayas.

The involvement of his disciples (and also sympathizers) in this type of volunteer work and the funding that it requires can, and in many senses should, be understood within the context of "non-formal education" as advocated by Lama Gangchen. Through humanitarian assistance, people from the West come into contact with realities very different from their own, thus acquiring a more global vision of the world and its problems – a type of learning that, as we have seen, was also the objective of the lama's pilgrimage trips. In spiritual practice, in his humanitarian aid work and in his "spiritual tourism" trips, as he likes to call them, Lama Gangchen developed a network, connecting people around the world with the different facets of his activities. The notion of interdependence between all phenomena, so central to Buddhism, is what lies behind his wider range of activities and his conception of non-formal education. Thus, with the idea of "world peace" he finds the (almost natural) confluence of his aspirations. This becomes a central theme and, in a way, it is the ultimate meaning of the type of spiritual search he is proposing. As he usually says, "interior peace is the best basis for world peace." These notions are encapsulated in the LGWPF's objectives:

> The principal proposed aims of the foundation are to support the development of World Peace by creating the conditions for a real inner peace educational system at all levels, and by promoting a concrete cultural, spiritual and material exchange between East and West. In essence, this also includes the promotion of dialogue between science and religion, a necessary condition for real human growth, as well as a "reconciliation of spirituality with economics and politics", that is a "reconciliation between the material and the non-material world".
>
> (www.lgpt.net/Foundation/foundation_intro.htm)

The affiliation of LGWPF with the United Nations in 1995 represents the formal acknowledgment of his efforts to establish the foundations for his spiritual practice, and his activities in general, where the local and the global, the micro and the macro are always in dialogue. According to Isthar Adler,

> Lama Gangchen has always said that he wasn't here to attain a limited peace, but to contribute to world peace. "It won't work," he says, "unless there is peace everywhere." It follows that the UN is the perfect place for him.

The opportunity to become affiliated with the UN occurred during the organization's Jubilee celebrations. Lama Gangchen was invited to participate in the festivities and he used the occasion to propose the creation of a permanent spiritual forum that could advise on matters related to world peace, something that has not yet materialized. In any case, as Isthar tells us,

> At the time this idea was still at a very early stage, but it caused a stir. Lama Gangchen received positive feedback from many people and at this point we decided to apply for affiliation and our request was accepted.

In many ways, affiliation with the UN represented the most important aspect of the institutionalization of Lama Gangchen's activities outside traditional networks. In this way, the Tibetan Lama entered a terrain that not even the Dalai Lama has had access, due to Chinese pressure.

II Ritual

Rio de Janeiro, 1979: the small statue of a yogi immediately awakened his mind to the memory of visions that had been with him for a long time. It was the yogi that used to float in the air right in front of him! Antônio asked the owner of the statue for the name of the yogi, but he did not know it. He went to talk to Xazyr II, who was then the leader of the Irmandade Espiritualista Verdade Eterna (IEVE) [Eternal Truth Spiritualist Brotherhood] where Antônio was one of the most active mediums. They made a small circle and the leader entered into a trance, channeling the Venerable Master Shidha. Even before the box with the statue was opened, he said: "Be aware of Master Tsongkhapa!" Pointing to Antônio, he said: "You are one of his followers and you are going to disseminate his teachings in Brazil." After this day, the image of the yogi, who turned out to be Tsongkhapa, appeared just once more to Antônio, only to disappear in smoke. "Now," thought Antônio, "I am on the path."

Kathmandu, 1999: from dawn to dusk, in a ceremony which would last for three whole days, the Segyu monks were carefully performing the Guhyasamaja puja, one of the most complex rituals in Tibetan Buddhism. Sitting on the highest throne, above the elders, young people and children, was Segyu Rinpoche, dressed in the appropriate attire for the occasion. Though he did not understand the meaning of the verses recited in Tibetan, he attentively followed all the stages of the ritual and presided over each movement of the chöpöns, the Tibetan ritual assistants. In the reality constructed by the tantric imagination, the monks had to visualize him as the main deity of the ceremony – he was Guhyasamaja.

Nearly 20 years separated these two moments in the life of this single man, a period of time in which he underwent a profound identity transformation, a long spiritual metamorphosis, which is still incomplete today. The loose ends in his trajectory do not prevent us from recognizing, precisely in this period of time, the crucial point of mutation. It is this period of transition, a period marked by the meeting of two spiritual universes apparently very distant from each other, which interests us most here. It is in the threshold that this process of identity formation, still ongoing, is most transparent.

During this liminal stage, Antônio was no more, while Segyu Rinpoche, his future identity, was yet to emerge. Then, he was known as Lama Shakya Zangpo, the Brazilian lay lama only informally recognized as the reincarnation of a sixteenth-century Tibetan abbot by Jampel Shenpen, the 98th Ganden Tripa Rinpoche, head of the Gelug school of Tibetan Buddhism.

Contrary to most tulkus, who are usually identified during childhood, Lama Shakya was only recognized when he was already over 30 years old and after a long trajectory in Brazilian spiritualist traditions, the Umbanda tradition[16] in particular. Thus, his case is exceptional in many respects. It is exceptional due to the high status of the lama that identified him. It is also exceptional because of the difficult conditions that Lama Shakya had to face from not having been immersed from early on in the world of Tibetan Buddhism, as is the case with many western tulkus. Finally, and perhaps most importantly, it is exceptional because of his spiritual trajectory and the inevitability of having to integrate his previous experiences into his new religious career.

The relationship he developed with his Umbanda past is, in this context, clouded in ambiguity. As we shall see, this lama's Umbanda spiritual inheritance was to become key for his insertion in the field of Tibetan Buddhism, while at the same time, it also represented a vestige that slowly but surely had to be flushed out. Thus, without ever totally discarding this Brazilian spiritual heritage, Lama Shakya became increasingly more Buddhist – from the point of view of his discourse and spiritual practice – creating, often unconsciously, an extremely dynamic interchange between the Brazilian and Tibetan religious traditions.

Here I will discuss this interchange, seeking to reveal the various layers of meaning through which it unfolds. I believe that the best starting point for this task is to investigate the construction of Lama Shakya's autobiographical narrative. I aim to identify in this narrative a common thread, which, amidst stories immersed in pre-destination and revelation, links all his experiences.

Lines of destiny

Lama Shakya tells that he was only four when he had his first contact with the spiritual world. He used to play with spirits at this age. But as nobody else could see them, his mother started to worry. Although she was a Catholic, she decided to take Lama Shakya, then known by his name Antônio, to a healer, Lucinda. To Antônio's surprise, Lucinda could also see his spiritual friends. She told his mother that her son would have great healing abilities in the future.

However, as he grew older, Antônio became more skeptical. He even used to sneer at the "despachos" (religious offerings in Afro-Brazilian spiritual traditions) that he encountered on the streets. On one occasion, some friends decided to play a trick on him, taking him to a spiritualist center of a "mãe de santo" (a priestess in Afro-Brazilian spiritual traditions), Zanira. Antônio was furious. Despite this, he decided to keep the appointment with Zanira. In a dramatic gesture, Zanira threw a coin up in the air and said to him, leaning close to his face: "Listen, this is your life. Your life has two facets. One is suffering, the other is your spirituality. If you don't look after your spirituality, you will suffer."

At that time Antônio was going through an intense period of suffering and a year later his situation would get worse. From the perspective of onlookers, he did not seem to have a very good reason for being so upset. He was healthy, had a job he enjoyed and enough money to live. On the whole, such a predicament is said to be quite common among those who are considered mediums but do not develop their capabilities. As the anthropologist Dolores Shapiro explains, "together with the privilege comes great responsibility which most mediums do not want to assume and which, in fact, many resist for a long time" (Shapiro 1992). Shapiro studied the trajectory of eight new mediums and concluded that the activity of the "medium" is associated with some sort of problem, large or small, which according to religious traditions will only be resolved when they accept their religious role.

Antônio's trajectory seems to confirm this idea. When his suffering reached a level that was truly unbearable, he decided to contact Zanira and become her apprentice. Zanira and her guide Vovó Miquelina [Grandma Miquelina] initiated him into Umbanda, allowing him to develop his role as a medium and recover his clairvoyance. This learning process would last eight years, until Zanira's death. Shortly before Zanira died, however, Vovó Miquelina, told him that she was not his real spiritual mentor. According to him, Vovó Miquelina said that she was "only a spirit" and that the real spiritual mentors were yet to reveal themselves. His next significant spiritual meeting would happen as unexpectedly and magically as the first.

Antônio was in the Garota do Ipanema bar in Rio de Janeiro when he sensed a strong smell of incense. He followed the smell to a door, on which he knocked.

> When they opened the door, there was an image of him [the venerable Master Shidha]. I embraced the image and started to cry uncontrollably. I felt a deep love, a love of many, many lives. I was in a different plane. I did not notice that the room with the image was full of people attending a lesson. The next day I went to a healing session there [this was the IEVE]. The leader recognized me and said: you took your time, but you have come.

At the IEVE, Antônio would get to know another type of spiritualist tradition, with a number of lineages, including the so-called "oriental lineage." It was within this unusual context that he would come into contact with Buddhism and other Asian traditions. As we have seen in the scene described above, it is the Venerable Master Shidha himself, the "mentor of the spiritual brotherhood," that would reveal to Lama Shakya his connection with the founder of the Tibetan Buddhist Gelug School, Tsongkhapa. This revelation would make clear to Lama Shakya that the IEVE "was not his true path," but a "short cut" to his final destination.

An initial conclusion that can be reached from these autobiographical accounts is that the division between the spiritual and the earthly worlds is essential for understanding the type of relationship Lama Shakya would develop with Umbanda, even after entering the Buddhist path. For the Brazilian lama, Umbanda was more than anything a "bridge" which took him towards his "true path." This idea of a "bridge" can be clearly understood when we analyze the outcome of each phase of his spiritual life. Each of these phases was marked by his mentors revealing that his true path was to be a different one.

His relationship with the spirits that fill the world of Umbanda, albeit often imbued with this understanding of "bridge," seems to transcend this notion. Through the clairvoyance of his spirit guides — mentors that recognized Lama Shakya's qualities and showed him his path — the exceptional character that the lama attributes to these spirits is perceived. As we shall see, Lama Shakya did not leave behind the relationships he developed at the spiritual level, but deeply re-signified their nature.

Nothing is lost, nothing is gained, everything is transformed...

Among all the spirits that Lama Shakya had had contact with in Umbanda, after he was recognized as a reincarnate Tibetan lama it was certainly Venerable Master Shidha that played the most significant role. In 1996, when I visited the Healing Buddha Foundation, Lama Shakya's center in California, an enormous thangka (traditional Tibetan painting) of Master Shidha adorned the meditation hall. At the time, Lama Shakya spoke of him as his main spiritual mentor. According to the lama, Venerable Master Shidha was present in all practices, coordinating the work at a spiritual level. In the past Lama Shakya had received the teachings of Master Shidha only indirectly through Xazyr II. In the American context, however, he came to incorporate him and receive his teachings directly, "mind to mind."

In many respects, this was not the same Venerable Master Shidha that the Brazilian lama had known at the IEVE. In statues and even in the thangka at the Healing Buddha Foundation, Master Shidha was characterized as a Buddhist monk wearing a saffron-colored tunic typical of Theravada Buddhism commonly practiced in the countries of Southeast Asia. According to the IEVE webpage on the Internet, Master Shidha lived 2,000 years ago (hpm.com.br/ieve.html). For Lama Shakya, however, Master Shidha was an important leader of the Gelug School (founded in the fifteenth century) who used a false name "in order to avoid conflict among his followers."

This process of the re-signification of the figure of Venerable Master Shidha has been extremely dynamic. Later, the identity and status of Master Shidha within Lama Shakya's spiritual universe would once again be given new meanings. In 2000, three years after his official investiture as the reincarnation of a Tibetan lama,[17] the Brazilian lama, now renamed Segyu Rinpoche, would maintain that Master Shidha belonged neither to the Segyu lineage, his particular lineage, nor to any other of the Gelug School's many lineages. In fact, according to Lama Shakya, he was not even an enlightened being, as he had earlier proclaimed. In the words of the lama:

> We are talking about a being, in fact a spirit, who is extremely evolved, but not enlightened. Within IEVE he belongs to the 'Seventh Law' and is therefore evolved. But I no longer work with him. He was very important at a particular time – he showed me the path. Today, I am very grateful for his guidance, for the path.

In this way, the lama's career in Umbanda had only been a transition, a "bridge" which led him to his "true path."

This lama's account of the translation and re-translation of the identity of Master Shidha reveals the workings of a complex process: the re-signification of his own understanding of the cosmos based on Tibetan categories. This was a conscious effort and became the foundation upon which the Brazilian lama re-structured his system of spiritual practices. By his own account, the first step was to re-classify the hierarchy of Umbanda spirits according to the six realms of existence within Buddhist cosmology: the realms of gods, demi-gods, human beings, animals, "pretas" (or hungry spirits) and finally, hell beings.

> What is a conscious manifestation of elemental spirits and of a being that is already evolved? What is the consciousness of a being that is in the infernal planes, of the wandering spirits which surround us or even the spirits which appear as animals in degenerated forms? Humans, classifications of humans and non-humans, or demi-gods, who are more elevated spirits, more evolved, but which are in the form of an actual spirit as such, of energy? And what about the gods themselves, divinities and entities which are present as our spiritual masters, spiritual divinities of light, though still tied to this world of samsara, that is, tied to the cycle of existence, within the desire realm? In this way I was able to reclassify my whole vision of Umbanda, of the Umbanda rites.

Indeed, a cursory analysis of his effort to reclassify the spirits of Umbanda in accordance with the Buddhist vision indicates that while Lama Shakya's under-standing of Umbanda and its spiritual hierarchy had been deeply modified by his contact with Tibetan Buddhism, the categories of Buddhism too were directly re-signified in this process.

In fact, within Buddhism, when we talk about, for example, the realms of gods and demi-gods, what stands out is their luxurious environment. According to Buddhist teachings, the inhabitants of these realms can live in a world of sensual pleasures for eons without ageing.[18] Despite this apparently privileged existence, these beings do not have the opportunity to practice Dharma. In other words, Buddhist teachings present this type of incarnation as less than optimal. Buddhism maintains that within cyclic existence, or samsara it is human birth that is supreme, because this is the only kind of existence that allows for the attainment of enlightenment. Therefore, in Tibetan Buddhism, humans do not generally seek spiritual advice from gods and demi-gods. Lama Shakya, however, believes that the more elevated spiritual masters live in these god and demi-god realms. Moreover, other spirits inhabit other realms such as the animal or human realms, depending on their condition and "degree of evolution." Lama Shakya's view about the degree of evolution of these spirits is unusual, as in Buddhism there is no notion of linear evolution.[19] In fact, we may be human in this life and reborn as an animal in the next, or even in one of the hells, depend-ing on the merits and virtues we have accumulated in this and past lives. Lama Shakya is certainly aware of this concept, but as a result of his Umbanda past he recasts this doctrinal notion in terms of an "evolving hierarchy."

This notion of evolution is present in an explanation he gave regarding the types of purification that a person may experience in a lifetime. In his words, the more I evolve the less I need my physical body. As I become a more elevated spirit, let us call it this, I become more subtle, an extremely subtle, mental being, I become a bodhisattva, until I become a complete Buddha, out of this cycle of existence.

Once more, the notion put forward by Lama Shakya, in this case the relationship between the presence or absence of a body and the level of spiritual evolution, derives more directly from Brazilian spiritualist traditions than from Buddhism. To be sure, Lama Shakya's vision does agree to some extent with the Buddhist tantric notion of working with a refined subtle body and gaining mastery over its coarser elements through yogic practice. However, Tibetan Buddhist tantra overall emphasizes the necessity of having a physical human body in order to attain final enlightenment. Lama Shakya de-emphasizes this doctrinal mainstay, and instead charts spiritual progress in terms of his Brazilian spiritualist tradition. In Tibetan Buddhism, the relationship between the "degree of evolution" and the need (or not) for a physical body is not stated in the same way. According to Buddhism, a bodhisattva is a being that sets out to delay his or her full enlightenment until all other beings have reached it. Very often, the "task" of helping other beings may demand that a bodhisattva manifest as a human being (or even as a dog[20] or another animal). This is the case of the Dalai Lama. As we saw in the second chapter of this work, the Dalai Lamas are seen as emanations of Avalokiteshvara, the bodhisattva of compassion.

It is clear, therefore, that in the perspective of Lama Shakya, it is necessary to understand both Umbanda and Tibetan Buddhism as languages, which constitute the basis from which the lama reorganizes his own vision of the cosmos. These languages are largely fluid, and in an extremely dynamic process, end up influencing each other. A good example of how this mutual influence between two different languages happens in practice was the performance of a tantric initiation within a more traditional Tibetan format, where Master Shidha appeared as the main deity. During a tantric Buddhist initiation that took place at IEVE in 2001, Master Shidha, who had in another context only been classified as an "evolved spirit," was described by Lama Shakya as a Buddha, that is, an enlightened being. From this we can clearly observe the malleability of the categories in which Master Shidha and the entities of Umbanda are "re-classified" within a spiritual hierarchy based on a foreign system. It is also clear that in this new phase of his spiritual trajectory, Lama Shakya, now known as Segyu Rinpoche, not only re-signified Umbanda and Tibetan Buddhist practices and concepts within a Buddhist context, but also did so within his old sphere of action.

Transformation through ritual

Language, as a system of knowledge and communication, should also be taken into account when analyzing the rituals through which Lama Shakya materializes and confers a practical meaning to his attempts at reclassifying the Umbanda spirits. It is precisely through ritual that the Brazilian lama makes public and intelligible his internal process of reorganizing the cosmos, directly implicating his disciples in this process. At this point in the discussion, I will concentrate specifically on a type of ritual Lama Shakya performed to help the spirits in his "egregore," or spirit family, enter the path of Buddhism. According to the lama, his "pretos velhos," "caboclos" and children[21] were, in certain ceremonies, "placed in a mandala" and together with the Tibetan masters, now help him in his work of "psycho-spiritual healing."

In the 1990s, it was in the encounter between these two spiritual universes that the originality of Lama Shakya's religious practice was revealed. In fact, the Brazilian lama claimed that he was literally creating a new type of Buddhism, "Brazilian Buddhism," through the "alignment of the forces of the shamanic world (that is, the world of Umbanda) with the forces of Tibetan Buddhism" (Healing Buddha Foundation 1994). We could even say that the vision of religious practice cultivated by Lama Shakya has always been imbued with a missionary element. Generally speaking, Lama Shakya believed that he was sowing the seeds for a true revolution in which the Brazilian spiritual traditions "which had little or hardly any philosophical content" would be transformed and improved through contact with Buddhism (or even become a new type of Buddhism).

This missionary element was also present in the relationship he developed with his disciples and even with some of the patients that came to his healing sessions. In fact, when he used to visit the Shi De Choe Tsog Dharma Center in São Paulo, Lama Shakya performed rituals, which were analogous to those he had performed for his Umbanda guides. In April 1995 I had the opportunity to observe these rituals stage by stage. At that time, Lama Shakya was living in the United States, where he ran the Healing Buddha Foundation, but he used to visit the Brazilian center founded by Lama Gangchen twice a year. Even when he was not present, the so-called "Buddha Medicine sessions," which took place under his directions were performed by his disciples on Tuesdays and Thursdays. Very quickly these became the most popular sessions at the dharma center, attracting over 200 people when the lama came to São Paulo.

The 1995 visit was exceptional because it included the active participation of Xazyr III, the successor to Xazyr II, as the new patriarch of IEVE. He had been invited by Lama Shakya to help with the diagnosis and prescription of treatments. Among other things, the presence of an IEVE member during these sessions confirmed the strong and ongoing connections between Lama Shakya and the ritualistic structures of Umbanda. It brought to light certain conflicts, which naturally emerged in Lama Shakya's internal struggle to fit his own conceptions into Tibetan Buddhism categories.

On the first day of the "session" at the dharma center, people came to ask Lama Shakya and Xazyr III for guidance. The healers' eyes were semi-closed, as if they were both in a trance. Both Lama Shakya and Xazyr III prescribed treatments, which demonstrated that at the time the healing performed by the lama was not very different from that carried out at the IEVE.

That night, after a series of consultations, Xazyr III spoke to the public, defending the idea that we belong to a "fifth race":

The fifth race is the race of service. We, human beings, are in the "law of service," we need to donate our energy because we have too much. Every human being is a medium and this is a karmic condition, since in this way, spirits take energy and transfer it to beings that need it.

Without getting into the details of Xazyr's discourse, I would like to emphasize here its missionary tone, which in many ways goes against Lama Shakya's aims, that is, to put his Umbanda spirit guides on the path to Buddhism. Despite this clear opposition, or perhaps, precisely because of it, we can assume that the missionary zeal that I have emphasized in Lama Shakya's discourse was, as we shall see, a counter-response to the type of idea presented by Xazyr III.

The day after the consultations Lama Shakya performed another diagnostic session at the dharma center. This time, some of those present were invited to position themselves inside an "energy circle" formed by Lama Shakya, Xazyr III and two other disciples, chosen because they had also attended Umbanda centers in the past. Upon entering the middle of this circle some people went into a trance or even incorporated other entities. On this day, Xazyr III, who had also become possessed, once more helped Lama Shakya in the task of diagnosing "psycho-spiritual disturbances" among those present. Invariably, Xazyr III said to each person entering the circle that he or she should be working with his or her spiritual guide, visibly irritating Lama Shakya. In some cases, Lama Shakya even managed to discretely tell people "there is no need to work with any guides at all."

One of the people present, Fernanda, also heard from Xazyr III that she should be working with a spiritual entity, but according to Lama Shakya's diagnosis she was suffering from a "psycho-spiritual disorder," or more specifically, she was being disturbed by her "pomba gira"[22] and should do some ritual[23] to send the entity away.

Two weeks later, Fernanda came back to the dharma center with 12 yellow roses and three ribbons – blue, yellow and white – as requested by the lama. Xazyr III was not present and only a few people watched the ritual. Lama Shakya slowly led Fernanda to the center's meditation hall and signaled to his assistant to turn on the tape recorder, filling the room with the echoes of the voices of Tibetan monks. Ringing a small bell and beating a hand drum (damaru), Lama Shakya approached the girl and she gradually went into a trance. Lama Shakya moved a mirror around Fernanda while he continued to play the drum. Then he threw a little rice over her. The lama placed ribbons, reminiscent of Senhor do Bonfim ribbons,[24] over her head. They were decorated with Buddhist mantras and he called them "protection ribbons."

He braided the blue, yellow and white ribbons and tied them around Fernanda's head while chanting a Tibetan mantra. Then, he placed her in the center of a square white cloth on which a circle and some Tibetan syllables had been drawn in blue chalk (pemba[25]). This represented the mandala where the pomba gira had to be inserted. According to Lama Shakya, Tibetan spiritual masters were inside this mandala, waiting to take the entity on its path towards Buddhism. The yellow roses were placed on a small altar with Tibetan images. Lama Shakya rang the bell once again and then made Fernanda lie on the cloth. While moving an "arruda" tree branch[26] over the girl's body, Lama Shakya prayed in a low voice. He clapped three times[27] and then helped Fernanda rise to her feet. He announced that the pomba gira had been "sent away" and would no longer bother her.

The recreation of a myth

First and foremost, it is worth noting the public character of the ritual in question, which is consistent with the open nature of similar practices within Tibetan Buddhism.[28] This coincidence may indicate two things: first, a vestige of Umbanda, as in this tradition rituals are generally open; second, we can assume that Lama Shakya's option for openness comes from his need to communicate through ritual with his disciples, and perhaps more importantly, with Tibetan lamas. The direct reference the ritual makes to a founding myth of Tibetan Buddhism reinforces this second supposition, though it does not exclude the first.

As we have seen in Chapter 2, according to Tibetan historiography, at the end of the eighth century, the Indian tantric master Padmasambhava was invited by king Trisong Detsen to visit Tibet in order to help another Indian master, Shantarakshita, who had unsuccessfully been trying to build the first Buddhist temple in this country. In one of the versions of this mythohistorical narrative, every night local gods would go to the building site and undo the work completed during the day. Padmasambhava not only put an end to this destructive practice of the local gods, but "tamed" them, putting them at the service of the new religion.

The terms used by Lama Shakya to describe his practice of putting Umbanda spirits at the service of Buddhist masters point to a re-interpretation of this founding myth. In fact, Lama Shakya refers directly to Padmasambhava's story. In his words, "Padmasambhava put local entities at the dharma's service, as protectors, didn't he? Well, on a different scale, I am doing the same thing. It is not syncretism, but the conciliation of our cultural entities with the Buddhist structure."[29]

By identifying himself with the figure of Padmasambhava, Lama Shakya makes his Buddhist practice and his past in Brazilian spiritual traditions more comprehensible to both his western disciples[30] and to Tibetan lamas. The underlying missionary meaning in rituals such as those performed for Fernanda is backed up by the myth. We could say that the issue here is, above all, the insertion of the Brazilian lama and his idiosyncratic practices within the religious field of Tibetan Buddhism.

Ritual through transformation

Another crucial aspect that surfaces through analyzing the ritual performed for Fernanda and the "diagnosis session" is the reformulation of the concepts of disease and cure and also of "disciple" and "patient." Lama Shakya first acquired these concepts within the context of Umbanda. As evident from the conflicts with Xazyr III at the dharma center, Lama Shakya was not concerned with identifying mediums who were able to "work" with their entities. Quite the opposite, he wanted to treat mediumship as a "disturbance." Clearly, Lama Shakya seeks to substitute the discourse "you are a medium and need to be using this skill" with "you have a psycho-spiritual disturbance and need to treat it (through a ritual)." Something, which in the Umbanda tradition could be considered a gift (and also a cure), becomes an "illness." As we will see, the revision of these concepts is one of the central points of the process of reorganization, not only of Lama Shakya's practice, but of the inner hierarchy of his circle of followers, above all in the United States.

In the first few years following his recognition as a tulku, Lama Shakya did not make any radical changes to his spiritual activities. His work was largely geared towards healing and he continued to do this, using practices that were directly derived from Brazilian spiritualist traditions. In Brazil, Lama Shakya had transmitted only one type of practice to his disciples. This was the so-called "psycho-spiritual healing," or "the healing circle," a therapeutic system which involved, among other things, the application of "passes" (laying on of hands) by four people positioned in a circle around the patient. This format had originally come from IEVE, as I already mentioned. In the United States, the "healing circles" were also the main activity of the Lama Shakya group. However, there were also other practices, which could not have been easily introduced within the context of a Buddhist center in Brazil. In fact, his center in California was, in many ways, an Umbanda center, although Lama Shakya has always claimed that what took place there was Buddhism. Giras, or Umbanda trance sessions, renamed by Lama Shakya as "shamanic drumming rituals," were performed weekly. Lama Shakya also used to channel caboclos and pretos velhos when conducting consultations with his followers.

During the first half of the 1990s, however, Lama Shakya started a process that would definitively alter the overall format of his spiritual practice. He announced to his circle of American disciples that his Foundation would be gradually abandoning practices characteristic of Umbanda to become increasingly more Buddhist in nature. One of the main directives set for the group was to more clearly differentiate the status of disciples and patients. In Lama Shakya's words,

> From that point on, it was expected that people would be performing Buddhist practices. Patients would no longer be confused with disciples. Patients are patients and disciples are disciples. And whoever wanted to leave the organization was free to do so.

Within this new context, the giras, for instance, where everyone had participated on a somewhat equal footing, became gradually more exclusive, until they finally disappeared altogether. The trance possessions were also not conducted in the public eye. According to Lama Shakya, only his most advanced disciples would be able to channel entities. In the face of these resolutions, many saw themselves losing prestige, because they were not involved in the giras as much as they had been before. The majority, in fact, did not approve of the changes and left. Even most of those that remained with Lama Shakya missed the giras. And in a short time, his group was reduced to a small number of students. It was then that Lama Shakya once and for all implemented the changes he had previously announced. From that point on, no one was to refer to him as Antônio, as he had been previously known, but as Lama Shakya Zangpo, the name given to him by his master Lati Rinpoche (1922–2010), and everyone had to start treating him in a way that was in line with the respectful protocol with which lamas are treated in traditional Tibetan contexts.

In practice, only one of his disciples from the American group, a woman, continued to channel entities. Lama Shakya said that she was the oracle of his group: "In Tibetan Buddhism isn't there also a lama that channels entities. These lamas are oracles and this is exactly the case with Misa." In fact, in Tibetan Buddhism deities which still reside in the so called "spheres inhabited by animated beings" can take "possession" of mediums and make predictions and prophecies in general (Nebesky-Wojkowitz 1993: 409). This Tibetan Buddhist practice is very close to Brazilian spiritualism.

Lama Shakya's decision to restrict trance with entities to only one person in the group seems a clear attempt to adapt his spiritual activities to the norms of Tibetan Buddhism, as in this environment very few mediums are possessed by spirits.[31] We could go further and say that what is going on here is another reorganization of his group of disciples, which is clearly reflected in the organization of ritual itself. Thus, the fact that the "healing circles" were the only practice originating from Brazilian spiritualism which continued in the new phase indicates, among other things, a search for a structure in the ritual in which a new cosmology (as we saw, this was being constructed by Lama Shakya and his disciples) and a new hierarchical organization of the group could be established. In contrast to the giras, in these circles it was possible to define clearer limits between "patients" and "disciples." Thus, ritual, understood as a language, was able to "communicate" to the practitioner, impressing on his or her mind these new models of organization, since knowledge can only be fully assimilated if it is transformed into experience in one way or another (Turner 1982). Ritual here represents a possible means of experience.

It is worth mentioning that the "healing circles" are (or came to be) conceived by Lama Shakya as mandalas, in which each person is positioned under the influence of a particular Buddha and works with that Buddha's qualities. "In the Dalai Lama's initiation you were within Chenrezig [Avalokiteshvara]'s circle," says Lama Shakya. "I am doing the same thing here with the people in the healing circle. They will enter this healing mandala. The patient arrives and experiences a strong visualization. [...] Within this environment, things happen in a structured way."

Through his re-classification of the Umbanda entities within his own vision of the traditional Tibetan cosmology, it could be said that a new cosmology was created in which Lama Shakya gradually inserted not only the entities that follow him, but also his followers. Thus, the idea of community extends beyond the physical limits to also embrace the invisible realms. This community and its extensions in other planes of existence are organized in mandalas by the Brazilian lama.

> We are born connected. You create these conditions during this process of dying and being born and therefore you are not left behind. You belong to a family, which protects you and this act of protecting is the egregore, from the hells to the highest realms. Inside this mandala you have everything that you need to continue your evolutionary process. Nothing is lost. So, how do you keep all this emanation together? Without the mandala you would not be able to. How is the mandala created? Through initiation sessions. Then the causes and conditions lead you on. It is likely that through initiations received in earlier incarnations or due to factors which led to your evolution, you start to become conscious of the fact that you belong to a community that you continue to follow. Was I not another person? Was I not reborn somewhere else but belong to the same lineage? Don't the spirits continue to follow me? Don't I have followers in Brazil? Yes, I do. Don't I have followers here (in the United States) too? Yes, I do. Then, all this is energy and I draw people in. People who I meet on the way, but who are no longer with me, they might think: "Ah, this does not matter anymore." Then there are other people also thinking: "Ah, this does not matter any more," but they are on the path. Things vary. But then it does depend on which point of the mandala you place yourself, that is, either you are outside or you are inside. You can be inside the circle, but outside the essence, but at least you are protected by the egregore that surrounds you, until you create the causes and conditions for you to enter inside the mandala.

It is clear that the gradual abandonment of more orthodox Umbanda practices, such as the gira and trance possessions, was supported by this symbolic reorganization, which practically resulted in the creation of a new cosmology. In a way, Lama Shakya makes the "invisible" spiritual world "visible" (Yamaguchi 1991: 58) every time he practices a ritual such as the one performed for Fernanda. He finds a particular place for the Umbanda entities in this new phase, and thus, he allows his followers to interact with this other reality, even without trance. As we have seen, this process involves a "dialectic" in which the visible also emerges from "the invisible background that surrounds it" (ibid.: 62). This brings to his group of disciples a new hierarchical meaning.

III Study

Among the various examples of lamas that have established themselves and created organizations in the West, Geshe Kelsang Gyatso's case stands out as one of the most significant. He has established a vast network of centers and disciples around him. In fact, the New Kadampa Tradition (NKT) created by Geshe Kelsang in 1991 is today the largest organization led by a Tibetan monk in the West.[32] James Belither, who was General Secretary of NKT in 2002, estimated that at that time there were over 500 centers and discussion groups linked to this tradition worldwide. Evidence of this incredible expansion is the so-called Summer Festival held every year, which brings together thousands of people at NKT's headquarters, the Manjushri Institute, an old eighteenth century castle located in the small town of Ulverston in the North of England. The fact that only the Dalai Lama has managed to stage events of a similar size in the West puts this event into perspective.

In 2002 I participated in NKT's Summer Festival, and was able to observe from close quarters the dimensions of Geshe Kelsang's organization. During the Festival at the Manjushri Institute all languages were spoken. Disciples came from distant and unlikely countries, such as South Africa – Africa is by far the continent with the least number of Buddhist centers. The commitment of Geshe Kelsang's students could be measured, albeit in a superficial way, by the impressive number of monks and nuns circulating in the gardens of the Institute. Without a doubt, the number of NKT's ordained community far exceeds that of any other Tibetan Buddhist group in the West.

There are, of course, many reasons for Geshe Kelsang's huge success and we will move on shortly to discuss some of these. However, first it is important to acquaint ourselves with the story of his arrival in the West, and more specifically, the account of how he broke with the lama who first invited him to teach in England. This was an important initial step in the unparalleled expansion of Geshe Kelsang's activities to its current international scope (although, for at least a decade, his activities, despite being relatively well known, remained limited to England).

It was Lama Yeshe, briefly introduced in Chapter 3, who facilitated the initial encounter between Geshe Kelsang and the West. In 1975, Lama Yeshe created the Manjushri Institute in the London area (two years later, the Institute was transferred to Ulverston) as part of the Foundation for the Preservation of the Mahayana Tradition (FPMT). He needed a teacher who could manage the center, so he asked his tutor, Trijang Rinpoche, to recommend someone. According to Geshe Kelsang, Trijang Rinpoche then asked him to move to England and teach three fundamental texts of the Tibetan Buddhist curriculum – *The Way of the Bodhisattva*, a classic text by the Indian master Shantideva (eighth century), the *Introduction to the Middle Way*, Chandrakirti's seventh-century commentary on the philosophical work of Nagarjuna, and the Lamrim, a commentary on Atisha's *Lamp on the Path to Enlightenment* – and then assess whether it was worth staying on (New Kadampa Tradition 1997: 6–7). Geshe Kelsang arrived in England in 1977. Although he did not speak English very well, he quickly gathered around him a group of faithful students. Soon, however, there were a number of conflicts between Geshe Kelsang's disciples and the FPMT. This scenario resulted in the Manjushri Institute, under the guidance of Geshe Kelsang, breaking away from the Foundation.

In 2002, James Belither, who was one of Geshe Kelsang's first pupils, occupied one of the most important positions within NKT, General Secretary. In an interview with him in his office during the Summer Festival, he stated:

> There were many of us who were devoted to Geshe-la, and we had a different way of thinking in relation to FPMT, which was not very strong at the time. As the year progressed, they started to insist: "you should do this, you should do that." And there was a time when they tried to impose a new director. Well, we were happy with our director, Roy Tyson, and also, we believed that the new director did not like Geshe Kelsang. And for this reason Geshe Kelsang had to leave. So we decided to break away from FPMT. And there were many problems, many difficulties with this.

Following his disengagement from Lama Yeshe's Foundation, Geshe Kelsang gradually established his own style of teaching Buddhism to westerners. His starting point, however, was the same type of academic education advocated at FPMT. Geshe Kelsang himself had gone through the long period of academic education which was required to become a "geshe."[33] This involved approximately 20 years in the study of philosophy, logic and monastic rules. Geshe Kelsang, however, was not content to simply transpose to the West the curriculum exactly as it was taught in the Tibetan monasteries. In this sense, those first years in England were in general quite experimental.

As some of his disciples told me, Geshe Kelsang closely observed the western way of life and made gradual adjustments. According to the Swiss disciple, Morten Clausen, who has been with the geshe since 1981 and was in 2002 a Resident Teacher at the main center in New York, Geshe Kelsang quickly realized that the educational program for geshes did not work for westerners: "it was too complex, too focused on theory and very distant from practice." Thus, gradually, according to Clausen,

> Geshe Kelsang introduced the element of practice, because he believed that westerners liked to put things into practice when they learn. They want to experience it immediately, they do not want to wait years and years to refine something intellectually.

The balance between practice and theory also played a part in the life trajectory of Geshe Kelsang himself. In fact, the long intellectual effort that his education as a geshe demanded was counter-balanced by a period of meditation retreat of almost the same length. After he fled Tibet, Geshe Kelsang's periods of retreat lasted almost 18 years altogether.

Nevertheless, it is important to stress that though meditation practice has become an important, and even a central part of Geshe Kelsang's teachings, the systematic study of Buddhist texts is the pillar upon which his activities in the West are based. His study program focuses on two main points: first, how to effectively put studies into practice, in one's personal life and in meditation; and, second, how to transmit the teachings, something that became more significant over time within Geshe Kelsang's organization. Morten Clausen says that Geshe Kelsang has always stressed, right from the start, that Buddhism should be transmitted to westerners by westerners. He wanted a type of Buddhism that "spoke the local language of each country." Teacher training thus became one of the most significant factors in the expansion of centers and groups associated with Geshe Kelsang.

Beginning in 1979, the year of the establishment of his first center, the Madhyamaka, in the British city of York, Geshe Kelsang allowed his main pupils to teach Buddhism. At the beginning, however, there was not much coordination with the study program at the Manjushri Institute. Lucy James, who met Geshe Kelsang in 1981 and was part of the Madhyamaka community, recalls how during those first years everything was very experimental: "As there were no books, we used transcriptions to study the teachings of our teacher. And he taught very different things such as texts that we do not study now particularly. We had no idea about Geshe-la's[34] vision."

As Lucy's declaration indicates, the books would gradually become the basis for establishing new centers. Lucy herself had a crucial role in publishing the books written by Geshe Kelsang, which are largely commentaries on traditional texts. She was just over 20 when she went to live in the recently established Madhyamaka Center. It was there that in 1982 Geshe Kelsang asked her to transcribe and publish a very short text for the first time. "I was not aware at the time, but it was a test." Lucy started to publish books with another disciple. At first, Geshe Kelsang used a Tibetan translator to write his books. With time, however, he started to dictate his commentaries directly into his own personal style of English. It was up to his pupils, in particular Lucy, to edit the texts later.

Geshe Kelsang took an essential step in the process of preparing westerners to teach Buddhism when he stressed the importance of directly applying his commentaries on traditional texts to daily life and spiritual practice. The history of the foundation of the first Geshe Kelsang center in Brazil reflects the central role of publications in the development of his global activities. It also mirrors the process that was then taking place in England. In fact, in a very informal way (and without noticing the similarities), while organizing the first Brazilian Kadampa center, Kelsang Pälsang, Geshe Kelsang's first disciple in Brazil, reproduced the same experimental phase that the centers in England had gone through.

Parallel paths

Kelsang Pälsang came into contact with Geshe Kelsang's teachings at the end of the 1980s. The son of a friend who was a disciple of Geshe Kelsang in England, where Pälsang was living at the time, gave her a set of tapes containing teachings about the Lojong, or the *Eight Verses for Training the Mind*.[35] "When I came back to Brazil," says Pälsang:

I decided to listen to these tapes a bit, just like that. I had no great motivation. My motivation was to see if I could understand the English, but then these teachings touched me deeply because they were very direct and their perspective was that by improving our own mind, by working on ourselves, we would then be able to help others. This coincided exactly with my beliefs, my desire to help others. During the days of the student movement in Brazil [protesting the dictatorship in Brazil] many people wanted to help [at the end of the 1960s, Pälsang was part of this movement]. The methods may have been completely wrong and deluded, but the basic idea, our motivation, was that there should be justice, that there should be less suffering.

In 1987, Pälsang discovered through a friend that a Tibetan lama was going to Brazil. This was Lama Zopa, who together with Lama Yeshe had established the FPMT. She decided to take part in a retreat and to her amazement Lama Zopa's teachings were precisely about Lojong. "I was so excited about this coincidence, I was very, very taken by this coincidence and for me this retreat was very powerful, it touched something inside me," says Pälsang. At Lama Zopa's retreat she got in touch with people who were involved in the creation of a new Buddhist center in São Paulo, Lama Gangchen's Shi De Choe Tsog Dharma Center. At the end of the year, when everyone was going on holiday, Pälsang offered to look after the center. For a month she organized a group of friends and relatives who took turns cleaning the center and renewing the offerings.

I said to my friends: as we are going to clean it, let's try something, let's imagine that we are cleaning our own minds. But, I didn't know anything. I had never read anything. At that time I new almost nothing – I only had the *Eight Verses* course. I had not read any of Geshe-la's books. I did not know much about Buddhism. I only knew the course, the tapes, nothing else. Then I found out that this is one of the most common Buddhist practices.

Pälsang is referring here to the practice of Lam Chung,[36] where people who are carrying out practical tasks, such as cleaning a shrine, imagine that cleaning is taking place at a more subtle level. It was during the time when Pälsang was looking after the dharma center that she decided to translate the tapes. She was thinking about organizing a study group and she asked Lama Gangchen for permission.

I asked if I could organize a group to study the tapes that I had and that I liked so much and he asked to see the tapes. I showed him the first two and he seemed very happy because the teachings were from the lineage of Trijang Rinpoche, who was his root guru. Then, to my surprise, he was giving a presentation, the center was full, absolutely packed, and he told everyone that they should come and study with me, that I had a lot of experience, that it was very auspicious as the teachings came from the

lineage of this root guru. He said that, can you believe it? But I knew
nothing. I hardly knew anything about Buddhism.

Pälsang was able to move between the various groups and without being aware
of it, she was sowing the first seeds for the future Geshe Kelsang center in
Brazil. This was due to the connection that existed between the teaching contained in the tapes and the master of Lama Gangchen, Trijang Rinpoche, who
was also the master of Geshe Kelsang, Lama Zopa and many other important
Gelug lamas, including the current Dalai Lama. Coincidentally, the style of the
course she proposed to hold at Lama Gangchen's center was very close to what
was taught at Geshe Kelsang's centers. Pälsang established two groups that met
weekly for approximately one year. There were often 30 or 40 people at these
sessions. Due to the fact that so many people were clearly interested in the
course, she decided to send the textual materials she had prepared for the course
to her friend in England. A few months later, Pälsang was contacted by the Manjushri Institute, though she had never personally met Geshe Kelsang. They asked
her to translate the book *Universal Compassion* (1988), Geshe Kelsang's commentaries on Lojong, from the English.

> So, I started to translate *Universal Compassion* and at that time my husband
> was going to spend time working on a project linked to an American univer-
> sity. We could choose where to go. It could either be near New York or
> Madison, I don't know, he had a number of options. He ended up opting for
> Santa Cruz in California, and by coincidence, the only center Geshe-la had
> in the United States at that time was in a town called San Jose, very near
> San Francisco. So I was very happy.

In the United States, Pälsang was able to work on the translation of *Universal
Compassion* with one of Geshe Kelsang's oldest disciples, Losang Kelsang, who
was a Resident Teacher at the San Jose center. The first translation of a book by
Geshe Kelsang into Portuguese was not the only outcome of this collaboration.
Perhaps more significantly, Pälsang established a method that she used for all
her translations. She told us that Losang explained to her the terminology, which
was expressed in English in detail.

> In this way he gave me a feeling, my English isn't great, but he gave me a
> feeling and I would find a term in Portuguese. Then I would bring the trans-
> lation together, I would refine it, constructing a base, because Geshe-la uses
> very exact terms, his vocabulary is very exact.

Pälsang believes that translating Geshe Kelsang is very different from translating
other Tibetan authors. According to her, there is still no unified translation of
terms from Tibetan: "therefore, they vary from author to author and from book
to book, even when they are by the same author. Sometimes they are books for
disseminating ideas and the concepts are not very well defined." Pälsang points

out that Geshe Kelsang started the translation process from the concepts themselves.

> For example, what is mindfulness? What is this concept? What is the concept of attention? This was one of the terms I had great difficulty in translating. Then I would discuss it with Losang and he would give me various examples. We not only discussed the Buddhist concept, but he gave me an example of its current use in English, he gave me various examples. But it would not work, because in Portuguese it all leads towards "attention," "paying attention," "full attention," "complete attention." There is a different mental state described by the word "attention" and it has nothing to do with mindfulness. So it was very difficult to find a translation, until I became inspired. I said: "Losang, and in Tibetan, what does it mean?" As Losang did not speak Tibetan, he gave me a more literal translation. He said: "It is remembering, it is memory, but it is a memory that remains." Then I came up with the term *"contínua lembrança"* [continuous remembrance] and it worked very well, it received very positive feedback.

Despite the fact that with regard to this specific term Pälsang went back to the Tibetan to find a translation into Portuguese, in her opinion, a profound knowledge of the language is irrelevant.

> In our case, it is not important to know Tibetan, because the concept exists. If you understand the concept, you find the word. For example, although I did not know the Tibetan word for "mindfulness," I knew that the concept was different from "attention" because I understood the concept of "attention."

Thus, gradually, as was the case with the English translation, a specific technical vocabulary was established in Portuguese, where terms were very often only deciphered after careful study.

The elaboration of this technical and hermetic vocabulary contributed directly to the process of building an identity for the group now being established worldwide. From this point of view, it is clear why, in 1990, when Pälsang finally met Geshe Kelsang to ask his permission to open a center in Brazil, the geshe requested that, first, more books should be translated. According to him, there was no point in opening a center unless there was material to study. "If they don't have this, then they will not progress," Geshe Kelsang said. Pälsang tells us, "with a well defined vocabulary" and a "solid base" it was easy to translate the texts. In a few months, she translated three books and wrote to Geshe Kelsang, who finally gave her permission to open a center in Brazil.

The history of the foundation of the first Geshe Kelsang center in Brazil coincided chronologically (and, in many ways, in general terms) with the incubation period the geshe's activities were undergoing as a whole. Symbolically and in practice this period was marked by Geshe Kelsang's three-year retreat between

1987 and 1990. From that period on, there were significant changes in his activities. During his seclusion, Geshe Kelsang continued to work on his books between meditation sessions. He concluded *Joyful Path of Good Fortune* (1990), *Universal Compassion* (1988) and wrote *The Meditation Handbook* (2001) and *Guide to the Dakini Land* (1991). At this time, Geshe Kelsang set up three study programs, which would become the core of his activities. He based them on these texts (and on others already written or in the final stages of editing). These were the General Program, the Foundation Program and the Teacher Training Program (New Kadampa Tradition 1997: 10).

The creation of the New Kadampa Tradition

Soon after he emerged from retreat, Geshe Kelsang announced a project which, once put into practice, would totally change the direction of his activities in the West: the creation of a central organization to coordinate the activities of all his centers. In 1991, when this was proposed, 27 centers had already been established in England and there were also a small number abroad. Geshe Kelsang invited representatives from most of these centers to discuss this idea. During the meeting Geshe Kelsang introduced the term "New Kadampa Tradition" for the first time, "so as to give the centers under his spiritual direction a distinct identity within the Buddhist world" (ibid.: 12).

In May 1991, the New Kadampa Tradition was officially inaugurated. Its main objectives were to provide general spiritual assistance to the centers, to ensure the purity and authenticity of spiritual programs and to oversee the examinations of both the General and Teacher Training programs in each center (ibid.: 13). Among all the new features, which the creation of NKT brought to Geshe Kelsang's group, the establishment of the three study programs was perhaps the most significant. Therefore, it is worth briefly describing here the content of these programs.

First is the General Program, which, according to Pälsang, is possibly the most important.

> As Geshe-la would say, if it were not for this program, we could meet each other in our houses and there would not be such hard work. The aim of the program is to welcome people. Points are discussed in broad terms, seeking to help everybody, even if that person is not an actual Buddhist practitioner. The General Program also seeks to teach some relaxation techniques so that people can know themselves better, so that they can discover themselves.

If this General Program aims to "welcome" new students, the so-called Foundation Program focuses on "Buddhist practitioners who wish to gain more knowledge and experience of the Dharma and attain authentic spiritual achievements, through a structured program of Buddhist studies" (New Kadampa Tradition *undated*: 1). This program aims to provide the practitioner with the intellectual basis for his daily practice. Thus, it is based on fundamental Tibetan Buddhist literature genres such as Lamrim, Lojong, Lorig,[37] and also more generally on texts from Indian Mahayana Buddhism, such as the *Heart Sutra* and Shantideva's *Guide to the Bodhisattva Path.* The books studied in the Foundation Program are also part of the third program established by Geshe Kelsang, the Teacher Training Program, which, in addition, covers literature on tantra. This program is recommended to all those wishing to become teachers. However, it is not necessary to complete this course before starting to teach.

It is possible to observe not only a clear progression in the sequence of these programs, but also a structure to guide the opening and operation of new centers. The General Program, as we have seen, "welcomes" new disciples. The Foundation Program provides them with further knowledge, guiding them in their spiritual practice, and the Teacher Training Program creates the direct conditions for new centers to be opened. It is apparent that in practice this "division of functions" is not so clear-cut. Progress in the Foundation Program, for example, can provide the student with enough knowledge to become a teacher at the General Program level. In any event, I believe that the manner in which the programs were structured was the most significant factor for the progressive increase in the number of centers associated with Geshe Kelsang during the last decades.

However, other factors were also important. The publication of some of Geshe Kelsang's books, with a wider public appeal, was certainly a means of introducing Kadampa Buddhism to a larger audience. Some books such as *The Meditation Handbook* and *Introduction to Buddhism* had already sold over 60,000 copies in the United Kingdom around the beginning of the last decade.

Another factor that also seemed to contribute to the significant growth in the number of centers was the legal and financial independence of centers in relation to NKT. In general terms, each center is responsible for its own fundraising in order to keep itself afloat. In Brazil, the group chose to be independent both in financial terms and with regard to its courses, as it never requested teachers from abroad. "In this way," Pälsang said, "we stood on our own two feet and grew in accordance with our own capabilities." Teachers and even monks need to support themselves. Some monks even have regular jobs. Such financial independence allowed them to grow in a short period of time. On the other hand, during a second phase of growth, NKT developed organizations, such as the New Temples Fund and the New Center Development Fund, to assist with the establishment of new centers and temples.

Concluding remarks

The three paths of healing, ritual and study – each with its own missionary and proselytizing spirit – helped ensure the rebirth of Tibetan Buddhism in the diaspora through complex processes of re-signification in dialogue with western cultures. In the cases of both Lama Gangchen and Geshe Kelsang, one of the most visible aspects of this process of re-signification is the intense institutionalization of their activities along western lines. This dynamic can perhaps best be understood as a parallel movement to the "official" process of re-institutionalizing Tibetan

Buddhism in exile, a process which mainly involved the reconstruction of monasteries in India and Nepal. At least during his first phase, Lama Shakya also positioned himself outside this "official" process. The basis of his dialogue, however, is mainly built from his reorganization of the vision of the cosmos based on his knowledge of Tibetan Buddhism and Brazilian spiritualism. In his case, the meeting of two spiritual universes becomes public through elaborate rituals.

Notes

1 This chapter was initially translated by Julia Spatuzzi Felmanas and Phillip Wigan. Later, several changes were made to the text.
2 *The Noble Great Vehicle Sūtra "The Play in Full"* (*Āryalalitavistaranāmamahāyāna-sūtra*), trans. Dharmachakra Translation Committee, 275 (www.84000.com, 2013).
3 The precise origins of the Tibetan medical system and its relationship with Buddhism has been an issue of contention within Tibetan intellectual circles for several centuries, and more recently among university scholars. For more on this issue, see Janet Gyatso's upcoming monograph.
4 The book *Self-Healing I*, from which this information was extracted, was first published in Brazil in 1991 as *Autocura I* (Gangchen 2001 [1991]), and then translated into other languages. All the passages in the present study quoted from *Self-Healing I* have been translated by me from the Brazilian edition.
5 In his book *Self-Healing I*, Lama Gangchen explains the meaning of each syllable in the mantra:

> OM: absolute mental tranquility and happiness.
> MUNI: determination to renounce Samsara, an intense desire to be free from all suffering.
> MUNI: determination to maintain the motivation of an altruistic mind, the mind of Bodhicitta which wants to help everyone
> MAHA MUNI: represents the correct vision of reality, that is, the perception that all phenomena have an empty nature, they are free from concepts and do not exist independently.
> SHAKYA MUNYIE: represents the secret (tantric) path, which is the quickest.
>   Thousands of Buddhas have come to our world, but Buddha Shakyamuni was the only one to transmit tantric teachings.
> SOHA: means "Please, make these things happen for the benefit of healing."
> (Gangchen 2001 [1991]: 61)

6 If Lama Gangchen was a great influence in Mônica's life, we could also say that the opposite was true. In fact, Mônica played a fundamental role in Lama Gangchen going to Brazil and in the foundation of his first center in this country in the 1980s. A French astrologer introduced her to Isabel Villares and her husband Daniel Calmanowitz. They collected the funds to make the visit of Lama Gangchen to Brazil possible. Mônica decided to get in touch with the astrologer because she was thinking of bringing Lama Gangchen to Brazil and wanted advice or perhaps the name of other people who might help her in this "project." She states:

> One day he [the astrologer] telephoned me and said: there's a couple here, they have a very interesting astral chart and I think that they may be able to help you to bring the lama over. It was mad, don't you think? I went to Bel's house on her birthday, she was holding Fê [her daughter] in her arms. I think she was about a year and a half. I was coming back from Goa ... can you imagine? I must have looked really strange. My hair was all cut short and messy, my nails were metallic green, I was full of scorpions, rings and other stuff ... I thought I looked

really cool: "My friend, the Tibetan lama...." And she was involved in a campaign in São Paulo against radioactive milk from Chernobyl. She looked at me, but she did not look down on me. We started to talk and I told her about my trip with Lama Gangchen. We started to see each other. On the weekend, I went to Ilhabela and then she came to my house. Two months later, Rinpoche was in São Paulo.

In 1987, a year after this first visit to Brazil, Isabel, with the help of other people who were to become important disciples of Lama Gangchen, such as Ely Inoue, founded the Shi De Choe Tsog Dharma Center. Around this time, Lama Gangchen recognized Michel, Isabel and Daniel's son, as the reincarnation of one of his masters, thus planting important seeds for the continuity of his work in Brazil and also around the world.

7 The "Four Limitless Thoughts" refer to four types of virtuous mental states – love, compassion, altruistic rejoicing and equanimity. They are limitless because they relate to all beings. Every time he gathers with his disciples, Lama Gangchen recites the following famous aspiration of the Four Limitless Thoughts in a number of languages:

May all beings have happiness and its causes.
May all beings be free from suffering and its causes.
May all beings never be separated from the great happiness that is beyond all misery.
May all beings dwell in equanimity, unaffected by attraction to dear ones and aversion to others.

(Gangchen, 2001[1991])

Recently, Lama Gangchen added another three thoughts to the four limitless thoughts: health, ecological regeneration and peace:

May all beings recover from the sicknesses of mind and body pollution and enjoy relative and absolute health now and forever.
May all beings relax in a pure and healthy outer and inner environment now and forever.
May all beings enjoy inner and world peace now and forever.

(Gangchen 1999: 15)

As it will become clear throughout the present work, this adaptation of a classic teaching is directly related with Lama Gangchen's activities in the West. Health, ecology and world peace represent, in fact, the pillars upon which all his activities are based.

8 Tara represents the feminine principle of enlightenment. Tara is a bodhisattva of compassionate activity and considered to be the mother of all Buddhas. There are innumerable manifestations of Tara, such as White Tara, who is usually associated with longevity. For more on the role of Tara in Tibetan religious life, see Beyer (1988).

9 Puja (Skt. *pūja*) literally means "worship." It usually refers to an offering associated with a ritual, or the recitation and performance of a liturgy.

10 For an explanation of the three bodies of the Buddha, see Makransky (1997).

11 Lama Gangchen, as we shall see in the next chapter, affirms that these practices constitute *termas*, or "treasures." As I briefly discussed in Chapter 2, these treasures are sacred texts and objects that were hidden in the past in rocks, caves, pillars, in the mind, in space and so forth, to be discovered in the future, when the time is appropriate for their dissemination. The tradition of discovering treasures is mainly practiced among representatives of the Nyingma School, but in all the schools of Tibetan Buddhism it is possible to find examples of it.

12 I must point out that Lama Gangchen directly associates the practice of tantric self-healing with a set of teachings that belongs to his lineage. The preface of his *Self-Healing II* states, for example: "This secret teaching of chakra purification is passed down through a direct lineage, from Buddha Vajradhara to my root guru, (*Ganden Kargyu Chagya Chenpo*) [who is a Gelug lama]" (Gangchen 1997 [1993]: 21).

13 In Chapter 6, we will look in greater detail at the Kalachakra tantric system.
14 This seems to be an interesting inversion of the more classical Buddhist idea of enlightening or "healing" ourselves in order to enlighten or heal the universe.
15 Despite the fact that Lama Gangchen lives in Italy, for bureaucratic reasons the LGWPF was established in Spain. Apparently it was easier to set up this type of organization within Spanish law. In any case, the LGWPF has in practice always operated in Italy.
16 Umbanda, an urban spirit-possession cult, emerged in Rio in the 1950s, bringing together influences of three major matrices: African traditions brought to Brazil, Catholicism and the theories and beliefs of the nineteenth-century French educator Allan Kardec. For more information on this tradition, see Diana Brown (1994).
17 Lama Shakya was recognized as the reincarnation of a Tibetan Lama in the 1980s; his formal investiture, however, only took place almost 15 years later, in part due to the lama's own wavering. After being ordained a monk and enthroned, Lama Shakya received a new name: Segyu Choepel Rinpoche. "Segyu" refers to his lineage, the history of which is marked by the foundation of the first tantric school in the Gelug tradition. "Choepel" means "the one who spreads the Dharma" in Tibetan; this means that Lama Shakya came to occupy the most important position in the Segyu tradition. Rinpoche means "precious" in Tibetan and it is usually added to the name of tulkus as an honorific sign of respect and veneration.
18 For a discussion of the lifespan of gods according to the Buddhist Pali canon, see for instance Rupert Gethin (1998).
19 See Gethin (1998: 112–32).
20 According to Robert Thurman (personal communication) some bodhisattvas manifest themselves as dogs to help human beings who have difficulties showing their feelings. Tibetans believe that even showing affection to an animal can make people virtuous.
21 Pretos velhos, caboclos and children are entities which possess mediums in the context of Umbanda. According to Diana Brown, pretos velhos, or

> "Old Blacks" are the spirits of Africans enslaved in Brazil, generally slaves from Bahia. All are elderly [...]. They are characterized as humble, patient, long-suffering, and good [...]. In contrast to the Caboclos, they are considered to be naturally endowed with humility and extremely anxious to help humans in any way they can. It is said that they love to exercise their many talents in curing and resolving family problems.
>
> (1994: 67–8)

Caboclos are the spirits of Brazil's native inhabitants and the "crianças," or "children" refer simply to the spirits of young children.
22 Known as the "Ladies of the Cemetery," "Queens of the Crossroads," and "Mistresses of the Night" (Hayes 2008), pomba giras are female spirits characterized by their sensuality. They are usually depicted in gypsy looking outfits that are predominantly red and black. In the words of Kelly Hayes, "often represented as a bawdy, demon-like figure clad in red and black, Pomba Gira embodies dominant notions of femininity and female sexuality as both alluring and perilous" (ibid.: 1).
23 The Portuguese term used in this context was "trabalho," literally meaning, "work."
24 "Senhor do Bonfim ribbons" are ribbons sold in Salvador, the capital of Bahia, for wish making.
25 A pemba is a piece of chalk used in the Umbanda context to design pontos riscados, magical diagrams very similar to the magical diagrams of yantra in the Indo-Tibetan tantric context. On the use and significance of yantra in Tibetan Buddhism, see Nebesky-Wojkowitz (1993).
26 Arruda (*Ruta graveolens*) is a medicinal plant in common use within Afro-Brazilian religious traditions to ward off evil spirits and influences.

27 While clapping the hands is a common practice in the Umbanda tradition done for a variety of reasons, clapping the hands is also done in Tibetan Buddhism specifically to expel spirits. This practice, despite its divergent meanings across these two traditions, is an interesting coincidence which, along with other coincidences, enables points of contact between the two traditions that allow for the re-signification process we observe in the spiritual theory and practice of Lama Shakya.

28 In Tibetan Buddhism, exorcisms may be performed in settings ranging from semi-private healing sessions to public dance ceremonies. The *'chams*, or public lama dancing rituals performed every year around the time of the Tibetan New Year is one particularly visible instance of this ritual type. For more on the *'chams* ritual as public exorcism, see Nebesky-Wojkowitz (1976).

29 See Mumford (1990), Ortner (1978), and Paul (1982) for analyses of the role of the myth of Padmasambhava's conversion of local spirits in the spread of Tibetan Buddhism throughout the Himalayan border regions of highland Nepal.

30 It is interesting to note that the idea of the "indoctrination" of spirits, very common in Umbanda, has a parallel in this ritual. Thus, in yet another way, the task of "putting entities on the path of Tibetan Buddhism" becomes more likely to be understood by Brazilian disciples.

31 It is interesting to note that despite conforming to Tibetan Buddhist practices, in the diaspora, spirit possession has in general been restricted to Tibetan circles.

32 For a detailed discussion on the emergence and development of the New Kadampa Tradition in Great Britain, see Kay (2004).

33 For more on the Gelug scholastic curriculum, see the excellent work by George Dreyfus, *The Sound of Two Hands Clapping: The Education of a Tibetan Buddhist Monk* (2003).

34 "Geshe-la" is a respectful way of referring to a geshe.

35 Lojong, literally "mind training," refers to a genre of meditation manuals. There are many traditions of Lojong teachings. In the case of NKT, this practice is based on aphorisms of the Tibetan master Geshe Chekawa (1102–1176). For more on Lojong, see Cabezón and Jackson (1996).

36 Lam Chung refers to a monk that lived during the time of the Buddha who had a reputation for being dull and unteachable. After numerous failed attempts at traditional modes of monastic and lay training, including even the ability to memorize a single verse, Buddha finally taught him just a few words of dharma and assigned him as a temple sweeper, by which he attained the highest realization. For more details on this story, see Geshe Kelsang Gyatso (1990: 42–5).

37 Lorig refers to a Tibetan Buddhist genre that defines and explains the different types of cognitions and their subdivisions. For more on this genre, see Lati Rinpoche (1980).

5 Etiquette, fantastic tales and the construction of sacred space[1]

Constructing a sacred space is one of the many crucial aspects that provide a foundation for the process of transmitting Tibetan Buddhism to western disciples. There are many ways in which this construction is materialized. In a literal sense, we could consider this in terms of the building of Buddhist centers, material constructions that are merely the most visible part of a wider process ultimately leading to the creation of a universe, which in many ways is magical.

The figure of the guru nearly always lies at the heart of this creation process. In fact, one of the most striking characteristics of Tibetan Buddhism is precisely the emphasis given to the role performed by the spiritual mentor in relation to a practitioner's path towards enlightenment. Within this context, the building of a transcendental image of the guru is crucial. Mechanisms involved in this process range from word-of-mouth accounts – narratives which have more than a touch of the fantastical about the life, or past lives, of the guru – to the transmission of dharma etiquette, that is, rules of behavior to be adopted when in the presence of a guru (these rules also apply to objects and physical space itself). Rituals, and even well defined rules, are the foundations that sustain this process of creating a sacred space around the guru, leading at the same time to the main consequence of this process, the construction of hierarchy.

I Segyu Rinpoche

April 2000: over 150 people gathered outside the Lama Je Tsongkhapa Buddhist Center for its inauguration. Watched by the crowd, Segyu Rinpoche went up the steps of his first center in Brazil and cut the ribbon he himself had tied around the door. The space, a hall measuring around 30 square meters, was not large enough to accommodate the small crowd that was waiting outside. Some people had to make do with standing on the narrow steps of the two-story house in Cidade Baixa, the bohemian quarter of the city of Porto Alegre, in the southern Brazilian state of Rio Grande do Sul.

The center was carefully decorated. Segyu Rinpoche had considered every detail. Some days earlier, upon arrival in Porto Alegre, he had spent almost an hour talking to his main disciple there, Elton de Oliveira, and to the cabinet-maker about the height of the throne on which he would sit. The throne was lower than what he had specified and the small table higher than what it should have been. The solution to the problem was not to simply shorten the length of the legs of the table, as the most important issue was the height of the throne, which had to be in proportion to the altar. In the end, Segyu Rinpoche decided to cut the legs of the table and raise the throne by placing a wooden base underneath it.

With the same eye for detail, Segyu Rinpoche – helped by his assistant, the American nun Christina Juskiewicz – prepared his disciples for the opening ceremony of the center's activities. Each of his five main disciples in Porto Alegre, a group Segyu Rinpoche had designated as the "inner mandala" of his center, had to give him the five traditional offerings, representing the three qualities of the Buddha – body (a statue of Buddha), speech (a book) and mind (stupa) – and his two ordinary and extraordinary activities, represented by two mandalas made out of rice. Segyu Rinpoche had to symbolically accept the offerings, thus agreeing to transmit to them his teachings.

Elton, Jussara, Isadora, Maria do Karmo and Varni got up from their places and prostrated themselves with some difficulty in the small area in front of the throne. Christina then passed them the offerings, which they in turn gave to Segyu Rinpoche. Elton formally requested the teachings: "We want to ask our Venerable Segyu Choepel Rinpoche to give us teachings so that we can enlighten ourselves for the benefit of all".

Segyu Rinpoche then spoke, reminding everyone who Tsongkhapa was.

> There may be many stories I could tell … this is the Lama Je Tsongkhapa Buddhist Center. Today's ceremony is very simple, but perhaps very profound. Around 23 years ago, I consecrated a plot of land to build the Lama Tsongkhapa Temple, perhaps the first [Tibetan] Buddhist ritual temple in Brazil. I left the country and I am still living in the United States, where I have my center. I have a monastery in India and one in Nepal and now I return to establish a Buddhist center from the Lama Tsongkhapa lineage. Lama Tsongkhapa lived in the fourteenth century, from 1357 to 1419. He was a reformer of Tibetan Buddhism. He studied with masters from all the Tibetan Buddhist schools, identifying the positive points of each school. He then established his own school. This book we are offering and these five objects represent the body, speech, mind, qualities and activities of the Buddha. We call this book *Lamrim – Lam*, path and *Rim*, stages – the stages of the path, which will definitely lead us to internal peace and harmony. This book was written by this great master.

This fragment, taken from my ethnographic transcript of the inauguration of the Lama Je Tsongkhapa Buddhist Center, is significant when we take into account its elements, the raw materials from which sacred, symbolic and physical spaces connected to the Tibetan Buddhist tradition are being built in the West. First, there is the actual construction of Buddhist centers, the care taken with the measurements of furniture, the position of objects and colors, etc. Second is the preparation of the disciples, so that they know how to behave in a sacred environment. Finally comes the reference to the lineage. The insertion into a lineage is essential to Buddhism as a whole and particularly in the case of Segyu Rinpoche, a Brazilian lama who was "discovered" when he was already over 30 years old.

The inauguration of the center in Porto Alegre marked the beginning of a new phase of the lama's activities in Brazil. Since his departure from Lama Gangchen's dharma center in 1995,[2] Segyu Rinpoche, then known as Lama Shakya, no longer had a clear route to follow in Brazil. He would come and visit relatives every now and again and give talks about his healing work and Tibetan medicine in general. It was during one of these talks that he met Elton, who was from Porto Alegre. Elton started to organize meetings and retreats with Segyu Rinpoche in Rio Grande do Sul. Gradually, Segyu Rinpoche gathered a group of students in the capital, Porto Alegre. The inauguration of the center sealed this relationship. Apart from his departure from Lama Gangchen's center, another significant factor was the new style that Segyu Rinpoche now embodied through his decision to take monastic vows and his subsequent official enthronement. The Brazilian lama once again found himself at a juncture marked by the re-configuration of his activities, thus rendering visible the mechanisms involved in the construction of sacred space in Tibetan Buddhism.

Although it seems to be almost a natural consequence of the path that Lama Shakya had followed after his first transformation into a fully-fledged Tibetan Buddhist lama, his decision to take monastic vows was made with a certain amount of resistance on his part. When I interviewed him in 1996 in San Francisco, he firmly expressed his aversion to the idea of being ordained as a monk within Tibetan Buddhism, even if this decision implied that he would never be officially enthroned as a reincarnate lama. All lamas are monks within the Gelug School, with few exceptions. At the time, Lama Shakya was mainly concerned about his freedom to act. He believed that by becoming a monk, he would be too involved in the Tibetan hierarchy and this would interfere with his healing work with westerners. As we previously observed, his situation was quite stable in the United States: he ran the Healing Buddha Foundation, a dharma center with a number of faithful followers. Up to that point, he had kept a certain distance from the Tibetan hierarchy, and more specifically, from the hierarchy of the Gelug School.

Just over a year after this interview in the American summer of 1996, I briefly returned to San Francisco and was surprised to see him with his head shaven and wearing a monastic habit. He explained at the time that he had been pressured by his spiritual master, Lati Rinpoche to take monastic vows and thus initiate the process of official recognition as a reincarnate lama. He said he was content with his new condition. His disciples also seemed to approve of these changes, though not without a dose of irony. Miguel, for example, who had been his disciple since the end of the 1980s, warned me, before I had even met the lama himself, that he had become "more Tibetan than the Tibetans themselves."

Miguel's observation was astute, as this change effected much more than his external appearance. By then Lama Shakya had already become Segyu Rinpoche. His ordination as a monk was a significant moment in Segyu Rinpoche's spiritual career, leading to changes in his relationship with the lineage to which he belonged. Now, more than ever, he would have to join hands with a culture to which he did not belong, at least not originally. Within this new context in which he found himself, it was neither useful nor desirable to make his connections with Umbanda explicit. Indeed, his gradual abandonment of explicitly Umbanda practices had been underway for a number of years. "Placing his spiritual guides within a Buddhist mandala" was also part of this process, which was now becoming even more marked. A seemingly banal though significant example is his biography posted on the Healing Buddha Foundation website (www.healingbuddha.org[3]). It reads as follows:

> The Venerable Segyu Choepel Rinpoche is the founding director and Head Lama of the Healing Buddha Foundation – Segyu Gaden Dhargye Ling. In 1985, the 98th Gaden Tri Rinpoche, the Venerable Jampal Shenpen, holder of the Gelugpa lineage founded by Lama Tsongkhapa, identified him as the re-incarnation of Dorje Zangpo. At a ceremony at the Segyu Monastery in Kathmandu, Nepal, on 19th February 1997, the Venerable Segyu Rinpoche was formally recognized as a tulku [re-incarnation] of the Venerable Gyudchen Dorje Zangpo, the 16th Century tantric master from the Segyu lineage.
>   Following the healing tradition of the Medicine Buddha, the Venerable Segyu Rinpoche developed his own therapeutic system, a psycho-spiritual cure based on tantric medicine and Buddhist psychology. This system pays special attention to emotional and psychosomatic imbalances, providing successful treatment for different types of psycho-spiritual emergencies and crises.

In this short biography, there is no reference to his connection with Umbanda, his Brazilian nationality or even to the fact that Segyu Rinpoche is from the West. As we have seen, the so-called "psycho-spiritual cure" developed by Segyu Rinpoche from his experiences at the Eternal Truth Spiritual Brotherhood (IEVE) in Rio de Janeiro was transformed into a system "based [only] on tantric medicine and Buddhist psychology," although in actuality some elements more common to Umbanda than to Tibetan Buddhism, such as candles and a glass of water mixed with coarse-grained salt, are nonetheless used. It is also possible to ascertain a link with Umbanda by the fact that his disciples wear white clothes during the healing sessions. In the past, Segyu Rinpoche himself explained this characteristic as being a vestige of his time in Umbanda. He used to say, "wearing white clothes is part of our spiritualist culture." Then he started to associate the use of white clothes with the requirement that his disciples wear some type of uniform in order to differentiate themselves from patients.[4] Segyu Rinpoche also used to wear white robes, giving him a slightly ambiguous reputation within the Gelug School, as in Tibetan Buddhism white is usually reserved for lay yogis, who are more common in other schools. He explained his choice of color with the same arguments used to justify the uniform of his disciples: it was a cultural vestige. During one of our conversations in 2001, however, Segyu Rinpoche explained his decision to use white clothes as a tradition based on the history of his school.

> The Segyu School was very powerful due to its large number of spiritual masters, real masters who manifested incredible powers. The eleventh master [the abbot of the school] was poisoned, but before he died, he prophesized that the Segyu School would experience a period of decline, until the karma of the family, which had poisoned him, disappeared. Only then would the school return with the presence of an "upasaka." "Upasaka" is the Sanskrit term for "religious layman," that is, one who takes the [Buddhist] lay precepts, but not monastic vows. I was, therefore, this person. I was the upasaka and for this reason I used to wear white.

It is clear from both his discourse and the documents produced by the Healing Buddha Foundation that since his official recognition Segyu Rinpoche started to use his connection with the Segyu lineage as his principal source of legitimacy. His foundation then came to be called the Healing Buddha Foundation – Segyu Gaden Dhargye Ling, a clear reference to the Segyu lineage. His website stated that the main aim of the foundation was to "disseminate Buddhist teachings, particularly those from the Segyu lineage." Other sections on the site recounted the history of the lineage and asked for donations in order to preserve it.

The so-called Segyu Tantric School was the first Gelug institution established in Tibet exclusively dedicated to teaching Tantric Buddhism. It was founded in the fifteenth century at the request of Tsongkhapa himself. Despite its historical importance, the Segyu School had been going through a period of decline even before the Chinese invasion. Two other schools teaching Tantra, the Gyume School and the Gyuto School, closer to the Tibetan capital of Lhasa, became predominant, while the Segyu School became less important. According to Segyu Rinpoche, in 1999, there were only six senior monks of the 40 who went into exile that were able to keep the Segyu tradition alive. From the moment of his official recognition and his subsequent investiture as abbot of the school, Segyu Rinpoche directed his efforts towards preserving the teachings that were at risk of being lost forever.

Thus, a combination of different factors, such as a concern with preservation and also his position as an outsider, made Segyu Rinpoche, in a certain way, become a more traditional lama than many other Tibetan lamas active in the West. This is clearly seen in his opinion of Lama Gangchen. Despite the fact that he admires Lama Gangchen's work, Segyu Rinpoche does not believe that the new practices introduced by him are in fact "consistent with the lineage." Segyu Rinpoche said:

> He is working for peace. He does very good work by the way, it will become a landmark, but I do not see in him the continuation of the lineage.

The practice of self-healing is an unblocking mechanism. It is very efficient, but it is independent of time and space.

Segyu Rinpoche even claimed that a number of the spiritual practices introduced at Lama Gangchen's dharma center, particularly those introduced by some of his disciples, resembled New Age practices. In relation to the work of Isabel César, founder of the Center, Segyu Rinpoche said:

Bel's classes were very popular. I think that's great! I've said to Bel: "Bel, you're doing great work." But it is very much self-help stuff. About menstrual cycles, for example: She does workshops in which women can bleed on the earth. Ok, it's ok. She started with the winds, and she is right, because that's where the PMS processes start. It is precisely the energy that is not moved around by the winds that cause this. But this type of work is really outside the concept of dharma. It becomes a New Age thing, you can do this type of work, but you cannot call it dharma.

This tendency to adopt a more traditionalist posture is also reflected, as I mentioned above, in the transmission of the so-called dharma etiquette to his pupils, a very important theme for Segyu Rinpoche. During the retreat he conducted in São Francisco de Paula (in the state of Rio Grande do Sul, Brazil), during the Easter holiday of 2000, his assistant, Christina, taught Segyu Rinpoche's pupils some rules of conduct. She explained, for example, that they have to prostrate themselves in front of a guru when he enters a meditation hall and also the meaning of prostrating. She talked about the fact that it is not permitted to point one's feet towards the guru and how to look after dharma objects such as books, never leaving them on the ground or sitting on top of them.

Apart from the etiquette classes, Segyu Rinpoche also distributed among his disciples the famous *Fifty Verses on Guru Devotion* (Aryashura and Geshe Ngawang Dhargyey 1992). This is a classic text that Tibetan tradition attributes to the Indian poet Ashvaghosha who lived in the first century BCE. These verses describe various rules about how to behave in front of a guru. In the second verse, for example, Ashvaghosha writes: "All the Buddhas residing in every land in the ten directions have prostrated three times (each day) to the tantric masters from whom they have received the highest empowerments. (Is there need to mention that you should too?)" (ibid.: 2). Ashvaghosha provides more practical advice in other verses:

In the presence of your teacher never do such things as spit, (cough or sneeze without covering your head. Never) stretch out your legs when at your seat, nor walk back and forth (without reason before him. And never) argue.

(ibid.: 16)

It is worth pointing out that this concern with the rules of conduct that the community must follow is not something new for Segyu Rinpoche. In a retreat that took place in 1996 in Santa Cruz, California, Christina taught Segyu Rinpoche's American disciples the "dharma etiquette." As we have seen, at that time his group of pupils was going through a period of transition in which old Umbanda practices such as the gira were being gradually abandoned. The lama's efforts to integrate the Umbanda spirits within the Buddhist mandala had a parallel on the physical level. As the anthropologist Geoffrey Samuel rightly observes, "The work of the lama is to tame. This is true in two ways. The lama tames demons and hostile forces and he also tames his disciples" (Samuel 1993: 220). Thus, it could be said that the process of "placing Umbanda entities inside a Buddhist mandala" was relevant to the new stage the lama was going through, in that it could be equated with the task of "taming disciples," either through meditation or dharma etiquette. The way this act of "taming" is performed in each group is not necessarily the same, but it ends up involving similar elements, which are often used in converse ways.

II Geshe Kelsang Gyatso

São Paulo, 2000. On a sunny Saturday a small group studying the Foundation Program at the Mahabodhi Center, the first Geshe Kelsang Gyatso center founded in Brazil, crossed the banks of the River Pinheiros in a convoy of cars to take part in a day of practical teachings in Osasco. A small meditation room was set up at the back of a house belonging to one of the pupils. The idea was that in the future a new center would be established there, a branch of Mahabodhi to serve the Osasco community. The decision to conduct the teaching there was in fact a way of supporting the nascent center. Two pupils in the Foundation Program told me about the subjects being taught, such as the preparation of the mandala rice offering and the way to set up an altar. They were both beginners in the study of Buddhism and yet they were reasonably confident when talking about these practical activities along general lines. Something caught my attention that day and shed light on a particular procedure common to all New Kadampa Tradition (NKT) centers: despite the fact that they were beginners, we had to prostrate ourselves before them, that is, before their teachings. While doing my fieldwork I had noted the rule about prostrating oneself before Foundation Program teachers. This episode in Osasco, however, made the universal nature of this rule clear.

If at NKT centers there is a serious concern with dharma etiquette rules, as can be observed from the example of prostration – one of the strongest signs of respect to a spiritual guide – in this case, the application of these rules also reveals, and this may be more important, how their use can vary in accordance with different contexts. In fact, differently from other Tibetan Buddhist traditions, where prostration is generally reserved for highly learned and accomplished figures, and sacred symbols (such as thangkas representing deities), at NKT the practice is to prostrate before any person who is teaching, regardless of their position in the traditional hierarchy or their level of "spiritual attainment." This protocol must be understood in relation to different factors and by emphasizing the privileged position that the study programs occupy in the New Kadampa Tradition.

In fact, the object which Geshe Kelsang's disciples prostrate themselves before seems to be the actual act of teaching, which at first sight appears to be at least as important as "spiritual attainment" through meditation in other traditions. The idea that dharma etiquette helps to establish a place for each individual within a religious hierarchy does not seem to apply here. On the contrary, I would venture to say that the primary function of etiquette – especially that which relates to the act of prostration – is to establish a "democratic sense" or at least "equal opportunities" for the NKT community. In fact, the study program offers a clear path, which, in theory, everyone can follow in order to become a teacher. In other Tibetan Buddhist traditions, the act of teaching the dharma is restricted to a few individuals and it generally depends on the head lama's direct and personal approval.

Another factor, perhaps crucial, in order to understand the direction followed by the Geshe Kelsang centers is the issue of the recognition of incarnations. Whereas in other Tibetan Buddhist schools the recognition of incarnations is usually fundamental to the process of choosing "spiritual guides," in NKT this procedure has been abandoned. As Kelsang Khyenrab who in 2002 was the resident teacher at the Tara Center in London explains, Geshe Kelsang believes that there is considerable abuse of this practice and that the criteria involved are not sufficiently precise. For this reason he decided to prohibit it in his organization. The implications of this decision are manifold. The first (and perhaps more immediate implication) is what could be called the decentralization of the power of decision over who can teach. When there is the recognition of reincarnations, the responsibility of deciding who teaches ends up in the hands of a few incarnate lamas.

Indeed, as mentioned earlier, in NKT senior teachers have the autonomy to decide who is apt to teach in their centers, not unlike geshes in Gelug monasteries of past and present. To become a teacher, it is necessary to be studying, at the very least, in the Foundation Program, and to become a Resident Teacher one must be taking the Teacher Training Program. However, an essential criterion for deciding who can teach is also assessing the pupils' faith in their "spiritual guide." According to Venerable Chöwang, one of Geshe Kelsang's most important disciples as of 2002,

> some people have faith, others have impressions of past lives. So, you can ask people to teach, even if this is beyond their capacity; due to the faith they have in their spiritual guide they are able to transmit their teachings. In this way, people can quickly start teaching because of the faith they have in their spiritual guide.

In fact, according to various teachers I have spoken to, pupils do not need to be fully qualified in order to start teaching. As Venerable Chöwang usually quotes Geshe Kelsang saying: "A mother cooks for her children and eats at the same time."

It is important to remember that the intention here is that, in part, the teacher becomes a "channel" through which Geshe Kelsang's teachings can flow. The same principle is followed when permission is given to disciples to perform initiations. In the words of Morten Clausen:

Who performs the initiation? Geshe-la performs it. But Geshe-la cannot be everywhere at the same time. So I try to imagine myself as his representative. On a good day, when I am performing an initiation, I only try to leave the path, and allow ... I only try to feel that Geshe-la cannot be physically present and that is why he has placed my body here, in order to perform an initiation through me.

We can detect here a delicate balance between the local power of the centers (and their effective decentralization in institutional terms) and the obvious centralization (in magical terms, if we can call it this) embodied in the person of Geshe Kelsang. This is a balancing act, which in many ways reflects the set of rules on which the whole of the NKT structure is based. As Morten Clausen explains:

There are two different things. There is "spiritual attainment" and there is also the organization. And the way that Geshe-la established the basis for the New Kadampa Tradition was ingenious, as each center is independent in constitutional, financial and legal terms. This basically allows them to be real grassroots organizations. People feel that it is their center, in contrast to some of the large centralized institutions. The connection between the centers is of a spiritual nature. However, these connections are very, very important, as otherwise, over time, institutions will become fragmented as teachers may wish to establish their own practices. Spiritual affiliation is what defines us, by all studying the same study programs and so on. Therefore, it is important that there is an overall Spiritual Director of NKT and National Spiritual Directors in each country, so that we can all gather these fellow practitioners in festivals. This is very, very important, this huge gathering. So you might say in that sense that the next General Spiritual Director will be like the official lineage holder, but that's like more from the point of view of the organization. You see what I'm saying? It all helps us all stay "one family," work things together, because there is so much more power, there is a protection, we protect the lineage.

The hierarchy issue, which seems to be rather confusing at the most immediate level of the application of etiquette rules, is thus clarified. It is a fundamental element in the internal organization of NKT. It is therefore worth describing in general terms how NKT is structured according to its constitution, entitled *A Moral Discipline Guide: The Internal Rules of The New Kadampa Tradition.* The highest power in NKT is the Education Council whose objectives are the same as those of the organization itself, that is, to provide spiritual assistance to all centers affiliated to NKT and to ensure the purity and authenticity of the New Kadampa Tradition. Members of the Education Council are the Resident Teachers of all NKT centers. The Council is responsible for electing representatives from among its members as follows: two from the United Kingdom, two from the Americas, two from Europe (excluding the UK), one from Asia, one from

Australia and one from Africa. "These representatives must be elected by all members of the Education Council in their respective continent."

The functions of the Education Council consist of a number of activities on which the principles of the hierarchy are based:

(A) to oversee the general standard of examinations for Foundation Program and Teacher Training Program; (B) to act as the final arbiter in any dispute; (C) to ensure that all the centers act according to internal regulations; (D) to ensure that the General and Deputy Spiritual Directors, National Spiritual Directors and Resident Teachers act in accordance with these Internal rules and do not cause division among the students. It is also the responsibility of the Council to elect the spiritual director-general and vice-director every four years and the director can be re-elected.

(New Kadampa Tradition 2001: 6–7)

Geshe Kelsang has been until 2009 the General Spiritual Director of NKT. He then decided to retire. Even before his voluntary retirement, elections were organized every four years and his name was put forward. Obviously in practical terms there was no possibility of removing him from this position through the voting process (a situation somewhat similar to how it used to be with the Dalai Lama within the Tibetan community living in exile). The National Spiritual Directors, on the other hand, are elected by the Resident Teachers of each country, who themselves are appointed by the General Spiritual Director. Finally, it is worth pointing out at least two other responsibilities of the General Spiritual Director: to ordain new monks and nuns and to authorize Heruka and Vajrayogini initiations which belong to the so-called Highest Yoga Tantra, the highest and most secret level of tantric Buddhist practice.[5] In each country National Spiritual Directors can, under the orientation of the General Spiritual Director, preside over these initiations.

Despite the adequacy of the NKT framework for western sensibilities due to its democratic principles, this configuration is also clearly influenced by the bureaucratic organizational structure of mass Gelug monasteries of the past.[6] In part owing to their enormous populations, such monasteries were less hierarchical and more bureaucratic and "democratic" than many religious institutions belonging to non-Gelug traditions.[7] In the NKT's case, however, we can see how a combination of institutional democracy and the highly (and necessarily) hierarchical structure of Tantric Buddhism created unexpected and even unimaginable situations within a traditional context.[8] An example is the idea that the person responsible for the highest and most secret initiations, or even those who are the "holders of the lineage," may be chosen through an election of sorts. While Geshe Kelsang is alive, however, these two organizational tendencies should work side-by-side, very often superimposed upon one another. Even after he stepped down as General Spiritual Director, his influence over every level of internal decision certainly continued to be felt.

Important issues emerge from a brief analysis of NKT's internal makeup. Of particular relevance here is the concern with the future of the organization, after the death of Geshe Kelsang. Certain institutional mechanisms exist precisely to avoid divisions, thus preserving the "purity" of the school. But what exactly does "purity" mean here? Or rather, what are the bases from which it is built? The fact is that in practice the effort to safeguard the purity of the school by institutionalizing it and subscribing to the NKT constitution goes hand in hand with another movement in the same direction, where the founding myths and structures inherent to Tibetan Buddhism are the fundaments to building a new religious tradition and breaking with the traditional Tibetan order.

The name "New Kadampa," which Geshe Kelsang used to baptize his new religious tradition, carries both the notion of rupture and the search for seminal purity. The origins of the Gelug School can be traced back to the Kadampa School of Tibetan Buddhism, founded in the eleventh century based on the teachings of the Indian master Atisha. Atisha was considered by many to be a Buddha and was partially responsible for the second dissemination period of Buddhism in Tibet.[9] Tsongkhapa, a follower of Atisha's tradition, attempted to reform the supposed corruptions that accrued over the centuries of transmitting these teachings (Powers 1995: 418). Tsongkhapa and his followers thus became known as the "New Kadampas," and later as Gelugpas.

The image of Geshe Kelsang Gyatso and his spiritual activities in the West is clearly associated with the role of Tsongkhapa, the reformer and founder of the Gelug School. Geshe's aim is to return to the "original purity" of this school. His short biography on the Internet, at www.tharpa.com/gkg.htm,[10] is an example of the emphasis Geshe Kelsang Gyatso places on the "originality" and "purity" of the teachings he transmits. According to his biography, after fleeing Tibet in 1959, Geshe Kelsang Gyatso spent the next 17 years in meditation retreat in the Himalayas. His online biography states,

> During this period, he concentrated on the practices of Kadampa Buddhism, a form of Buddhism dating back to the times of the Buddha himself which was transmitted through the great Indian pandits and Tibetan lamas to pure practitioners such as Geshe Kelsang Gyatso.

All the books written by Geshe Kelsang are, according to the geshe himself, commentaries on the teachings of Tsongkhapa. As the aforementioned Kelsang Pälsang says, "Geshe Kelsang took from the 19 books written by Tsongkhapa the essence of all his teachings, presenting them [now outside the monasteries] in a way befitting the modern world." More synthesized study plans, directed towards the practical application of the teachings – and in this sense certainly more appropriate to the modern style – substituted for the traditional monastic curriculum inspired by Tsongkhapa in Tibet. In the same way, the restoration of the strict monastic discipline adhered to by the great fourteenth century Tibetan master is echoed in modernity, making the spiritual community of the New Kadampa Tradition one of the most original in modern times.

One of the most striking characteristics of NKT is precisely the close everyday contact between male and female monastic and lay disciples. As the

English monk Losang Kelsang, who was Geshe Kelsang's first western disciple to take monastic vows at the beginning of the 1980s, told me:

> The experience of monks, nuns and lay practitioners living together is something that is somewhat unique, because it would be impossible to experience a similar situation in Tibet. In Tibet, monks and nuns live in different monasteries. Buddhist teachers never mix with the local population. The idea was: "this is what monks do" and "this is what nuns do" and our task [that of the lay community] is to make offerings, to look after the monks and so on. Right from the start, Geshe Kelsang did not separate monks and nuns, except for in the rooms, of course! So, in this tradition you can be a female lay teacher and be extremely qualified to do the job. It is a question of lifestyle and people can choose the one that suits them. We need to have a monastic community and we need to have a lay community, one supports the other. People can choose the role model they wish to follow. In Asian traditions there is a very strict hierarchy: monks are at the top, then the nuns and finally the lay population. In our case there is no hierarchy between the monastic and lay practitioners.

This bombastic sentence comes from Geshe Kelsang himself: "Tibet is not a Buddhist country. There are great masters in all the traditions, but Tibet is not a Buddhist country." Here Geshe Kelsang is referring precisely to the separation between practitioners, generally monks, and the lay population of Tibet, mentioned by Losang Kelsang above. By valuing lay practitioners and more specifically lay teachers, who are rare within the traditional Gelug order, Geshe Kelsang is, in a way, taking his reform further than Tsongkhapa's, including the lay community in a system of strict discipline geared towards practice. Despite this, I would not go so far as to say that there is no hierarchy between the two styles of community. Perusing NKT's constitution, we can see that the monastic community enjoys more prestige. The General Spiritual Directors must be monks or nuns because the regulation states that they are responsible for the ordination of disciples.

Furthermore, the higher prestige of the monastic community can be easily observed in practice. The NKT community has more monks and nuns than any other group connected to Tibetan Buddhism in the West. In the 2002 Summer Festival they represented around a quarter of the 1,800 people that were present at the event. And the general feeling at the event was that the number of monastic practitioners had grown dramatically over the previous few years. José Antônio Bacchin, from Brazil, who had been a disciple of Geshe Kelsang since the 1990s took part in 2002 in the International Teachers Training (ITT), an exclusive course for Resident Teachers held at the Manjushri Institute. He said that out of the 82 people that took part only 14 were from the lay community.

Bacchin was then part of the lay group, but expressed his wish to become a monk, although he had been married for over 20 years to another pupil of Geshe Kelsang. According to him, this was the natural path: "if you are a layman, you have to make twice as much effort to show that you are good and this also applies to moral discipline." In May 2003, Bacchin's wish became reality. He would henceforth be known by his monastic name: Kelsang Panchen. The Brazilian nun Kelsang Pälsang was also married when she decided to take her monastic vows. Although she was happy in her marriage, she felt at the time that it was essential that someone be ordained in Brazil. For Kelsang Pälsang, an "ordained person" would bring a new dimension to the work.

> You can physically see the monk. That's where it starts. Despite the fact that it is not the habit that makes the monk, that is where it starts. You can see what happens in a hospital. I think that this comparison is excellent. Just imagine you go to a hospital to give blood and see someone wearing jeans, with dirty hands and they say they are going to take your blood. You would feel totally insecure. But if a nurse comes, you don't ask her for her diploma. You trust her naturally. Because she is wearing white, you can see that. You don't ask for a monk's diploma, you don't ask him to describe his education. That is the role of the monk. People naturally approach us because they know that physically we are signaling that we are not interested in material things, that we have taken this option. Therefore, the identification with Geshe-la is very close, very direct. People naturally recognize this. There is no 100 per cent guarantee because a monk's motivation can change and he can be useless. Of course! But this signaling is important. So, this is how it works. Well, a monk has certain commitments, which are very similar to those of any teacher. Teachers in our tradition have the same or almost the same commitments that monks have, except monks cannot be sexually active. Apart from this, both have to at least be disciplined and not drink or smoke and so on.

Thus, despite the fact that lay teachers have "almost the same commitments" as the monastic community, the external signal of wearing a monastic habit has the fundamental function of making the role of the teacher within NKT more professional. This issue also touches on another important point highlighted by Kelsang Pälsang: identification with the guru. In every religious tradition the figure of the spiritual leader is always a model for moral conduct, a spiritual life and so on. In Tibetan Buddhism, this is no different, but the centrality of the guru within this tradition gives extra meaning to the notion of a model.

In fact, the promise that we have, within each of us, the full potential to reach enlightenment, and that this perfect state is attainable in this life, is only possible through trust, through having faith in the guru. The key word here is inspiration. According to Lama Yeshe, who was a very influential Tibetan lama among westerners, "it is not enough to know why this self-transformation is necessary and possible, we must create the strength and trust which will allow us to follow this radical approach to personal realization. In other words, we need to be inspired" (Yeshe 1987: 95). In the tantric tradition, the source of this inspiration is the guru who represents, among other things, the living proof of the possibility of enlightenment.

The aforementioned Venerable[11] Chöwang, an English disciple who came into contact with Geshe Kelsang's tradition for the first time at the beginning of the 1990s, was captivated precisely by a teaching about "trusting the guru." As she states:

> I felt very strongly that I had finally met my true guru. When I had previously been involved with another eastern tradition, I was not fully committed. When I heard people talking about "trusting the spiritual guide" I thought: "This is it!" I immediately felt that Geshe-la was the right person.

The inspiration that her relationship with the guru provoked was so strong that in less than a year Chöwang would turn her life upside down. She left behind her business, boyfriend and apartment, moved to a Geshe Kelsang center in London and took monastic vows. In Tibetan Buddhism, changes in daily life are considered to be merely a bridge to a greater change. Thus, to see the guru as a fully enlightened Buddha could act as powerful impetus towards self-transformation. According to Venerable Chöwang:

> There are different ways of relating to your spiritual guide. You can think: "this is a really good person!" Thinking like this, you can already attain something special. But you could go further and think: "I want to trust this person as if he were a Buddha." And how do you do this? I think that this really depends on your understanding of knowledge, of the teachings about knowledge. Some people have natural faith: "Here is a Buddha." And this is really beautiful. But, deep inside you need to understand that there is nothing apart from your mind, you need to understand that everything is a projection of your mind; you yourself are only a projection of your own mind. And from this basis you can think: "This is only a projection of my mind, if I have an impure mind, I will have a normal person in front of me, but if I develop a pure mind, I will manage to understand the benefits of trusting the spiritual guide, seeing him as Je Tsongkhapa, I will be blessed straight away." From a certain point of view, my mind is creating Je Tsongkhapa, but everything is created by my mind. If my mind creates Je Tsongkhapa, I will receive Je Tsongkhapa's blessings. Because there is no Tsongkhapa outside my mind, there is no "normal" geshe, there is no human being. There is only space, there is nothing that is really there! In this way, if I see the spiritual guide as a Buddha, I will gradually be able to relate to people in the same way. This is by far the most profound way of relating to a spiritual guide. So, between something like simple faith and something like the basis for understanding the experience of emptiness, the latter is far more profound.

There are, therefore, various levels through which a disciple can see his master as a fully enlightened being. At a deeper level, as Venerable Chöwang puts it, we should think that what must sustain the identification of the guru with a

Buddha is "the basis for understanding the experience of emptiness." At a relative level, however, the association of Geshe Kelsang with Tsongkhapa has a direct impact in the symbolic construction that lies behind the idea that NKT, like the "New Kadampas" of the fourteenth century, is reforming Buddhism.

III Lama Gangchen

Of all the Buddhist communities I spent time with during my fieldwork, Lama Gangchen's group was, without a shadow of a doubt, the one that seemed least concerned with dharma etiquette. According to his longest-standing disciples, this informality has always been part of Lama Gangchen's style and that of his spiritual community. As we have seen, Lama Gangchen did not impart any formal teaching when he first came to stay in the West. In those seminal days, his contact with new disciples occurred mainly through physical or emotional healing. Some disciples describe their first contact with Lama Gangchen as simply an "energetic contact," a non-verbal type of communication, which takes place mainly through action. His disciple, Mônica Bienvenutti, for example, compares Lama Gangchen's style to the behavior of the mahasiddha yogis:

> Rinpoche was like the mahasiddhas. The first mahasiddhas who arrived in places like Mongolia for example were fantastic, because they had to deal with barbaric people who killed everyone. The mahasiddhas did not seek to convert: "Look, don't do like this, as it isn't good." No, they first integrated themselves by their actions. They hunted with them, they did exactly the same things, but subliminally they showed them something that was good. This is exactly how Rinpoche reached us. Rinpoche also used to go with us everywhere, to bars and nightclubs. Wherever we went, he wanted to come.

The mahasiddha tradition evolved between the seventh and the ninth century in India.[12] In the traditional hagiographical literature they are depicted as tantric practitioners from different social strata whose behavior was often eccentric, rebellious and iconoclastic. Some of the most famous mahasiddhas were mendicant yogis who lived amongst common people, "teaching them through psychic vibration, posture and attitude – *mantra*, *mudra* and *tantra* – rather than through discourse" (Dowman 1985: 21). Thus, the identification of Lama Gangchen with the figure of the mahasiddha is far from coincidental. In fact, as we shall see, Lama Gangchen adopts the ideal of the mahasiddha practitioner in various ways, both for himself and also for his disciples. An example of this occurred in the summer of 2002 at the Albagnano Healing Meditation Center, his "headquarters" in Italy, when Lama Gangchen made a direct reference to this idea during a retreat about the 84 mahasiddhas. "The mahasiddhas," he said, "lived like normal people, they were fishermen, blacksmiths, hunters … exactly like us!!!" Lama Gangchen believes that like the mahasiddhas our search for enlightenment should start precisely from the point at which we find ourselves.

The adoption of this ideal has many implications for Lama Gangchen's activities in the West. Among these, disregard for etiquette rules is only one of the most visible signs of the type of impact that Lama Gangchen intends to have in the world through his spiritual practice. Francesco Prevosti, an Italian who has been a disciple of Lama Gangchen since 1985 says:

> Some lamas are very interested in keeping within tradition. As Lama Gangchen transcends formality, he is able to do anything. That is why he has this freedom; he has a lot of courage. He is a manifestation of "the spiritual power of all Buddhas," represented by the deity Vajrapani. Lama Gangchen's main incarnation in Tibet is considered to be an emanation of Vajrapani. If you think about it, his ways consist of power, the power to do things. I think that is how he manifests himself, but in order to do this you have to transcend all formalisms. You have to go beyond the formality required to be a lama, a monk, a Buddhist. He goes beyond all this. And, in fact, enlightenment is beyond all this. To be a Buddha is to be beyond etiquette, beyond all things, we could say. Enlightenment ... enlightenment is a "total phenomenon," it is global, it goes beyond any limitations, doesn't it?

In a certain sense, Francesco tells us that it is by going beyond the cultural formality related to his status as a lama that Lama Gangchen builds his image of the sacred, to the point of creating new identities for himself: "healer of the world," defender of world peace, and UN affiliate. The mahasiddha ideal accommodates well this multifaceted profile. The representatives of this Indian tradition ostensibly try not to conform to rules, but to take from the world things that very often seem banal and use them as raw materials for spiritual practice. Thus, as a mahasiddha who is able to teach "the living ideal in the world," Lama Gangchen is able to build the bases for his activities.

Indeed, "live in the world" but not in any kind of world. There is a sense among his students that the ground Lama Gangchen walks on is constantly re-enchanted by him. Perhaps one of the most striking hallmarks of Lama Gangchen's teachings is precisely the fact that, from the perspective of his students, he brings a "magical dimension" to everyday life in the modern world. This process of "re-enchantment" starts with somewhat fantastical word-of-mouth narratives and accounts that surround his life (or lives), and clearly shows how the sacred image of the guru is also constructed through the interweaving of these present and past histories.

In April 2000, the British-born Lama Caroline (b. 1965), one of Lama Gangchen's main disciples, went to São Paulo to give a series of teachings. Among the topics covered in her presentations were "Lama Gangchen's past lives." It is worth pointing out three tendencies in his past lives, whose narratives, full of fantastical deeds, illuminate his current life and help to symbolically sustain his activities while imbuing them with a magical dimension. First, the three mahasiddha incarnations must be emphasized. As we have seen, they represent a fundamental paradigm for Lama Gangchen and his disciples. According to Lama Caroline:

> The first incarnation of Lama Gangchen as a mahasiddha is Laksminkara, a female reincarnation. Laksminkara is a very important practitioner of Tantric Buddhism. She was a princess who was born in Oddyana, the "land of the Dakinis," which today is in modern Pakistan. This is why Lama Gangchen always says he is in favor of women's liberation, because he was a completely liberated woman. And she ended up going to Sri Lanka, where she became known as the "mad Dakini." Then there is the Indian mahasiddha, Darikapa. He was a king that became famous as the slave of prostitutes. So many of the women who were in this brothel with Darikapa became enlightened. So, our joke is that the women who are today with him are the ones who were not enlightened at the time. Everyone is very proud of the same idea: "I have known Lama Gangchen for centuries." But this is because we are very sick. If we walked a little faster, we would already be in the pure lands. The next apparition is Drugpa Kunley[13] who lived between 1454 and 1529. Drugpa Kunley means the Mad Dragon, the Mad Dragon of Bhutan. Bhutan was very influenced by Drugpa Kunley and that's why it became a Buddhist country and this influence continues today. He used to travel constantly between Tibet and Bhutan.

Thus, from stories such as that of Laksminkara, the "mad princess," Darikapa, "the slave of prostitutes," and Drugpa Kunley, one of the most revered "mad wise men" of Tibet, Lama Caroline provides Lama Gangchen's disciples with paradigms. They give meaning to the lama's unconventional attitudes and they also provide his disciples (who are also very often unconventional) with models of how to recognize themselves within Tibetan Buddhism.

Returning to the set of stories about Lama Gangchen's past lives, I would also like to stress the fact that, according to Lama Caroline, her guru retraces his past incarnations to the four main schools of Tibetan Buddhism, emphasizing a non-sectarian tendency. This posture is essential for his activity in organizations such as the UN, where, as we have seen, he defends the creation of a "Permanent Spiritual Forum," bringing together representatives of all religions, forming what could be called a "council of wise men" to discuss issues related to world peace. As the English lama playfully remarks:

> Lama Gangchen has always appeared in different schools of Tibetan Buddhism. The different schools of Tibetan Buddhism are like Brazilian schools of samba. Everything is samba, but there are different forms of practicing, there are different masters. And generally most lamas always stay in the same school. Just like a person who is from a particular school of samba spends his whole life in that school. On the other hand, Joãosinho Trinta[14] is one of those who are everywhere. Just like Lama Gangchen! He has always belonged to different schools. Hence, it is very difficult for Lama Gangchen

to be sectarian, as he has belonged to all schools. And one of Lama Gangchen's current projects is the Spiritual Forum, which is precisely a non-sectarian religious project. Just to recall some of his past incarnations: Trophu Lotsawa[15] [1172–1224] was Kagyu; Buton Rinchen Druppa[16] [1290–1364] was Sakya; Drugpa Kunley was Nyingma [*sic*]; and the famous Panchen Zangpo Tashi [1410–78/79], the second holder of the throne of the Tashilhunpo Monastery, was Gelugpa.

Furthermore, it is also important to stress that Lama Caroline directly connected to the practice of "self-healing" at least two of Lama Gangchen's incarnations, Trophu Lotsawa and Buton Rinchen Druppa, bringing the non-sectarian tendency into his spiritual practice. Buton Rinchen Druppa, from the Sakya tradition, was perhaps the most important spiritual master of his generation. Among his many writings are five volumes dedicated to the Kalachakra Tantra, which include books covering all the main aspects of this tradition (Mullin 1991: 109). As previously mentioned, Lama Gangchen used the Kalachakra system as a foundation for his practice of the self-healing of the environment. The fact that Buton Rinchen Druppa is considered one of his past lives certainly contributes to substantiate this practice and his activity as global healer.

Trophu Lotsawa has a more direct role in legitimizing the spiritual practices conceived by Lama Gangchen. In fact, according to the lama, his Ngalso Self-Healing texts were originally written by Trophu Lotsawa, who hid them "in the heavens to be rediscovered in future times." They are, therefore, mind termas (treasures). As Lama Gangchen explains in a very modern way, "they were imprinted onto my inner Space disc eight centuries ago and now the right dependently arising causes and conditions have arisen for these Self-Healing programmes to print out from my inner heart computer" (Gangchen 1994: 22). Lama Caroline says that some time ago she had read in *Blue Annals*, an important fifteenth-century Tibetan religious history, the biography of Trophu Lotsawa. She states: "I then noticed that Trophu Lotsawa's practices were exactly the same as those that Lama Gangchen performs today, even the terminology he uses is the same. I wrote these words in my computer," said Lama Caroline, who is the main editor of Lama Gangchen's books.

With regard to Trophu Lotsawa, one of his most renowned acts is today being re-enacted by Lama Gangchen: the commissioning of Maitreya Buddha statues, the so-called Buddha of Love, or Buddha of the Future. During his lifetime Trophu Lotsawa built three large images of Maitreya, which ended up being destroyed during the Chinese Cultural Revolution. In the words of Lama Caroline:

Recently, Lama Gangchen initiated a project consisting of the building of ten statues of the Maitreya Buddha, not as large as those built by Trophu Lotsawa, they are in fact three meters tall [the original statues were ten meters] and these statues have been put in various places and monasteries in India, Nepal [Kathmandu] and Tibet. One is in fact at the Trophu monastery in Tibet, where one of the large statues used to be. We can see from this that the feeling of pure reincarnation, as experienced by Lama Gangchen, never disappears. Because he was the one who built those three statues. They were destroyed, but he still had the same feeling inside him. He did not build large statues since they would have cost millions of dollars. Instead he built ten smaller ones.

This is a clear example of how Lama Gangchen sacralizes, and thus re-enchants the world around him through the histories of his past lives. The account of another life outside Tibet clarifies this point further. Going further back in time we encounter one of Lama Gangchen's most important reincarnations, Saliendra, the Javanese king that built the famous Borobudur stupa. According to Lama Caroline: "For us the Borobudur stupa is very important, because this is where the practice of self-healing emerged. All our practice and everything that we do is inspired by the Borobudur stupa." She explains further:

> In one of the monuments near Borobudur, we [the disciples] saw written in Javanese that Saliendra was a bodhisattva of the tenth bhumi[17] and he attained enlightenment thanks to the merit he accumulated by building Borobudur. Borobudur is a monument built for inner peace, for world peace. And Lama Gangchen has been there 12 times so far, once a year for the last 12 years. One can imagine the feeling of *déjà vu* he had when he went there for the first time. In December 1992 Lama Gangchen was in Borobudur and he had visions. It was as if the bodhisattvas came and said "Look, Lama Gangchen, come on, don't you want to write a new practice to help the people from the West?" That's when he returned to Europe to write the self-healing practice. "Call it self-healing!" So it is not only the practice of self-healing referred to here as *Self-Healing II,* which is directly linked to Borobudur, but all the practices that Lama Gangchen shows us, including Vajrayogini, are directly linked to Borobudur, they are all based on the practice of self-healing from Borobudur.

The creation of the self-healing practice, as was previously mentioned, represented an important milestone in Lama Gangchen's trajectory in the West. It could be said that his activities were organized around different versions of this practice that emerged throughout the years. The constant reference to Borobudur in his teachings is therefore an almost natural consequence of this fact. In 2001, Lama Gangchen decided to commission various statues in Borobudur, from the same volcanic rocks used to adorn the great stupa. A set of statues called the "five Dhyani Buddhas," archetypal deities representing the five types of wisdom, among other things,[18] and which form the basis of the self-healing practice, were sent to each of the main countries Lama Gangchen has links with: Italy, Brazil and Tibet. Lama Gangchen said that in this way he is trying to reproduce in these places the same energy that exists in Borobudur. Lama Gangchen thus gives a new meaning and at the same time re-enacts the mythical history of king

Saliendra through his practices and the material construction of sacred spaces. Moreover, it is important to point out that the lama is symbolically creating a connection between these different parts of the world through the image of Borobudur. He creates, in this way, a sense of interdependence linking all his practices and activities.

Furthermore, in the Amazon, during a retreat he conducted between the end of 2000 and the beginning of 2001, Lama Gangchen once more evoked the image of Borobudur when on the sandy bank of the Tapajós River he performed a practice, which involved the symbolic re-creation of the famous stupa. While walking on the sand, disciples were invited to mentally reproduce the walls of the Javanese monument. In a circular movement, they visualized the regeneration of the forest by imagining lotus flowers in various colors spreading out in all directions. Sometimes Lama Gangchen would pronounce: "Amazon, the center of the world, the lungs of the world." They walked inside this "virtual reality" to the center of the mandala, the "top of the stupa," where Lama Gangchen sat down and together with Lama Caroline delivered teachings.

Lama Caroline commented that this practice was exactly like self-healing, "except that in self-healing we go from top to bottom and in the case of this mandala we start from the sides, in all directions." According to her:

> At the time Borobudur was built, it was at the center of the island of Java and represented the center of the world. Now we can imagine this mandala of Borobudur in the center of the world, with the continents we know all around.

Lama Gangchen then explained that what we were doing there was a sort of environmental education: "We are here with the lama himself, transforming impure elements into pure ones. This is therefore a type of practical, rather than theoretical, environmental education."

Another important point to understand is that often these mythical narratives become part of our reality. Almost at the end of the retreat with Lama Gangchen in the Amazon, the opportunity arose to experience one of these moments first hand, as I narrate in the following vignette from my ethnographic journal.

Account of a foretold storm – or the fantastical in the real

That night, we went back to Suruacá, a riverside village on the Tapajós, to watch a circus show performed by the local community. We were a group of around 35 or 40 people. Some people stayed on the boat. During the day, we were unsure as to what was going to happen in the evening. The presentation had been more or less planned, but when we docked at the "Abrigo dos Golfinhos" [Dolphin's Haven], Eugênio Scannavino, a doctor with "Saúde e Alegria," the NGO which had organized the trip together with AACHAA (Association of the Healing Arts of the Himalayas, Andes and the Amazon), sent a speedboat up to Suruacá to find out whether the event was taking place. We received word that the population had been waiting for us since midday. However, it was known since earlier that day that a storm was approaching and it was decided that Lama Gangchen would not go to Suruacá.

When we arrived in Suruacá most of the community received us with banners welcoming Lama Gangchen, even though the lama was not with us. They sang songs while we went through a tunnel of people. We watched a clown presentation for about one hour and then went to buy some of the local handicrafts. Finally, extremely exhausted by the long day, we started to prepare for our departure. We arrived at the bank of the river and discovered that the boatmen had disappeared. Ten minutes later, two boats returned. Some people had already confirmed their place on the first trips that would take us back to the dormitory-boat. After the first run, we received the news: the river was too turbulent and the dormitory-boat could not remain where it was. We later found out that the speedboat that had taken the others to the dormitory-boat was swaying a lot and that the boatman had said that with the river as it was, it was impossible to take more people. The plan was to dock the speedboat in front of the jungle hotel where we had spent New Year's Eve a few days before. Only those with physical disabilities or with children were taken back to the speedboat from Suruacá beach.

That's when our small adventure started. We walked along the beach for over one hour with just a few torches. Lightening lit the path and forewarned us of the approaching storm. We could see the boat in the distance, and contrary to what we expected, it seemed to be getting further and further away from us. When we arrived at our rendezvous, the boat was nowhere to be seen. We sat on the sand for a while. Some people started to question the coordinators of the trip in order to understand what was going on, but they replied impatiently or nervously. Their motto was: "do not panic, let us stay calm and chant some mantras." People were obviously not happy with their reply and the treatment they received and continued to ask for an explanation. Then Sassá, a local man who was working with the NGO "Saúde e Alegria" explained that the speedboat that could have taken us to the dormitory-boat was used to rescue a person from the local community who was not feeling well. Sassá told us that this person had had a heart attack. He also said that the boat would not be able to dock there, because the river was too strong. Everyone calmed down with this simple explanation.

After waiting for some time, someone suggested we try to sleep in the foyer of the jungle hotel. Christian, an Argentinean who had joined Lama Gangchen's group in the middle of the trip, went to the hotel and asked the staff if we could stay there. With their permission, we all went to the hotel. Around 15 minutes later, Rui, a friend of Dr. Scannavino who was not a Lama Gangchen disciple, told us that the boat had docked some 20 minutes away from where we were. We left in a convoy once again. This was our hardest walk, we went past stretches where there was practically no sand and we were constantly stepping on tree trunks. Some people really started to panic and some even started to cry. We had walked further than the first time. When we arrived at the place where

Rui was, we sat down and waited for the speedboat. Nobody understood anything; once again the speedboat was not there. Ten minutes later, Márcia, one of Lama Gangchen's disciples arrived. She was very nervous and started to shout at Christian. She explained that the speedboat had capsized and for over an hour she had attempted to turn it over with the help of the boatmen. All the men went to help turn the speedboat around. They managed to turn it around in a couple of minutes, but now the engine would not start.

While they were fixing it, some people tried to talk to the coordinators of the trip to convince them to go to the place we had been before in order to get into the boat. The river seemed to be calmer at that point. The coordinator not only did not want to listen, but he was rude. "One step at a time, at the moment we are fixing the boat." When the boat was working and people were boarding, they tried to talk to him again. And he gave the same answer. It almost ended in a fight.

As people were getting on board, the storm finally arrived. That was certainly the most confusing and dramatic moment of our escapade. Despite this, some people were running to get on board, though the river had suddenly become violent. Among this group there was even a female disciple who could not swim. Another group preferred to wait on the banks of the river until the storm was over. Gradually the speedboat started to take people back. Our boat had a light, so we could finally see where we were going. It was raining torrentially, but fortunately the lightening was far away. Everything started to calm down.

I went on the last boat. By that time, the river was much calmer. When we arrived at the dormitory-boat, Débora Laruccia, a representative of AACHAA, was there to welcome us. It was three in the morning. We then discovered that the person who wasn't feeling well was being treated on our boat by Dr. Scannavino and Bel, Isabel Villares, Lama Michel's mother. The patient's relatives gathered around the room where he was lying down in silence. I asked Dr. Scannavino how he was, and he said that he probably would not survive the night. Talking to Bel a while later, she also said that he was going to die in a few hours. In the morning we saw him being carried away groaning to the speedboat.

It was only the next day that we heard more about what had happened. Dr. Scannavino told us that he had been called while he was at the presentation. The patient, Manuel, a man of over 60 years old, had had a cardiac arrest. Manuel was unconscious even before he was put on the boat and had suffered a heart failure. When he was being taken onto the speedboat his heart stopped again, at the exact moment the engine failed. Dr. Scannavino had to massage his chest there and then. He had also had fits. All in all, he had three heart failures and five fits.

Dr. Scannavino also said that Lama Gangchen was called to see the patient. The lama put a Tibetan medicine in his mouth and blew a few times. Manuel, who had been unconscious for hours, woke up immediately. And he started talking. His relatives were very surprised. After this, his paralysis – he had become paralyzed from the waist down – started to recede. Dr. Scannavino said that he had never seen a patient improve in this way. "Another one that at least does not die in my hands." Manuel was taken on the speedboat to Alter do Chão, the biggest city nearby. Then he had to go by land to Santarém, a city with better hospitals. We only found out later from Dr. Scannavino after I had returned to São Paulo that Manuel had fully recovered and had returned home walking and talking. He also said that the doctors did not believe what they had seen, especially because there were no aftereffects.

The day after the storm we met under a beautiful tree and Lama Gangchen talked a little about the events of the previous night. He talked about the storm mainly in terms of the elements and how they manifested themselves in this context. The element air, or wind as gales; the element water as the turbulent river; the element fire as lightening, and so on. He claimed that it was important for us to know about the external elements and learn from them, and from that, to understand the inherent relationship between those external elements and the elements as these make up our own bodies. This was in his opinion an essential step for the group to overcome the fear it had felt during the storm. Lama Gangchen also said that it was important that everyone be able to express how he or she had experienced the events of the previous night. Thus, in a real group therapy session, everyone talked about his or her experiences of the storm.

Dr. Scannavino was the first to talk – he reported the then partial healing of Manuel. Next, everybody talked about his or her experiences with the storm, some exchanged accusations, some just expressed the fear they felt, others made references to mantras and prayers that they claimed to have done during the most dangerous moments. After this collective act of catharsis, Lama Gangchen transmitted to his pupils a practice of Tara, a female Buddha associated with removing fear.[19] While introducing the practice, read aloud by Daniel Calmonowitz, Lama Michel's father, the fear felt by almost everybody during the storm took on a new dimension.

> Our world has been permeated by fear. People have experienced suffering and fear. All that we see and touch can cause harm and suffering. If our relationships are inappropriate, even the most miraculous western medicine can become poisonous. If we pay attention we will observe that all the phenomena in our dualistic world are mutable. In our samsaric world, phenomena change. Even the experience of pleasure is like honey on a shaving blade. One day our best friend can become our worst enemy. Our hair will go grey, our clothes out of fashion. All the objects in our world are transient. We are also scared of things that cause us pain and suffering. Life is a nightmare. Fame and social status are fleeting. We are scared of being alone, of being bored. There is fear in the relationship between parents and their children. We are scared of the environment [...].
>
> Politicians are scared of losing power. Poor people have "financial" and "social" fears. Many of us may think that we are strong. However, if we look carefully at our most basic everyday actions we will find some sort of fear associated with them. Instead of being overcome by our fears, we need

to find a natural way of becoming fearless. In the Tibetan tantric tradition there is a method we can use in order to become familiar with our own fears. Tara is liberating, she is the consort of Buddha Amoghasiddhi,[20] the absolute therapist of fear. Her practice can help us to free ourselves from our fears.

Perhaps the most fascinating aspect of the foretold storm and the way in which Lama Gangchen dealt with the "crisis" later is the interaction between the many levels of understanding both "fear" and "cure." In the passage quoted above, Lama Gangchen extends, both philosophically and therapeutically, the localized fear felt during the storm to a broader framework that included all our daily and most fundamental fears. If the experience of fear was expanded and its causes directly correlated with the imbalances between our bodily inner elements and the external elements manifested in the storm, likewise was the way this fear could be healed. In fact, the healing methods gained new dimensions, being transposed to a cosmological level in the self-healing of the environment practice. In the context where all those aspects converged – a cathartic "group therapy" session enchanted by the news of a miraculous healing during a trip to the Amazon forest in which the self-healing of the environment was the central theme and so forth – Lama Gangchen's identity can not and does not remain the same. The range of his healing powers is certainly symbolically expanded.

IV Between local and global powers

The tension between the local and the global illustrated by Lama Gangchen's activities permeates my research as a whole, engendering complex and interdependent outcomes. As we have seen, while Lama Gangchen's power of curing illness was emphasized at the beginning of his time in the West, later this power gained new connotations both within the context of his spiritual practice and in his work with the UN, giving rise to a multi-faceted image of a "lama healer of the world." His practice of the self-healing of the environment associates each of our bodies with the environment that surrounds us, representing an allegorical tension between the local and the global, as mentioned above. At the same time, this practice indicates how a relatively private event, such as a miraculous cure performed by Lama Gangchen in the Amazon, can be understood on a planetary scale, in terms of its symbolic dimensions in the articulation of ritual practices, and in terms of the global institutionalization of this lama's activities.

I believe that the capacity of this lama's particular practices to fashion his identity is present, albeit less directly, in other tantric rituals practiced by Tibetan lamas. In fact, the role of visualization techniques inherent to these rituals is precisely to create a "virtual reality," a "simulation" of the ultimate and enlightened reality of everything. This process starts with the identification of the guru as a fully enlightened being. Invested with this status, he commands each stage of the rite, leading the practitioner to finally imagine that he and the surrounding universe are perfect in every way, replete with their enlightened and ultimate nature. In this way, the importance of the guru within the realm of tantric ritual becomes particularly evident in the process of creating a magical universe, a sacred space, where he occupies a central position.

In the cases of Geshe Kelsang and Segyu Rinpoche, it is clear that ritual is also fundamentally important in the creation of sacred space, as well as in the construction of the roles that these lamas play in relation to their community and beyond. In each case, however, the relationship between ritual and the construction of the sacred is established in a different way.

In the New Kadampa Tradition, it is through an institutional base structured according to a certain model of democracy that Geshe Kelsang acts as a vajra master (the one who presides over the ritual) and the holder of the lineage. This re-alignment is able to combine democratic rules with a necessarily hierarchical model. The fact that this model is centered on the transcendental figure of the vajra master has many consequences, contributing in particular to a redistribution of spiritual power at a number of levels. The interplay between the local and the global generates, mainly through institutional channels, an extremely dynamic situation. For example, even at a distant center like Osasco, where the teachers are still beginners, the authority of the geshe is present through the role of the teacher, a role that each one of his pupils takes on sooner or later. This dynamism has made it possible, among other things, for NKT to grow to an extraordinary size.

It is from this strong basis of support that the role of Geshe Kelsang undergoes a marked process of re-signification, where his quality as a transcendental guru is strengthened by quasi-democratic structures. Within the traditional Tibetan context, his authority would have had a limited reach, as he is not recognized as a reincarnation of a lama, or a tulku. It is worth remembering that within Tibetan society reincarnate lamas occupy the pinnacle of spiritual and social hierarchies. Geshes can also have great prestige, but usually their status is inferior to that of tulkus. The scope of his activities in the West, however, through the combination of the modern with the traditional and the local to the global, has reached proportions that would have been unthinkable within the traditional Tibetan Buddhist context.

In a way, Segyu Rinpoche is moving in the opposite direction from Geshe Kelsang, in that he finds in traditional institutions the main mechanisms for his insertion within the realm of Tibetan Buddhism. By becoming "more Tibetan than the Tibetans" the Brazilian lama is mainly seeking to lay claim to his status as a reincarnate lama. At the same time, he cannot simply do away with his Umbanda past, but must address it directly in terms of the Tibetan ritual system. It is the spatial dynamics of tantric ritual – where taming local landscapes is analogous to taming disciples – and the associated rules of etiquette, which enable Segyu Rinpoche to absorb the local (deities and disciples) within the global field of Tibetan Buddhism.

Notes

1 This chapter was initially translated by Julia Spatuzzi Felmanas and Phillip Wigan. Later, several changes were made to the text.
2 Some directors thought that the "healing sessions" were not in line with the philosophy of the center and therefore decided to suspend this activity.
3 This Internet address now takes us to the new organization of Segyu Rinpoche, Juniper, which was recently created to promote "Buddhist training for modern life." In this new organization Segyu Rinpoche shares the role of teacher with other westerners, including his old assistant Christina Juskiewicz. This new turnaround in his activities seems to indicate that Segyu Rinpoche has somewhat distanced himself from the Gelug hierarchy, but not totally. His emphasis is now on bringing Buddhist wisdom to a modern setting. Even while he still makes reference to his reincarnation status, he no longer cites his Tibetan lineage. As the page states:

> Juniper's work involves how that insight and tradition of inner development might take shape in modern times. We are an extension of a long Indo-Tibetan Buddhist lineage, bringing its wisdom and practices into modern culture. Juniper's Segyu Rinpoche was recognized in 1983 by the 98th Gaden Tri Rinpoche as a master and holder of the renowned Tibetan Buddhist Segyu lineage, part of the Gelug school that is the school of the Dalai Lama.

For more see www.juniperpath.org/.
4 After a while, even the uniforms had traditional Tibetan colors.
5 For more on the Tibetan classification schemes for Indian tantric literature translated between the tenth through the twelfth centuries, see Gibson (1997), Snellgrove (1988), and more recently, Dalton (2005).
6 Also in this respect it is worth citing at length Goldstein's (1990) discussion of the organizational structure of the "three seats:" Drepung, Ganden and Sera monasteries. Note the many points in common with NKT's internal structure.

> The Three Seats somewhat resembled the classic British universities such as Oxford in that the overall entity, the monastery, was in reality a combination of semi-autonomous sub-units, known in Tibetan as tratsang (*grwa tshang*). By analogy with British universities, these are commonly called "colleges" in English. Monks belonged to a monastery only through their membership in a college, and although there was a standing committee that functioned with regard to monastery-wide issues, there was no abbot for the whole monastery, only for individual colleges.
>
> Each tratsang had its own administration and resources, and in turn was comprised of important residential sub-units known as khamtsen (*khams-tshan*) which contained the actual domiciles (apartments or cells) of their monks. Like the college, they had their own administration and, to a degree, their own resources.
>
> A potential monk could enter any of the Three Seats but within the monastery had to enroll in a specific khamtsen depending on the region he was from. Membership in a khamtsen, therefore, was automatic and mutually exclusive. For example, a monk from Kham (Eastern Tibet), or more likely, from one of a number of regions in Kham, had to enter one and only one khamtsen. Thus, khamtsen exhibited considerable internal linguistic and cultural homogeneity. Since different khamtsen were affiliated with different colleges, the college level also often had a regional flavor. Colleges and their khamtsen units occupied a specific spatial area within the monastery, and were the center of ritual, educational, social and political activities for their members.
>
> Each of these units – the monastery, the various colleges and the khamtsen – were corporate entities. They had an identity and a name which continued across

generations, owned property and wealth in the name of the entity, and had internal organization. While the monks came and went, the entity and its property continued. Moreover, it is essential to note that a monk's loyalties were primarily rooted at the khamtsen and college levels, and there was often little feeling of brotherhood between monks of different colleges despite their being from the same monastery.

(234–5)

7   For a detailed explanation of these contrasting religious organizational structures and their various implications, see Samuel (1993).

8   The mass Gelug monasteries were not places of tantric study and practice. This role was reserved for the specifically tantric colleges of the tradition.

9   The "second dissemination," also called the "later dissemination" (Tib. *phyi dar*) of Buddhism in Tibet, refers to the period roughly between the eleventh and thirteenth centuries during which Tibetans shared a renewed interest in the mass importation of Indian Buddhist texts and traditions. This period, which began after roughly 150 years of political and social fragmentation in the wake of the disintegration of the Tibetan Empire, has recently come to be called the Tibetan renaissance in Ronald Davidson's study of this period bearing that name. For more details, see Davidson (2005).

10 This website has since changed to kadampa.org/en/, a revamped version of the previous site.

11 The title of "Venerable," like the title of Gen-la, reserved for National Directors and director-generals, is used exclusively for members of the monastic community, which is another indication of the high regard in which monks and nuns are held within NKT.

12 For more on the mahasiddhas see Davidson (2002) and Gray (2007).

13 See Keith Dowman (2000) for a complete life-story of this master.

14 João Clemente Jorge Trinta (1933–2011), a.k.a Joãosinho Trinta, was a Brazilian visual artist known for revolutionizing Carnival in Rio de Janeiro with his innovative contributions to the parades.

15 For a complete life-story of Trophu Lotsawa (Tib. *Khro phu lo tsā ba*), see *Blue Annals* (Roerich 1976: 705–11).

16 For a life-story of Buton Rinchen Druppa (Tib. *Bu ston rin chen sgrub pa*), see *Blue Annals* (ibid.: 793–5).

17 *Bhūmi* (Sanskrit) refers to the ten levels of attainment of a bodhisattva in Mahayana Buddhism.

18 For detailed description of the iconography and meanings of the Five Dhyani Buddhas, see Alice Getty (1914: 25–42).

19 For a detailed description of the beliefs and practices associated with Tara, see Stephan Beyer (1988).

20 Amoghasiddhi, or Amoghasiddha, is one of the Five Dhyani Buddhas, particularly associated with enlightened activity. For more details, see Getty (1914: 41).

6   The divine theater of Kalachakra[1]

Wonderful!
Behind the rocky mountains, powerfully robust
Amazing!
On the peak of the mountains in front, adorned by snow
In all directions, encircled by mist, rainbows appear.[2]

Shabkar Tsogdruk Rangdröl (1781–1851)

On a cold day in late October 2002, the sun was not yet up in the city of Graz. Yet, the reddening of scattered clouds announced its imminent appearance. This would have been just another dawn, if it were not for the giant rainbow that strangely extended across the skies of that Austrian city without any ostensive signs of sunrays or rain. A Buddhist practitioner would have seen this as an auspicious sign, for at the precise moment the rainbow defied the laws of physics in the skies of Graz, inside the main auditorium of the recently built Stadt Hal the Dalai Lama began the last day of the most important event in the international Tibetan Buddhist circuit: the Kalachakra initiation rite.[3]

For nearly two weeks, about 10,000 people from over 70 countries[4] transformed the landscape of the quiet city of Graz with fresh hues (especially the traditional Tibetan colors of maroon and yellow), various accents, and in particular, a religious aspiration very different from the Catholicism traditionally practiced in Austria. This was the third time the Dalai Lama had bestowed the Kalachakra initiation rite in Europe, and the eighth time in the West. In each instance, this cosmopolitan mini-scenario was repeated. It should be said that the series of Kalachakra initiations conferred by the Dalai Lama is an unprecedented phenomenon. Never before in Europe or in the United States had an event related to an eastern religion brought together in such a consistent manner such a large and eclectic group. The first Kalachakra initiation held by the Dalai Lama in the West took place in the US state of Wisconsin in 1981 and attracted about 1,500 people – a number that would grow with every subsequent performance of the event.

The charisma and high visibility of the Dalai Lama, who has won over a massive legion of fans and followers through his writings and public teachings, certainly help explain the huge popularity of the Kalachakra ritual. However, the Tibetan leader has bestowed other initiation rites in the West and in Asia without repeating (in numerical terms, at least) the success of the Kalachakra initiations. Bearing this in mind, I believe that to more fully understand the mass appeal of the Kalachakra ritual it is important to situate it in its Asian contexts.

The Dalai Lama has granted the Kalachakra initiation in Asian countries on 22 occasions. While in Tibet, before going into exile, the Tibetan leader presided over the ritual in question twice (1954 and 1956), bringing together about 100,000 people for each initiation. During his exile in India, the Dalai Lama would attract 200,000 people to these events.[5] According to Glenn Mullin, in Asia the Kalachakra initiation has all the characteristics of a major Buddhist festival:

> Entire villages and tribes come, with babies, adolescents, middle-aged people and grandparents. Those too young, old or weak to walk are carried. Businesses spring up everywhere, to buy from and sell to the crowd. Most pilgrims bring a few items to sell in order to pay their way back home, small articles of antiquity being the most usual. Roadside shops-on-a-blanket are everywhere. In the Bodhgaya initiation of 1985 some entrepreneur even brought in a circus, with ferris wheels and merry-go-rounds.
>
> (Mullin 1991: 27)

The tradition of granting the Kalachakra to the masses, certainly one of the most unique features of this initiation rite, underscores its exceptional and at the same time paradoxical role in the context of Tibetan Buddhism. Despite its association with large multitudes of people, the *Kalachakra Tantra* is considered one of the most intricate systems of Vajrayana Buddhism. Its basic literature covers subjects as diverse as astrology, geomancy, geography, history, human psychophysiology and eschatology (Geshe Lhundub Sopa *et al.* 1985: 31). And although it has played a vital role in Tibet over the years – the Tibetan calendar and medicine, for example, are extensively based on that system – due to its great complexity, few engage in an in-depth study of Kalachakra.[6] For example, it has never been included in the official curriculum of any of the great Gelug tantric colleges (ibid.: 116).

What is the purpose then of initiating people into such a complex system through a mass ritual? First, there is the belief that these rituals can sow seeds in participants' *mental continuum*[7] that will bear fruit in a future life, when they will have better opportunities to deepen their practice of the tantra in question. Second, most people take part in these initiation rites in hopes of receiving "incidental blessings," or "jinlab" (Tib. *byin brlabs*) in the Tibetan language (Samuel 1993: 260).

The aura of a major festival that surrounds the Kalachakra initiation rite in Asia seems to confirm the appeal of possible blessings and the idea of creating future opportunities for spiritual practice. In the West – where the initiation rites per se are also charged with a festive atmosphere – the situation is not very different. In Graz, the Dalai Lama, with his characteristic good humor, ironically observed that the number of participants was visibly larger on the three days when the initiation actually took place.[8] On the other days the Dalai Lama and other lamas gave several teachings on the *Kalachakra Tantra* and other essential texts for the practice of Vajrayana Buddhism.

On that occasion, the Tibetan leader also pointed out that he considered his preliminary teachings, which focused on transmitting some of the basic precepts of Buddhism, such as compassion, to be more important than the initiation rite itself. Clearly, the Dalai Lama does not expect most of the people in his audience to devote themselves to the complex practice of the *Kalachakra Tantra*. In fact, he always says that he performs this initiation merely as a blessing, setting aside the more secret practices involved. According to Robert Thurman, "with his habitual modesty, the Dalai Lama always advises the public that 'this initiation is being given by an unqualified lama to people who are also unqualified'" (personal communication, 1997).

Another unique feature of Kalachakra directly explains its performance as a major mass ritual: its relationship with the mythic realm of Shambhala. The connection between Kalachakra and Shambhala makes this system a unique case in the category of the Unexcelled Yoga Tantra.[9] According to the Dalai Lama, other Unexcelled Yoga Tantras

> have their origin in relation to individual persons or adepts, as was the case with the *Guhyasamāja Tantra* and the King Indrabhuti. The *Kālachakra Tantra*, however, has been intimately connected with the country of Shambhala – its ninety-six districts, its kings, and retinue.
>
> (Tenzin Gyatso and Hopkins 1999 [1985]: 166)

As we will see, this reference to Shambhala has many implications. Let us therefore begin with a discussion of the mythic origins of the *Kalachakra Tantra*.

Interwoven realities

According to the writings and teachings on the *Kalachakra Tantra*,[10] Shakyamuni Buddha, the historical Buddha, taught the *Kalachakra Tantra* inside the stupa Shri Dhanyakataka, in southern India, one year after his enlightenment. In John Newman's words:

> In the form of Kalachakra, the Buddha stood on the vajra lion throne in the middle of the great mandala of the "Sphere of Vajra" (vajradhatu), the abode of great bliss. He was absorbed in the Paramadibuddha (Kalachakra) samadhi. Inside the mandala he was encircled by a host of buddhas, bodhisattvas, wrathful kings, gods, nagas and male and female deities. Outside the mandala were the disciples. These included the ninety-six satraps of Shambhala, headed by the requestor of the tantra, King Suchandra of Shambhala, an emanation of Vajrapani.

The entire three realms (the desire, form, and formless realms) saluted the feet of the Buddha, and bodhisattvas, demons and gods made copious offerings of divine flowers, food, music, and so forth. Representing the entire assembly, Suchandra miraculously entered the dharmadhatu mandala, circumambulated the Teacher, and offered jeweled flowers at his feet. He saluted the Buddha again and again, and sat down before him. With folded hands, Suchandra requested initiation into, and instruction on, the Kalachakra.

(Newman 1985: 53–4)

Pleased with Suchandra's request, the Buddha taught him the 12,000 verses of the *Kalachakra Mulatantra* (the root text for the *Kalachakra Tantra*) and gave the Kalachakra initiation to all those present. After receiving these teachings, king Suchandra returned to Shambhala, where he wrote a 60,000-verse commentary on the *Kalachakra Mulatantra*. Then, he propagated the Kalachakra tradition among his subjects. His successors maintained the tradition, gradually spreading the Kalachakra teachings throughout the country. The seventh sovereign after Suchandra, Manjushriyashas, made Kalachakra the official state religion, initiating so many people (approximately 35 millions according to the literature on this tantra) into the Kalachakra mandala that "he and subsequent kings became known as *kulika* (*rigs ldan*), 'one who bears the lineage'" (Tenzin Gyatso and Hopkins 1999 [1985]: 59). Manjushriyashas wrote another 1,000-verse summary of the *Kalachakra Mulatantra*, and his son, Pundarika, wrote a 12,000-verse commentary on that text. These two writings, respectively known as *Laghutantra* (*Abbreviated Kalachakra Tantra*) and *Vimalaprabha* (*Immaculate Light*), were "brought to our world"[11] by two Indian visionaries in the tenth and eleventh centuries. This is the first historical record of Kalachakra and the mythical narrative of the kingdom of Shambhala.

Shortly after this "first contact" with our "ordinary reality," the *Kalachakra Tantra* and its system of measuring time were introduced into Tibet by the Indian master Somanatha. This is why the Tibetan calendar begins in 1026 AD, the year that marked the beginning of these teachings (Bernbaum 2001 [1980]: 16). It would not be long before Buddhism (and consequently the *Kalachakra Tantra*) ceased to have a strong institutional presence in India. The literature on the Kalachakra and the realm of Shambhala continued, nevertheless, to develop outside of India, more specifically in Tibet and Mongolia.

Much has been written (and recounted) in these two countries regarding the Kalachakra and Shambhala. And naturally, these teachings have been propagated on many levels. As Edwin Bernbaum, author of the most complete study of Shambhala published in the West, tells us, a strong folk tradition about this kingdom – including stories about the "the war and golden age to come, and others about mystics who have gone there and the treasures they brought back" – spread among the Tibetans and Mongols. However, "the most secret aspects of the realm of Shambhala" have never been consigned to paper, and are only passed on orally from guru to initiate disciple (ibid.: 5). Thus, like the

Kalachakra initiation itself, which combines highly esoteric teachings[12] with the exuberance of mass rituals, the imagery regarding the mythic realm of Shambhala shifts back and forth between the sphere of secrecy and the easily accessible world.

In many senses, this ambiguity is also reflected in the very structure of the myth of Shambhala. As we have seen, the roots of this mystical kingdom lie in more than one reality, something that is in perfect harmony with the predominant worldview of Tibetan Buddhism. Tibetan Buddhist texts speak of a multidimensional universe: there are ordinary perception, extraordinary perception (Thurman 1995a: 6) and multiple gradations therein. Thus, the realm of Shambhala is believed to exist in our world, but hidden behind a "ring of mountains" or a "barrier of mist," and therefore invisible to those who lack pure perception. According to Edwin Bernbaum:

> Although many lay Tibetans regard Shambhala as a heaven of the gods, most lamas consider it a Pure Land, a special kind of paradise meant only for those on their way to Nirvana. According to the texts, the kingdom provides the conditions under which one can make the fastest possible progress toward enlightenment.
>
> (Bernbaum 2001 [1980]: 9)

It should be added that, for those lamas concerned, Shambhala is the only Pure Land on this planet. The paths leading to this Buddhist paradise have been described in detail in countless "travel guides" (Tib. *gnas yig)*. Although the "coordinates" given in these guides combine real and mythical elements, which makes them almost impossible for an ordinary person to follow, they give the feeling that the kingdom of Shambhala is actually within everyone's (physical) reach (ibid.: 29–30). In many senses, the most fascinating aspect of Shambhala appears to be precisely that it affords the possibility of a meeting of two worlds. As we will see, there are several "paths" leading to Shambhala, and, particularly, several instances in which the meeting between our reality and mythical realms can occur. In any event, this meeting is predicted to happen on at least one occasion. According to the mythical narrative, 3,000 years after the enlightenment of Buddha Shakyamuni (so in roughly 300 to 400 years) the kingdom of Shambhala will emerge from behind the barrier that makes it invisible. After a long period of degeneration during which men will lose sight of the truth and spirituality and the world will be dominated by a materialist dictatorship, the king of Shambhala, Rudra Chakrin, will lead an army of enlightened warriors against the "barbarians," or lalos (Tib. *kla klo)*. Once the battle is won, the "rule of Shambhala will extend over the rest of the world," ushering in a new, perfect era, "better than anything that has happened before" (ibid.: 22–3).

The difficulties Tibetans faced after the Chinese invasion and in the wake of the Cultural Revolution are sometimes interpreted as a sign that we are entering the period of degeneracy that precedes the era of liberation. This interpretation of historic events on the basis of myth provides important clues for understanding the worldview that guides the work of some lamas, demonstrating that "mythical consciousness" and "historical consciousness" are not mutually exclusive. Jonathan Hill's theoretical reflections in *Rethinking Myth and History* are especially pertinent in relation to this point. Although his work focuses on indigenous South American societies, it is still extremely relevant to us, since it discusses precisely the impossibility of drawing clear boundaries between the notions of myth and history. Among the many points that Hill discusses in his book, the notion that history is "the totality of processes whereby individuals experience, interpret, and create changes within social orders" (Hill 1988: 2–3) is particularly important to this discussion, because it enables us to understand how myth can be a powerful "machine for negating time" and therefore history, as Lévi-Strauss (1995) has stated, while being at the same time an instrument for interpreting historical changes, such as those experienced by the Tibetans after the Chinese invasion. In this sense, it could be said that mythic atemporality and historical temporality are often combined in a certain Tibetan sensibility towards history, as we have seen, for instance, in the case of the Fifth Dalai Lama.

The use of these parameters in the interpretation of historical events seems to be essential in the understanding of recent developments in Tibetan Buddhism, since the interpretation of realities on the basis of myth has a direct impact on the work of some lamas in the diaspora, including the Dalai Lama. Indeed, the association between the Shambhala myth and the tragic fate of Tibet gives a feeling of urgency to the transmission of the Kalachakra initiation in particular. According to the Dalai Lama,

> The higher meditations of the *Kalachakra Tantra* can be practiced only by a select few; but because of past and future events, and in order to establish a strong karmic relationship with Kalachakra in the minds of the people, there is now a tradition of giving the initiation to large public gatherings.
>
> (Geshe Lhundub Sopa *et al.* 1985: xviii–xix)

It is interesting to note that the missionary connotation present here can also be perceived in the work of other lamas in exile. This is particularly the case with Lama Gangchen. As we have seen, Lama Gangchen structures his activities, and particularly his spiritual practice, on the basis of preparing his disciples for the final battle of Shambhala.

Unlike Lama Gangchen, however, the Dalai Lama rarely, if ever, makes references to Shambhala in terms of the need to prepare for the struggle alongside the illuminated warriors in the battle ahead (Gangchen 1997 [1993]). The Tibetan leader primarily discusses the mythical kingdom in the form of scholarly digressions, presented during the initiation ceremony. Furthermore, the Shambhala myth is implicit in the very structure of the Kalachakra ritual. Such associations with the Shambhala myth have numerous implications. The most prominent one – as in the case of Lama Gangchen – is once again the question of world peace. The full title of the event that took place in Graz expresses this clearly: "Kalachakra for World Peace – Graz 2002." Therefore, the main focus here is the numerous ways in which the question of peace (certainly worldwide but also within the institutions of Tibetan Buddhism, as we will see) comes together in the Kalachakra ritual.

Ritual time, mythical time

First of all, it is crucial to emphasize that commentaries on the Kalachakra describe the battle of Shambhala not only in historical terms but also as a "spiritual battle" in which each individual must struggle against his or her own negative feelings and barbarous attitudes, which arise from ignorance of the true nature of reality. As Khenpo Noryang explained to Bernbaum:

> We can talk about three Shambhalas corresponding to the three divisions of the Kalachakra teachings. The outer Shambhala exists as a kingdom in the external world, the inner lies hidden in the body and mind, and the other [alternative] is the Kalachakra mandala with all its deities.
>
> (Bernbaum 2001 [1980]: 141)

Clearly, based on this description of the kingdom of Shambhala in its different layers of meaning, the mythical narrative not only figures in the history of the origins of the *Kalachakra Tantra*, but it is also directly incorporated into the ritual. This proximity with the myth spotlights, among other things, a highly unique elaboration of the concept of time. Literally, "Kalachakra" means "wheel of time." Nonetheless, "*Kala*, or time is not linear time, but the flow of all events, past, present, and future. This is similar to our concept of space, which does not imply any particular direction or limitation" (Bryant 1992: 24). The Kalachakra system includes three time cycles: external, which has to do with the passing of hours, days, months, years, etc.; internal, which deals with the sequence of daily breaths that an individual takes; and finally, the alternative cycle, which deals with all of the spiritual practices related to the tantra in question. Therefore, "the external and internal cycles deal with time as we normally conceive it, while the alternative cycle refers to the methods that lead to liberation from the first two" (Berzin 2010 [1997]: 27).

A unique characteristic of the *Kalachakra Tantra*, the correspondence that the ritual establishes between the external and internal time cycles, or in a broader sense, between the macrocosm and microcosm, brings the system as a whole closer to the concept of myth as it is discussed by Lévi-Strauss. Comparing myth with music, the French anthropologist concludes that both operate on the basis of a "twofold continuum."

> [O]ne part of it is external and is composed in the one instance of historical, or supposedly historical, events forming a theoretically infinite series from which each society extracts a limited number of relevant incidents with which to create its myths; and in the other instance, the equally infinite

series of physically producible sounds, from which each musical system selects its scale. The second aspect of the continuum is internal and is situated in the psychophysiological time of the listener, the elements of which are very complex: they involve the periodicity of cerebral waves and organic rhythms, the strength of the memory, and the power of attention.

(Lévi-Strauss 1979: 16)

In many ways, the form in which the Kalachakra ritual deals with what Lévi-Strauss calls a "twofold continuum" sheds light on the conscious and unconscious mechanisms involved in the narration and reception of myths. For example, it is precisely through the imaginary performative alignment in the external and internal cycles that the power of "suppressing time" that the French anthropologist directly associates with myth is transformed into "experience" in the ritual. Robert Thurman's interpretation of the etymology of the word "Kalachakra" is particularly germane to this discussion. Thurman gives the extended meaning of the term "chakra," which can also mean "machine." According to this interpretation, "Kalachakra" would mean "Time Machine," "not in the science-fiction sense that it travels through time, but in the special sense that it is the artistic creation with which universal compassion turns time into a machine to produce the enlightenment of all sentient beings" (Rhie and Thurman 1991: 384).

In this context, the idea of a "time machine" is very close to the effects wrought by myth and ritual: the suspension of the "normal" course of time. This is one of the most essential properties of tantric practice, which consists of accelerating the process of spiritual development, making it possible to "reverse" the logical order of the religious path. In the tantra, the practitioner takes the future outcome of his or her practice as the starting point. This means that during the ritual, initiates "act," "speak" and "think" as if they were already fully enlightened. In this regard, the ritual could primarily be thought of as a "chain of mirrors" in which the body, speech and mind of the practitioner are "transformed" into the body, speech and mind of the chief deity, in this case, the Kalachakra deity, through the meditation techniques of mudra, mantra and visualization.[13] In the ritual, the method of identification can be interpreted as a theatrical performance. In a carefully constructed scenario based on the elaborate art of citation, the practitioner plays his part in what can be poetically describe as a "cosmic drama without beginning or end."

The theatre of enlightenment

Just as in most initiation rites in all cultures, the basic structure of the Kalachakra ritual is based on the cycle of death (the former personality) and rebirth (as a new person), therefore constituting at some level a rite of passage.[14] During the initiation process, this cycle is repeated several times, culminating in the initiate's final rebirth as the Kalachakra deity. To a great extent, the main idea here has to do with rebirth in an idealized form. Following the lama's instructions, practitioners mentally construct a "virtual reality" in which they and the world that surrounds them are viewed as perfect, in their fully enlightened nature. According to Jeffrey Hopkins, "much of tantric practice is structured around mimicking ordinary, uncontrolled processes in a manner that serves to purify those processes and bring them under control. In this case, the process of taking rebirth is being mimicked, purified, and brought under control" (Tenzin Gyatso and Hopkins 1999 [1985]: 94).

Here, we see the structural proximity that clearly exists between tantric ritual and theatre. While there are many points of similarity that confirm this proximity,[15] two are particularly relevant for the present discussion. First, it is important to stress the direct relationship between text and performance – even imaginary performance – within the sphere of tantric ritual. The text that the lama follows when conducting the rite can, in a way, be understood as a script (clearly a very rigid one) that "leads" the practitioner along an imaginary route – or an equally imaginary performance – throughout the initiation rite. In this context, there is little or no room for improvisation. Recalling Hopkins's words once again, habitual processes are reproduced in a controlled environment for the ultimate purpose of perfecting them. To a great extent, the text of the ritual can be considered the chief basis for creating this controlled environment.

The idea of repetition is another important factor. Both in the initiation rite and the daily practice of Kalachakra, the steps involved in the practitioner's imaginary transformation are repeated countless times. It can generally be said that transformation is expected to occur through repetition – during which the body and mind gradually become "accustomed" to the new principles. Basically, the practitioner arrives at a sense of *experience* by directly superimposing imaginary performances involving similar (or even identical) cycles of transformation (Turner 1986, 1982).

The concept of experience has been an important part of Buddhism since the doctrine first developed. Among other things, the emphasis on experience has had the practical result of creating a varied range of methods ostensibly aimed at furthering spiritual growth. However, it is only within the context of Vajrayana Buddhism – to which the Kalachakra rite pertains – that meditation methods have given special meaning to the concept of *performance* in Buddhist rituals by proposing an imaginary identification between practitioners and meditational deities. This brings us to a second aspect of the structural similarities between ritual and theatre that I would like to spotlight: the close connection between performance and experience, and its place in the religious system as a whole. The entire range of tantric ritual practice has proven to be an effective way of presenting abstract concepts – such as non-duality, emptiness and Buddha nature – in a concrete form, or performance. It could be said that this method is capable of focusing all of the practitioner's energy and concentration on the assimilation of the doctrine.

In this regard, it is essential to stress that all tantric initiation rites form part of a dramatic narrative. In the specific case of the Kalachakra rite, this narrative mirrors birth and the other seven stages of childhood that are represented by the seven main initiations into which the rite is divided.[16] The central place of the concept of narrative within tantric ritual cannot be overstated. According to Hayden White,

> [N]arrative might well be considered a solution to a problem of general human concern, namely, the problem of how to translate knowing into telling, the problem of fashioning human experience into a form assimilable to structures of meaning that are generally human, rather than culture-specific.
>
> (White 1990: 1)

In this sense, it could be said that the overall structure of tantric ritual sums up the abstract concepts of Mahayana/Vajrayana doctrine. Through this "narrativization" – a practice that, as White observes, is capable of creating a form of trans-cultural communication – practitioners are prepared to experience these abstract concepts in the course of the performance.

A brief description is in order here to give an example of the "internal initiation" that, as the first step in the ritual, introduces the practitioner to tantric reality, preparing him or her for the principal initiations – the seven initiations that represent seven different "stages" of childhood.[17] In any event, without delving too deeply into the complexities of these concepts, we can say that this process involves the abovementioned mechanism of imitating "routine processes that are out of our control" and thereby controlling them. In this case, the initiations as a whole represent the initiates' conception, gestation and birth. At the end of the ritual, the practitioner is reborn as the "child of the lama" or the "child of the deity" and thus, an "uncontrolled" process – birth, or better yet, re-birth – has been placed under control within the context of the initiation.[18] This is also true for "childhood" – the time of learning in society and the practice of Buddhist teachings beyond the ritual – which should follow the same logic and be controlled in accordance with the divine sequence of "stages" represented by the seven initiations mentioned above. Therefore, it could be said that the "internal initiation" – the initial stage of the Kalachakra ritual – plays an important structural role that, in a way, reflects the significance of the ritual as a whole.

It is important to stress that within the context of tantric ritual the practitioner's performance begins with the construction of the setting in which he or she will "perform." On the basis of the ritual text, which is a "script" permeated with doctrinal and historical/mythological references, the Dalai Lama invites the practitioners to set aside their usual view of reality, replacing a perception that is considered "impure" with "a pure perception." The Dalai Lama himself should be seen as a Kalachakra deity and, similarly, the place where the initiation takes place should be seen as the deity's divine palace. The Dalai Lama "manifests" as Kalachakra, with a blue body, four faces and 24 arms, in sexual union with his consort, Vishvamata, who is pictured with a yellow body, four faces and eight arms. There are countless complex references behind this description of Kalachakra and Vishvamata. For now, however, I will focus on their essential meaning: the depiction of a fully enlightened being.

Placing their trust in this basic understanding, practitioners must visualize rays of light emanating from the lama's heart. Each practitioner is then captured by a ray of light and transported inside the lama's mouth, travelling through the lama's body to fall into the womb of Vishvamata, who is understood here as an archetypal mother. Within Vishvamata's womb, practitioners are transformed into emptiness. This is the critical moment of the initiation rite, because it is the time when the practitioner becomes aware of the emptiness of existence inherent to all phenomena. According to the Dalai Lama, the mind that perceives and understands emptiness "serves as the substance of each student's appearance as Kalachakra" (Tenzin Gyatso and Hopkins 1999 [1985]: 175). This mind that "understands emptiness" is successively transformed into the seed-syllable[19] *hūm*, into a vajra[20] and finally into the form of the Kalachakra deity – not with all the faces and arms of the mandala's tutelary deity, but with just one face and two arms.

This brief example provides a glimpse into an important aspect of the ritual's general structure: the dramatic narrative in which the practitioner's actions take place is replete with metaphors. Thus, if there is a direct reference to the concept of emptiness during the initiation, there is also an indirect reference to it through a figure of speech. In fact, the multiple transformations that each practitioner undergoes before emerging as Kalachakra can be interpreted as a powerful metaphor for the concept of emptiness. They express the multiple possibilities for representing something, and its consequent lack of inherent existence (Dagyab Rinpoche 1995: 6). The realization and experience of emptiness plays an essential role in the ritual, as it forms the basis for self-transformation in the context of this esoteric practice. Emptiness can be understood as an antidote for the reification of the self. The glimpse of the non-existence of a fixed identity creates some of the conditions for a concrete change.

Here, Victor Turner can help us understand other elements of the language of this ritual. Indeed, the concept of emptiness and its role within the sphere of tantric ritual are, in a way, analogous to Turner's concept of "anti-structure." Turner uses this term to describe the moment in rituals when social structures and roles are not present, emphasizing that it is not a reference to a "structural reversal, a mirror-imaging of 'profane' workaday socioeconomic structure, or a fantasy-rejection of structural necessities, but to the liberation of human capacities of cognition, affect, volition, creativity, etc." (Turner 1982: 44). Just as anti-structure is the basis for social change in Turner's interpretation of ritual, so the notion of emptiness is the basis for inner transformation that is sought in tantric ritual.

One of the most interesting points Turner discusses in regard to the concept of anti-structure has to do with the nature of the language used at this stage of the ritual. Based on the findings of Van Gennep, Turner observes that in ritual, language "moves from the *indicative* mood of cultural process, through culture's *subjunctive* mood back to the *indicative* mood, though this recovered mood has now been tempered, even transformed, by immersion in subjunctivity" (Turner 1982: 82). The *subjunctive* mood is related to the anti-structural aspect of the ritual, and indicates a wish, a desire, a possibility or a hypothesis. It is, in fact, the language of "wishful thinking." In Turner's words: "It is 'as if it were so', not 'it is so'" (ibid.: 83).

In esoteric Buddhist ritual, the subjunctive mood is always coupled with the indicative mood. In the rite in question, if the multiple transformations that practitioners undergo before emerging as Kalachakra can be interpreted as a powerful metaphor for the concept of emptiness, then this method of transformation also aims to reveal their true essence, which is already "fully enlightened." This is implicit in the identification between each practitioner and the deity. However, if each of us is *already* fully enlightened in the latter sense, we are "imprisoned" on a relative or conventional level by our mental defilements. One of the aims of the tantric ritual is precisely to "purify" these defilements, thereby enabling the *emergence* of the practitioner's true "self." Thus, the tantric ritual combines the indicative and subjunctive moods to create a basis for transformation. Paraphrasing Turner, it is "as if it were so" now, because "it is so" *already.*

Implicit in this coupling of the subjunctive and indicative moods is one of the main concepts developed by Mahayana thought, which has become one of the pillars of the practice of Vajrayana Buddhism: the notion of the non-duality of samsara and nirvana. Achieving liberation or enlightenment ceases to become a question of leaving this world. Nirvana is taking place in the here and now, but the impurity of our vision prevents us from seeing it. In this sense, the idea of personal transformation that is expressed in various ways in tantric ritual can be translated, first and foremost, into a transformation of the practitioner's perspective. In effect, the "stage of creation" that is being dealt with in the Kalachakra initiation concentrates essentially on transforming each practitioner's perception, informing and shaping it through symbols and concepts that are potentially capable of shaking the foundations of their worldview. The purpose of the imaginative performance of the tantric ritual may be precisely to influence this perception in practice by encapsulating abstract doctrinal concepts in "concrete metaphors" that are lived out through the performance. By means of the enacted experience of the ritual, the image that the practitioners themselves have of their bodies and surrounding environment (extending as far as the entire universe) is remodeled and takes on new meaning.

In regard to this transformation, the ritual contains a double progressive movement that confers new meanings not only on the practitioner's body but also on his or her environment. During the second part of the ritual, the practitioners who had previously been outside the mandala palace visualize themselves entering one of its doors. During this process, they circle around the mandala, climbing each of its levels in their imaginations until they reach the center. The lama narrates this journey, describing every detail of the environment while the practitioners proceed through the mandala. The varied aspects of the mandala are associated with the signs of the Zodiac, the main planets and constellations, as well as the 360 days of the year (following the lunar calendar). Here, each month is symbolized by a deity, who is accompanied by 30 assistants, one for each day of the month. A comparison can be made here with the

Japanese method of accentuating the obscure aspects of an object, known as *mitate*. As Masao Yamaguchi explains, "The Japanese use *mitate* to extend the image of an object. By so doing they transcend the constraints of time" (Yamaguchi 1991: 58). According to Yamaguchi, in the Japanese context, *mitate* – which, in many regards, could be described as an "art of citation" – is a universal tendency to bring the invisible to light through the visible organization of objects. In the case of the Kalachakra ritual, which gradually becomes visible bit by bit – albeit in the practitioners' imaginations – it is a certain conception of the universe that is inherent to this system, and in which microcosms and macrocosms are closely connected.

In this cosmic environment, practitioners are invited to carry out the so-called "internal initiation" four more times in conjunction with the main initiations of the ritual. The first of these four internal initiations is received together with the "water" and "crown" initiations on the northern (white and peaceful) face of Kalachakra represented by the mandala. Following the same pattern, the second initiation is received together with the "silk ribbon" and "vajra and bell" initiations on the southern (red and voluptuous) face of Kalachakra. The third initiation, which is associated with the "conduct" and "name" initiations, occurs on the eastern (blue and wrathful) face of Kalachakra. Finally, the fourth initiation and the final "permission" initiation are received on the western (yellow and contemplative) face of Kalachakra (Tenzin Gyatso and Hopkins 1999 [1985]: 74). The four "faces" or aspects of Kalachakra are respectively associated with the body, speech, mind and "bliss." The initiations held on the first three of these faces are therefore directly related to the purification of the body, speech and mind.

The sequence of the four sets of internal initiations reproduces the circular movement inherent to the figure of the principal deity. Thus, the dramatic experience of being "reborn" countless times in four different directions gives practitioners the means to achieve awareness of the concept of the simultaneity of time during the performance. As Paul Mus explains, the multiplication of faces or aspects confers the power of blessing in not just one direction but in all directions at once. In this regard, the four-faced form of Kalachakra indicates some type of succession in time. This image denotes a circular movement, constituting an "axis" for a ritual procession (Mus 1964: 6). It could be said that the performance in the Kalachakra ritual has the power to convert time into space in the practitioners' imaginations, giving them elements that can influence the manner in which they perceive time.

In the ritual, this particular characteristic of Kalachakra is expressed in more than one way. One of the most inspiring and concise forms of transformation of time into space may be the representation of the 360 days of the year in the mandala. According to Edwin Bernbaum:

> [A]s a particular deity, each day takes on a divine quality that partakes of eternity. Along the way he comes to see them as different manifestations of the main tutelary deity of the Kalachakra, who embodies the timelessness

of every passing moment. Through the visualization of these deities, he experiences the secret that past and future are but different phases of one time that happens now. By identifying himself with the tutelary deity who rules them all, he eventually becomes master of time itself.

(Bernbaum 2001 [1980]: 129–30)

In many regards, it could be said that the *Kalachakra Tantra*'s capacity of "manipulating" time gives it a special connection to the idea of world peace. Jhado Tulku Rinpoche, who between 1997 and 2004 served as abbot of Namgyal Monastery, the Dalai Lama's personal monastery, addressed this question directly in a lecture he gave in Graz:

Although in the other major tantric systems like the *Guhyasamaja*, *Vajrab-harava*, *Chakrasamvara*, there is a meditation and analogy regarding the paths to be purified. Nevertheless, you do not have a result, which is similar to this. You do not have an extensive system of analogy as you have in the Kalachakra. In the Kalachakra, you have a presentation of the external world to be purified with the passage of the years and months and days and the signs of the zodiac. We have an internal basis to be purified, which refers to the body with the passage of the 21,600 breaths during the course of one day, analogous to the 21,600 hours in the course of the year, and we have a meditation in analogy with this in order to purify both the internal and exter-nal basis. And doing this purification we are able to overcome the effects of the influence of these internal and external cycles. Now in connection with world peace, if on the external level the passage of the year, and month and day happens in a peaceful way, we can bring about a peaceful situation. And if it is confused, we know the way the time passes is filled with a great deal of problems. Similarly [this is what happens] with the body and the passage of breaths and so on. If this is all confused and the basis of it is confused, then we experience great difficulties, problems with health and so on, whereas, if it goes smoothly, we experience our bodies in a peaceful situation.

The basic idea expressed here is that external peace begins with inner peace, which is a central idea in just about every line of Buddhism. However, because it is incorporated into a ritual, this notion takes on new outlines and has different offshoots. This reference to peace was probably the main reason why the Kalach-akra has become an important stage of activities for the Dalai Lama. The cause of peace enables the Dalai Lama to rub shoulders with the world's political leaders and has raised the Tibetan cause to a universal level. In a way, the Kalachakra initiation rite permits the Tibetan leader to implement in practice (albeit through an action "of a magical nature") his theoretical discourse on defending world peace. There are several ways through which the question of peace is voiced in the Kalachakra initiation. We have already seen some exam-ples of this in the ritual performance. Nevertheless, there is an underlying meaning to the ritual as a whole that can only be discussed on the basis of the elements of the Shambhala myth.

Myth and peace

It can generally be said that the construction of the sacred setting in which ritual practitioners "act" goes beyond the strict boundaries of ritual practice. As a mass ritual, the Kalachakra initiation has a broader significance that must be understood in this light. Every time the Dalai Lama stages the divine theatre of Kalachakra for thousands of people he makes an explicit reference to the mythic kingdom of Shambhala. As we have seen, after receiving initiation from Buddha Shakyamuni, king Suchandra returned to Shambhala and made Kalachakra the state religion. Also according to tradition, after king Suchandra received the Kalachakra initiation from the Buddha, 26 kings would govern the kingdom of Shambhala, and all of them would propagate the teachings of Kalachakra. Every year, each of these kings gave, gives and will give the Kalachakra initiation to his entire kingdom.

Among all the stories of the sovereigns of Shambhala, one is particularly relevant to Kalachakra as a mass ritual related to world peace. Manjushriyashas, the seventh king after Suchandra, initiated so many subjects during his reign that, as mentioned earlier, he became known as the first *kulika*, or "he who bears the lineage." According to Alex Berzin and Jhado Rinpoche, the association with the concept of peace is derived from the occasion on which king Manjushriyashas gave the Kalachakra initiation to the entire population of his kingdom in order to unite his people against the threat of a barbarian invasion. In Berzin's words:

> At that time, Shambhala was a land comprised of people from many different backgrounds and religions. Most, in fact, were Hindu. Caste prejudice was rampant and different groups within society refused even to eat with one another. *As a divided society, Shambhala was weak.*[21]

It was not king Manjushriyashas's intention to convert his subjects.[22] The sovereign knew that most people would take part in the initiation as observers – which is precisely what happens in the rituals presided over by the Dalai Lama today. As stated by Berzin:

> The King of Shambhala said that he gathered his people in the Kalachakra mandala palace to join them together and convince them to re-examine their own customs and religions. He hoped to provide the circumstances for them to think about ethics and examine if they were really living up to the standards that their religions taught.[23]

In many ways, the Dalai Lama also reproduces the spirit that drove Manjushriyashas to disseminate the Kalachakra in the mass initiation rites. The Tibetan leader literally states that the most important part of the event occurs before the ritual is held. As we have seen, for the Dalai Lama, the preliminary teachings that generally deal with subjects like compassion, love and ethics are the most essential part of the event. He also says that the main reason for giving the Kalachakra initiation is to lead a large and diverse group of people to spend ten days in a peaceful atmosphere. He made this clear on the first day of teachings:

> Among the people who are gathered here, it is possible that there are some who practice their own religion. It is also possible that there are people who do not have any religious practice. Among those who already follow a religious tradition, it is possible that listening to Buddhist teachings will provide you some new insights. In the past, I had the opportunity to give talks in many places to Protestants, Catholics, and many of them came to me and said that it has benefited [them] in strengthening their own religious tradition. And even if that is not the case, it will definitely help to bring harmony and unity among the different traditions.

In fact, the Dalai Lama goes beyond his inter-religious statements, encouraging those present to follow the traditions of their "forefathers," or at least, not to disrespect them. During the event, an inter-religious conference was also held at a Graz university. "On this occasion," the Dalai Lama declared later during his farewell speech, "the religious leaders of five major religions of the world spoke of the need for peace and harmony in the world," thereby calling on everyone, Buddhists and non-Buddhists alike, to follow this advice. It is also important to stress that the Dalai Lama takes pains to ensure that Buddhists from other traditions play an active role in the event. Every day, before he began his teachings, the Tibetan leader invited a group of Buddhists present there to recite a text or recite a prayer. In his words:

> Normally, when I give this initiation in India, there is a recitation in Pali, and then if there is a large number of Chinese audience members this will be followed by the recitation of the Heart Sutra in Chinese. But today the recitation of the Heart Sutra will be done in Vietnamese. After this, we are going to do the refuge prayer in Tibetan.

Here we have examples of how the Kalachakra initiation is one of the most ideal platforms for the Tibetan leader's activities, for it enables him to spread his message of peace and harmony throughout the world and among all faiths from a prominent position, with the support of a mythical narrative.

Kalachakra and the state

Another aspect of the Kalachakra initiation that correlates with the widespread teaching of the value of peace, but whose outcomes can be very different, is the Dalai Lama's trans-sectarian posture in relation to the different lines of Tibetan Buddhism. Without a doubt, the Kalachakra initiation has become one of the most (if not the most) important events related to Tibetan Buddhism in the diaspora, bringing together representatives of all of its traditions. In Graz, lamas from the four schools of Tibetan Buddhism,[24] and also the Bön tradition, gave lectures and took part in the ritual alongside the Dalai Lama. One of the event's organizers, Chungdak Koren – a Tibetan woman who for many years was the representative of the Dalai Lama's government in Geneva – says that the initial intention was to invite leaders from all lineages to the initiation, but some could not attend – only the head of the Sakya School, Sakya Trinzin, was present in Graz. In any case, it is important to stress that all the other schools were represented by important lamas.

The Dalai Lama's significant opening address showed clear signs of his trans-sectarian posture on multiple levels. On the first day of teachings, the Tibetan leader discussed the introduction of Buddhism in Tibet. He particularly mentioned the roles that Abbot Shantarakshita and Padmasambhava played in establishing Buddhism in his country. He also spoke about Atisha and his role in the second period of the dissemination of Buddhism in Tibet. Finally, he observed:

> When you hear all these accounts, it becomes very clear that the tradition of Buddhism that is practiced in Tibet is none other than the Nalanda tradition. Texts like Nagarjuna's *Fundamental Wisdom*, Chandrakirti's *Introduction to the Middle Way*, and Aryadeva's *Four Hundred Verses*, are still studied in the main establishments. [...] In the Indian Nalanda Monastic University there was a complete practice of all the traditions that have been preserved in Pali, and Sanskrit. So all these teachings were available there in Nalanda Monastic University. It is very clear that all these teachings that were practiced in Nalanda were preserved in Tibet itself.

These words express the Dalai Lama's clear intention of stressing the common origins of all schools of Tibetan Buddhism. This aim was further confirmed because, in the course of his talk, he also underlined the common provenance (the Nalanda Monastic University) of the precursors of each of the Tibetan traditions. In this regard, it is also worth citing another reference that the Dalai Lama made to Nalanda at Graz. The Tibetan leader introduced his western audience to a prayer he had written in honor of the founding masters, entitled "A Prayer to the 17 Great Pandits of the Glorious Nalanda." With this prayer, which was to be said every day before the teachings, the Dalai Lama cemented his trans-sectarian posture in a moment of religious communion.

Echoes of the Dalai Lama's trans-sectarian discourse could also be heard in the lecture given by Sakya Trinzin, the leader of the Sakya School, on his own spiritual tradition. Sakya Trinzin also stressed the points that the different lineages share in common.

> Inside Tibet there are many different spiritual lineages. Now we speak of four. All those four have followed a common path, which begins with the

bodhicitta, generating the altruistic mind of enlightenment, and culminate with the union of the path of the sutras and the secret mantra. And there have been lots of extraordinary beings that could write about the fruit of their accomplishments in all four traditions. So in truth all those main schools and traditions and lineages are certainly not contradictory expressions of the Buddha's teachings. And, promoting beneficial and enlightened activities for the benefit of all sentient beings, all of them have worked in the same way.

Sakya Trinzin also discussed the other three schools' influences on his own school. Thus, both speakers expressed an alignment with a certain non-partisan view of Tibetan Buddhism.[25] In fact, the Dalai Lama does not limit himself to the framework of spiritual practice pertaining to Gelug, his school of origin. On more than one occasion he has given initiations and lectures on the traditions of other schools, and in particular, Dzogchen, the spiritual practice exclusive to the Nyingma and Bön schools. Moreover, the Tibetan leader also often expresses a personal interest in finding academic support for his defense of the harmony among the many and varied viewpoints of the different schools. According to Alex Berzin, the Dalai Lama personally asked him to carry out an in-depth study of the four Tibetan Buddhist traditions in order to create a "unified field theory" that shows how they all fit together (personal communication, 2002).

This trans-sectarian posture regarding the other schools of Tibetan Buddhism sheds light on the clearly political aspect of the Kalachakra initiation, because, in many ways, it indicates a structural relationship with the state as it was organized in Tibet. Recall the discussion in Chapter 2 concerning the establishment of the state of the Dalai Lamas that demonstrates how the Fifth Dalai Lama skillfully united religion and politics in a governmental structure that endured for centuries. The Fifth Dalai Lama sought to go beyond the bounds of his own school in order to create a symbolic apparatus for the state that assimilated references from most of the other Tibetan Buddhist traditions, in particular the Nyingma School.[26] By taking a trans-sectarian stance, the current Dalai Lama follows in the example of his predecessor. This strengthens his position as the leader of Tibetan Buddhism as a whole, which is proving to be crucial to the Tibetan cause.

It should also be underscored that probably more than at any other performance of the Kalachakra initiation before it, this political aspect was expressed in many ways at the event held in Graz.[27] First, unlike previous events, the Dalai Lama was not invited to give the initiation by a Buddhist organization. In fact, it was the mayor of Graz himself, Alfred Stingl, who formally requested the Kalachakra teachings. Stingl, a recognized champion of human rights, was declaredly more interested in the ethical and humanitarian message the Dalai Lama could communicate at the event than in the religious aspect per se. Second, partly due to that official invitation, different levels of government – including city, state and federal – provided ample funding: roughly three million euros. Generally, funding for these events is obtained from the private sector, through donations. Graz was designated the cultural capital of Europe in 2003, and a number of activities were already scheduled. The generous supply of government funding, and the mayor's invitation, were therefore justified in light of the belief that the Kalachakra would be a good way to publicize how the city proposed to fulfill its designated role. Finally, a number of side-programs spotlighting the cause of Tibetan independence were also held during the ten-day initiation entitled "Kalachakra for World Peace – Graz 2002." To a great extent, the presence of Chungdak Koren (who, as we have seen, was the representative of the Dalai Lama's government in Geneva) among the organizers is directly related to the publicity for the Tibetan cause throughout the initiation. As she explains:

> Normally, wherever His Holiness gives teachings, the organizers do not have much political issue awareness of Tibet. They are just focused on the teaching. Whereas here ... it is lucky that I have been here, and that I had the responsibility for Hall 12 [where the restaurants and the stores selling Buddhist-related products were located], which I made a condition. I said, "I'll come, but then I'll have responsibility for the marketing, and the control of the side-programs," because I knew how it normally works.... Of course this is a religious teaching, but you cannot ignore the political issue if His Holiness is there. After all, His Holiness is the head of 6 million people, and he has been working for the Tibetan issue for the last 40 years. So how can you ignore this? If you really respect him, you have to support his concern, his interest. And his interest is to solve the problem of Tibet, in a peaceful solution. So I was happy I could organize these three things.

The side-programs that Chungdak Koren organized included screenings of several films, including a documentary about the boy recognized by the Dalai Lama as the reincarnation of the Panchen Lama, whom the Chinese imprisoned together with his family in 1995. As we have seen in Chapter 1, the Panchen Lama's current whereabouts are unknown, and many believe that he has been assassinated. Koren is also a member of the International Campaign for Tibet (ICT), which has organized an exhibition on the Chinese occupation of Tibet and was presented the "Light of Truth" award. This annual award is bestowed to "individuals who have made a significant contribution to public understanding of the situation in Tibet and the cause of independence." In Graz, the honorees were Petra Kelly (*in memoriam*), co-founder of the German Green Party and a leading champion of the Tibetan cause in Europe, and Heinrich Harrer,[28] the Austrian mountaineer who recounted his adventures in Tibet during World War II in the celebrated book *Seven Years in Tibet*. (As mentioned before, Brad Pitt played Harrer, a native of Graz, in the film version). Therefore, a setting could be carefully built up around the ritual, making transparent what was once implicit: the political meaning of the event presided over by the Dalai Lama.

Spectacle as politics

In the past, mass rituals like the Kalachakra initiation were exceptional "theatres" in which the power of the Tibetan state was staged and reaffirmed. As I have already indicated, in the Austrian performance of the Kalachakra initiation, this connection with political power was also far from peripheral. In fact, it is an integral part of the very structure of the ritual and the underlying myth. In a way, the ambivalence surrounding Kalachakra – not only the most esoteric of all the secret tantric systems but also a mass ritual – has a close connection to the very concept of power, something that is held by few but which concerns everyone. It is therefore no coincidence that the two main niches in which the Kalachakra Tantra received particular attention were Tashilhunpo, the headquarters of the Panchen Lamas (second in the Gelug School's hierarchy), and Namgyal, the personal monastery of the Dalai Lamas.

It was precisely the representatives of these two spiritually and politically high-ranking lineages that popularized the practice of Kalachakra in Tibet. Several Panchen Lamas and Dalai Lamas have written commentaries and prayers on Kalachakra. According to the anthropologist Geoffrey Samuel, major Kalachakra initiations were given by the Panchen Lama in the 1920s, and in those years, the audience numbered in the hundreds of thousands (Samuel 1993: 260).

There is also a connection between these lamas and two important kings of Shambhala. As Jhado Rinpoche explained during his lecture at the Graz initiation:

> Like Pundarika, son of Manjushriyashas [the first *kulika* king], who wrote down the *Stainless Light*, the commentary on the *Root Kalachakra Tantra*, was an emanation of Chenrezig [Avalokiteshvara], so is the Dalai Lama. Also receiving the initiation from the Panchen Lama is very significant, for like Manjushriyashas, he too is an emanation of Manjushri. So, receiving the Kalachakra initiation from both the Dalai Lama and the Panchen Lama is very special.

This association of the Dalai and Panchen Lamas with kings of Shambhala certainly has a wealth of implications. For the purposes of this discussion it is particularly germane to remark that allying politics and religion in the mythical context as well points to the tendency of the Kalachakra initiation rite to expand into multiple levels of meaning, in which the same "story" is told and retold. In the end, this is a story of power, the power of the Dalai Lamas, which unfolds in settings that seem to extend (almost) infinitely from the core of the ritual.

In this regard, much like the example of the Yellow Procession described in Chapter 2, the Kalachakra is excessive in its profusion of symbols. This sense of excess, and its accompanying expression of exuberance, could be seen as one of the reasons why this particular initiation came to be the most popular among the initiations conferred by Dalai Lama in exile (and certainly before). In the particular case of the Kalachakra ritual, the connection between excess, beauty, superiority and glory put forth by Paul Veyne in his famous article (1988) gains yet another dimension. The keyword here is experience, and any experience "would be incomplete," to quote Victor Turner, "unless one of its 'moments' is performance" (Turner 1982: 18), even if it is an imaginary one, as in the context of tantric ritual. The crucial moment of the initiation, the internal initiation – in which disciples imagine their rebirth as the children of the lama – creates in this setting an experiential glimpse of the kingdom of Shambhala, or at least a sense of belonging to a larger community that has at its center the figure of the Dalai Lama.

In view of all of that, it could be said that the Dalai Lama, by staging the Kalachakra ritual (even after formally stepping down as the secular leader of Tibetans in 2011), keeps the symbolic power of the former Tibetan state alive, using similar means to those utilized in the past, such as recourse to the spectacle. However, if in the past the ritualization of power made reference to the religious dimension that sustained the state, today it is the sacred that takes on a political dimension or, better yet, which gives power one of its possible forms outside the former Tibetan context, after the dismantling of the social and political structures that once served as the foundations for the religion and the state.

Notes

1 This chapter was initially translated by Sabrina Gledhill. Later, several changes were made to the text.

2 This poem by the great Nyingma master Shabkar Tsogdruk Rangdröl can be found in his autobiography (Shabkar Tsogdruk Rangdröl 2003: 320b). For the works of Shabkar in English, see Ricard (2002; 2001).

3 Some texts in the tantric literature actually recommend that practitioners look for internal and external signs of a ritual's effectiveness. A rainbow also appeared, for example, during the Kalachakra initiation presided by the Dalai Lama in Wisconsin in 1981. In that case, too, there was no rain (Lopez 1997: 227).

4 This is according to the figures in the final report produced by the event's organizers.

5 These numbers are official numbers of the Office of His Holiness the Dalai Lama; see www.dalailama.com/teachings/kalachakra-initiations.

6 An exception is the followers of the Jonang School, who have practiced and still continue to practice the tantra in retreat. In any event, the exclusivity surrounding the *Kalachakra Tantra* endangered its survival after the invasion of Tibet. According to the Buddhist Studies scholar Alexander Berzin, who studies this system, during the initial years of exile, just one lama who managed to escape the Chinese occupation, Kirti Tsenshab Rinpoche (1926–2006), had the lineage of one of the two basic texts of the *Kalachakra Tantra* (personal communication, 2002). Over the years, Kirti Tsenshab passed on this text to a few lamas, including the Dalai Lama himself. After spending 19 years in retreat, Kirti Tsenshab began travelling the world at the Tibetan leader's request in order to give the Kalachakra initiation. In December 2001, the lama visited Rio de Janeiro to preside over the first performance of that ritual ever held in Brazil.

7 According to Robert Thurman, the term *mental continuum* – or *life-continuum*, as this author puts it – has to do with what could be called the "energy-continuity" of a living being that flows from one moment to another, and from one life to another. "It is an important concept, because the Buddhist critique of fixed self makes language of 'soul' and 'essence' relatively rare – though not totally absent – in most contexts" (Thurman 1994: 252).

8 This proximity between East and West in what concerns the general festive atmosphere of the Kalachakra's initiations puts into relief, on the one hand, the uniqueness of this religious event, and on the other, a certain (and perhaps unforeseen) common basis between western and eastern Tibetan Buddhists in their devotional propensities. Even if it is true that westerner lay followers tend to be more focused on the meditational aspects of Tibetan Buddhism than Tibetan lay followers, very few participants in the Kalachakra initiations – be they from Asian or western countries – have the hope of becoming serious practitioners in the intricate Kalachakra tantric system. I recently (2012) had a chance of attending the Kalachakra for World Peace in Bodhgaya and once more this assessment was confirmed: clearly the absolute majority of the people I came across, regardless of their region of origin, were there first and foremost to obtain blessings from the Dalai Lama and to accumulate merit. On the occasion, the Tibetan leader even mentioned that the harsh conditions the participants were facing in Bodhgaya – such as air and sound pollution, extremely dry weather, the crowds, power failures and so forth – would increase by seven times the merit accumulated through taking the initiation. It is important to note furthermore that in other initiations, the Dalai Lama makes sure that only people willing to take the commitment of doing the related practices for the rest of their lives would take part. This discussion brings to mind the controversial book by Stephen Batchelor, *Buddhism Without Beliefs* (1997). Underlining the book is the idea that karma and rebirth are difficult concepts to be reconciled with modern "Euroamerican" mentalities. Without making any definitive statement, one could venture to say that the ever-growing interest among westerners in the Kalachakra initiations conducted by the Dalai Lama seems to suggest quite the opposite.

9 According to the classification of Indian Buddhist scriptural teachings among the "New Translation" (Tib. *gsar ma*) traditions of Tibetan Buddhism, the tantras are divided into four main classes: Krya, Upa, Yoga and Anuttara Tantra, the latter of which is also known as the Unexcelled Yoga Tantra. The tantras in this class are considered the most superior, complex and secret of all.

10 The Kalachakra teachings' narrative of origin is told in the *Laghutantra* (*Abbreviated Kalachakra Tantra*) and in its commentary, the *Vimalaprabha* (*Immaculate Light*), and subsequently reproduced in the vast literature connected to this tantra. For an authoritative discussion on the view of the "nature of the individual and one's place in the universe and society" in accordance to the *Kalachakra Tantra* and the *Vimalaprabha*, see Wallace (2001).

11 The idea here is very close to the practice of discovering termas, or treasures, in Tibetan Buddhism. As we have seen in previous chapters, termas are texts that were hidden by the old masters and discovered later by tertons, or treasure-finders. Therefore, the Indian visionaries cannot be considered the authors of the texts in question, but only the "revealers," or "receivers."

12 Despite the highly esoteric nature of the Kalachakra, this tantra is considered to be the "most explicit *tantra*," according to Vesna Wallace, since it "imparts its teaching by revealing the actual meanings; whereas the other *anuttara-yoga-tantras*, which are regarded as secret, or concealed, *tantras*, convey their meanings only in an implicit manner" (Wallace 2001: 6).

13 The tantras pertaining to the category of Unexcelled Yoga Tantra often include two stages known as the "stage of creation" and the "stage of perfection." During the stage of creation, practitioners cultivate the construction of their self-image as a deity. The stage of perfection, which involves complex yogic techniques, is believed to complete this transformation, giving rise to a new physical structure through the transformation of the body, speech and mind of the practitioner into the body, speech and mind of a Buddha. In the Kalachakra initiations usually given by the Dalai Lama, the participants are only authorized (and instructed) to practice the "stage of creation."

14 Van Gennep describes "rites of passage" as rituals accompanying all changes of place, state, social position and age. According to Van Gennep, these rites are characterized by three stages: separation, margin or liminarity and aggregation. As described by Victor Turner,

> The first phase (of separation) comprises symbolic behavior signifying the detachment of the individual or group either from an earlier fixed point in the social structure, from a set of cultural conditions (a "state"), or from both. During the intervening "liminal" period, the characteristics of the ritual subject (the "passenger") are ambiguous; he passes through a cultural realm that has few or none of the attributes of the past or coming state. In the third phase (reaggregation or reincorporation), the passage is consummated.
>
> (Turner 1995: 94–5)

As we will see, this same ritual structure can be detected in the Kalachakra initiation.
15 In a sense, the Tantric ritual "redoubles" theatre. If the Dalai Lama, invested with the Kalachakra "character," is the lead actor, he is also the director of this unique performance, guiding the actor-spectators on an imaginary journey to the heart of the mandala.
16 The Kalachakra initiation is considerably different from other initiation rites pertaining to the category of Unexcelled Yoga Tantra. According to Glenn Mullin,

> the mainstream tantric initiations are comprised of four individual empowerments, known as vase, secret, wisdom, and sacred word, each of which is given only once during the ceremony. In Kalachakra, however the initiation process is in three separate sets: "entering like a child," which is comprised of seven phases; the four higher initiations; and the four higher than higher initiation. The four phases of each of the last two sets have the same names as the four initiations of the mainstream tantras, and the meditations pursued during them are similar to those in the mainstream tantras.
>
> (Mullin 1991: 101)

The seven initiations in the first stage of the Kalachakra rite – the only ones covered by the Dalai Lama in the mass initiations over which he presides – authorize the pupil to practice within the sphere of the "stage of creation," which, as we have seen, has the overarching aim of building a self-image as a fully enlightened deity. The eight final initiations authorize the pupil to practice the advanced yoga techniques pertaining to the "stage of perfection" in order to transform his body, speech and mind into the body, speech and mind of a Buddha.
17 During the second part of the ritual, however, other "internal initiations" – given this name because they occur "within" the womb of the principal deity's consort – will also take place in association with the principal initiations.
18 Here there are clear similarities between the psycho-physiological processes initiated in the Kalachakra rite and the "symbolic effectiveness" of the healing ritual analyzed by Lévi-Strauss (1983), which displays, among other things, the "magical" aspect of the Tibetan initiation rite.
19 Seed-syllables are monosyllabic mantras that contain the essence of a deity or a state of absorption (samadhi).
20 *Vajra* (Sanskrit) means "lightning," "diamond," "unbreakable," etc. The vajra is the most significant symbol in Vajrayana Buddhism, and essentially refers to the "unbreakable," "indivisible," "immutable" enlightened aspect of the mind and enlightenment itself. In Tibetan Buddhist iconography, vajras are depicted in the form of scepters in the case of peaceful deities, or even as "weapons" in the case of wrathful deities.
21 www.berzinarchives.com/web/en/archives/advanced/kalachakra/kalachakra_world_peace/attending_kalachakra_initiation.html.

22 Vesna Wallace discusses the same account of king Manjushriyashas's mass initiation event with a slightly different take. In her words,

> The Kālacakra tradition expresses the concern that due to the similarity between the Vedic and Barbarian Dharmas with regard to killing, future generations of Brāhmaṇical communities may well convert to Islam, unless they join their Buddhist compatriots in the *vajra*-family. The *Vimalaprabhā's* account of Mañjuśrī Yaśas's teaching of the *Kālacakratantra* to thirty-five million Brāhmaṇic sages in Sambhala attests to that concern. According to the *Vimalaprabhā*, the king Yaśas was aware that Brāhmaṇas in Sambhala were originally from different countries with contrary customs regarding eating meat, drinking liquor, and the like. Therefore, he deemed it necessary to unite them into a single *vajra*-family by initiating them into the *kālacakra*-maṇḍala, which he constructed in a sandalwood grove, south of the village of Kalāpa [the capital of Shambhala].
>
> (Wallace 2001: 117)

23 www.berzinarchives.com/web/en/archives/advanced/kalachakra/kalachakra_world_peace/attending_kalachakra_initiation.html.

24 There are four principal schools of Tibetan Buddhism. The Nyingma School was the first school of Buddhism established in Tibet in the eight and ninth centuries. During the second stage of the spread of Buddhism in that country (beginning in the eleventh century) there emerged the other three of the four most important schools in Tibetan Buddhism: Kagyu, Sakya and, as we have discussed in Chapter 2, a few hundred years later, in the fourteenth century, the Gelug School. The schools created during the second period belong to the sarma tradition. In the Tibetan language, "sarma" basically means "new translation." In contrast, the only important school that emerged during the previous period became known as Nyingma, or the "old translation."

25 This kind of non-sectarian posture is sometimes controversially referred to as "rime" (Tib. *ris med*) after the homonymous nineteenth century movement. For a detailed discussion of the Rime movement, see Smith (2001: 235–72).

26 Despite the Fifth Dalai Lama's trans-sectarian posture in what concerns the creation of a symbolic apparatus for the nascent state, after gaining power he persecuted representatives of other schools. The Fifth Dalai Lama established a particularly harsh policy against the Kagyu and Jonang schools since their representatives were allies with the Tsang king.

27 In a certain sense, a more recent performance of the Kalachakra initiation rivaled the event at Graz in terms of its explicitly political nature. Partly due to the evident political symbolism of Washington D.C., the "Kalachakra for World Peace 2011" that took place at the Verizon Center in the American capital, was particularly revealing of the alliance between the political and the spiritual that, I believe, underlines these initiations. During the event, for instance, the Dalai Lama was received by president Obama at the White House and invited to Congress by Speaker John Boehner and congressional leaders from both the Republican and the Democratic parties. Also during the event, more specifically on July 6, 2011, the day the Dalai Lama celebrated his 76th birthday, he gave a very significant speech in the presence of several illustrious guests, such as Arun Gandhi, the grandson of Mahatma Gandhi, and Martin Luther King III, the son of Martin Luther King, Jr. After the guests and the Dalai Lama himself proffered words about world peace, the Tibetan leader announced that he would deliver a speech in his native tongue to be broadcast to the people in Tibet. In a statement rich in historical associations and positioning, the Dalai Lama reiterated his decision to abdicate as political leader of the Tibetan people – which, as we have seen in Chapter 3, was announced a few months earlier that year – and his deep commitment to democracy. Between the lines we can also read messages being delivered indirectly to the Chinese Government. In 2009, when I was staying at Harvard University as a visiting scholar, I had the opportunity to witness another

instance of this kind of indirect dialogue with the Chinese government in the context of a conference about Sino-Tibetan relations. Lobsang Sangye, the current Prime Minister of the Tibetan government in exile, was then a Ph.D. student at Harvard and one of the main organizers of the conference. The event also included other Tibetan scholars active in the United States and Chinese scholars coming from China. During the talks, the exchange of political messages between the two parties was quite clear.

28 Heinrich Harrer died a few years later, on January 7, 2006, aged 93.

Part IV

Once more death...

7 Spiritual politics[1]

Kathmandu, Earth-Rabbit year (1999). The streets of Boudhanath in Nepal's capital were buzzing with the preparations for the last day of Losar – the 15-day period of Tibetan New Year festivities. The maroon and yellow of the monks' robes cast warm colors on the landscape already busy with local commerce. In this area of Kathmandu, where most of the valley's Tibetan Buddhist temples and monasteries are located, one also finds the small complex of buildings that harbors some of the Segyu monks, who sought exile in neighboring countries after the Chinese invasion of Tibet.

In the rooms of this monastery, Segyu Rinpoche worked out the last details of the preparation for the Guhyasamaja puja to be performed the next day, a day after the end of Losar, a Segyu tradition. Between one command and another made to his assistants, his thoughts wondered to other spheres. Despite the festive atmosphere, he felt that he did not have much to celebrate. He was, in his own words, in the "eye of the hurricane" with respect to an internal schism in his lineage.

Only two years had passed since he was officially enthroned as the abbot of the two Segyu monasteries in exile. Now he was taking upon himself the responsibility of bringing an end to the dissolution of the Segyu lineage, a process that had started even before the Chinese invasion and occupation of Tibet. In his understanding, a first step in this direction would be to eliminate dissensions among Segyu representatives, dissensions that were, in fact, the outcome of a conflict that pertained to Tibetan Buddhist institutions as a whole. The Brazilian lama was dealing here with disputes that go back more than three centuries and that, in the context of the Tibetan diaspora, acquired a global scope, involving some of the most important representatives of the Gelug School.

Like many other followers of the Gelug School, the Segyu monks were divided between those who abandoned the worship of the spiritual protector Dorje Shugden and those who insisted (due to conviction or necessity) to continue with this practice. The decision to advise against the propitiation of this protector deity came from the Dalai Lama himself, who declared, among other things, that Dorje Shugden would be responsible for the spread of sectarianism among followers of the Gelug School in relation to the other schools of Tibetan

Buddhism. Already in 1979, the Dalai Lama had suggested restrictions on Dorje Shugden worship, but it was only in 1996, the year in which the Tibetan leader more forcefully and openly spoke against it, that the conflicts surrounding this protector gained surprising proportions, with repercussions inside and outside the Tibetan community.

Among the most shocking events related to the Dalai Lama's decision to advise against the propitiation of Dorje Shugden was the murder of an important lama of the Gelug School, Geshe Lobsang Gyatso,[2] founder of the Institute of Buddhist Dialects in Dharamsala, India, along with two of his students. Geshe Lobsang Gyatso was openly against the cult of this protector, and advised his disciples to abandon it.[3] The Tibetan government in exile, a major portion of the Tibetan community in Dharamsala, and the Indian press all attributed the killings to a group of Dorje Shugden followers. The case remains unsolved to this day.

The Tibetan community in exile had not yet totally recovered from the devastating effects engendered by these events, when, in Kathmandu, Segyu Rinpoche tried to prevent the monks of his monastery from performing Dorje Shugden pujas. The internal schism of the Segyu lineage occurred after a senior monk parted ways with the rest of the group due to his opposition to the cult of this protector. The other monks – in fact, the majority of the Segyu monks in Kathmandu – seemed not to have much choice. In the face of the meager resources of their monastery, they had no option but to respond to the requests for Dorje Shugden pujas made by Tibetans who became rich in Nepal due to carpet manufacturing. Segyu Rinpoche was extremely preoccupied with the image of his lineage in the Tibetan community at the time. According to Segyu Rinpoche, the dissident monk had already publicized among a few persons close to the Dalai Lama that the monastery and its activities were closely connected with the protector.

The main ammunition of the Brazilian lama in his efforts to put an end to the practice of Dorje Shugden within his community was to invest financially in the monastery. Segyu Rinpoche had already bought some land for a new temple to be built in the future. He also had created structural conditions for the reception of new young monks. In the beginning of 1999, around 20 monks less than ten years old were living and studying in the monastery – two years before, only one monk this age lived there. Gradually, Segyu Rinpoche became a crucial sponsor for the Segyu monasteries – the one in Kathmandu and the other in Kalimpong, India. It is no exaggeration to say that at least in this initial moment sponsorship was the role that the Segyu monks expected him to perform. When I asked, for example, a monk – the main figure responsible for the education of the children – what he thought about having a Brazilian as the abbot of his monastery, he responded that Segyu Rinpoche could bring more resources to the monastery. The intentions of the Brazilian lama, nevertheless, went well beyond the project of simply raising funds for the Segyu monasteries.

On that last day of Losar what occupied his mind most was the meeting that would take place in a couple of days bringing together the senior Segyu monks to discuss the future of the lineage. The meeting was at the initiative of Segyu Rinpoche and had as its main topic the Dorje Shugden issue and the internal schism of the lineage. Segyu Rinpoche was performing here an exercise in *realpolitik*. The Brazilian lama thought it was important to be on good terms with the Dalai Lama and the Tibetan government in exile. In his opinion, a good relationship with Dharamsala was the essential condition for the Segyu monks to have access to the knowledge of qualified geshes educated in the great monasteries of the Gelug School, which would certainly represent an important step towards the revitalization of the lineage.

The meeting, however, did not go as he had expected. The dissident-monk did not show up and the other senior monks were still resistant to abandoning their old sponsors. Despite the pragmatism of Segyu Rinpoche's concerns, his vision of things clashed with even more concrete and pressing questions, which related to well-established commitments between lamas, monks and sponsors, commitments that in many cases preceded the exile period. Before long, the repercussions surrounding the measures which Segyu Rinpoche was trying to implement in the Segyu community of Kathmandu extended beyond the walls of the monastery, engendering the discontentment of one of his main allies in the Tibetan world, Lama Gangchen. In the past, as we have seen, Lama Gangchen had opened the doors of his center in Brazil to Segyu Rinpoche. More recently, he played a crucial role in making the arrangements for Segyu Rinpoche, then known as Lama Shakya Zangpo, to be enthroned as the lineage holder of the Segyu tradition. In effect, the news about Segyu Rinpoche's efforts to prevent the monks of his tradition from performing pujas for Dorje Shugden reached Lama Gangchen almost immediately, since the Tibetan lama's sponsors were in almost every case the very same ones "hiring" Segyu monks to perform the pujas.

In exile, Lama Gangchen had formed a solid connection with these men, who helped him in many ways over the years. Not very far from the Segyu Monastery, for instance, one of these sponsors had built a clinic with an adjacent guesthouse – the complex was baptized "Himalayan Healing Center" by Lama Gangchen and is until today his headquarters in Kathmandu. Among other things, it was there that his disciples would stay while visiting the Nepalese capital. In his autobiographical introduction to the book *Self-Healing I*, Lama Gangchen highlights the "important" help that his sponsors had been giving him. In 1981, says the "Introduction," his sponsors from Kathmandu invited him to visit Nepal, and offered on the occasion a "long-life puja," a "long and complex" ceremony that enabled him to "give more teachings and take care of all the beings" (Gangchen 2001 [1991]: 17). In the introduction, moreover, it is said that these same Tibetans that were helping him now were also his sponsors in previous incarnations.

It is not hard to imagine then, in light of this context, why Lama Gangchen was so outraged by Segyu Rinpoche's strategy to regain the trust of Dharamsala. As soon as he heard about the Brazilian lama's plans, Lama Gangchen invited him for a conversation at the Healing Center. Segyu Rinpoche reports the general tone of the meeting as follows:

Lama Gangchen has already started to "fume." Why? Because I didn't let my monks take part … [in a Dorje Shugden puja]. This is Lama Gangchen's interest, not mine. This is a fact! "Aren't you afraid of the sponsors?" I think … so what? The fact is that I'm not afraid of these things […]. But if we are talking here about someone who wants to make things right, but then stab one in the back because he turned his back just a little? I'm talking here about the sponsors in relation to Lama Gangchen. It was yesterday morning … the conversation was not very pleasant. The consequences are difficult to digest: insinuations of betrayal…

Thus, when trying to solve a problem that seemed to be, at least at first glance, internal to his lineage, Segyu Rinpoche had to contend with the small, but cohesive, social network formed within the Tibetan community of Kathmandu throughout the years. Beyond these aspects, the conflict with Lama Gangchen was also evidence of the difficulties that Segyu Rinpoche would face in dissociating his own image from that of the protector Dorje Shugden in light of connections established in the past.

As we have seen in the introduction to this work, in 1996, during an Avalokiteshvara initiation bestowed by the Dalai Lama in Pasadena, Los Angeles, Segyu Rinpoche, then known as Lama Shakya, expressed his hesitation at seeing his name associated with that of Lama Gangchen. A few months earlier, the Dalai Lama had come down more forcefully against the cult of Dorje Shugden, and during the initiation in Pasadena, a list containing the names of lamas that insisted on worshiping this protector circulated among participants. Lama Gangchen was among those names. Visibly tense with the comments the Dalai Lama made about people who were not following his advice, Segyu Rinpoche would later tell me, "this is why I like to make it clear that I am only a guest in Lama Gangchen's center."

However, even after the council of the Shi De Choe Tsog Dharma Center (Lama Gangchen's center in São Paulo) decided to put an end to the "healing sessions" of Segyu Rinpoche a few years later, the connection with the Tibetan lama remained. In fact, his involvement with Lama Gangchen was even traced back to his past lives, one of his presumed incarnations of the sixteenth century, in particular.

A project which Segyu Rinpoche had been working on since 1997, and which was concluded in the beginning of 1999 with the bilingual publication (English-Tibetan) of the book *The History of Segyu Gaden Phodrang Monastery (1432–1959)*, reveals an example of the strong connection between these two lamas. Authored by Champa Thubten Zongtse, one of the senior monks of the Segyu lineage, the book tells the history of this tantric school since its foundation until the year 1959. Among the many biographies present in the book is the biography of the previous incarnation of Segyu Rinpoche as the abbot of Segyu Monastery. "Gyudchen Dorje Zangpo," the short biography tells us, "received spiritual teachings from many incomparable spiritual masters. Particularly, in the monastery Gangchen Chosphel [Lama Gangchen's monastery], he studied extensively the contemplation of the *Tripitaka*, the Three Baskets of Teachings" (Thubten Zongtse 1999: 30).

And in Segyu Rinpoche's words:

> My connection with Lama Gangchen is much bigger, because it comes from other incarnations. So before I became the Gyudchen – "chen" means "master" [*sic*], "gyud" means "tantra" – Dorje Zangpo, I received my education at the Gangchen Monastery. So, I come from Gangchen Monastery. It is blood, spiritual blood, right? But it is very dangerous to talk about any link [with Lama Gangchen] that I have, even in past lives – it is extremely dangerous for me.

The unfolding of events in Kathmandu, instigated by Segyu Rinpoche's presence on the scene, suggests that the entire Gelug School was involved, in one way or another, with disputes connected to the protector Dorje Shugden. Amplified by the lenses of the small Tibetan community of Kathmandu, connections and fissures surfaced, highlighting the unavoidable international implications of this conflict and its direct influence on the balance of power in the religious field of Tibetan Buddhism.

Between the political and the spiritual

India, June 1996. In all the main monasteries of the Gelug School in exile, thousands of monks were summoned to large meetings in which signatures and fingerprints of all who supported the end of the cult of Dorje Shugden were being collected. Some abbots and even the Ganden Tri Rinpoche himself, the head of the Gelug School, tried to be present to the maximum number of meetings in order to illuminate the reasons that led the Dalai Lama to advise against Dorje Shugden worship.

The Brazilian Lama Michel, recognized by Lama Gangchen as a tulku when he was still a boy, was then a monk in the monastery of Sera-me in South India. As advised by his tutor, Lama Gangchen, who thought that because he was not Tibetan he should avoid getting involved in the issue, Lama Michel decided not to go to the meetings. The consequences engendered by this decision would manifest soon. Like many of those who decided not to sign the lists that were circulating, the Brazilian lama would be labeled a "Shugden devotee." Accounts of violence against those who decided not to endorse the Dalai Lama's decision began to circulate among the monks. According to Lama Michel – who did not have to endure more than a few "dirty looks" himself[4] – one of his monk-friends had his house burned to the ground due to being identified as a Shugden devotee.

The signature campaign represents a clear example of the kind of tension that resulted from the entanglement between the political and the spiritual in Tibetan Buddhism. In the words of Lama Michel:

> Because they consider the Dalai Lama their guru, they cannot lie to him. And when they signed the document [forswearing Dorje Shugden] it was as

if they were stating this directly to the Dalai Lama. It is a political thing, since spiritually you do not have to sign for your guru if you do something or not. It is a political thing, but they also see it as religious since it is being done in the name of the Dalai Lama, even if it was not necessarily his idea.

Actually, it is not always easy to know where ideas of the Dalai Lama start and finish, as his statements about the Dorje Shugden issue have often been accompanied by government resolutions. In May 1996, for instance, the Kashag (the executive Cabinet of the Tibetan government) issued a statement condoning the Dalai Lama's words against the cult of Dorje Shugden. In June the same year, the Tibetan Parliament in exile unanimously passed a series of resolutions to endorse the decision of the Tibetan leader to advise against the worship of Dorje Shugden. "In the interest of Buddhism and the Tibetan national cause," goes the document,

> His Holiness the Dalai Lama has openly advised against the propitiation of Shugden. On behalf of the Tibetan people, both in and outside Tibet, the Assembly of Tibetan People's Deputies would like to express our thanks and gratitude to His Holiness the Dalai Lama and make a pledge that we will abide by his every advice.
> (www.dalailama.com/messages/dolgyal-shugden/atpd-resolutions)

Another document, this time from the Department of Information and International Relations of the Tibetan Government in exile stated that contrary to what Dorje Shugden devotees were claiming, "there had been no forced signature campaign of any kind against the propitiation of this spirit." It goes on to say:

> Soon after His Holiness the Dalai Lama advised the Tibetan Buddhists to stop propitiating Dholgyal [i.e., Dorje Shugden], the Kashag issued a circular explaining why heeding his advice is in the best interest of the Tibetan national cause and the personal security of His Holiness the Dalai Lama. The *Tibetan people* responded to His Holiness the Dalai Lama's advice by *voluntarily* submitting signed statements: the majority saying that they have never propitiated the spirit while some vowing to give up this practice for good. This is now being misinterpreted by vested interests as a forced signature campaign.[5]
> (Department of Information and International Relations 1996)

According to the same document,

> the allegations against the Tibetan Women's Association and Tibetan Youth Congress (TYC) are totally false and defamatory. [. . .] Following His Holiness' advice, the TYC held a general body meeting to chalk out a course of plan to *educate* the Tibetan people about the need to stop propitiating Dholgyal.[6]
> (Ibid.)

The complete alignment of these governmental entities with the Dalai Lama's position on the matter, while understandable from the religious point of view, seems to run contrary to their claims to democracy. This political style of the Tibetan government in exile, as we are going to see below, finds its parallel in the invisible world of spirits and in its influences within the material world.

The *Yellow Book*

The starting point of the modern phase of the controversy surrounding the protector Dorje Shugden can be located to the year 1975, when Dzeme Rinpoche (1927–96), an important lama in the Gelug School, published the book *Thunder of the Stirring Black Cloud: The Oral Transmission of the Intelligent Father*, also known as the *Yellow Book*. In general terms, the *Yellow Book* consists of a series of histories orally transmitted to the author of the book by his guru (who was also the senior tutor of the Dalai Lama, Trijang Rinpoche, 1901–80). The text tells in detail calamities brought on by Dorje Shugden for monks and lay people of the Gelug Tradition who engaged in practices of the Nyingma School. Some of these practitioners, cited by name in the book, even died due to their trans-sectarian activities. In sum, the *Yellow Book* highlights one of the main attributions of Dorje Shugden, which is to protect (also through violent means) the "purity" of the Gelug School, especially against the influence of the Nyingma School.

The publication of this work had implications inside and outside the Gelug School. Such effects were certainly accentuated, moreover, by the fact that the year of 1975 was also marked by another important event in the life of the Tibetan community in exile: the attempt to institute a great annual ceremony connected to Padmasambhava, otherwise known as Guru Rinpoche. The initiative to institute such a ceremony came from the Dalai Lama himself. This was one of the key elements in his project to restore the ritual system underlying the government of the Fifth Dalai Lama. According to the Tibetan Buddhist scholar (and also one of the first westerners to become a geshe) George Dreyfus, the Fourteenth Dalai Lama came to greatly appreciate the political project of the Fifth Dalai Lama over the years. The current Dalai Lama described this project as a "masterplan" to transform Tibet from "a marginal state governed by religious hierarchs mostly preoccupied with the power of their monasteries and estates" into a nation capable of finding its place in the history of the region (Dreyfus 1998: 262).

As we have seen in Chapter 2, the Fifth Dalai Lama looked for inspiration to the old Tibetan Empire to unify the country and build the symbolic basis of his state. The elaborate system of rituals that supported the Tibetan state had, in this way, many elements pertaining to the Nyingma School, since this was the first school of Tibetan Buddhism – "Nyingma" refers to "old school" – and has as it founding figure the semi-mythical tantric master Padmasambhava, who was invited by Trisong Detsen, one of the kings of the old empire, to visit Tibet. The cult to the transcendental figure of Padmasambhava, or Guru Rinpoche, hence constituted one of the most essential aspects of the state ritual system. The Fourteenth Dalai Lama's plan to institute a great ceremony in honor of Guru Rinpoche reinstated this tradition. Nevertheless, his plan failed, since the majority of Gelug monks and nuns would not take part in the event, probably frightened by the intimidating message of the *Yellow Book.*

According to George Dreyfus, an eye-witness of the events of 1975, the Dalai Lama felt directly attacked by the publication of this book, not only because it frustrated his attempts to restore the state ritual connected with Guru Rinpoche, but also because it attacked him personally on the issue of his own spiritual practices. He had already become a student of Dilgo Khyentse Rinpoche, one of the great Nyingma masters of the twentieth century, and in his personal monastery of Namgyal, the monks traditionally performed Nyingma practices,[7] along with other Gelug practices. One of the first public manifestations of his discontentment with the then recent events occurred in the Tibetan New Year of 1976, when the Dalai Lama refused the long-life offerings made by the Tibetan government.

> Traditionally, the Dalai Lama accepts such an offering after the new year as a sign of the pure bond that exists between him and Tibetans: this bond is based on his commitment to continue his work as Dalai Lama and the Tibetans' allegiance. His refusal signaled in effect that the bond had been undermined and that the behavior of Tibetans was incompatible with his remaining as Dalai Lama.
>
> (Dreyfus 1998: 257)

The Dalai Lama would only accept the long-life offerings in the middle of the year 1976, just a few months prior to his decision to advise restrictions to the cult of Dorje Shugden.

History repeats (and perpetuates) itself

In the beginning of the twentieth century, Thubten Gyatso, the Thirteenth Dalai Lama, another distinguished representative of the lineage of Dalai Lamas, also tried to limit the cult of Dorje Shugden within the Gelug School. As in the case of the Fourteenth Dalai Lama, strong connections with the Nyingma School figured behind his decision to restrict the cult. The Thirteenth Dalai Lama was also connected with the Nyingma School. "He had several teachers from the Nyingma School, practiced with them in the Potala Palace, and wrote commentaries to the Nyingma texts of his predecessor the Fifth Dalai Lama" (Batchelor 1998: 62). Besides the conflict in relation to his personal spiritual practice, the Thirteenth Dalai Lama too had political reasons for limiting the cult of this protector. The Tibetan leader believed that the broad diffusion of Dorje Shugden worship in Drepung Monastery – the largest monastery in the country, and one of the main reservoirs of monks that were to occupy high ranking positions in the government – represented an attempt to expropriate from the deity Nechung his duties as the official protector of this monastery and of the Tibetan government (Dreyfus 1998: 244).

Nechung is part of a group of deities known as "the five kings," who are considered to be a manifestation of Pehar, the deity appointed by Padmasambhava as the main guardian of Buddhism in Tibet. According to tradition, the temple of Pehar, the Nechung Gompa, a Nyingma establishment strongly connected to Drepung, keeps its southern door closed. Tradition has it that Dorje Shugden will be waiting outside this door to occupy the place of Pehar once this deity has transcended the "six spheres of existence" (Nebesky-Wojkowitz 1993: 444–5).

Behind the relatively recent broad dissemination of Dorje Shugden worship is Pabonka Rinpoche (1878–1941), one of the most important Gelug lamas of the twenty-first century. As is the case with many other Gelug lamas, Pabonka Rinpoche received teachings from Nyingma lamas. Nevertheless, after getting very ill and having a series of visions and dreams of Dorje Shugden, he convinced himself that the illness that befell him was a sign sent by this protector indicating that he should stop practicing Nyingma teachings (Batchelor 1998: 63). Pabonka Rinpoche started from then on to intensively disseminate the cult of Dorje Shugden, but due to the command of the Thirteenth Dalai Lama, he ended up swearing "from the depths of his heart" never to worship this protector again (ibid.). The unfolding of more recent events seems to contradict this sentiment. Trijang Rinpoche, the main disciple of Pabonka Rinpoche, put even stronger emphasis than his guru on the cult of Dorje Shugden, highlighting the "fully enlightened nature" of this protector.

Trijang Rinpoche would become in exile the main source of inspiration for the Gelug School, and also the root-guru of all the figures involved in the Dorje Shugden controversy. The "spirit" of the contention between the Thirteenth Dalai Lama and Pabonka Rinpoche has been kept alive through the teachings of Trijang Rinpoche and the conduct of some of his disciples. Nevertheless, because this spirit materialized in disputes that have since unfolded on a planetary scale, it presents, as we shall see, a much more direct influence on the balance of forces within the Tibetan Buddhist transnational religious field.

New developments of the controversy

For almost 20 years, the Fourteenth Dalai Lama himself kept the Dorje Shugden issue within a more restricted circle, being circumscribed to the Tibetan community in exile. Starting from the middle of the 1990s, however, the Dalai Lama decided to make public his position on Dorje Shugden to western followers of Tibetan Buddhism as well. During this time, as discussed above, the Tibetan leader hardened his position against the cult of the protector. Since then, the Tibetan leader has almost always mentioned the Dorje Shugden issue in his teachings around the world, requesting the people who practice this protector not to receive initiations bestowed by him. On the occasion of the Kalachakra initiation in Graz, for instance, the situation was no different:

And I'm sure that among those who are here there are none who propitiate the spirit Dogyal [i.e., Dorje Shugden] and as I have on many occasions asked the people who are propitiating the controversial spirit Dogyal not to come to receive my teachings, or my initiations, and I'm sure that there will be none here. If there is anyone here who is still propitiating this controversial spirit Dogyal, or Shugden, then I advice you not to receive this initiation. Because to receive this initiation it is important that there be a pure bond between the lama who is conferring the initiation and the students who are receiving the initiation. So therefore those of you who claim to be Buddhists and my followers, and are still practicing the controversial spirit, then it is not good to receive the initiation from me. With regard to this controversial spirit, the Fifth Dalai Lama has clearly said that this spirit is a malevolent force, an evil spirit that is born out of wrong prayers. And therefore I have advised people against such practice, so I request you not to attend this initiation.

Statements like this have been shaping, in a certain sense, the network of relations between lamas of the Gelug School and other schools, in light of the position adopted by each in relation to the controversy surrounding Dorje Shugden. Since the announcement of the unequivocal advice against the cult of Dorje Shugden, some of those who decided to openly defy the Dalai Lama's decision have been gradually isolated from the Tibetan community in exile and other Tibetan Buddhist groups. In the end, even the lamas who did not necessarily agree with the decision of the Tibetan leader were obliged to cut relations with the "rebels."

Lama Gangchen was one of the lamas who decided not to go along with the advise against the cult of Dorje Shugden. In his center in Milan the effect of the Dalai Lama's statements were devastating. His disciple, Tiziana Ciasullo, tells that before 1996, the self-healing sessions in the downtown area of the Italian city – of which she was responsible – would attract up to one hundred people. After the Dalai Lama more forcefully advised against Dorje Shugden worship, the sessions, she tells us, started to become less and less popular. Moreover, the social work that Lama Gangchen does through his NGO Help in Action faced obstacles created by the controversy surrounding the protector. According to his Brazilian disciple who lives in Italy, Mônica Benvenuti, in many places in India and Nepal where Help in Action is strong Lama Gangchen has become *persona non grata*. A lot of people in these countries have even refused the help offered through Help in Action. On the institutional level as well there has been great hesitancy with regard to the participation of the Tibetan lama's group in the meetings of the Unione Budista Italiana. In the words of Francesco Prevosti:

The Dalai Lama came to Italy in 1996. And even though he was speaking exclusively to the Tibetans present in the audience [about the Dorje Shugden issue], the translator decided to translate his speech to everyone. That was the beginning of a real mess around here. From that a great disarray emerged within the Unione Budista Italiana, which is an association that includes Zen, Theravada, Nyingma, Gelug, Sakya and Kagyu centers. Disciples of Namkhai Norbu – who is originally a Bön master, from the Bön tradition, but who is also a Dzogchen master, hence connected to the Nyingmas – were the ones leading the opposition against Lama Gangchen. There was a strong lobby to "chase us away." And we have four centers in this organization! A lot of discussion about the issue happened, and also a lot of problems.

There was the thought that we were against the Dalai Lama. The Dalai Lama spoke against the protector, from his own point of view – that is his opinion. It is not that we are against anyone – we are not against anyone! We were not against the Dalai Lama before, and we are not against the Dalai Lama now. The truth is the majority of the people here [connected to Lama Gangchen's centers] consider themselves to be disciples of the Dalai Lama too. From their point of view, they [the affiliates of the Unione Budista Italiana] claimed that they had a pure samaya with the Dalai Lama: "We cannot be affiliated with people that are against the Dalai Lama" etc.

In the end, the executive committee of the Unione Budista Italiana decided that the organization should not interfere with the spiritual practice of its groups, and thus allowed the group of Lama Gangchen to remain a member. In any event, the account of this episode is a clear illustration of the impact of the Dalai Lama's statements in a context that was slightly outside the sphere of Tibetan Buddhism. On a more personal level, some of the disciples of Lama Gangchen also resented the fact that while before they were in contact with many lamas residing in western countries, today they are isolated from the Tibetan community in exile. In some cases, disciples of Lama Gangchen who had previously cultivated a close relationship with the Dalai Lama himself had to take sides after the advent of the controversy. This is the case with the Italian Claudio Cipullo. In his words:

> I used to be very close to His Holiness the Dalai Lama and to see him I didn't need passes or something like that. This is because I was one of the first westerners to become a monk in Tibetan Buddhism. We were friends. When His Holiness talked to me, I felt great emotion. We had the same guru, Trijang Dorje Chang, so there was this strong connection.

In the beginning of the controversy, when the Dalai Lama had only advised that the cult of Dorje Shugden should not be practiced in public, Claudio did not face major problems. He tells that in the 1980s he directly asked the Dalai Lama how he should proceed in relation to the cult of the deity. The Tibetan leader told him then that he could continue to practice, but in a private way. Nevertheless, over the years this situation would change. Gradually, Claudio was obliged to part ways with friends from that time, such as Robert Thurman and Glenn Mullin, who became two important scholars in the academic field of Tibetan Buddhist studies and are still very close to the Dalai Lama. His access to the Dalai Lama also became more restricted. Claudio says that the last time he met with the Dalai Lama everything was very different:

> It has been a while [probably 1997]. I went to one of His Holiness' teachings in the Lama Zopa center in Pomaia [Italy]. When I saw him one of those days, I went to talk with him: "His Holiness, His Holiness, give me your blessings!" But he only gave me his blessings after checking if nobody was watching us.

Since this last encounter, Claudio decided not to see the Tibetan leader again, and to follow the advice he had given him two decades before: he would keep doing his Dorje Shugden practice in private. In his words:

> From my point of view, His Holiness is Buddha, so what he says – 20 years before or 20 years after – is always the same. The words of a Buddha are not interpretable – they are the truth – above all if he speaks directly to me in private. And that is what happened. He spoke to me in private and not to a big assembly with thousands of people, or in a political situation. I understand though [that the Dalai Lama acts as a political man], I understand…

An important idea implicit in the statements of Claudio is the notion that the Dalai Lama might be acting against his will. Among some lamas that have chosen to continue to worship Dorje Shugden there is the idea (almost generalized) that the Dalai Lama is being forced to make certain decisions, or that his entourage is doing a poor job in advising him. For instance, Gonsar Rinpoche – spiritual director of the important Rabten Choeling Center for Higher Buddhist Studies in Switzerland and one of the most criticized figures in the controversy – believes that the Dalai Lama is surrounded by "narrow-minded and incompetent" people. By his account:

> Before, the Dalai Lama had at his side his two excellent enlightened masters, Ling Rinpoche and Trijang Rinpoche, and also some other great masters, like my master Geshe Rabten Rinpoche, who was among his closest philosophical assistants. Moreover, he was surrounded by some politicians from the older generation, really very sincere, really dedicated. Since the beginning of the 1970s, this situation started to change. A new team and a new context started to form around him. Later, his two excellent masters passed away [in the beginning of the 1980s]. In a way, His Holiness actually became very alone. This new team is spoiling many things.

Like Gonsar Rinpoche, many Tibetan lamas that decided to continue to propitiate Dorje Shugden refrain from publicly and directly attacking the Dalai Lama, especially in relation to his skills as a spiritual master. Often the criticism is directed against the Tibetan government, and in some cases, attempts to separate the political sphere from the spiritual sphere are evident. For instance, in the Rabten Choeling Center, contrary to what one might have imagined, there were pictures of the Dalai Lama everywhere in 2002, when I did my fieldwork. This fact is all the more striking considering that the director of the center, Gonsar Rinpoche, is considered by many the most ardent opponent of the Tibetan leader. Over the years, Gonsar Rinpoche has become quite isolated from the Tibetan community and other lamas in exile. In Switzerland, where, as mentioned before, the largest Tibetan community in Europe is located, Gonsar Rinpoche was even prevented by the local Tibetan community through public demonstrations from continuing with his annual visits to Rikon monastery, where he was once abbot. In any event, Gonsar Rinpoche claims that he still considers the Dalai Lama one of his spiritual masters, but states that he cannot abandon the propitiation of Dorje Shugden due to his commitment to his root-guru.

> My relation to the deity Dorje Shugden has its roots in my precious masters, like Geshe Rabten Rinpoche. There are eight lamas from whom I have receive teachings in my life, but among them, Geshe Rabten Rinpoche is the lama to whom I owe everything. If I have some little qualities anywhere I have him to thank. He is really my spiritual father, my spiritual mother, spiritual brother, my spiritual friend, my protector, my teacher and guide and everything. I've received this practice from him; my relation to Dorje Shugden also came through him. It has also come from this master [points to a picture of Trijang Rinpoche], who is also the master for all of us – the master of His Holiness the Dalai Lama, too.

Clearly, what is at stake here is devotion towards the guru. In all cases of lamas that do not follow the Dalai Lama's advice, Trijang Rinpoche was one of their main gurus. Hence, the controversy emerges from a very restricted group of lamas, very close to each other in terms of the lineage of knowledge transmission. The ramifications that the actions of this small network of lamas would have in the world, as I have tried to demonstrate, are surprising to say the least. In a country like Brazil, which is situated at the periphery of the broader Tibetan Buddhist transnational religious field, the conflict was not – at least at first – clearly distinguishable. When the Dalai Lama went to Brazil in 1999, for example, he did not make any comments about Dorje Shugden.[8] Moreover, many of the main followers of Lama Gangchen in Brazil were present at the events in the city of Curitiba and in the capital, Brasília. Along with representatives of the other communities in Brazil, they helped organize the visit of the Tibetan leader, sat at the stage during the teachings and were granted an audience with the Dalai Lama. This does not mean, however, that echoes of the controversy had not at that point arrived on Brazil's tropical shores. In fact, just as it happened in other countries, among the other Brazilian communities, and in particular, the centers connected with the Nyingma lama Chagdud Rinpoche (1930–2002), who moved to Brazil in 1995, there has been great hostility against Lama Gangchen. Several years earlier in 1979, one of the most revered Nyingma masters alive, Chatral Rinpoche (b. 1913), wrote a response in Tibetan to the *Yellow Book* entitled *The Rain of Adamant Fire: A holy discourse based upon scriptures and reason, annihilating the poisonous seeds of the wicked speech of Dzeme Tulku Lobsang Palden* (Chatral Rinpoche 1979). This work is certainly one of the main sources substantiating the support of Nyingma lamas for the Dalai Lama's decision to advise against Dorje Shugden worship. Chatral Rinpoche describes the *Yellow Book* as follows:

> It is a poisonous seed of biased sophistry and ill intent aimed explicitly at causing people to supplicate a demon as the awakened mind of something exalted; causing the monastic community and patrons that uphold the doctrine of the yellow hat tradition [i.e., the Gelug School] to rely on a demon for refuge and thereby create the cause for destroying the refuge vow; implicating the author and all others in the terrible karma of holding wrong view and abandoning the Dharma by proposing that the Old School tradition [i.e., the Nyingma School] and its upholders are outside Shakyamuni's doctrine of sūtra and tantra; and what's more, inciting within persons in the present and future the intent of sectarianism, divisiveness, argumentation, and ruinous contention.
>
> (Ibid.: 5)[9]

In his treatise, Chatral Rinpoche emphasizes both the demonic nature of the protector and its sectarian penchant. Chatral Rinpoche defends the idea that we should see the traditions as not contradictory, but each as valid expressions of the Buddha's singular and all-encompassing awakened intentionality. The "negative speech" of the *Yellow Book* should be "openly criticized," in his opinion, otherwise "many monks and laypersons of meager intelligence will follow the negative speech, like the 'plop' sound of [a fruit fallen in water, as reported by a paranoid][10] rabbit, and wander in unpleasant hell realms as retribution" (ibid.: 13). Chatral continues:

> So to avert beings from the ongoing sin of accumulating the severe karma of abandoning the Dharma, we should take as our basis the pure perception of devotion for the avenues through which Dharma appears; stay clear of resentments and jealousies between fellow followers of the Sage; and not regard any of the teachings as contradictory, in the manner of heat and cold, through keeping a harmonious attitude and pure samaya with one another, like siblings of the same parents. Through thus knowing how to integrate the textual traditions with oral teachings, the remnant of the doctrine still present only as the glow of nearly extinguished lamp will not swiftly vanish.
>
> (Ibid.: 13–14)

The publication first of the *Yellow Book*, and later the influential book by Chatral Rinpoche created an unbridgeable gap between Nyingma followers and Dorje Shugden's devotees. In a certain sense, it made even more evident that the controversy over the protector Dorje Shugden constituted, first and foremost, an organizing factor, capable of determining political alliances and their positioning in the Tibetan Buddhist international circuit of lamas and disciples (western and Asian). This is particularly true with respect to the Gelug School.

Transgression and identity

New York, May 1998. A group of around 50 western monks and nuns prayed peacefully in front of the theatre where the Dalai Lama gave teachings about Manjushri, the bodhisattva of wisdom. Posters petitioning for religious freedom in the hands of a maroon robed crowd addressing one of the main spiritual leaders of our times imbued the scene with an unusual atmosphere. However, between 1996 and 1998, demonstrations like this one became commonplace at many of the Dalai Lama's events in the United States and Europe. Behind this campaign against the Dalai Lama's decision to recommend the abandonment of Dorje Shugden worship was Geshe Kelsang Gyatso, a disciple of Trijang Rinpoche.

I cannot emphasize enough the magnitude and novelty of the breach of traditional protocol represented by those public demonstrations promoted by a Gelug lama against the Dalai Lama. Even though disregard for the Dalai Lama's advise occurs at many levels, few lamas have dared to go beyond the private sphere of their spiritual practices to publicly defy the Tibetan leader. As I mentioned above, Lama Gangchen and Gonsar Rinpoche are among those few lamas. Nevertheless, Geshe Kelsang went even further than these lamas when he directed his criticisms directly and openly against the Tibetan leader.

The extreme nature of the demonstrations against the Dalai Lama illustrates how the controversy surrounding Dorje Shugden became important as a political identity marker for each one of the groups involved.[11] In more than one conversation that I had with some of Geshe Kelsang's older students, they voiced the idea that the demonstrations represented, more than anything else, an assertion of Geshe Kelsang's independence in relation to Tibetan politics, and more specifically, the Dalai Lama. In this sense the demonstrations have had an important role in the construction of the group's identity. According to Björn Clausen, national director of NKT in Switzerland in 2002 and organizer of some of the demonstrations, this was precisely the main consequence of the protests. When I asked him whether or not the demonstrations had helped NKT, he said:

> No, in fact, the only thing they established for the NKT was its identity. I say sometimes it was a reputation-suicide. There you go and you demonstrate against the most popular man in the universe. What more stupid thing can you actually do? I think that in terms of identity there is no doubt now that the NKT is not the Dalai Lama. We are quite distinct from the Tibetans, which makes us immune to this sort of politicizing of religion. Because this is what happened to the Tibetans: everything was very political. That is the way it used to be in Tibet in the past. The monasteries were also the centers

of political life. And I think Geshe-la is very much against that [...] I don't think that the politics now are Buddhist; I don't think this kind of repression of the Dorje Shugden practice is Buddhist.

Kelsang Pagpa, an English NKT monk who worked as a press attaché during the height of the controversy, corroborated Björn Clausen's opinion. According to Pagpa,

> All the debate that happened at that time in newspapers, magazines and maybe especially on the Internet helped to make clear that we did not have anything to do with Tibetan politics and the Tibetan government. In the future, this separation will be of benefit, since what we do here has to do with a new development of Buddhism in the West.

Ultimately, for Geshe Kelsang and his students, the falling-out with the Dalai Lama represented a rejection of the "contamination by politics" that has "taken over Tibetan Buddhism in the last few centuries." I heard more than once that one of Geshe Kelsang's main feats was precisely to "distinguish the Tibetan independence movement from Buddhism." According to some of the disciples of Geshe Kelsang with whom I talked, such as the brothers Morten and Björn Clausen, Buddhism was being used by the Dalai Lama and by the Tibetan government ("a lot of the times," according to them, "with some kind of corruption involved") in favor of the Tibetan cause, "a conflation which would destroy the essence of this religion." Still, in accordance with the logic behind this point of view, the activities of the Dalai Lama, which mix religion and politics, were only one instance of a thoroughly disseminated practice in Tibetan Buddhism as a whole. In effect, there is a generalized notion among NKT Buddhists that the majority of the lamas who circulate in the West are solely concerned with raising funds for their monasteries in India, Nepal or even Tibet. The disciples of Geshe Kelsang seem to unanimously agree on the fact that their master is one of the few, if not the only Tibetan lama, who is transmitting Buddhism to westerners in its totality without any additional interests.

The English monk Kelsang Tharpa, one of Geshe Kelsang's oldest students and in 2002 responsible for an important NKT center in Spain, believes that Geshe Kelsang's "generosity is one of the main motivators behind the attacks against his guru." In his words:

> He is the only Tibetan lama who has wanted to give Buddhism away, out of Tibetan influence. He wanted to give Buddhism to the world, not just to the West, but also to the world. This has created a certain jealousy in the Gelug tradition's hierarchy. They basically were using Buddhism like the Church used the Catholic doctrine. The Catholic Church founded the Portuguese Empire and then the Spanish Empire. The Catholic tradition conquered new territories, and brought back [to Europe] the wealth they found there. So the Tibetans would send a lama over here to give some initiations, hardly any

commentary to his initiations and then he goes back to India. And then maybe set up a monastery here, but the teachers would be Tibetans, the focus would be to interest people in the Tibetan cause, get people to go to India to support their monasteries, support the Tibetan government in its fight against China. That was basically the use of Tibetan Buddhism by, I think, 90 per cent of Tibetan lamas.

Clearly, the identity of Geshe Kelsang's group is defined in contrast to the idea that the Dalai Lama and other lamas are supposedly more interested in making political use of the religion. Geshe Kelsang and his disciples affirm that their tradition is not part of Tibetan Buddhism. It is simply "Kadampa Buddhism," a spiritual practice free from the "influence of Tibetan culture," i.e., Tibetan politics. In many senses, what is being criticized here is not only the conduct of the current Dalai Lama, but the essence of the Tibetan political project, such as it was conceived by the Fifth Dalai Lama in the seventeenth century. The project of combining politics and religion to give rise to the Tibetan state allowed, among other things, the spectacular development of Tibetan Buddhism through the concentration of resources in the hands of religious hierarchs. And it is not without irony that in positioning themselves "against politics," the "new Kadampas" are precisely demarcating their identity in a field, allowing them to legitimate *politically* the interests of NKT in their competition for disciples within the religious market (Bourdieu 1998), opened up by the controversy about what would be "authentic" Buddhism, Tibetan or Kadampa?

Finally, it is important to call attention to the fact that the radical NKT position against other Tibetan lamas does not seem to be confirmed when observing the conduct of lamas in the West. In fact, innumerable contemporary lamas are clearly committed to transmitting Buddhism to westerners. It is clear too that the role played by the Dalai Lama in today's world extends well beyond that of a spokesperson for the Tibetan cause. That said, it is also true that Tibetan lamas, animated by a sense of responsibility for their communities (monastic or not), often try to raise funds to rebuild their monasteries and to help the local population. In this sense, it is important to highlight here that because Geshe Kelsang is not considered to be a reincarnate lama, or a tulku, he does not have responsibility for a community, or a monastery. This fact certainly gives him more freedom to concentrate his activities solely in western contexts. Then again, there is also the case of Lama Gangchen, who in an interesting contrast with Geshe Kelsang is able to help more directly his old community in Tibet, the Gangchen village, precisely due to his position in relation to the Dorje Shugden issue.

The other face of transgression

In the case of Lama Gangchen, his decision to continue to openly worship Dorje Shugden caused the Chinese to have more tolerance with respect to his projects of humanitarian aid in Tibet. According to his disciple, Tiziana Ciasullo, the

Chinese let him carry out his projects in Tibet precisely because they knew about his dispute with the Dalai Lama. In Tibet, especially in the region of his monastery, Lama Gangchen helps local communities and monasteries in different ways.

In 2000, the lama inaugurated a renovation of his old monastery, which had been almost completely destroyed during the Cultural Revolution. His project, moreover, went beyond simply rebuilding the monastery. In an article published in *Peace Times*, Lama Gangchen World Peace Foundation's newsletter, one of his disciples, the aforementioned Sharon Dawson, relates:

> Gangchen Village Project was formally initiated in 1998 by Lama Gangchen, with the decision to rebuild the local Monastery – the heart of every Tibetan community. However, to improve the quality of life for these people, the completed project also foresees the creation of educational and healthcare facilities in the entire area, the supply of electrical and solar power, and the provision of a system which will transport to the villages the very precious element of water.
>
> (Lama Gangchen Peace Publication 2000: 12)

Also in Tashilhunpo, the monastery of the Panchen Lamas, which is located in the same region as Gangchen Monastery, Lama Gangchen financially contributed to a series of improvements, such as the construction of a new hospital and the creation of a school for boys who aspire to become monks. The money to fund this humanitarian work comes from the donations of Lama Gangchen's disciples in the West, and also in Asian countries, like Malaysia, where the lama has a center. In many senses, Lama Gangchen takes on the role of a public authority, which certainly accords with the traditional role played by lamas and their monasteries in relation to their communities.

Another relevant question here is the diplomacy that this lama exercises in relation to the Chinese government. In a ceremony held at Tashilhunpo by the local authorities to welcome Lama Gangchen, for instance, the representative of the monastery in the government, a monk of around 70 years old, congratulated Lama Gangchen for his work "around the world," and in particular for his defense of the environment, peace and, finally for his projects in Tibet. "These projects", he added, "are very hard to be accomplished. Lama Gangchen *can only do them, because he is not involved in politics*,[12] otherwise it would be impossible!"

The supposed "non-involvement" of Lama Gangchen in political issues mentioned here by the Tashilhunpo government representative does not mean that this lama "is not involved in politics," but more directly that he is not involved in the Tibetan cause of autonomy. His position with respect to the Dorje Shugden issue was for the Chinese a clear sign of this. In this regard it is important to highlight another of his positions: Lama Gangchen is one of the few Tibetan lamas that directly supports the Chinese government's decision to officially recognize the controversial reincarnation of the Panchen Lama (cf. Chapter 1). During Lama Gangchen's trip to Brazil, in June of 2002, he touched upon this subject:

> The communists did not believe in many things. Also, when Mongolia was taken over by the communist Soviets, the search for reincarnate lamas was forbidden. What happened in China – that the Panchen Lama was officially recognized by the government – is really exceptional.

The situation is, nevertheless, far more complicated and delicate than that. We cannot ignore here, for instance, the political intentions behind this exceptional decision of the Chinese government, and also the fact that there are historical precedents for Chinese policies attempting to control the recognition of reincarnate lamas.[13] The fact that the boy recognized by the Chinese government is not the same one recognized by the Dalai Lama adds insult to injury. The Tibetan government, along with many international organizations, continues to protest this decision of the Chinese government, especially because the boy chosen by the Dalai Lama, Gendun Choekyi Nyima was arrested with his family in 1995 and their fate remains unknown to this day.

Consequently, despite their different and almost opposing motivations, both the position of Lama Gangchen to not interfere with the political plans of China towards Tibet, and the position of Geshe Kelsang to separate Buddhism from the Tibetan cause altogether seem to find a common denominator. In effect, both positions indicate a falling-out with the political project of the Dalai Lama to reclaim some level of Tibetan autonomy, a project that even after 50 years of occupation has not ceased to be one of the main concerns of the Tibetan leader, who naturally embodies the main source of hope for his people.

Trijang Rinpoche

A final ramification of the Dorje Shugden issue must be broached here. In what was certainly one of the hardest blows suffered by the Dalai Lama due to his decision to advise against the cult of the this protector, the youth who was considered to be the reincarnation of Trijang Rinpoche (b. 1982) fled to Europe. In 1997, the young reincarnation of Trijang Rinpoche, then only a teenager, visited Europe and never came back, settling in Austria for a number of years. The circumstances surrounding this exile are rather murky. In the opinion of some of the Dalai Lama's allies, like Robert Thurman, Trijang Rinpoche was "kidnapped" by Gonsar Rinpoche.[14] Gonsar Rinpoche, however, talks about "a happy coincidence." According to Gonsar Rinpoche's rendition, the life of Trijang Rinpoche was in danger after the Dalai Lama publicly advised against the cult of Dorje Shugden, since his previous incarnation had so emphasized the practices connected with this protector.

> Some people threatened Trijang Rinpoche. He was then only 14 years old, what would he know about all that? That happened because of his

predecessor. [...] Trijang Rinpoche was there in his teaching, when His Holiness started to talk more severely about the Dorje Shugden issue. The problem was that His Holiness used very harsh words. That was unfortunate. He said: "if you want me to be dead, then you worship this deity." And "if you don't care about Tibetan freedom," continue to worship Dorje Shugden. Later, after the teaching was over, some monks, even though they respect very much Trijang Rinpoche, were telling him, "do you understand?", "do you know?", already abusing. After this there came a few letters [from instances connected to the Tibetan government in exile] about how we should respect His Holiness, and how the Tibetan government is so important etc., etc. And then further down, they said "the former Kyabje Trijang Rinpoche and Song Rinpoche, they did not do things in accordance with the wishes of His Holiness and now the two reincarnations, if they also do the same, we Tibetan people cannot respect you."

According to Gonsar Rinpoche, it was necessary to guard the residence of Trijang Rinpoche in India 24 hours a day due to threats. Gonsar Rinpoche affirms that it was fear that something bad happen to Trijang Rinpoche that led him to invite him and his main tutor, Chogtrul Rinpoche, to stay in Europe. Gonsar Rinpoche appointed the old property of the Rabten Choeling Center in Austria, close to the border with Switzerland and Italy, as the residence of Trijang Rinpoche. In Europe, the young Tibetan received his education exclusively from private tutors, even while in India he had been studying in the big monastery of Sera-me. In this new context, Gonsar Rinpoche became, in many senses, the main guardian of Trijang Rinpoche, paying his expenses and creating conditions for his formal education. Once more, the controversy surrounding Dorje Shugden produced a situation with few precedents.

As we saw above, Trijang Rinpoche's previous incarnation was one of the most important Gelug masters of the last century. The fact that the reincarnation of such an important figure was raised outside a more traditional context is exceptional, and created (at least for a short period[15]) another axis of political and spiritual power away from the influence of the Dalai Lama and Gelug monasteries. Lama Gangchen has had an active role in this new ordering of conflicting forces. Besides contributing financially with frequent donations to Gonsar Rinpoche and Trijang Rinpoche, Lama Gangchen has also continually invited both lamas to visit his center in Italy.

Moreover, it is important to underline the fact that not all the lamas isolated due to the Dorje Shugden issue had an interest in playing a part in this new power niche. Geshe Kelsang Gyatso, for instance, does not even believe in the legitimacy of this incarnation of Trijang Rinpoche. In the words of Kelsang Khyenrab, one of Geshe Kelsang's main disciples and director of the Tara Center in London in 2002,

Geshe Kelsang Gyatso does not recognize this incarnation of Trijang Rinpoche. One reason is the fact that methods for recognizing reincarnations are very unreliable. Another reason is due to the fact that this reincarnation was recognized by the Dalai Lama. Finally, [the previous] Trijang Rinpoche explained … he didn't explain clearly, but Geshe-la believes Trijang Rinpoche's last incarnation was his last life. It is not necessary for him to return.

Kelsang Khyenrab believes that the "supposed new incarnation" of Trijang Rinpoche was in the middle of a struggle within Tibetan Buddhism between the lamas who want to continue with the Dorje Shugden cult and those who want it banned. "He is like a pawn in the game: before he was in India, and now he is in Switzerland [*sic*]." Indirectly, Kelsang Khyenrab is saying here that before Trijang Rinpoche was manipulated by the Dalai Lama and his political allies, whereas now he is manipulated by people who are in favor of the continuation of the Dorje Shugden cult. Geshe Kelsang's group certainly reinforces its "divorce" from Tibetan Buddhism as a whole. More than that, however, what also comes to light here are the *many faces* of a single protector, indicating, ultimately, different expressions of a general process of identity re-signification.

Where history (once again) encounters myth

It might behoove us to return to the beginnings of this controversy, or at least to a beginning, since the versions of Dorje Shugden's origin myths are many.[16] Perhaps the most classical of these versions is the account[17] that interweaves historical and mythical elements to contextualize the birth of this protector in the court of the Fifth Dalai Lama.

According to this version, the history of this protector begins during the process of choosing the successor of Yonten Gyatso, the Fourth Dalai Lama. Among the main candidates were Dragpa Gyaltsen (1619–56) and Ngawang Lobsang Gyatso. As we have seen in Chapter 2, Ngawang Lobsang Gyatso was chosen and enthroned as the Fifth Dalai Lama. Dragpa Gyaltsen was recognized as the reincarnation of one of the most important Gelug lamas of the sixteenth century, Panchen Sonam Dragpa (1478–1554). Even after the resolution of this first "dispute," the tension between the two lamas continued, since they came to occupy two traditionally rivaling positions in the hierarchy of Drepung monastery.

As we have seen, in 1642, the Fifth Dalai Lama rose to power under the auspices of the Mongols who defeated the Tsang rulers of Tibet. In the meantime, Dragpa Gyaltsen completed his studies with brilliance, becoming one of the most famous spiritual masters of his time, and rivaling the Dalai Lama, also a notable erudite, in philosophical knowledge. In a debate between the two lamas, Dragpa Gyaltsen was victorious over the Tibetan leader. That was the last straw for the Dalai Lama's party, who moved by "jealousy" and "resentment," decided to eliminate this adversary. After several murder attempts, Dragpa Gyaltsen finally let himself be killed, only to exact, from another dimension, his revenge. Dragpa Gyaltsen returned as a ghost to haunt the Dalai Lama and his allies. Disturbed by the spirit, they could not even eat their meals in peace – as soon as they sat to eat, their plates full of food would be turned upside down. In a direct attack on his trans-sectarianism, the Fifth Dalai Lama was obliged to use the yellow hat of the Gelug School each time he wanted to cross the threshold of his palace. Otherwise, the earth would shake around him. After suffering numerous attacks like these, the Dalai Lama decided to do practices and rituals with the goal of appeasing the ghost of Dragpa Gyaltsen, who agreeing to become a protector of the Gelug School, would from then on be known as Dorje Shugden, or Powerful Thunderbolt.

Implicit in this narrative is, among other things, the resistance of members of the Gelug hierarchy in relation to a strong Fifth Dalai Lama and his project of a trans-sectarian government. In many senses, the history of Dorje Shugden seems to express through a mythical language the conflicts involved in the creation of Dalai Lama rule. It is no coincidence, then, that the controversy surrounding Dorje Shugden has resurfaced precisely during the times of two other powerful Dalai Lamas, the Thirteenth and the Fourteenth. It is not too farfetched to say then that in both cases a good portion of the power disputes between the Dalai Lama and other lamas of the Gelug School was transferred, through mythical reference to Dorje Shugden, to the symbolic field of religion.

According to George Dreyfus, before Pabonka Rinpoche there was no dissention surrounding Dorje Shugden. It was Pabonka Rinpoche who identified the protector with Dragpa Gyaltsen, and attributed to him the responsibility to protect the "purity" of the Gelug School against the interference of other schools, in particular the Nyingma School. If today the followers of Dorje Shugden are the ones who identify this protector with Dragpa Gyaltsen, in the past it was precisely the rivals of this lama, i.e., the Fifth Dalai Lama and his entourage, who first made this association (Dreyfus 1998: 237). The supporters of Dragpa Gyaltsen even considered it an insult, according to documents of the time, to see the name of their lama associated with a ghost. Hence, the identification of Dorje Shugden with Dragpa Gyaltsen, first made by the Fifth Dalai Lama and his allies, could be interpreted as the transference to the symbolic field of conflicts internal to the Gelug School. In this case, however, what is highlighted is the power of the Dalai Lama to "tame" these oppositions.

The current Dalai Lama and his allies also defend, based on extensive bibliographical research, a version of the Dorje Shugden origin myth that is not very different, structurally speaking, from the one presented above. In the case of the version defended by the Tibetan leader, however, what is emphasized are the qualities of a "perfidious spirit," or "ghost" attributed to Dorje Shugden. George Dreyfus also highlights that the oldest references (also cited by the Dalai Lama's official website) impute to Dorje Shugden a close connection with the Tsampo area and the Yarlung valley in the central region of Tibet. In those references, Dorje Shugden is called "Dolgyal" – a pejorative term – and appears as a "dangerous red spirit of a religious figure, who died after breaking his monastic vows, or who was murdered" (ibid.: 240).

Another question that interested the current Dalai Lama in his research is the sectarian character of Dorje Shugden. In this terrain, the histories surrounding the figure of Pabonka Rinpoche represent the main focal point. Many accounts mention that Pabonka Rinpoche's followers, "fanatics with respect to Dorje Shugden," converted by force many monasteries belonging to other traditions, and in particular Nyingma monasteries. In sum, two main characteristics of the protector are evinced from this perspective: the sectarian tendencies of Dorje Shugden and his nature as a simple spirit, which evokes the risk of Tibetan Buddhism degenerating into a kind of "spirit worship" tradition. Dorje Shugden devotees, however, disagree vehemently with this depiction of the protector's characteristics. Through their activities in the context of diaspora, they reveal other particularities of Dorje Shugden that do not always find echoes in traditional contexts.

The many faces of Dorje Shugden

In the beginning of the 1980s, the British Lama Caroline, then known simply as Caroline Gammon, made a decision that would change the direction of her life: she was going to live in the Manjushri Center of Geshe Kelsang. At that time, Geshe Kelsang had only a few students. Caroline tells that the protector was a "top secret" subject. His statue was locked in a box. "In those days they had this protector – top secret. We didn't know what it was. Everything was top secret in Manjushri [Center]. And they had this kind of secret protector practice." One day, however, Geshe Kelsang's oldest students decided to invite all who lived there to take part in the protector puja. The experience that Caroline had that day could not be compared to anything that she had lived through before. In the puja, Caroline became, in her words, "possessed." "It was a very strong experience. You know, this ego-loss experience, as if somebody else took your body." When she was still in a trance, she thrashed about, making sounds that seemed terrifying to the others present in the puja. Ten people tried to take her outside. In vain! Her force became extraordinary. Réne de Nebesky-Wojkowitz, author of *Oracles and Demons of Tibet*, calls attention precisely to this particularity of possession practices in Tibetan Buddhism. In his words,

> the proof of the fact, however, that the Tibetan oracles develop in their trances if not unusual mental capabilities, then at least great physical powers, are the swords which they bend or even twist in spirals while in the state of possession by a deity.
>
> (Nebesky-Wojkowitz 1993: 440)

In Tibet, the practice of consulting oracles is quite common. Mediums possessed by deities give consultations and make predictions in private matters or even in matters of state. In the case of Caroline, however, she found herself in quite an embarrassing situation with respect to her group. She did not feel comfortable taking part in the pujas, since each time she had similar experiences. "Everybody thought that I was a freak or something. It was like a horror movie." Geshe Kelsang requested then that oracles in India be consulted about her case. The general recommendation was that Caroline should go into a one-year retreat. And that's what she did. After this period of time, a medium that channeled one of Dorje Shugden's emanations came from India to visit Geshe Kelsang's center. "The oracle told me I was embodying one of the deities of his retinue, a female deity called Dorje Khenyon Lhamo. He said also that I would be of benefit to the Gelug tradition."

Despite the encouraging words of the Dorje Shugden oracle, Caroline was still uncomfortable in the centers of Geshe Kelsang. She lived for another two years at the Madhyamaka Center in York, but decided later that she would leave the center, with the thought that she was "going in different ways from them." Some years later, she met Lama Gangchen and ended up becoming his disciple. Lama Gangchen, contrary to Geshe Kelsang's group, had a direct interest in the practice of oracles. Both he and Gonsar Rinpoche continued to cultivate and emphasize, even in the European context, this particular aspect of the protector Dorje Shugden. A medium of Dorje Shugden's oracle resided for a few years at Gonsar Rinpoche's center in Switzerland. Periodically, the medium used to visit the center of Lama Gangchen in Italy, and often, the disciples of Lama Gangchen went to the Swiss center for consultations.

It was with Lama Gangchen that Caroline learned how to deal with her mediumship. For some time Caroline continued to channel the energy of Dorje Khenyon Lhamo, until she learned how to control it. However, eventually she made the decision to stop channeling this deity.

> People in the West ask stupid things like "Is my husband having an affair?", or about their business, etc. And I didn't want to be a part of that. Dharma protectors should protect the dharma and should not get involved in this worldly stuff. I think that this is misusing it, because people don't have the culture.

Caroline says that she prefers to deal with the energy of Dorje Khenyon Lhamo through her teachings, in dreams, or even when she advises her disciple – without, however, going into a trance. The trajectory of Caroline – who would later be recognized by Lama Gangchen as a tulku – in the communities of two of the main lamas involved with the Dorje Shugden controversy offers insightful hints about the different approaches that one can have in relation to the same protector. For instance, despite being very traditional in its original context, the practice of oracle consultation was with time institutionally forbidden within centers of the NKT. In the NKT constitution it is stipulated:

> All NKT Dharma Centres shall follow the same tradition regarding rituals, retreats, pujas, and granting and receiving empowerments. To prevent Dharma being used for political aims or worldly achievement, no NKT Dharma Centre shall follow any tradition of recognizing and relying upon oracles, or any system of divination.
>
> (New Kadampa Tradition 2001: 17)

The main concern expressed here is clearly related to the preservation of NKT internal organization, which could be theoretically put at risk due to the misuse of oracles, or any other system of divination. Moreover, the excerpt above also indicates a generalized tendency within the NKT to relegate to secondary status Tibetan Buddhist features with a magical nature. I believe that the practice of oracle consultation was banned within the NKT precisely because it represents a more mystical, and hence, supposedly more "obscure" aspect of Tibetan Buddhism. The above-mentioned ban on the recognition of tulkus, or reincarnations, also seems to express this tendency. In both cases, the difficult to attest character of the efficacy and truth of these practices is what reportedly triggered their exclusion from the NKT's activities.

Even without conducting an exhaustive analysis, we can notice a clear influence of the British protestant environment – in which the NKT was born and formed – in this process of "de-mystifying" Tibetan Buddhism. The reactions of surprise and even aversion in the face of Caroline's mediumship, and the impossibility of developing it in Geshe Kelsang's centers are a clear indication of such. The emphasis placed on the creation of study programs in the NKT can be considered the other side of this same tendency, and indicates, in its turn, a "rationalization" of Tibetan Buddhism, through stressing aspects that already existed in traditional contexts. In effect, as we saw before, one of the strongest traits of Tibetan Buddhism, and more specifically, the Gelug School, is precisely the attention given to philosophical studies.

In many senses, the re-signification of Dorje Shugden's role within NKT follows this dual movement of de-mystification and rationalization. In the context of the NKT, the controversial protector gains new contours, without losing some of its more traditional attributes in the Gelug School. Hence, just as NKT followers regard Geshe Kelsang as associated with Tsongkhapa, the founding figure of the Gelug School, they also consider Dorje Shugden to be a manifestation of this figure. In the Summer Festival of 2002, Geshe Kelsang himself declared that Dorje Shugden and Tsongkhapa are to be considered the same "person." The direct association of Dorje Shugden with Tsongkhapa is based on the fact that both of these figures are traditionally considered emanations of Manjushri, the bodhisattva of wisdom. However, even though such an association is supported on doctrinal grounds, this is not a usual reference in other milieus. What is put into relief in the context of the NKT is Dorje Shugden's role as protector of the "purity" of Tsongkhapa's spiritual legacy, a role that is particularly reinforced by teaching it to be a manifestation of Tsongkhapa himself. It is worth noting here that this role attributed to Dorje Shugden confirms the Dalai Lama's claims that Dorje Shugden is a sectarian protector.

Lama Gangchen, however, does not seem to emphasize the protector's role as guardian of the purity of the Gelug School. On the contrary, the Tibetan lama attributes much more universal features to this protector. In the words of his disciple Francesco Prevosti:

> In Lama Gangchen's approach, Dorje Shugden becomes the world peace protector. This is a completely different way of practicing the protector.

234 Once more death …

In fact, one of the functions of the protector is to protect the Gelug School, but, in Lama Gangchen's group, we don't talk much about Gelugpas, or something like that. We are not traditional Gelugpas. Lama Gangchen's approach is more open, so there is no sense in practicing Dorje Shugden as the Gelug School protector.

Hence, in conformity with the direction he gave to his own spiritual activities in the context of exile, Lama Gangchen attributes to Dorje Shugden direct responsibility over issues that concern humanity as a whole. Francesco explains that Dorje Shugden is considered a manifestation of Manjushri, but, because he is a protector, he is close to us.

Lama Yeshe, for example, was a lama who did great work for the Gelug School in Europe and the United States. He created a lot of centers. He used to say that without the help of the protector, he could not have accomplished all these feats. The protector acts in this way. He helps to do this kind of work: opening centers, organizing, eliminating obstacles and so forth. In the case of Lama Gangchen, probably the main work that he does is for world peace, together with the United Nations. The help that he requests of this protector is in this field. The relation of Lama Gangchen with this protector, then, has to do with this kind of work. In the Dorje Shugden initiation, when Lama Gangchen introduces the audience to the protector, he introduces him as the guardian of world peace, so that is what we have in mind when we practice the protector.

If Dorje Shugden spiritually supports Lama Gangchen in his projects within the UN, the protector's activities are certainly not limited to this indirect function. Since the terrorist attacks of September 11, 2001, for instance, Lama Gangchen has performed daily a guru puja – a ritual honoring the guru – featuring Dorje Shugden mantra accumulation dedicated to world peace. During the months that followed the terrorist attacks Lama Gangchen stopped travelling, and by his own account, dedicated himself to these daily prayers directed toward world peace. Hence, once more, the role attributed to this protector is re-signified. In the case of Lama Gangchen, nevertheless, his new attributes seem to go beyond the protector's traditional domain of action. In any event, in the case of both Lama Gangchen and Geshe Kelsang, the many faces of Dorje Shugden represent, above all, important reflections of the unprecedented activities of each of these lamas in the context of diaspora.

New alliances, new directions

As we have seen, the conflicts surrounding Dorje Shugden – especially after they extended to a global scale after 1996 – work in many senses as a regulating mechanism, which defines political positions through transgression or obedience with respect to the Dalai Lama's wishes. In some regards, what is being described here is the reappearance of previous conflicts, which emerged out of the reorganization of the Tibetan Buddhist religious field in old Tibet. In the context of diaspora, however, these have gained new dimensions. In the face of the fragmentation of Tibetan culture, new political alliances were formed, giving birth to a situation that, although rooted in a traditional setting, acquired unexpected meanings.

First, among the determining factors of the new power balance that emerged due to the fragmentation of Tibetan Buddhism is the financial, and often, political power acquired by Tibetan lamas through their connections with western and Asian disciples encountered in exile. It is not by chance, then, that Lama Gangchen, Geshe Kelsang and Gonsar Rinpoche, three lamas with very strong activities in western countries, became some of the main "adversaries" to the Dalai Lama in the contemporary phase of the controversy. It is not by chance either that a lama like Segyu Rinpoche, who did not posses the same kind of financial power as these other lamas and who was still in the process of positioning himself in the field, was caught in a delicate situation, having to act as a juggler in the face of forces much stronger than his own.

Publicly defying the Dalai Lama's authority demanded more than a vigorous network of political and financial support. It demanded, among other things, a reconfiguration of the absolute and relative role played by each of the actors within the Tibetan Buddhist transnational religious field, since such confrontation meant, ultimately, questioning some of the symbolic foundations not only of the religion, but also of the Tibetan nation. In this way, having as a parameter precisely the image of the Dalai Lama, these lamas built for themselves a new position within the field, expanding traditional boundaries to broaden considerably the scope of their activities.

In the case of Lama Gangchen, the falling-out with respect to his traditional role started with the re-signification of his own spiritual practice. In effect, when he created the so-called "self-healing" practice – which did not fit in any traditional model and which was born directly from his qualities as a healing lama – Lama Gangchen put into relief and amplified his own particular qualities, at the same time that he disconnected himself from orthodox patterns and the hierarchical structure of the Gelug School. This tendency is even more visible in his self-healing practice focused on the environment. As we have seen, in this practice the lama invites his disciples to "heal" the planet from its "wars, violence, pollution etc." Through ritual, his healing powers acquire worldly, or even cosmic dimensions. Hence, Lama Gangchen constructed for himself a role as defender of ecology and world peace that is in many respects very similar to the part played by the Dalai Lama as a spiritual leader who champions non-violence for the planet. The creation of the NGO Lama Gangchen Foundation for World Peace, and his representation in the UN – a domain inaccessible to the Dalai Lama due to Chinese pressure – consolidated this role for Lama Gangchen through granting him a solid institutional basis.

Geshe Kelsang, on the other hand, acquired complete independence from the Gelug School when he founded the New Kadampa Tradition and promoted public demonstrations against the Dalai Lama. His falling-out with the Gelug School, however, is not explained exclusively by his antagonism for the Dalai Lama. Since 1979, when the Tibetan geshe and his students decided to part ways with the Foundation for the Preservation of the Mahayana Tradition, his activities became more and more independent of Tibetan institutions. The creation of the NKT and the promotion of demonstrations not only made this rupture with Tibetan Buddhist institutions official. It also gave a new sense – a political one – to the role of spiritual leader played by Geshe Kelsang Gyatso, who is now directly associated by his followers with the founder of the Gelug School, Tsongkhapa.

Gonsar Rinpoche emerges in this scenario as guardian of Gelug orthodoxy, taking upon himself the responsibility to care for the reincarnation of Trijang Rinpoche. This function, which extends well beyond what would constitute the scope of his activities in a more traditional context, afforded him powerful bargaining chips in the dispute with the Dalai Lama over Dorje Shugden.

Finally, just as the roles played by these lamas have undergone an intense process of re-signification, the scope of the Dalai Lama's activities has also expanded. The Tibetan leader has become one of the main spiritual leaders of our times, a historical figure that will certainly be remembered and revered for generations to come. The Dalai Lama's great strength, moreover, comes in part from his activities in multiple countries, Asian and western – in sum, a field of influence that encompasses the planet nearly in its entirety. It is from this privileged position that the Dalai Lama also exercises his function as spiritual leader for Tibetans. In this domain, his task is far from simple, as we have seen. In the face of the fragmentation of Tibetan Buddhism, the Dalai Lama has had to build a coalition that is similar to the one realized by the Great Fifth in the seventeenth century. In the diaspora, however, without a strong political and religious institutional basis, the authority of the Tibetan leader has been attacked in ways that would have perhaps been improbable in the past.

Notes

1 Due to the highly sensitive subject matter treated in this chapter, I would like to clarify two points. First, my involvement with all the groups studied in this book was solely for research purposes; I am not, nor have I ever been personally involved with any of the parties. In this and previous chapters, I try my best to present an academic discussion of the topics. Second, I would also like to make clear that I informed all the persons interviewed in this and previous chapters of my position as a researcher and the purpose of my research prior to our interview sessions.
2 In this lama's autobiography (Geshe Lobsang Gyatso 1998: 307–22), edited by one of his students after his death, the Geshe's public opposition to the practice of this protector and the details of his gruesome assassination are described. All the elements of the murder seem to indicate that it was a ritual killing involving elements of black magic.
3 Geshe Lobsang Gyatso expressed this opposition as early as the late 1970s, and wrote a series of further articles elaborating upon his position in the 1990s. In the 1970s, the Geshe directly criticised in writing Trijang Rinpoche for his promotion of the cult

(Geshe Lobsang Gyatso 1998: 321). In 1996, remarks Gareth Sparham, the Geshe's long-time oral interpreter and the translator and editor of his memoir, the Geshe responded in a series of articles to "attacks against the intregrity of the Dalai Lama by groups of Indian and foreign-based Shugden supporters" (ibid.: 318). These articles were later published as the Tibetan text entitled *An Honest Statement* (Tib. *Bden pa'i tshang tshig*), and, as Sparham states, "these appear to have been the catalyst for his murder" (ibid.).

4 Some time later, another Brazilian disciple of Lama Gangchen, Lama Kalden, would not be as lucky as Lama Michel. At the apex of hostility against Dorje Shugden devotees, he was, according to his own account, attacked at his home, also in the Monastery of Sera-me (South India), by a group of monks. In his words:

> At the time I rented a house in a remote location in relation to the monastery, not very far from a forest. On one of these terrible days, in which there was no electric power, I heard a small crowd outside my house. Soon they started to knock on my door, to kick my door. I ran to get a knife. I put it on my waist and got hold of a piece of wood. When I opened the door, there were 30 monks with their faces covered. "We are going to kill you," they said. "You practice Dorje Shugden!" We got into a fight. In the middle of the confusion, a bird of prey started to squawk on top of the roof. We heard also wild animal noises coming from the forest – maybe they were hyenas. The monks got scared and ran away.

According to the literature related to Dorje Shugden, this protector can often manifest himself as a bird of prey. Lama Kalden believes that the bird, as well as the animal noises, were manifested by Dorje Shugden to protect him.

5 The italics are mine.

6 The italics are mine.

7 Jhado Rinpoche (personal communication, 2012).

8 The situation would change during his next visits to Brazil. In 2006 and 2011, the Dalai Lama directly mentioned the protector Dorje Shugden, explaining his point of view and once more asking people not to take initiations from him if they propitiate this protector.

9 I would like to thank James Gentry for sharing his translation of excerpts of Chatral Rinpoche's book with me.

10 This is a proverb often given to warn against senselessly and uncritically acting based on the groundless fears of others. The story involves a rabbit, who upon hearing the "chal" sound of a fruit falling into a nearby stream, runs away in fear and provokes other animals to senselessly follow him.

11 For another discussion about Dorje Shugden as a key component of NKT's identity, see Kay (2004: 100–3).

12 The italics are mine.

13 As I discuss in Chaper 1, the Chinese attempt to institute the Golden Urn in the selection of high profile lamas such as the Panchen Lamas and the Dalai Lamas is perhaps the most classical example of this.

14 Personal communication, 2002.

15 A relatively recent ramification of Trijang Rinpoche's case changed once more the balance of forces around this important lama. In the beginning of 2005, Trijang Rinpoche decided to disrobe and move to the United States. In this way, Gonsar Rinpoche (and also in a certain sense, Lama Gangchen) lost one of their biggest political assets.

16 For another discussion on the many myths that account for Dorje Shugden origins, see Kay (2004: 44–52). Moreover, recently the Dogyal Shugden Research Society released a book (in kindle format) that discusses the origins of Dorje Shugden and the recent controversy around this protector, shedding some light also on the legal problems faced by the NKT since mid-1990s related to Cult-formation accusations. For more, see Dogyal Shugden Research Society (2014).

17 Following the Lévi-Straussian idea that "a myth consists of all its versions" (Lévi-Strauss, 1983), the first version of the Dorje Shugden's origin myth presented here is a combination of the many stories about the origins of this protector that I heard, while doing fieldwork. It should be noted that this first version was composed mainly from the stories told by Dorje Shugden devotees. Later in this chapter, other interpretations of this protector's nature and origin, and in particular the Fourteenth Dalai Lama's point of view, will be discussed.

Final considerations

From the "space of death" created in Tibet by the Chinese occupation, an intensive process of fragmentation and subsequent reorganization of Tibetan Buddhism and its institutions in the context of diaspora was put in motion. The spectacular dissemination of Tibetan Buddhism that issued from this is directly connected with the wider globalization process that we can observe in the world today. As we have seen, the activities of the lamas studied herein take place in different locations around the planet, exemplifying the kind of globalized interconnectedness, cultural interchange, and mobility that mark our current age. Amidst these new contexts, the Fourteenth Dalai Lama emerges as one of the most important spiritual leaders of all times, having acquired renown and influence in unexpected domains within just a few decades of his exile.

The Tibetan leader is at the center of a transnational religious field, which brings together lamas, Tibetan Buddhist practitioners, his wider circle of admirers and Tibetan refugees, among others. This field, as this book has shown, has strong political overtones precisely due to the centrality that the Tibetan leader occupies within it and the fragile political situation of Tibet and Tibetans. The gradual autonomization of other lamas, moreover, has had the effect of accentuating the field's political nature, in light of the novel financial, and often, political powers that they have acquired through their connections with western and Asian disciples encountered in exile. In the larger sphere of the transnational religious field of Tibetan Buddhism, these lamas preside over a multitude of transnational and translocal communities of different dimensions, which are connected to one another by means of a number of distinct channels.

The multi-cored network that characterizes the transnational religious field of Tibetan Buddhism points once more to the "Galactic Polity" (Tambiah 1976, 1985) as a suitable model to describe the principles that govern the power relations among the many agents involved. Once again, we have the figure of the Dalai Lama as a kind of exemplary center, who through different means or "dialogue zones," such as scientific encounters, academy-related activities, world peace and environmental conferences, the publication of books, the performance of rituals, the dispensation of Buddhist teachings and so forth, gives a sense of cohesion to a global and fragmentary field. At the same time, his and other lamas' activities around the world strongly contribute to the creation of Tibetan

Buddhist culture on a planetary scale. The core position occupied by the guru in Tibetan Buddhist traditions simultaneously engenders movements of centralization and devolvement that imbue the transnational religious field in question with a robust dynamism.

As we have seen throughout this work, many of the elements that were previously associated with the old institutions of Tibetan Buddhism continue to play a central part in the diaspora, but in the current context they acquire new configurations. On the one hand, we have the persistence of the symbolic power of Dalai Lama as king of Tibet, through the reactivation of the old Tibetan state power and its symbols in new settings as diverse as conferences with scientists, and mass rituals that bring together thousands of western and Asian sympathizers. On the other hand, charismatic lamas bearing their sense of affiliation to traditional lineages and schools have been able to expand their traditional roles, totally refashioning their identities in a globalized context. Following this double movement towards centralization and devolvement, the insertion into the transnational religious field of Tibetan Buddhism of the other three main characters of this book – Lama Gangchen Rinpoche, Segyu Rinpoche and Geshe Kelsang Gyatso – takes place, on one level or the other, negatively or positively or both, in a sort of dialogue with the Dalai Lama.

In the end, nothing remains (exactly) the same. At this precise moment of the field, in which lamas who directly lived through the old traditional systems in Tibet are still quite active, the process of the re-signification of Tibetan Buddhism displays itself in its full transparency and potency. The centrality of the guru in Tibetan Buddhism engenders a very particular example of the more general process of globalization. Within the dynamics at work in the transnational religious field of Tibetan Buddhism, the effects of globalization are brought into focus through the lenses of innovative individuals. This particularly "individualistic" expression of globalization is not contradictory to the centrality of mass migration and electronic media in the promotion of the "work of imagination" as a major and "constitutive feature of modern subjectivity" (Appadurai 1996a: 3), but it does bring back into the scene "archaic" elements, such as myth and ritual, which still operate as powerful binding instruments. Echoes of the Fifth Dalai Lama's self-presentation in the seventeenth century are still faintly heard in the diaspora – through the myriad ways that lamas present their abilities in new contexts, and also through the writing of autobiography as an act of political resistance – thus keeping a certain Tibet alive in the globalized imagination.

Bibliography

Addy, Premen (1994) "British and Indian Strategic Preceptions of Tibet," in Barnett, Robert and Akiner, Shrin (eds) *Resistance and Reform in Tibet*. London: Hurst & Company.

Ahmad, Zahiruddin (1995) *A History of Tibet by the Fifth Dalai Lama of Tibet*. Bloomington, Indiana: Research Institute for Inner Asian Studies (Indiana University).

Ahmad, Zahiruddin (1970) *Sino-Tibetan Relations in the Seventeenth Century*. Rome: Istituto Italiano per il Medio ed Estremo Oriente.

Alper, Harvey P. (ed.) (1989) *Mantra*. New York: State University of New York Press.

Appadurai, Arjun (ed.) (2001) *Globalization*. Durham, North Carolina: Duke University Press.

Appadurai, Arjun (1996a) *Modernity at Large: Cultural Dimensions of Globalization*. Minneapolis: University of Minnesota Press.

Appadurai, Arjun (1996b) "Sovereignty Without Territoriality: Notes for a Postnational Geography" in Yaeger, Patricia (ed.). *The Geography of Identity*. Ann Arbor: The University of Michigan Press, pp. 40–58.

Anderson, Benedict (2006 [1983]) *Imagined Communities: Reflections on the Origin and Spread of Nationalism*. London and New York: Verso.

Ani Pachen and Donnelley, Adelaide (2000) *Sorrow Mountain: The Journey of a Tibetan Warrior Nun*. New York, Tokyo and London: Kodansha International.

Aris, Michael (1988) *Hidden Treasures and Secret Lives: A Study of Pemalingpa (1450–1521) and the Sixth Dalai Lama (1683–1706)*. Simla and Delhi: Indian Institute of Advanced Study and Motilal Banarsidass.

Arjia Rinpoche (2010) *Surviving the Dragon: A Tibetan Lama's Account of 40 Years under Chinese Rule*. New York: Rodale.

Aronson, Harvey (2004) *Buddhist Practice on Western Ground: Reconciling Eastern Ideals and Western Psychology*. Boston and London: Shambhala Publications.

Aryashura and Geshe Ngawang Dhargye (1992 [1975]) *Fifty Stanzas on the Spiritual Teacher*. Dharamsala, India: Library of Tibetan Works and Archives.

Avedon, John F. (1994) *In Exile from the Land of Snows*. New York: HarperPerennial.

Badiner, Allan Hunt (ed.) (1990) *Dharma Gaia: A Harvest of Essay in Buddhism and Ecology*. Berkeley, California: Parallax Press.

Bankart, C. Peter (2004) "Five Manifestations of the Buddha in the West: A Brief History," in Dockett, Kathleen H., Dudley-Grant, G. Rita and Bankart, C. Peter (eds) *Psychology and Buddhism: From Individual to Global Community*. New York: Kluwer Academic Publishers.

Barnett, Robert (2009) "Introduction," in Lixiong, Wang and Shakya, Tsering (eds). *The Struggle for Tibet*. London and New York: Verso.

Barnett, Robert (2008a) "Preface," in Barnett, Robert and Schwartz, Ronald (eds) *Tibetan Modernities: Notes from the Field on Cultural and Social Change*. Leiden, Holland and Boston: Brill.

Barnett, Robert (2008b) "Authenticity, Secrecy and Public Space: Chen Kuiyuan and Representations of the Panchen Lama Reincarnation Dispute of 1995," in Barnett, Robert and Schwartz, Ronald (eds) *Tibetan Modernities: Notes from the Field on Cultural and Social Change*. Leiden, Holland and Boston: Brill.

Barnett, Robert (1997) "Preface," in Panchen Lama (1997) *A Poisoned Arrow: The Secret Report of the 10th Panchen Lama*. London: Tibet Information Network, pp. ix–xx.

Barnett, Robert and Schwartz, Ronald (eds) (2008) *Tibetan Modernities: Notes from the Field on Cultural and Social Change*. Leiden, Holland and Boston: Brill.

Barnett, Robert and Akiner, Shrin (eds) (1994) *Resistance and Reform in Tibet*. London: Hurst & Company.

Barth, Fredrik (ed.) (1969) *Ethnic groups and boundaries: The social organization of culture difference*. Oslo: Universitetsforlaget.

Bataille, Georges (1985) *Visions of Excess*. Minneapolis: University of Minnesota Press.

Batchelor, Stephen (1998) "Letting Daylight into Magic: the Life and Times of Dorje Shugden," in *Tricycle: The Buddhist Review*, New York, 7 (3), pp. 60–9.

Batchelor, Stephen (1997) *Buddhism Without Beliefs: A Contemporary Guide to Awakening*. New York: Riverhead Books.

Batchelor, Stephen (1994) *The Awakening of the West: The Encounter of Buddhism and Western Culture*. Berkeley, California: Parallax Press.

Beer, Robert (1999) *The Encyclopedia of Tibetan Symbols and Motifs*. London: Serindia Publications.

Bell, Charles (1994) *The People of Tibet*. New Delhi: Motilal Banarsidass.

Bell, Charles (1987) *Portrait of a Dalai Lama: The Life and Times of the Great Thirteenth*. London: Wisdom Publications.

Bell, Christopher P. (2013) *Nechung: The Ritual History and Institutionalization of a Tibetan Buddhist Protector Deity*, University of Virginia, unpublished Ph.D. dissertation.

Beckwith, Christopher (1987) *The Tibetan Empire in Central Asia: A History of the Struggle for Great Power among Tibetans, Turks, Arabs, and Chinese during the Early Middle Ages*. Princeton, New Jersey: Princeton University Press.

Benjamin, Walter (1999) *The Arcades Project*. Cambridge, Massachusetts and London: The Belknap Press of Harvard University Press.

Benjamin, Walter (1989) *Reflections: Essays, Aphorisms, Autobiographical Writings*. New York: Schoken Books.

Benjamin, Walter (1988) *Illuminations: Essays and Reflections*. New York: Schoken Books.

Benson, Herbert *et al.*, (1982) "Body temperature changes during the practice of gTum-mo yoga," in *Nature*, 295, pp. 234–6 (January 21).

Berman, Marshall (1983 [1982]) *All that is Solid Melts into Air: The Experience of Modernity*. London: Verso.

Bernbaum, Edwin (2001 [1980]) *The Way to Shambhala: A Search for the Mythical Kingdom Beyond the Himalayas*. Boston and London: Shambhala Publications.

Berzin, Alexander (2010 [1997]) *Introduction to the Kalachakra Initiation*. Ithaca, New York: Snow Lion Publications.

Berzin, Alexander (2000) *Relating to a Spiritual Teacher*. Ithaca, New York: Snow Lion Publications.

Beyer, Stephan (1988) *Magic and Ritual in Tibet: The Cult of Tara.* New Delhi: Motilal Banarsidass Publishers.

Bhushan, Nalini, Garfield, Jay L. and Zablocki, Abraham (2009) *TransBuddhism: Transmission, Translation, Transformation.* Amherst, Massachusetts: University of Massachusetts Press.

Birnbaum, Raoul (1989) *The Healing Buddha.* Boston: Shambhala Publications.

Blofeld, John (1977) *Bodhisattva of Compassion.* Boston: Shambhala Publications.

Bogin, Benjamin (2006) "Royal Blood and Political Power: Contrasting Allegiances in the Memoirs of Yol mo btsan 'dzin nor bu (1598–1644)," in Cuevas, Bryan J. and Schaeffer, Kurtis R. *Power, Politics, and the Reinvention of Tradition: Tibet in the Seventeenth and Eighteenth Centuries.* Leiden, Holland and Boston: Brill.

Bourdieu, Pierre (1998) *Practical Reason.* Stanford, California: Stanford University Press.

Bourdieu, Pierre (1995) *The Rules of the Art: Genesis and Structure of the Literary Field.* Stanford, California: Stanford University Press.

Bourdieu, Pierre (1993) *The Field of Cultural Production: Essays on Art and Literature.* New York: Columbia University Press.

Bourdieu, Pierre (1984) *Distinction: A Social Critique of the Judgment of Taste.* Cambridge, Massachussets: Harvard University Press.

Brauen, Martin (2005a) *A Visual History of the Dalai Lamas.* Chicago: Serindia Publications.

Brauen, Martin (2005b) "Western Views of the Dalai Lamas," in Brauen, Martin. *A Visual History of the Dalai Lamas.* Chicago: Serindia Publications, pp. 230–41.

Brown, Diana (1994) *Umbanda, Religion, and Politics in Urban Brazil.* New York: Columbia University Press.

Bryant, Barry (1992) *The Wheel of Time Sand Mandala: Visual Scripture of Tibetan Buddhism.* New York: HarperCollins Publisher.

Buck-Morss, Susan (1989) *Dialectics of Seeing: Walter Benjamin and the Arcades Project.* Cambridge, Massachusetts and London: The MIT Press.

Büyükokutan, Barış (2011) "Toward a Theory of Cultural Appropriation: Buddhism, the Vietnam War, and the Field of U.S. Poetry," *American Sociological Review*, 76 (4) (August), pp. 620–39.

Burke, Peter (1994) *The Fabrication of Louis XIV.* New Haven and London: Yale University Press.

Cabezón, José Ignácio (1995) "Buddhist Studies as a Discipline and the Role of Theory," in *Journal of the International Association of Buddhist Studies*, 18 (2) (Winter), pp. 231–68.

Cabezón, José Ignácio and Jackson, Roger R. (ed.) (1996) *Tibetan Literature: Studies in Genre.* Ithaca, New York: Snow Lion Publications.

Carrasco, Pedro (1959) *Land and Polity in Tibet.* Seattle: University of Washington Press.

Cassinelli, C.W and Ekvall, Robert B. (1969) *A Tibetan Principality: The Political System of Sa sKya.* Ithaca, New York: Cornell University Press.

Cesar, Isabel Villares Lenz (2001a) *Morrer não se Improvisa.* São Paulo: Editora Gaia.

Cesar, Isabel Villares Lenz (2001b) Viagem Interior ao Tibete. São Paulo: Editora Gaia.

Cesar, Isabel Villares Lenz (1987) *Life in Relation to Death.* Junction City, California: Padma Publishing.

Chatral Rinpoche (1979) *dGa' ldan shar rtse dze smad sprul sku blo bzang dpal ldan gyi smra ngan dug gi sa bon gzhom pa'i 'bel gtam lung rigs rdo rje'i me char.* Ganktok, Sikkim and New Delhi: Sherab Gyaltsen, Palace Monastery and c/o Lakshmi Printing Works.

Chayet, Anne (2003) "The Potala, Symbol of the Power of the Dalai Lamas," in Pommaret, Francoise (ed.) *Lhasa in the Seventeenth Century: The Capital of the Dalai Lamas.* Leiden, Holland and Boston: Brill, pp. 39–52.

Chokyi Nyima Rinpoche (1997) *The Bardo Guidebook.* Hong Kong: Rangjung Yeshe Publications.

Clark, Barry (1995) *The Quintessence Tantras of Tibetan Medicine.* Ithaca, New York: Snow Lion Publications.

Clarke, J.J. (1997) *Oriental Enlightenment.* London and New York: Routledge. .

Clifford, James (1988) *The Predicament of Culture.* Cambridge, Massachusetts and London: Harvard University Press.

Clifford, James and Marcus, George (1986) *Writing Culture: The Poetics and Politics of Ethnography.* Berkeley, California; Los Angeles and London: University of California Press.

Clifford, Terry (1984) *Tibetan Buddhist Medicine and Psychiatry.* York Beach, Maine: Samuel Weiser, Inc.

Coleman, Graham (1994) *A Handbook of Tibetan Culture.* Boston: Shambhala Publications.

Connerton, Paul (1989) *How Societies Remember.* Cambridge, United Kingdom: Cambridge University Press.

Cooper, Paul C. (2010) *The Zen Impulse and the Psychoanalytic Encounter.* London and New York: Routledge.

Cooper, Paul C. (ed.) (2007) *Into the Mountain Stream: Psychotherapy and Buddhist Experience.* Lanhan, Boulder, New York, Toronto, Plymouth, UK.

Cornu, Phillipe (2002) "Padmasambhava, les Nyingmapa et leur influence sur le Ve Dalai Lama," in KARMAY, Samten Gyaltsen. *Rituels tibétains: visions secrètes du Ve Dalai Lama.* Paris: Édition de la Réunion des Musées Nationaux.

Cozort, Daniel (1998) *Unique Tenets of the Middle Way Consequence School.* Ithaca, New York: Snow Lion Publications.

Cozort, Daniel (1986) *Highest Yoga Tantra.* Ithaca, New York: Snow Lion Publications.

Craig, Mary (1999) *Tears of Blood: A Cry for Tibet.* Washington, D.C.: Counterpoint.

Cunha, Manuela Carneiro da (1986) *Antropologia do Brasil.* São Paulo: Editora Brasiliense and Edusp.

Dagyab Rinpoche (1995) *Buddhist Symbols in Tibetan Culture.* Boston: Wisdom Publications.

Dalton, Jacob (2011) *The Taming of the Demons: Violence and Liberation in Tibetan Buddhism.* New Haven and London: Yale University Press.

Dalton, Jacob (2005) "A Crisis of Doxography: How Tibetans Organized Tantra during the 8th–12th Centuries," in *Journal of the International Association of Buddhist Studies,* 28 (1), pp. 115–81.

Darlington, Susan (2012). *The Ordination of a Tree: The Thai Buddhist Environmental Movement.* Albany, New York: State University of New York Press.

David-Neel, Alexandra (2000) *Correspondance avec son mari: édition intégrale 1904–1941.* Paris: Plon.

David-Neel, Alexandra (1991) *My Journey to Lhasa.* Nova Delhi: Time Books International.

David-Neel, Alexandra (1978) *Immortalité et reincarnation.* Paris: Éditions du Rocher.

Davidson, Ronald (2005) *Tibetan Renaissance: Tantric Buddhism in the Rebirth of Tibetan Culture.* New York: Columbia University Press.

Davidson, Ronald (2002) *Indian Esoteric Buddhism: A Social History of the Tantric Movement.* New York: Columbia University Press.

Dawa Drolma, Delog (1999) *Delog: Journey to Realms Beyond Death.* Junction City, California: Padma Publishing.

Dawa Drolma, Delog (1976) *Tibetan Religious Dances. Tibetan text and annotated translation of the* 'chams yig. Ed. Christoph von Fürer-Haimendorf. The Hague: Mouton.

Dening, Greg (1996) *Performances.* Chicago: University of Chicago Press.

Deshung Rinpoche (1995) *The Three Levels of Spiritual Perception.* Boston: Wisdom Publications.

Dewatshang, Kunga Samten (1997) *Flight at the Cuckoo's Behest: The Life and Times of a Tibetan Freedom Fighter.* New Delhi: Paljor Publications.

Dilgo Khyentse Rinpoche (1999) *The Wish-Fulfilling Jewel: The Practice of Guru Yoga According to the Longchen Nyingthig Tradition.* Boston and London: Shambhala Publications.

Dilgo Khyentse Rinpoche (1996) *The Excellent Path Enlightenment.* Ithaca, New York: Snow Lion Publications.

Dilgo Khyentse Rinpoche (1993) *Enlightened Courage.* Ithaca, New York: Snow Lion Publications.

Dilgo Khyentse Rinpoche (1992) *The Heart Treasure of the Enlightened Beings.* Boston and London: Shambhala Publications.

Dirks, Nicholas, Eley, Geoff and Ortner, Sherry (eds) (1994) *Culture/Power/History: A Reader in Contemporary Social Theory.* Princeton, New Jersey: Princeton University Press.

Dirks, Nicholas (ed.) (1992) *Colonialism and Culture.* Ann Arbor, Michigan: The University of Michigan Press.

Dockett, Kathleen H., Dudley-Grant, G. Rita and Bankart, C. Peter (eds) (2004) *Psychology and Buddhism: From Individual to Global Community.* New York: Kluwer Academic Publishers.

Dodin, Thierry and Räther, Heinz (eds) (2001) *Imagining Tibet: Perceptions, Projections and Fantasies.* Somerville, Massachusetts: Wisdom Publications.

Dowman, Keith (2000) *The Divine Madman: The Sublime Life and Songs of Drukpa Kunley.* Varanasi, India and Kathmandu, Nepal: Pilgrims Publishing.

Dowman, Keith (1985) *Masters of Mahamudra.* Albany, New York: State University of New York Press.

Donnet, Pierre-Antoine (1994) *Tibet: Survival in Question.* London: Zed Books.

Dreyfus, Georges (2003) *The Sound of Two Hands Clapping: The Education of a Tibetan Buddhist Monk.* Berkeley, Los Angeles and London: University of California Press.

Dreyfus, Georges (1998) "The Shuk-den Affair: Origins of a Controversy," in *Journal of the International Association of Buddhist Studies,* Lausanne, 21 (2), pp. 227–69.

Dreyfus, Georges (1997) *Recognizing Reality: Dharmakirti's Philosophy and Its Tibetan Interpretations.* New Delhi: Sri Satguru Publications.

Dudjom Rinpoche (2002) *Petites instructions essentielles.* Saint-Léon-sur-Vézère, France: Éditions Padmakara.

Edou, Jérôme (1996) *Machig Labdrön and the Foundations of Chöd.* Ithaca, New York: Snow Lion Publications.

Ehrhard, Franz-Karl (2012) "'Flow of the River Gangā': The Gsan-yig of the Fifth Dalai Bla-ma and its Literary Sources," in Vitali, Roberto (ed.) *Studies on the History and*

Literature of Tibet and the Himalaya. Kathmandu, Nepal: Vajra Publications, pp. 79–98.

Eppsteiner, Fred (ed.) (1988) *The Path of Compassion: Writing on Socially Engaged Buddhism.* Berkeley, California: Parallax Press.

Epstein, Marc (1995) *Thoughts Without a Thinker: Psychotherapy from a Buddhist Perspective.* New York: Basic Books.

Evans-Wentz, W.Y. (2000 [1927]) *The Tibetan Book of the Dead.* Oxford: Oxford University Press.

Everskog, Johan (2003) *The Jewel Translucent Sutra: Altan Khan and the Mongols in the Sixteenth Century.* Leiden, Holland and Boston: Brill.

Fields, Rick (1992) *How the Swans Came to the Lake.* Boston and London: Shambhala Publications.

Frechette, Ann (2007). "Democracy and Democratization among Tibetans in Exile," in *The Journal of Asian Studies*, 66, pp. 97–127.

Frédéric, Louis (1995) *Buddhism: Flammarion Iconographic Graphics.* Paris and New York: Flammarion.

French, Rebecca Redwood (1995) *The Golden Yoke: The Legal Cosmology of Buddhist Tibet.* Ithaca, New York and London: Cornell University Press.

Fromm, Erich, Suzuki, D.T. and De Martino, Richard (eds) (1960) *Zen Buddhism and Psychoanalysis.* New York: Harper & Row.

Garfield, Jay L. (1995) *The Fundamental Wisdom of the Middle Way: Nagarjuna's Mulamadhyamakakarika.* New York and Oxford: Oxford University Press.

Gangchen, Lama (2001 [1991]) *Autocura I: Proposta de um Mestre Tibetano.* São Paulo: Editora Gaia.

Gangchen, Lama (1999) *A Solution for the Third Millenium.* Milan: Lama Gangchen Peace Publications.

Gangchen, Lama (1997 [1993]) *Self-Healing II: Tantric Self-Healing of Body and Mind, a Method to Transform this World into Shambala.* Milan: Lama Gangchen Peace Publications.

Gangchen, Lama (1996) *Making Peace with the Environment I: A Crystal Clear Vision of the Inner Wind System to Make Peace with the Outer and Inner Environment.* Milan and New Delhi: Lama Gangchen Peace Publications and Indian Institute of Ecology and Environment.

Gangchen, Lama (1994) *Ngal so – Self-Healing III: Vol. 1 – Guide to the Good Thought Supermarket.* Milan: Lama Gangchen Peace Publications.

Gangchen, Lama (1995a) *Messaggero della Chiara Luce Lunare per la Pace nel Mondo: Volume 2.* Milan: Lama Gangchen Peace Publications.

Gangchen, Lama (1995b) *Messaggero della Chiara Luce Lunare per la Pace nel Mondo: Volume 1.* Milan: Lama Gangchen Peace Publications.

Geertz, Clifford (1988) *Works and Lives: The Anthropologist as Author.* Stanford, California: Stanford University Press.

Geertz, Clifford (1983) *Local Knowledge: Further Essays in Interpretative Anthropology.* New York: Basic Books.

Geertz, Clifford (1980) *Negara: The Theatre State in Nineteenth-Century Bali.* Princeton, New Jersey: Princeton University Press.

Geertz, Clifford (1973) *The Interpretations of Cultures.* New York: Basic Books.

Gen Lamrimpa (2002) *Realizing Emptiness: Madhyamaka Insight Meditation.* Ithaca, New York and Boulder, Colorado: Snow Lion Publications.

Gentry, James D. (2014) *Objects of Power in the Life, Writings, and Legacy of the*

Tibetan Ritual Master Sog bzlog pa Blo gros rgyal mtshan. Harvard University, unpublished Ph.D. dissertation.

Geshe Kelsang Gyatso (2002) *Heart Jewel*. Ulverston, United Kingdom and Glen Spey, New York: Tharpa Publications.

Geshe Kelsang Gyatso (2001) *Transform Your Life*. Ulverston, United Kingdom and Glen Spey, New York: Tharpa Publications.

Geshe Kelsang Gyatso (2001) *A Meditation Handbook*. Ulverston, United Kingdom and Glen Spey, New York: Tharpa Publications.

Geshe Kelsang Gyatso (2000) *Living Meaningfully, Dying Joyfully*. Ulverston, United Kingdom and Glen Spey, New York: Tharpa Publications.

Geshe Kelsang Gyatso (1997) *Essence of* Vajrayana. London: Tharpa Publications.

Geshe Kelsang Gyatso (1995) *Clear Light of Bliss*. London: Tharpa Publications.

Geshe Kelsang Gyatso (1994) *Tantric Grounds and Paths*. London: Tharpa Publications.

Geshe Kelsang Gyatso (1991) *Guide to the Dakini Land*. London: Tharpa Publications.

Geshe Kelsang Gyatso (1990) *Joyful Path of Good Fortune*. Ulverston United Kingdom: Tharpa Publications.

Geshe Kelsang Gyatso (1988) *Universal Compassion*. Ulverston, United Kingdom: Tharpa Publications.

Geshe Lhundub Sopa and Donnelly, Paul (2012) *Like a Waking Dream: The Autobiography of Geshé Lhundub Sopa*. Boston: Wisdom Publications.

Geshe Lhundub Sopa, Jackson, Roger and Newman, John R. (1985) *The Wheel of Time: The Kalachakra in Context*. Ithaca, New York: Snow Lion Publications.

Geshe Ngawang Dhargyey (1994) *Kalacakra Tantra*. Dharmsala, India: Library of Tibetan Works and Archives.

Geshe Rabten (2001) *Les États de la Conscience*. Le Mont-Pèlerin, Switzerland: Éditions Rabten.

Geshe Rabten (2000) *The Life of a Tibetan Monk*. Le Mont-Pèlerin, Switzerland: Éditions Rabten.

Geshe Rabten (1992) *The Mind and its Functions*. Le Mont-Pèlerin, Switzerland: Éditions Rabten Choeling.

Geshe Sonam Rinchen (1997) *Atisha's Lamp for the Path*. Ithaca, New York: Snow Lion Publications.

Geshe Wangyal (1995) *The Door of Liberation*. Boston: Wisdom Publications.

Gethin, Rupert (1998) *The Foundations of Buddhism*. Oxford and New York: Oxford University Press.

Getty, Alice (1914) *The Gods of Northern Buddhism*. Oxford: Clarendon Press.

Gibson, Todd (1997) "Inner Asian Contributions to the Vajrayāna," in *Indo-Iranian Journal*, 40, pp. 37–57.

Giddens, Anthony (1990) *The Consequences of Modernity*. Stanford, California: Stanford University Press.

Gimian, Carolyn Rose (2003) "Introduction to Volume Two," in Gimian, Carolyn Rose, *The Collected Works of Chögyam Trungpa*. Boston and London: Shambala Publications, vol. 2.

Goldstein, Melvyn C. (2014) *A History of Modern Tibet, Volume 3: The Storm Clouds Descent: 1955–1957*. Berkeley and Los Angeles, California: University of California Press.

Goldstein, Melvyn C. (2007) *A History of Modern Tibet, Volume 2: The Calm before the Storm: 1951–1955*. Berkeley and Los Angeles, California: University of California Press.

Goldstein, Melvyn C. (1997) *The Snow Lion and the Dragon: China, Tibet and the Dalai Lama.* Berkeley, Los Angeles and Oxford: University of California Press.

Goldstein, Melvyn C. (1990) "Religious Conflict in the Traditional Tibetan State," in Epstein, L. and Shervurne, R. (eds) *Reflections on Tibetan Culture: Essays in Memory of T.V. Wylie.* Lewiston, New York: Edwin Mellen.

Goldstein, Melvyn C. (1989) *A History of Modern Tibet, 1913–1951: The Demise of the Lamaist State.* Berkeley and Los Angeles, California: University of California Press.

Goldstein, Melvyn C. (1971) "The Balance Between Centralization and Decentralization in the Traditional Tibetan Political System: An Essay on the Nature of Tibetan Political Macro-Structure," in *Central Asiatic Journal*, XV (3).

Goldstein, Melvyn and Kapstein, Matthew T. (eds) (1998) *Buddhism in Contemporary Tibet: Religious Revival and Cultural Identity.* New Delhi: Motilal Banarsidass Publishers.

Goldstein, Melvyn, Jiao, Ben and Lhundrup, Tanzen (2009) *On the Cultural Revolution in Tibet: The Nyemo Incident of 1969.* Berkeley, Los Angeles and London: University of California Press.

Goldstein, Melvyn, Sherap, Dawei and Siebenschuh, William (2004) *A Tibetan Revolutionary: The Political Life and Times of Bapa Phüntso Wangye.* Berkeley, Los Angeles and London: University of California Press.

Goldstein, Melvyn, Siebenschuh, William and Tsering, Tashi (1997) *The Struggle for Modern Tibet: The Autobiography of Tashi Tsering.* Armonk, New York and London: M.E. Sharpe.

Goleman, Daniel (ed.) (2003) *Destructive Emotions: How Can We Overcome Them, a Scientific Dialogue with the Dalai Lama.* New York: Bantam Books.

Goleman, Daniel (ed.) (1997) *Healing Emotions: Conversations with the Dalai Lama on Mindfulness, Emotions, and Health.* Boston and London: Shambhala Publications.

Goleman, Daniel (1995) *Emotional Intelligence.* New York: Bantam Books.

Goméz, Luis O. (1995) "Unspoken Paradigms: Meanderings through the Metaphors of a Field," in *Journal of the International Association of Buddhist Studies*, 18 (2) (Winter), pp. 183–230.

Gonçalves, Ricardo M. (1992) *Textos Budistas e Zen-Budistas.* São Paulo: Cultrix.

Goodman, Steven D. and Davidson, Ronald M. (eds) (1992) *Tibetan Buddhism: Reason and Revelation.* New York: State University of New York Press.

Gray, David (2007) *The Chakrasamvara Tantra.* New York: The American Institute of Buddhist Studies at Columbia University in New York, Columbia University's Center for Buddhist Studies and Tibet House.

Gyatso, Janet (1998) *Apparitions of the Self: The Secret Autobiographies of a Tibetan Visionary.* Princeton, New Jersey: Princeton University Press.

Gyatso, Janet (1996) "Drawn from the Tibetan Treasury: The *gTer ma* Literature," in Cabezón, José and Jackson, Roger (eds) *Tibetan Literature: Studies in Genre.* Ithaca, New York: Snow Lion Publications, pp. 147–69.

Gyatso, Janet (1994) "Guru Chos-dbang's *gTer byung chen mo*: An Early Survey of the Treasure Tradition and Its Strategies in Discussing Bon Treasure," in Kvaerne, Per (ed.) *Tibetan Studies: Proceedings of the 6th International Association of Tibetan Studies Seminar.* Oslo: Institute for Comparative Research in Human Culture, vol. 1, pp. 275–87.

Gyatso, Janet (1993) "The Logic of Legitimation in the Tibetan Treasure Tradition," in *History of Religions*, 33 (2) (November), pp. 97–134.

Gyatso, Janet (ed.) (1992) *In the Mirror of Memory: reflection on Mindfulness and*

Remembrance in Indian and Tibetan Buddhism. Albany, New York: State University of New York Press.

Gyatso, Janet (1987) "Down With the Demoness: Reflections on a Feminine Ground in Tibet," in *Tibet Journal*, 7 (4), pp. 38–53.

Gyatso, Janet (1986) "Signs, Memory and History: A Tantric Buddhist Theory of Scriptural Transmission," in *Journal of the International Association of Buddhist Studies*, 9 (2), pp. 7–35.

Hakeda, Yoshito S. (1972) *Kukai: Major Works.* New York: University of Columbia Press.

Halbwachs, Maurice (1992) *On Collective Memory.* Chicago and London: University of Chicago Press.

Harrell, Stevan (ed.) (1995) *Cultural Encounters on China's Ethnic Frontiers.* Seattle and London: University of Washington Press.

Harrer, Heinrich (1997 [1953]) *Seven Years in Tibet.* New York: Jeremy P. Tarcher/Putnam.

Harrer, Heinrich and Norbu, Thubten Jigme (1986 [1960]) *Tibet is My Country: Autobiography of Thubten Jigme Norbu, Brother of the Dalai Lama as told to Heinrich Harrer.* London: Wisdom Publications.

Harris, Ian (1997) "Buddhism and the Discourse of Environmental Concern: Some Methodological Problems Considered," in Tucker, Mary Evelyn and Williams, Duncan Ryūken (eds) *Buddhism and Ecology: The Interconnection of Dharma and Deeds.* Cambridge, Massachusetts: Harvard University Press, pp. 377–402.

Harris, Ian (1995a) "Buddhist Environmental Ethics and Detraditionalization: The Case of EcoBuddhism," in *Religion*, 25 (3) (July), pp. 199–211.

Harris, Ian (1995b) "Getting to Grips with Buddhist Environmentalism: A Provisional Typology," in *Journal of Buddhist Ethics*, 2, pp. 173–90.

Harris, Ian (1994) "Causation and 'Telos': The Problem of Buddhist Environmental Ethics," in *Journal of Buddhist Ethics*, 1, pp. 46–59.

Harris, Ian (1991) "How Environmentalist Is Buddhism?" in *Religion*, 21, (April), pp. 101–14.

Harris, Marvin (1976) *The Rise of Anthropological Theory.* New York: Harper and Row Publishers.

Harvey, David (1989) *The Condition of Postmodernity.* Malden and Oxford: Blackwell Publishers.

Hayward, Jeremy W. and Varela, Francisco J. (1992) *Gentle Bridges: Conversations with the Dalai Lama on the Sciences of the Mind.* Boston and London: Shambhala Publications.

Hayes, Kelly (2008) "Wicked Women and Femmes Fatales: Gender, Power, and Pomba Gira in Brazil," in *History of Religions*, 48 (1), pp. 1–24.

Hill, Jonathan D. (ed.) (1988) *Rethinking History and Myth: Indigenous South American Perspectives on the Past.* Urbana and Chicago: University of Illinois Press.

Hilton, Isabel (1999) *The Search for the Panchen Lama.* London: Penguin Books.

Hilton, James (1960 [1933]) *Lost Horizon.* New York: Pocket Books.

Hoffmann, Helmut (1986) *Tibet: A Handbook.* Bloomington (Indiana): Indiana University Research Institute for Inner Asian Studies.

Hollier, Denis (ed.) (1988) *The College of Sociology (1931–39).* Minneapolis: University of Minnesota Press.

Hopkins, Jeffrey (1997) *Emptiness Yoga: The Tibetan Middle Way.* New Delhi: Motilal Banarsidass Publishers.

Hopkins, Jeffrey (1996) *Meditation on Emptiness.* Boston: Wisdom Publications.

Hopkins, Jeffrey (1984) *The Tantric Distinction.* Boston: Wisdom Publications.

Houshmand, Zara, Livingston, Robert B. and Wallace, B. Alan (ed.) (1999) *Consciousness at the Crossroads: Conversations with the Dalai Lama on Brain Science and Buddhism.* Ithaca, New York: Snow Lion Publications.

Ishihama, Yumiko (1993) "On the dissemination of the belief in the Dalai Lama as a Manifestation of the Bodhisattva Avalokiteśvara," in McKay, Alex (ed.) *The History of Tibet: The Medieval Period.* London: RoutledgeCurzon, pp. 538–53.

Jackson, Michael (2002) *The Politics of Storytelling: Violence, Transgression and Intersubjectivity.* Copenhagen: Museum Tusculanum Press.

Jackson, Roger and Makransky, John (2003) *Buddhist Theology: Critical Reflections by Contemporary Buddhist Scholars.* London: RoutledgeCurzon.

Jagou, Fabienne (2011) *The Ninth Panchen Lama (1888–1937): A Life at the Crossroads of Sino-Tibetan Relations.* Paris and Chiang Mai, Thailand: École Française d'Extrême-Orient and Silkworm Books.

Jerryson, Michael and Juergensmeyer, Mark (eds) (2010) *Buddhist Warfare.* Oxford: Oxford Press.

Huber, Toni (2008) *The Holy Land Reborn: Pilgrimage and the Tibetan Reinvention of Buddhist India.* Chicago and London: The University of Chicago Press.

Kværne, Per (1995) *The Bon Religion of Tibet: The Iconography of a Living Tradition,* London: Serindia Publications.

Kamenetz, Rodger (1995) *The Jew in the Lotus.* San Francisco: HarperSan Francisco.

Kangyur Rinpoche (2001) *Treasury of Precious Qualities.* Boston and London: Shambhala Publications.

Kapstein, Matthew T. (2006) *The Tibetans.* Malden, Massachussets, Oxford and Carlton, Australia: Blackwell Publishing.

Kapstein, Matthew T. (2000) *The Tibetan Assimilation of Buddhism.* Oxford: Oxford University Press.

Karmay, Samten Gyaltsen (2002) *Rituels tibétains: visions secrètes du Ve Dalai Lama.* Paris: Édition de la Réunion des Musées Nationaux.

Karmay, Samten Gyaltsen (1988a) *Le Manuscrit d'Or: visions secrètes du Ve Dalai Lama.* Paris: Éditions Findakly.

Karmay, Samten Gyaltsen (1988b) *The Secret Visions of the Fifth Dalai Lama: The Gold Manuscript in the Fournier Collection.* London: Serindia Publications.

Kay, David N. (2004) *Tibetan and Zen Buddhism in Britain: Transplantation, Development and Adaptation.* London and New York: RoutledgeCurzon.

Khenchen Kunzang Pelde and Minyak Kunzang Sönam (1999) *Wisdom: Two Buddhist Commentaries.* Saint-Léon-sur-Vézère, France: Éditions Padmakara.

Khenpo Ngawang Pelzang (2004) *A Guide to the Words of My Perfect Teacher.* Boston and London: Shambhala Publications.

Khenpo Palden Sherab Rinpoche (1993) *Ceaseless Echoes of the Great Silence.* Boca Raton, Florida: Sky Dancer Press.

Khetsun Sangpo Rinbochay and Hopkins, Jeffrey (eds) (1986) *Tantric Practice in Nyingma.* Ithaca, New York: Snow Lion Publications.

Khétsun, Tubten (2008) *Memories of Life in Lhasa under Chinese Rule.* New York: Columbia University Press.

Khyongla Rato Rinpoche (1991) *My Life and Lives.* New York: Rato Publications.

Kitagawa, Joseph M. (ed.) (1989) *The Religious Traditions of Asia.* New York: Macmillan Publishing Company.

Kitagawa, Joseph M. and Cummings, Mark D. (eds) (1989) *Buddhism and Asian History*. New York: Macmillan Publishing Company.

Kloetzli, Randy (1983) *Buddhist Cosmology*. New Delhi: Motilal Banarsidass.

Kornfield, Jack (1993) *A Path with a Heart*. New York: Bantam Books.

Kraft, Kenneth (ed.) (1992) *Inner Peace, World Peace: Essays on Buddhism and Nonviolence*. New York: State of New York University Press.

Kvaerne, Per (1995) *The Bon Religion of Tibet*. London: Serindia Publications.

Landaw, Jonathan and Weber, Andy (1993) *Images of Enlightenment: Tibetan Art in Practice*. Ithaca, New York: Snow Lion Publications.

Larsen, Knud and Sinding-Larsen, Amund (2001) *The Lhasa Atlas: Traditional Tibetan Architecture and Townscape*. London: Serindia Publications.

Lati Rinpoche (1985) *Death, Intermediate State and Rebirth in Tibetan Buddhism*. Ithaca, New York: Snow Lion Publications.

Lati Rinpoche (1980) *The Mind in Tibetan Buddhism*. Ithaca, New York: Snow Lion Publications.

Lati Rinpoche and Denma Löcho Rinpoche (1997) *Meditative States in Tibetan Buddhism*. Boston: Wisdom Publications.

Leary, Timothy, Metzner, Ralph and Alpert, Richard (1992 [1964]) *The Psychedelic Experience: A Manual Based on the Tibetan Book of the Dead*. New York: Citadel Press.

Leidy, Denise Patry and Thurman, Robert (1997) *Mandala: The Architecture of Enlightenment*. New York and Boston: Asia Society Galleries, Tibet House and Shambhala Publications.

Lenoir, Frédéric (1999) *Le Bouddhisme en France*. Paris: Librairie Arthème Fayard.

Lévi-Strauss, Claude (1995) *Myth and Meaning*. New York: Schocken Books.

Lévi-Strauss, Claude (1983) *Structural Anthropology*. Chicago: University of Chicago Press.

Lévi-Strauss, Claude (1979) *The Raw and the Cooked*. New York: Octagon Books.

Lhalungpa, Lobsang (1979) *The Life of Milarepa*. New York: Penguin Books.

Lixiong, Wang (2009) "Reflections on Tibet," in Lixiong, Wang and Shakya, Tsering (2009) *The Struggle for Tibet*. London and New York: Verso, pp. 37–81.

Lixiong, Wang and Shakya, Tsering (2009) *The Struggle for Tibet*. London and New York: Verso.

Lobsang Thrinley (2002) *Dung dkar tshig mdzod chen mo*, Beijing: China Tibetology Publishing House.

Lodo, Lama (1987) *Bardo Teachings: The Way of Death and Rebirth*. Ithaca, New York: Snow Lion Publications.

Longchen Yeshe Dorje and Kangyur Rinpoche (2001) *Treasury of Precious Qualities: A Commentary on the Root Text of Jigme Lingpa*. Boston and London: Shambhala Publications.

Lopes, Ana Cristina (2013) "Visões Secretas do V Dalai Lama: Texto e Performance em uma Obra Literária Tibetano do Século XVII," in Dawsey, John C., Müller, Regina P., Hikiji, Rose Satiko G. and Monteiro, Marianna F.M. *Antropologia e Performance: Ensaios Napedra*. São Paulo: Editora Terceiro Nome.

Lopes, [Nina] Ana Cristina (2007) "Arqueologia de Uma Identidade Espiritual: O Caso da Inserção de um Umbandista no Campo Religioso do Budismo Tibetano," in Sampaio, Gabriela dos Reis; Bellini, Lígia and Souza, Evergton Sales. *Ensaios de História Religiosa do Mundo Luso-Afro-Brasileiro, séculos XIV–XXI*. Salvador: EDUFBA.

Lopes, [Nina] Ana Cristina (2006a) *Ventos da Impermanência: um Estudo sobre a Res-significação do Budismo Tibetano no Contexto da Diáspora*. São Paulo: Edusp.

Lopes, [Nina] Ana Cristina (2006b) "O Relato de uma Tempestade Anunciada: Histórias de Cura de um Lama Tibetano," in *Debates do NER*, year 7, no. 9, January–June, pp. 81–108.

Lopes, [Nina] Ana Cristina (2006c) "O Teatro Divino de Kalachakra: uma Discussão sobre um Ritual de Massa do Budismo Tibetano," in *Religião and Sociedade* (ISER), 23 (1), pp. 32–61.

Lopes, [Nina] Ana Cristina (1996) "Histórias da Diáspora Tibetana," in *Revista USP*, São Paulo, 31, September–November, pp. 150–62.

Lopez, Donald S. (2011) *The Tibetan Book of the Dead: A Biography*. Princeton, New Jersey: Princeton University Press.

Lopez, Donald S. (2010) *Buddhism and Science: A Guide for the Perplexed*. Chicago and London: University of Chicago Press.

Lopez, Donald S. (ed.) (2005) *Critical Terms for the Study of Buddhism*. Chicago and London: The University of Chicago Press.

Lopez, Donald S. (ed.) (2002) *A Modern Buddhist Bible: Essential Readings from East and West*. Boston: Beacon Press.

Lopez, Donald S. (1998a) *Prisoners of Shangri-la: Tibetan Buddhism and the West*. Chicago and London: Chicago University Press.

Lopez, Donald S. (1998b) "Two Sides of the Same God," in *Tricycle: The Buddhist Review*, New York, 7 (3), pp. 67–82.

Lopez, Donald S. (ed.) (1997) *Religions of Tibet in Practice*. Princeton, New Jersey: Princeton University Press.

Lopez, Donald S. (ed.) (1995) *Curators of the Buddha*. Chicago and London: The University of Chicago Press.

Lopez, Donald S. (ed.) (1993) *Buddhist Hermeneutics*. New Delhi: Motilal Banarsidass Publishers.

Lopez, Donald S. (1987) *A Study of Svatantrika*. Ithaca, New York: Snow Lion Publications.

Mackenzie, Vicki (1998) *Cave in the Snow: Tenzin Palmo's Quest for Enlightenment*. New York and London: Bloomsbury Publishing.

Mackenzie, Vicki (1996) *Reborn in the West*. New York: Marlove & Company.

Maher, Derek (2007) "The Dalai Lamas and State Power," in *Religion Compass* 1/2, pp. 260–78.

Maitreyanatha and Aryasanga (2004) *The Universal Vehicle Discourse Literature (Mahayanasutralamkara)*. New York: American Institute of Buddhist Studies at Columbia University, Columbia University's Center for Buddhist Studies and Tibet House US.

Makransky, John (1997) *Buddhahood Embodied: Sources of Controversy in India and Tibet*. Albany, New York: State University of New York Press.

Machiavelli, Niccolò (1988) *The Prince*. Cambridge, New York, New Rochelle, Melbourne and Sydney: Cambridge University Press.

Marcus, George (1998) *Ethnography through Thick and Thin*. Princeton, New Jersey: Princeton University Press.

Marcus, George and Fischer, Michael (1986) *Anthropology as a Cultural Critique*. Chicago and London: Chicago University Press.

Martin, Dan (2001) *Unearthing Bon Treasures: Life and Contested Legacy of a Tibetan Scripture Revealer, with a General Bibliography of Bon*. Leiden, Holland; Boston and Cologne, Germany: Brill.

McDonald, Kathleen (1994) *How to Meditate.* New Delhi: Timeless Books.

Merleau-Ponty, Maurice (1993) *Le visible et l'invisible.* Paris: Gallimard.

Michael, Franz (1982) *Rule by Incarnation.* Boulder, Colorado: Westview Press.

Michel, Lama (1996) *Uma Jovem Idéia de Paz.* São Paulo: Sarasvati Multimídia.

Midal, Fabrice (2000) *Mythes et dieux tibétains.* Paris: Éditions du Seuil.

Mills, Martin A. (2007) "Re-Assessing the Supine Demoness: Royal Buddhist Geomancy in the Srong btsan sgam po Mythology," in *Journal of the International Association of Tibetan Studies*, no. 3 (December): pp. 1–47.

Montes, Maria Lucia (1998) "As Figuras do Sagrado: entre o Público e o Privado," in Schwarz, Lilia Moritz (ed.) *História da Vida Privada no Brasil.* São Paulo: Companhia das Letras, vol. 4.

Moran, Peter (2004) *Buddhism Observed: Travellers, Exiles and Tibetan Dharma in Kathmandu.* London and New York: RoutledgeCurzon.

Mullard, Saul (2011) *Opening the Hidden Land: State Formation and the Construction of Sikkimese History.* Leiden, Holland and Boston: Brill.

Mullin, Glenn (2001) *The Fourteen Dalai Lamas: A Sacred Legacy of Reincarnation.* Santa Fe: Clear Light Publishers.

Mullin, Glenn (1997) *Readings on the Six Yogas of Naropa.* Ithaca, New York: Snow Lion Publications.

Mullin, Glenn (1991) *The Practice of Kalachakra.* Ithaca, New York: Snow Lion Publications.

Mullin, Glenn (1988) *Path of the Bodhisattva Warrior: The Life and Teachings of the Thirteenth Dalai Lama.* Ithaca, New York: Snow Lion Publications.

Mullin, Glenn (1987) *Death and Dying: The Tibetan Tradition.* London and New York: Penguin Group.

Mullin, Glenn (1985) *Selected Works of the Dalai Lama VII: Songs of Spiritual Change.* Ithaca, New York: Snow Lion Publications.

Mumford, Stan Royal (1989) *Himalayan Dialogue: Tibetan Lamas and Gurung Shamans in Nepal.* Madison, Wisconsin: The University of Wisconsin Press.

Murti, T.R.V. (1998) *The Central Philosophy of Buddhism: A Study of the Madhyamika System.* New Delhi: HaperCollins Publishers India.

Mus, Paul (1964) "A Thousand-Armed Kannon: A Mystery or a Problem?" in *Journal of Indian and Buddhist Studies*, 12 (1), pp. 1–33.

Nair, Urmila (2010) *When the Sun's Rays Are as Shadows: The Nechung Rituals and the Politics of Spectacle in Tibetan Exile*, University of Chicago, unpublished Ph.D.

Nebesky-Wojkowitz, René de (1993) *Oracles and Demons of Tibet: The Cult and Iconography of the Tibetan Protective Deities.* Varanasi, India: Book Faith India.

Ngawang Lobsang Gyatso, the Fifth Dalai Lama (1991–5a) *The Collected Works (gsung 'bum) of the Vth Dalai Lama Ngag-dbang-blo-bzang-rgya-mtsho*, 25 volumes. Gangtok, Sikkim, India: Sikkim Research Institute of Tibetology. (This collection is a reproduction of the Lhasa edition).

Ngawang Lobsang Gyatso, the Fifth Dalai Lama (1991–5b) *Deb ther dpyid kyi rgyal mo'i glu dbyangs*, in *The Collected Works (gsung 'bum) of the Vth Dalai Lama Ngag-dbang-blo-bzang-rgya-mtsho.* Gangtok, Sikkim, India: Sikkim Research Institute of Tibetology, vol. 19 (*dza*), pp. 1–228.

Ngawang Lobsang Gyatso, the Fifth Dalai Lama (1991–5c) *rJe btsun thams cad mkhyen pa bsod nams rgya mtsho'i rnam thar dngos grub rgya mtsho'i shing rta*, in *Collected Works of Vth Dalai Lama Ngag-dbang-blo-bzang-rgya-mtsho.* Gangtok, Sikkim: Sikkim Research Institute of Tibetology, vol. 8 (*nya*), pp. 1–246.

Ngawang Lobsang Gyatso, the Fifth Dalai Lama (1991–5d) *'Jig rten dbang phyug thams cad mkhyen pa yon tan rgya mtsho dpal bzang po'i rnam par thar pa nor bu'i phreng ba*, in *Collected Works of Vth Dalai Lama Ngag-dbang-blo-bzang-rgya-mtsho*. Gangtok, Sikkim: Sikkim Research Institute of Tibetology, vol. 8 (*nya*), pp. 247–350.

Ngawang Lobsang Gyatso, the Fifth Dalai Lama (1991–5e) *Za hor gyi ban-de ngag dbang blo bzang rgya mtsho'i 'di snang 'khrul pa'i rol rtsed rtogs brjod kyi tshul du bkod pa du kU la'i gos bzang (Dukūla)*, in *The Collected Works (gsung 'bum) of the Vth Dalai Lama Ngag-dbang-blo-bzang-rgya-mtsho*. Gangtok, Sikkim, India: Sikkim Research Institute of Tibetology, vols 5, 6 and 7 (*ca, cha, ja*).

Ngawang Lobsang Gyatso, the Fifth Dalai Lama (1972) *gSang ba'i rnam thar rgya can ma*. Leh, India: S.W. Tashigangpa.

Newland, Guy (1992) *The Two Thuths*. Ithaca, New York: Snow Lion Publications.

Newman, John Ronald (1987) *The Outer Wheel of Time: Vajrayana Buddhist Cosmology in the Kalachakra Tantra*. University of Wisconsin, unpublished Ph.D. dissertation.

Newman, John Ronald (1985) "A Brief History of Time," in Geshe Lhundub Sopa, Jackson, Roger and Newman, John R. *The Wheel of Time: The Kalachakra in Context*. Ithaca, New York: Snow Lion Publications, pp. 51–90.

Neuhaus, Tom (2012) *Tibet in the Western Imagination*. New York: Palgrave MacMillian.

Nhat Hanh, Thich (2013a) *Love Letter to the Earth*. Berkeley, California: Parallax Press.

Nhat Hanh, Thich (2013b) "The Bells of Mindfulness," in Vaughan-Lee, Llewellyn. *Spiritual Ecology: The Cry of the Earth*. Point Reyes, California: The Golden Sufi Center, pp. 25–8.

Nhat Hanh, Thich (2008a) *The World We Have: A Buddhist Approach to Peace and Ecology*. Berkeley, California: Parallax Press.

Nhat Hanh, Thich (2008b) "A History of Engaged Buddhism," in *Mindfulness Bell*, no. 49 Autumn issue, pp. 4–9.

Nietzsche, Friedrich (2001 [1887]) *The Gay Science*. Cambridge: Cambridge University Press.

Nishitani, Keiji (1983) *Religion and Nothingness*. Berkeley, Los Angeles and London: University of California Press.

Norbu, Jamyang (2004) *Shadow Tibet: Selected Writings 1989 to 2004*. New York: High Asia Press.

Norbu, Jamyang (2004 [1982]) "Atrocity and Amnesia: Goldstein and the Revision of Tibetan History," in Norbu, Jamyang *Shadow Tibet: Selected Writings 1989 to 2004*. New York: High Asia Press, pp. 49–61.

Norbu, Jamyang (1989) *The Illusion and Reality: Essays on the Tibetan and Chinese Political Scene from 1978 to 1989*. Dharamsala, India: TYC Books.

Norbu, Jamyang (1986 [1979]) *Warriors of Tibet: The Story of Aten and the Khampas' Fight for the Freedom of their country*. London: Wisdom Publications London.

Norbu, Jamyang (1983) "Tibetan Resistance movement and the role of C.I.A.," in Barnett, Robert and Akiner, Shrin (eds) *Resistance and Reform in Tibet*. London: Hurst & Company.

Ogyen Trinley Dorje, the Seventeenth Karmapa (2011) "Walking the Path of Environmental Buddhism through Compassion and Emptiness," in *Conservation Biology*, 25, issue 6 (December), pp. 1094–7.

Ortner, Sherry B. (1999) *Life and Death on Mt. Everest: Sherpas and Himalayan Mountaineering*. Princeton, New Jersey and Oxford: Oxford University Press.

Ortner, Sherry B. (1978) *Sherpas Through Their Rituals*. Cambridge: Cambridge University Press.

Pabongka Rinpoche (1993 [1991]) *Liberation in the Palm of Your Hand: A Concise Discourse on the Path to Enlightenment.* Boston: Wisdom Publications.

Palace, Wendy (2005) *The British Empire and Tibet, 1900–1922.* London and New York: RoutledgeCurzon.

Palden Gyatso (1997a) *The Autobiography of a Tibetan Monk.* New York: Grove Press.

Palden Gyatso (1997b) *Fire Under the Snow: Testimony of a Tibetan Prisoner.* London: The Harvill Press.

Paine, Jeffrey (2004) *Re-enchantment: Tibetan Buddhism Comes to the West.* New York and London: W.W. Norton & Company.

Panchen Lama (1997) *A Poisoned Arrow: The Secret Report of the 10th Panchen Lama.* London: Tibet Information Network.

Paul, Robert (1982) *The Tibetan Symbolic World: Psychoanalytic Explorations.* Chicago and London: University of Chicago Press.

Patt, David (1992) *A Strange Liberation: Tibetan Lives in Chinese Hands.* Ithaca, New York: Snow Lion Publications.

Petech, Luciano (1990) *Central Tibet and the Mongols: The Yüan–Sa-sKya Period of Tibetan History.* Rome: Istituto Italiano per il Medio ed Estremo Oriente.

Petech, Luciano (1950) *China and Tibet in the Early 18th Century: History of the Establishment of Chinese Protectorate in Tibet.* Leiden, Holland: E.J. Brill.

Pettit, John Whitney (1999) *Mipham's Beacon of Certainty: Illuminating the View of Dzogchen, the Great Perfection.* Boston: Wisdom Publications.

Pickering, Kevin T. and Owen, Lewis A. (1997 [1994]) *An Introduction to Global Environmental Issues.* London and New York: Routledge.

Pommaret, Francoise (ed.) (2003) *Lhasa in the Seventeenth Century: The Capital of the Dalai Lamas.* Leiden, Holland and Boston: Brill.

Powers, John (2004) *History as Propaganda: Tibetan Exiles versus the People's Republic of China.* Oxford and New York: Oxford University Press.

Powers, John (1995) *Introduction to Tibetan Buddhism.* Ithaca, New York: Snow Lion Publications.

Rampa, Lobsang (1956) *The Third Eye: Autobiography of a Tibetan Lama.* Garden City, New York: Doubleday & Company, Inc.

Revel, Jean-François and Ricard, Matthieu (1999 [1997]) *The Monk and the Philosopher: A Father and Son Discuss the Meaning of Life.* New York: Schocken Books.

Rhie, Marylin and Thurman, Robert (1999) *Worlds of Transformation: Tibetan Art of Wisdom and Compassion.* New York: Tibet House New York.

Rhie, Marylin and Thurman, Robert (1991) *Wisdom and Compassion: The Sacred Art of Tibet.* New York: Harry N. Abrams, Inc.

Ricard, Matthieu (2002) *Rainbows Appear: Tibetan Poems of Shabkar.* Boston: Shambhala Publications.

Ricard, Matthieu (2001) *The Life of Shabkar: Autobiography of a Tibetan Yogin.* Ithaca, New York: Snow Lion Publications.

Ricard, Matthieu (1996) *L'esprit du Tibet: la vie et le monde de Dilgo Khyentsé maître spirituel.* Paris: Éditions du Seuil.

Ricard, Matthieu and Trinh Xuan Thuan (2001) *The Quantum and the Lotus.* New York: Crown Publishers.

Richardson, Hugh (1993) *The Ceremonies of the Lhasa Year.* London: Serindia Publications.

Rinchen Dolma Taring (1986) *Daughter of Tibet.* London: Wisdom Publications.

Rocha, Cristina (2006) *Zen in Brazil: The Quest for Cosmopolitan Modernity*. Honolulu: University of Hawaii Press.

Roerich, George (1976) *The Blue Annals*. New Delhi: Motilal Banarsidass Publishers.

Roerich, Nicholas (1990) *Shambhala: In Search of the New Era*. Rochester, Vermont: Inner Traditions International.

Sadaka, Akira (1997) *Buddhist Cosmology: Philosophy and Origins*. Tokyo: Kosei Publishing.

Safran, Jeremy (2003) "Psychoanalysis and Buddhism as Cultural Institutions," in Safran, Jeremy. *Psychoanalysis and Buddhism: An Unfolding Dialogue*. Somerville, Massachusetts: Wisdom Publications, 2003.

Sakya, Jamyang and Emery, Julie (1990) *Princess in the Land of Snows*. Boston and Shaftesbury, United Kingdom: Shambhala Publications.

Sahlins, Marshall (1995) *How "Natives" Think: About Capitain Cook, for example*. Chicago and London: The University of Chicago Press.

Sahlins, Marshall (1997) *Historical Metaphors and Mythical Realities*. Ann Arbor, Michigan: The University of Michigan Press.

Sahlins, Marshall (1987 [1985]) *Islands of History* Chicago and London: University of Chicago Press.

Said, Edward (1979) *Orientalism*. New York: Vintage Books.

Samuel, Geoffrey (1993) *Civilized Shamans: Buddhism in Tibetan Societies*. Washington and London: Smithsonian Institution Press.

Sangye Gyatso (1973) *Mchod sdong chen po 'dzam gling rgyan gcig gi dkar chag*. New Delhi: T. Tsepal Taikhang (Volume 1).

Saso, Michael (1990) *Tantric Art and Meditation*. Honolulu: Tendai Educational Foundation.

Saunders, E. Dale (1985) *Mudra: A Study of Symbolic Gestures in Japanese Buddhist Sculpture*. Princeton, New Jersey: Princeton University Press.

Schaeffer, Kurtis (2006) "Ritual, Festival, and Authority under the Fifth Dalai Lama", in Cuevas, Bryan J. and Schaeffer, Kurtis R. *Power, Politics, and the Reinvention of Tradition: Tibet in the Seventeenth and Eighteenth Centuries*. Leiden, Holland and Boston: Brill, pp. 187–202.

Schaeffer, Kurtis (2005) "The Fifth Dalai Lama: Ngawang Lopsang Gyatso," in Brauen, Martin (ed.) *A Visual History of the Dalai Lamas*. Chicago: Serindia Publications, pp. 64–91.

Schaeffer, Kurtis, Kapstein, Matthew T. and Tuttle, Gray (eds) (2013) *Sources of Tibetan Tradition*. New York: Columbia University Press.

Schechner, Richard (1995) *The Future of Ritual: Writings on Culture and Performance*. London and New York: Routledge.

Schechner, Richard (1985) *Between Theater and Anthropology*. Philadelphia: University of Pennsylvania Press.

Schell, Orville (2000) *Virtual Tibet: Searching for Shangri-la from the Himalayans to Hollywood*. New York: Henry Hold and Company, LLC.

Schmithausen, Lambert (1991) *Buddhism and Nature: The Lecture delivered on the Occasion of the EXPO 1990: An Enlarged Version with Notes*. Tokyo: The International Institute for Buddhist Studies.

Schwartz, Ronald D. (1994) *Circle of Protest: Political Ritual in the Tibetan Uprising*. New York: Columbia University Press.

Shabkar Tsogdruk Rangdröl (2003) *Zhabs dkar tshogs drug rang grol gyi rnam thar rgyas pa yid bzhin gyi nor bu bsam 'phel dbang gi rgyal po*. New Delhi: Shechen Publications.

Shakabpa, Tsepon Wangchuk Deden (2010) *One Hundred Thousand Moons: An Advanced Political History of Tibet*. Leiden, Holland and Boston: Brill.

Shakabpa, Tsepon Wangchuk Deden (1976) *Bod kyi srid don rgyal rabs*, Kalimpong, India: W.B.: T. Tsepal Taikhang (two volumes).

Shakabpa, Tsepon Wangchuk Deden (1967) *Tibet: A Political History*. New Haven, Connecticut and London: Yale University Press.

Shakya, Tsering (1999) *The Dragon in the Land of Snows: A History of Modern Tibet since 1947*. New York: Columbia University Press.

Shantideva (1997) *The Way of the Bodhisattva*. Boston and London: Shambhala Publications.

Shapiro, Dolores (1992) *Symbolic Fluids: The World of the Spirit Medium in Brazilian Possession Groups*. Columbia University, unpublished Ph.D. dissertation.

Shiromany, A. A. (ed.) (1998) *the Political Philosophy of His Holiness the XIV Dalai Lama*. New Delhi: Tibetan Parliamentary and Policy Research Centre.

Siegel, Arianna (1989) "An Interview with Antonio Costa e Silva, Brazilian Spiritist," in *Shaman's Drum*, Williams (Oregon), 17.

Skilton, Andrew (1994) *A Concise History of Buddhism*. Birmingham, United Kingdom: Windhorse Publications.

Smith, Gene (2001) *Among Tibetan Texts: History and Literature of the Himalayan Plateau*. Somerville, Massachussets: Wisdom Publications.

Smith, Warren W. (2008) *China's Tibet? Autonomy or Assimilation*. Lanhan, Boulder, New York, Toronto and Plymouth, United Kingdom: Rowman & Littlefield Publishers, INC.

Smith, Warren W. (1996) *Tibetan Nation: A History of Tibetan Nationalism and Sino-Tibetan Relations*. Boulder, Colorado: Westview Press.

Snellgrove, David (1988) "Categories of Buddhist Tantras," in Gnoli, G. and Lanciotti, L. (eds) *Orientalia Iosephi Tucci Memoriae Dicata*. Serie Orientale Roma 56.3, pp. 1353–84.

Snellgrove, David (1967) *The Nine Ways of Bon, Excerpts from gZi-brjid*. London: Oxford University Press, London Oriental Series, vol. 18.

Snellgrove, David and Richardson, Hugh (1995) *A Cultural History of Tibet*. Boston: Shambhala Publications.

Sogyal Rinpoche (1992) *The Tibetan Book of Living and Dying*. New York: Harper-SanFrancisco.

Sørensen, Per K. and Hazod, Guntram (2007) *Rulers on the Celestial Plain: Ecclesiastic and Secular Hegemony in Medieval Tibet, A Study of Tshal Gung-thang*. Vienna, Austria: Verlag der Österreichischen Akademie der Wissenschaften (two volumes).

Spence, Jonathan D. (1990) *In Search for Modern China*. New York and London: W.W. Norton & Company.

Sperling, Elliot (2012) "Reincarnation and the Golden Urn in the 19th Century: The Recognition of the 8th Panchen Lama," in Vitali, Roberto. *Studies on the History and Literature of Tibet and the Himalaya*. Kathmandu, Nepal: Vajra Books.

Sperling, Elliot (2004) *The Tibet-China Conflict: History and Polemics* (*Policy Studies 7*). Washington, D.C.: East–West Center. Online Available at: www.eastwestcenter-washington.org/Publications/publications.htm (accessed May 24, 2014).

Stein, R.A (1972) *Tibetan Civilization*. Stanford, California: Stanford University Press.

Stearns, Cyrus (2007) *King of the Empty Plain: The Tibetan Iron-Bridge Builder Tangtong Gyalpo*. Ithaca: Snow Lion Publications.

Strong, John (1995) *The Experience of Buddhism.* Belmont, California: Wadsworth.

Surya Das (1992) *The Snow Lion's Turquoise Mane: Wisdom Tales from Tibet.* San Francisco: HarperSanFrancisco.

Swearer, Donald (1997) "The Hermenutics of Buddhist Ecology in Contemporary Thailand: Buddhadāsa and Dhammapiṭaka," in Tucker, Mary Evelyn and Williams, Duncan Ryūken (eds) (1997) *Buddhism and Ecology: The Interconnection of Dharma and Deeds.* Cambridge, Massachusetts: Harvard University Press.

Taklha, Namgyal Lhamo (2001) *Born in Lhasa: The Autobiography of Namgyal Lhamo Taklha.* Ithaca, New York: Snow Lion Publications.

Tambiah, Stanley J. (1990) *Magic, Science, Religion and the Scope of Rationality.* Cambridge, United Kingdom: Cambridge University Press.

Tambiah, Stanley J. (1985) *Culture, Thought and Social Action: An Anthropological Perspective.* Cambridge, Massachusetts: Harvard University Press.

Tambiah, Stanley J. (1984) *The Buddhist Saints of the Forest and the Cult of Amulets.* Cambridge, United Kingdom: Cambridge University Press.

Tambiah, Stanley J. (1976) *World Conqueror and World Renouncer.* Cambridge, United Kingdom: Cambridge University Press.

Tapontsang, Adhe (1997) *Ama Adhe: The Voice that Remembers.* Boston: Wisdom Publications.

Taring, Rinchen Dolma (1986 [1960]) *Daughter of Tibet: The Autobiography of Rinchen Dolma Taring.* London: Wisdom Publications.

Tarthang Tulku (ed.) (1989 [1975]) *Reflections of Mind: Western Psychology Meets Tibetan Buddhism.* Berkeley, California: Dharma Publishing.

Tarthang Tulku (1994) *Dynamics of Time and Space: Transcending Limits on Knowledge.* Berkeley, California: Dharma Publishing.

Taussig, Michael (1997) *The Magic of the State.* New York and London: Routledge.

Taussig, Michael (1994) *The Devil and Commodity Fetishism in South America.* Chapel Hill: University of North Carolina Press.

Taussig, Michael (1993) *Mimesis and Alterity: A Particular History of the Senses.* New York and London: Routledge.

Taussig, Michael (1992) *The Nervous System.* New York: Routledge.

Taussig, Michael (1987) *Shamanism, Colonialism and the Wild Man: A Study in Terror and Healing.* Chicago and London: Chicago University Press.

Tenzin Gyatso, the Fourteenth Dalai Lama (2011) *Beyond Religion: Ethics for a Whole World.* London, Sydney, Auckland and Johannesburg: Rider Books.

Tenzin Gyatso, the Fourteenth Dalai Lama (2005) *The Universe in a Single Atom: The Convergence of Science and Spirituality.* New York: Morgan Road Books.

Tenzin Gyatso, the Fourteenth Dalai Lama (1999) *The Art of Happiness: A Handbook for Living.* New York: Riverhead Books.

Tenzin Gyatso, the Fourteenth Dalai Lama (1998) *Ethics for the New Millennium.* New York: Riverhead Books.

Tenzin Gyatso, the Fourteenth Dalai Lama (1996) *The Good Heart: A Buddhist Perspective on the Teachings of Jesus.* Boston: Wisdom Publications.

Tenzin Gyatso, the Fourteenth Dalai Lama (1995) *The World of Tibetan Buddhism.* Boston: Wisdom Publications.

Tenzin Gyatso, the Fourteenth Dalai Lama (1994) *A Flash of Lightning in the Dark of Night.* Boston and London: Shambhala Publications.

Tenzin Gyatso, the Fourteenth Dalai Lama (1993) *A Policy of Kindness.* Ithaca, New York: Snow Lion Publications.

Tenzin Gyatso, the Fourteenth Dalai Lama (1990) *Freedom in Exile: The Autobiography of the Dalai Lama.* New York: HarperPerennial.

Tenzin Gyatso, the Fourteenth Dalai Lama (1988) *The Union of Bliss and Emptiness.* Ithaca, New York: Snow Lion Publications.

Tenzin Gyatso, the Fourteenth Dalai Lama (1987) *The Buddhism of Tibet.* Ithaca, New York: Snow Lion Publications.

Tenzin Gyatso, the Fourteenth Dalai Lama (1984) *Kindness, Clarity and Insight.* Ithaca, New York: Snow Lion.

Tenzin Gyatso, the Fourteenth Dalai Lama (1962) *My Land and My People: Memoirs of the Dalai Lama of Tibet.* New York, Toronto and London: McGraw-Hill Book Company, Inc.

Tenzin Gyatso, the Fourteenth Dalai Lama and Berzin, Alexander (1997) *The Gelug/Kagyü Tradition of Mahamudra.* Ithaca, New York: Snow Lion Publications.

Tenzin Gyatso, the Fourteenth Dalai Lama and Cutler, Howard (2000) *Dzogchen: The Heart Essence of the Great Perfection.* Ithaca, New York: Snow Lion Publications.

Tenzin Gyatso, the Fourteenth Dalai Lama and Hopkins, Jeffrey (2002) *Advice on Dying.* New York: Atria Books.

Tenzin Gyatso, the Fourteenth Dalai Lama and Hopkins, Jeffrey (1999 [1985]) *Kalachakra Tantra Rite of Initiation.* Boston: Wisdom Publications.

Tenzin Gyatso, the Fourteenth Dalai Lama, Jhado Tulku Rinpoche and Stril-Rever, Sofia (2002) *Kalachakra: Guide de l'initiation et du Guru Yoga.* Paris: Desclée de Brouwer.

Tenzin Gyatso, the Fourteenth Dalai Lama *et al.* (1991) *MindScience: An East and West Dialogue.* Boston: Wisdom Publications.

Thargyal, Rinzin (1993) "Forming the Nation: The Process of Polyarchic Laterality among the Tibetan Diaspora," in Kvaerne, Per and Thargyal, Rinzin. *Bon, Buddhism and Democracy: The Building of a Tibetan National Identity.* Copenhagen: NIAS Publishing.

Thinley Norbu Rinpoche (2001) *White Sail: Crossing the Waves of Ocean Mind to the Serene Continent of the Triple Gems.* Boston and London: Shambhala Publications.

Thinley Norbu Rinpoche (1985) *Magic Dance: The Display of the Self-Nature of the Five Wisdom Dakinis.* New York: Jewel Publishing House.

Thubten Zongtse, Champa (1999) *The History of Segyu Gaden Phodrang Monastery.* Sebastopol, California: Healing Buddha Foundation.

Thurman, Robert (2005a) *The Jewel Tree of Tibet: Enlightenment Engine of Tibetan Buddhism.* New York: Free Press.

Thurman, Robert (2005b) *Anger: The seven deadly sins.* New York: Oxford University Press.

Thurman, Robert (1998) *Inner Revolution: Life, Liberty, and the Pursuit of Real Happiness.* New York: Riverhead Books.

Thurman, Robert (1996) *The Holy Teaching of Vimalakirti: A Mahayana Scripture.* University Park, Pennsylvania: The Pennsylvania State University Press.

Thurman, Robert (1995a) *Essential Tibetan Buddhism.* New York: HarperSan Francisco.

Thurman, Robert (1995b) *Inside Tibetan Buddhism: Rituals and Symbols Revealed.* San Francisco: Collins Publishers San Francisco.

Thurman, Robert (1994) *The Tibetan Book of the Dead.* New York: Bantam Books.

Thurman, Robert (ed.) (1993) *Life and Teachings of Tsong Khapa.* Kangra, India: Library of Tibetan Works and Archives.

Thurman, Robert (1991) *The Central Philosophy of Tibet.* Princeton, New Jersey: Princeton University Press.

Tikhonov, Vladimir and Brekke, Torkel (eds.) (2013) *Buddhism and Violence: Militarism and Buddhism in Modern Asia*. New York and London: Routledge.

Trainor, Kevin (ed.) (2004) *Buddhism: The Illustrated Guide*. New York: Oxford University Press.

Trungpa, Chögyam (2005) *The Sanity We Are Born With: A Buddhist Approach to Psychology*. Boston and London: Shambhala Publications.

Trungpa, Chögyam (2003a [1977]) *Born in Tibet*, in Gimian, Carolyn Rose (ed.) *The Collected Works of Chögyam Trungpa*. Boston and London: Shambhala Publications, vol. 1, pp. 1–289.

Trungpa, Chögyam (2003b [1982]) "The Meeting of Buddhist and Western Psychology," in Gimian, Carolyn Rose (ed.) *The Collected Works of Chögyam Trungpa*. Boston and London: Shambala Publications, vol. 2, pp. 538–55.

Trungpa, Chögyam and Fremantle, Francesca (eds) (2000) *The Tibetan Book of the Dead*. Boston and London: Shambhala Publications.

Tsongkapa (1998) *The Principal Teachings of Buddhism*. New Delhi: Classics India Publication.

Tucci, Giuseppe (1999) *Tibetan Painted Scrolls*. Bangkok: SDI Publications.

Tucci, Giuseppe (1988) *The Religions of Tibet*. Berkeley and Los Angeles, California: University of California Press.

Tucker, Mary Evelyn and Williams, Duncan Ryūken (eds) (1997) *Buddhism and Ecology: The Interconnection of Dharma and Deeds*. Cambridge, Massachussets: Harvard University Press.

Tulku Thondup Rinpoche (1999) *Masters of Meditation and Miracles*. Boston and London: Shambhala Publications.

Tulku Thondup Rinpoche (1986) *Hidden Teachings of Tibet: An Explanation of the Terma Tradition of the Nyingma School of Buddhism*. Boston: Wisdom Publications.

Tulku Yeshi Rinpoche (2012) *A Modern Liberation Odyssey: An Autobiography of a Tibetan Buddhist Nomad Lama*. Minneapolis, Minnesota: Mill City Press, Inc.

Turner, Victor (1996) *Dramas, Fields and Metaphors*. Ithaca, New York and London: Cornell University Press.

Turner, Victor (1995) *The Ritual Process: Structure and Anti-Structure*. New York: Aldine de Gruyter.

Turner, Victor (1982) *From Ritual to Theatre: The Human Seriousness of Play*. New York: PAJ Publications.

Turner, Victor (1967) *The Forest of Symbols*. Ithaca, New York and London: Cornell University Press.

Turner, Victor and Burner, Edward (1986) *The Anthropology of Experience*. Urbana and Chicago: University of Illinois Press.

Tuttle, Gray (2005) *Tibetan Buddhists in the Making of Modern China*. New York: Columbia University Press.

Usarski, Frank (ed.) (2002) *O Budismo no Brasil*. São Paulo: Editora Lorosae.

Uspensky, V.L (1996) "The Illustrated Manuscript of the Fifth Dalai Lama's 'Secret Visionary Autobiography,'" in *Manuscripta Orientalia*, 2 (1), March, pp. 54–65.

Vahali, Honey Oberoi (2009) *Lives in Exile: Exploring the Inner World of Tibetan Refugees*. London, New York and New Delhi: Routledge.

Varela, Francisco (ed.) (1997) *Sleeping, Dreaming, and Dying: An Exploration of Consciousness with the Dalai Lama*. Boston: Wisdom Publications.

Veyne, Paul (1988) "Conduct Without Belief and Works of Art Without Viewers," in *Diogenes*, 36 (1), pp. 1–22.

Wallace, B. Alan (ed.) (2003) *Buddhism and Science: Breaking New Ground*. New York: Columbia University Press.

Wallace, B. Alan (1996) *Choosing Reality: A Buddhist View of Physics and the Mind*. Ithaca, New York: Snow Lion Publications.

Wallace, B. Alan (1993) *Tibetan Buddhism from the Ground Up*. Boston: Wisdom Publications.

Wallace, Vesna A. (2001) *The Inner Kālacakratantra: A Buddhist Tantric View of the Individual*. Oxford: Oxford University Press.

Wacquant, L.D. (1989) "Towards a Reflexive Sociology: A Workshop with Pierre Bourdieu," in *Sociological Theory*, 7.

Welwood, John (2000) *Toward a Psychology of Awakening: Buddhism, Psychotherapy and the Path of Personal and Spiritual Transformation*. Boston and London: Shambhala Publications.

Williams, Paul and Tribe, Anthony (2003) *Buddhist Thought: A Complete Introduction to the Indian Tradition*. London and New York: Routledge.

White, Hayden (1990) *The Content of the Form: Narrative Discourse and Historical Representation*. Baltimore: Johns Hopkins University Press.

Wu, David Y.H. (1990) "Chinese Minority Policy and the Meaning of the Minority Culture: The Example of Bai in Yunnan, China," in *Human Organization*, 49 (1), pp. 1–13.

Yamaguchi, Masao (1990) "The Poetics of Exhibition in Japanese Culture," in Karp, Ivan and Lavine, Steven D. (eds) *Exhibiting Cultures: The Poetics and Politics of Museum Display*. Washington and London: Smithsonian Institute Press.

Yamasaki, Taiko (1996) *Shingon: Japanese Esoteric Buddhism*. Fresno, California: Shingon Buddhist International Institute.

Yangchen, Soname and MacKenzie, Vicky (2007 [2006]) *Child of Tibet: The Story of Soname's Flight to Freedom*. London: Portrait.

Yeshe, Lama Thubten (1997) *Teachings of Lama Thubten Yeshe*. Boston: Wisdom Publications.

Yeshe, Lama Thubten (1987) *Introduction to Tantra*. Boston: Wisdom Publications.

Yeshe Tsogyal (1993) *The Lotus-Born: The Life Story of Padmasambhava*. Boston and London: Shambhala Publications.

Zajonc, Arthur (ed.) (2004) *The New Physics and Cosmology: Dialogues with the Dalai Lama*. New York: Oxford University Press.

Zangpo, Lama Shakya (1994) "The Winds of Change," in *Healing Buddha Center Newsletter* (May).

Zimmermann, Michael (ed.) (2006) *Buddhism and Violence*. Lumbini: Lumbini International Research Institute.

Documents and reports

Asia Watch Committee (1988) *Human Rights in Tibet: An Asia Watch Report*. Washington, D.C. and New York (February).

Department of Information and International Relations, Central Tibetan Administration (1997) *Shugden Versus Pluralism and National Unity: Controversy and Clarification*. Dharamsala, India (November).

Department of Information and International Relations, Central Tibetan Administration (1996) *The false allegations of Dholgyal devotees and clarifications*. Dharamsala, India, (July).

Healing Buddha Foundation (1994). *The Medicine Buddha Tradition and Brazilian Shamanism*. Sebastopol, California.

International Campaign for Tibet (2012), *Storm in The Grasslands: Self-immolations in Tibet and Chinese Policy.* Washington, D.C. (December).

International Campaign for Tibet (1996) *A Season to Purge: Religious Repression in Tibet*. Washington, D.C. (April).

International Campaign for Tibet (1990) *Forbidden Freedoms: Beijing's Control of Religion in Tibet*. Washington, D.C. (September).

International Commission of Jurists (1959) *The Question of Tibet and the Rule of Law*. Geneva.

Lama Gangchen Peace Publications (2000) *Peace Times*, no. 15 (April).

New Kadampa Tradition (2002) *Celebrating 25 Years of Kadampa Buddhism Worldwide: Directory of Kadampa Buddhist Centres and Branches* Ulverston, United Kingdom (August).

New Kadampa Tradition (2001) *A Moral Discipline Guide: The Internal Rules of the New Kadampa Tradition*. Ulverston, United Kingdom.

New Kadampa Tradition (2000) *The Kadampa Way of Life: The Essential Practice of Kadam Lamrim*. Ulverston, United Kingdom.

New Kadampa Tradition (1997) *Modern Day Kadampas: The History and Development of the New Kadampa Tradition*. Ulverston, United Kingdom.

New Kadampa Tradition (*undated*) *A Meaningful Life: The Foundation Programme in Kadampa Mahayana Buddhism*. Ulverston, United Kingdom.

Websites (last accessed on June 11, 2014)

www.84000.com
www.berzinarchives.com
www.china.org.cn
www.dalailama.com
www.deerparkcenter.org
www.fpmt.org
www.healingbuddha.org
www.hpm.com.br/ieve
www.juniperpath.org
www.kadampa.org
www.khoryug.com
www.lgpt.net
www.mindandlife.org
www.naropa.edu
www.scribd.com/doc/138857011/Affirm-Geoffrey-Samuel
www.songtsen.org
www.spcare.org
www.tharpa.com
www.tibetjustice.org
www.tibet.com
www.tibet.net
www.un.org

Index